Happy travels, Barbara! It's been a pleasure! Spencer

Happy trails! Bruce

Great Salt Lake

❖

An Anthology

Thanks for your enthusiastic participation. We'll miss you!
Lindsey

Dec. 2002

Barbara —
Happy trails and thanks for all your dedication to FRIENDS and our Great Salt Lake — Best - Lynn

Thanks for all your efforts! Your passion is inspiring.
Best Wishes
Chris Yorkam

Have a wonderful journey!
Brian

Great Salt Lake

An Anthology

Edited by

Gary Topping

UTAH STATE UNIVERSITY PRESS
Logan, Utah

Utah State University Press
Logan, Utah 84322

Manufactured in the United States of America

Printed on acid-free paper

08 07 06 05 04 03 02   1 2 3 4 5 6 7 8

Library of Congress Cataloging-in-Publication Data

Great Salt Lake : an anthology / edited by Gary Topping.
    p. cm.
Includes bibliographical references.
    ISBN 0-87421-436-X
    1. Great Salt Lake Region (Utah)—History—Sources. 2. Great Salt Lake Region
(Utah)—Description and travel—Sources. I. Topping, Gary, 1941–
    F832.G7 G74 2002
    979.2'42—dc21
                                            2002000781

Contents

⊶ Introduction ⊷

U tah's Great Salt Lake sounds like someone's literary fantasy: a vast interior sea bordered by marshes and dotted with islands that support thousands of shore birds of a great variety of species, yet flanked on other sides by an immense salt waste that forbids human habitation. This fantasy includes lore of sea monsters, whirlpools, pods of whales, prehistoric inhabitants riding elephants, and a river of colossal size draining into the Pacific Ocean. Although science and exploration have banished parts of that fantasy, Great Salt Lake remains one of the world's most remarkable geological phenomena, a place of beauty, drama, and complexity to challenge the most ambitious curiosity and imagination.

Curiously, the lake is at the same time both famous and obscure. Few visitors to Utah can resist the temptation to stand on its shore, to marvel at the anomaly of a huge lake in the midst of a desert, and perhaps to dip a finger into its brine to verify its high salinity. But native Utahns take the place almost totally for granted. Except for a few sailors, hunters, bird watchers, and those employed in the brine shrimp or salt industries—a total comprising less than a handful of the state's two million residents—most Utahns view the lake only while flying into or out of the airport or speeding along Interstate 80 to risk their money in the gambling emporiums of Wendover, Nevada.

Great Salt Lake is one of several remnants of an immense freshwater lake geologists call Lake Bonneville, which occupied most of western Utah during the latest Ice Age, fed by glacier melt and draining to the Snake River. As the earth warmed and the glaciers receded far to the north, the lake lost most of its influx of water and dropped below its outlet, becoming in time a salt lake because of mineral accumulations. Evidences of Lake Bonneville are still apparent in bodies of water like Utah and Sevier Lakes and Little Salt Lake in southwestern Utah, as well as, of course, Great Salt Lake itself. Also, one or more ancient shorelines of Lake Bonneville are visible as benches along the mountainsides flanking Salt Lake Valley, and residents of those benches commonly turn up seashells while cultivating their gardens in the sandy soil of the old beaches.

Historically, the lake has been both a blessing and a curse. Indians who moved into the area as early as ten thousand years ago found abundant supplies of carbohydrates in the cattails, pickleweed, and other plants that flourished in the marshes surrounding the lake and supplemented them with protein from small animals and insects. Archaeological investigations have identified a number of permanent and temporary occupation sites in caves around the lake and on its islands.

For early Euro-American explorers and settlers, the lake appeared less friendly. Although fur trappers ventured into Salt Lake Valley in the 1820s and traded with the Ute, Paiute, and Shoshone Indians they found there, the beavers that were their economic livelihood and the deer upon which they subsisted kept drawing them back into the mountains. Jedediah Smith, the most intrepid explorer among them, crossed the salt flats to the south and west of the lake twice during his explorations of the beaver streams of California, but narrowly avoided dying of thirst and found little of value in the region.

When reports of the abundant lands and easy living in California filtered back to the United States from explorers like Smith and John C. Frémont and sailors like Richard Henry Dana, land-hungry Americans began looking for ways to get there even before it became American territory in 1848. While the safest and most practical overland route to California branched off from the Oregon Trail southwesterly to follow the Humboldt River across Nevada, some adventuresome emigrants began experimenting as early as 1841 with more direct routes across the salt flats to the north or the south of Great Salt Lake. The Bartleson-Bidwell party, the first to attempt the northerly route, succeeded by following vague directions provided by the mountain man Tom Fitzpatrick and by their decision to abandon their wagons and fashion pack saddles for their animals. Those who attempted a southerly crossing in 1846, encouraged by California promoter Lansford W. Hastings, found the going much more difficult, and one contingent, the infamous Donner-Reed party, paid a ghastly price for their decision by starving and freezing to death in the Sierras.

Railroaders found the lake as much of an obstacle as did the overland emigrants. Golden Spike National Monument, which marks the point of the joining of the Union Pacific and Central Pacific railroads on May 10, 1869, at the summit of the Promontory Mountains north of the lake, also symbolizes the large detour the lake required in the railroad alignment. Straightening that alignment by means of a trestle spanning the lake presented immense engineering problems because of the porous lake bottom that swallowed up pilings almost like a straw pushed into a milkshake. It was not until early in the twentieth century that engineers arrived at the idea of binding several pilings together to spread the weight over a larger area, and the Lucin Cutoff routed the railroad across the lake. Heavier trains forced replacement of the trestle by a causeway in the 1950s.

The Mormons, who have placed their cultural stamp on Utah life as no other group, began arriving in Salt Lake Valley in 1847 and started exploring Great Salt Lake almost immediately to see what uses they might make of it. The best use they found, until they built the Saltair amusement park in the 1890s, was livestock grazing on Fremont and Antelope Islands. The latter herd was an official church venture, the income from which supported the Perpetual Emigrating Fund, a revolving loan fund that made it possible for some ten thousand impoverished European converts to emigrate to Utah before completion of the transcontinental railroad in 1869.

The islands of the lake, ranging in size from tiny atolls like Egg Island to the immense Antelope Island which looks like a lakeside mountain range from a distance, served as residences not only to the livestock herders and guano diggers who made their livelihoods on the lake, but also to the tubercular Judge U. B. Wenner, who used Fremont Island not only as a personal sanatorium, but turned it as well into an idyllic island residence for his wife and children. Alfred Lambourne, a dreamy artist and philosopher, left his family behind while he completed the residency requirement for a homestead on Gunnison Island, where he built a snug stone cabin and equipped it with a library and even a piano. Although his homestead claim eventually lost out to the business interest of the guano diggers who moved in on the other end of the island, Lambourne left us some memorable drawings of the lake, some magazine articles, and a book about his experience, *Our Inland Sea*, which has become a minor classic of Utah literature. Fremont Island even briefly had an involuntary resident, Jean Baptiste, a grave robber banished for life to the island as sentence for his heinous crime. The prisoner escaped almost immediately, making for shore on a raft fashioned from a dismantled building. His fate is unknown, though manacled skeletal remains discovered in the lake may indicate that he found a watery grave.

Boaters, whose sails dot the lake in colorful profusion on weekends, are heirs of a long tradition of recreational use of the lake. From the tiny boat built by early Mormon explorers of the Jordan River and Great Salt Lake in the 1840s to large excursion boats like today's *Island Serenade*, sailors and to a lesser degree power boaters have found the buoyant brine and the spectacular desert scenery an irresistible recreational recipe. That celebrated buoyancy and the bathwater warmth of the lake in the summer have lured bathers as well. While the beach at Bridger Bay on the north end of Antelope Island provides the only popular bathing area today, the Saltair resort on the southeast shore directly west of Salt Lake City, with its exotic Moorish architecture, its dining and dancing facilities featuring famous musical groups, its immense roller coaster, and its bathing lagoon, was once a national tourist destination. Fires twice ravaged the structure and radically fluctuating lake levels forced relocation of the bathing facilities, but Saltair finally lost out to the recreational appeal of movies and television. A new Saltair, which has also suffered from flooding by lake waters, and is a much smaller operation than the original establishment, provides tourist shops and concerts by popular bands.

Less visible to the visitor than Saltair and the sailboats are the various economic uses of the lake. When miners discovered rich gold and silver ores in the Oquirrh Mountains in the nineteenth century, steamboats on Great Salt Lake appeared to offer the most direct transportation to the railroad. Several such boats were operated through the years, and the town of Corinne, located near the railroad crossing of the Bear River, grew up as a supply depot for miners not only in the Oquirrhs, but far to the north in Idaho and Montana as well. The Gentiles (non-Mormons) who built the town hoped it would eclipse the economic power of the Mormons in Salt Lake City, but the eventual construction of railroad spur lines bypassed the community and its moment in the sun was brief.

Other economic resources have proved less ephemeral. The brine shrimp industry, for one, harvests the eggs of the tiny crustaceans who are among the few zoological inhabitants of the salty waters. Their eggs, which form dense cloudy patches covering acres of the lake surface, are sold as tropical fish food and food for prawns in commercial operations. The high mineral content of the lake water sustains large commercial salt factories who evaporate the water in huge shallow ponds, and Utah's MagCorp extracts magnesium from the lake waters in its plant on the west shore. Finally, the famously flat salt beds near Wendover, Utah, for many years provided a setting for land speed record attempts by a wide variety of high-powered cars and motorcycles.

A clash between economic needs and environmental concerns fuels an ongoing controversy. While pollution regulations attempt to minimize emissions from the Kennecott Copper Corporation smelter and the MagCorp factory, and seasonal regulations limit depletion of the brine shrimp population, solutions to other problems are more elusive. As Bountiful and other northern suburbs of Salt Lake City absorb more and more of the valley's expanding population, transportation needs have become increasingly acute, and plans for a parallel route to Interstate 15, called the Legacy Highway, aroused objections and even lawsuits from environmentalists who refuse to tolerate more encroachment on the hard-pressed bird habitat in marshlands on the lake's northeast shore. The railroad causeway, too, has come under attack from environmentalists who point out that the culverts built beneath it to allow water to pass between the north and south arms of the lake are insufficient to keep the salinity balanced. The Jordan, Weber, and Ogden Rivers, the south arm's major tributaries, carry much more fresh water into that part of the lake than the feeble Bear River, the only major tributary of the north arm, and the salinity imbalance is starting to have serious effects on the lake as bird and brine shrimp habitat. And so the lake, which has such economic and recreational importance for northern Utah, has come to the fore as a political issue as well.

This anthology has been assembled to encourage a deeper knowledge and understanding of the lake among tourists and natives alike. There are, to be sure, other reliable and readily available sources of information, like Dale Morgan's *The Great Salt Lake,* David E. Miller's *Great Salt Lake Past and Present,* and Marlin Stum and Dan Miller's *Visions of Antelope Island and Great Salt Lake,* and they are highly recommended. But Morgan's book, for all its virtues, appeared over a half century ago and has never been revised, David Miller's is a mere pamphlet, and Stum and Dan Miller's volume is mostly focused, as the title indicates, on the lake's largest island. Readers looking for more up to date and extensive information are faced with the prospect of digging through disparate scientific reports, historical journals, and newspaper archives.

The selections presented in this anthology are drawn from those very sources, including firsthand narratives by early explorers and settlers, later scientific and historical studies, and contemporary views. All are brief enough to be readable in one sitting, yet long enough to give the reader a substantial amount of information as well as to convey a good sense of the writer's personality and point of view. Each selection is accompanied by an introduction that identifies the writer and places the work from which it is chosen in historical or scientific context, as well as providing any corrections or explanations to make the reading accurate and meaningful. A brief bibliographical essay concludes each selection, focusing on readily accessible and relevant literature by which the reader can gain further knowledge of a topic that strikes his fancy. Those "suggestions for further reading" are particularly recommended, for the editor and publisher have felt themselves under considerable pressure to keep the volume within a manageable size and a reasonable price. Thus these selections are neither exhaustive nor comprehensive, and are intended to spark an interest that will lead to further exploration, both of the lake itself and of its extensive literature.

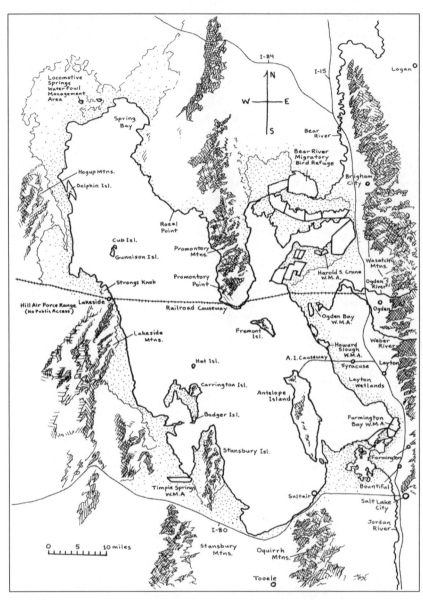

Great Salt Lake and vicinity, by Jose Knighton, from Marlin Stum, *Visions of Antelope Island and Great Salt Lake* (Logan: Utah State University Press, 1999).

I

An Overview of the Great Salt Lake

A Celebrated Historian and the Lake

Among Utah historians, Dale L. Morgan (1914–1971) enjoys preeminent rank. During his relatively short career, the prolific Morgan turned out dozens of books, articles, and edited sources on the fur trade, the Mormons, and overland emigration, many of which stand as classics today for their depth of research and literary excellence.

Morgan's life contained its share of adversity. An attack of spinal meningitis at age fourteen cost him his hearing, and with his deafness came a hampered social life and attenuated access to the kinds of career opportunities his immense talents would ordinarily have opened up. When he graduated from the University of Utah in the late 1930s, the moribund economy cut him off from an intended career in commercial art, but an opening on the Writer's Project of the Works Progress Administration enabled him to capitalize on his enormous literary ability, and he quickly rose to editorship of *Utah: A Guide to the State.* Morgan's deafness and lack of academic credentials in history prevented him from considering a teaching career, and his professional life became a succession of improvised sources of income. When the WPA disbanded at the beginning of America's entry into World War II, he shifted to the Office of Price Administration and moved to Washington, D.C., where he happily exploited the riches of the National Archives to feed his historical hunger during his spare time. A Guggenheim Fellowship gave him a year of financial independence during which he traveled from one archive to another researching a projected multivolume history of Mormonism. The fellowship was not renewed as he had hoped, but he secured a staff position in the Bancroft Library of the University of California, Berkeley, where he was still employed when cancer took his life at the youthful age of fifty-six.

The Great Salt Lake, from which the selection presented here is the introductory chapter, was a part of Bobbs-Merrill's American Lakes Series, and was Morgan's third commercially published book, after the WPA *Guide* (1941) and *The*

Humboldt: Highroad of the West (1943). It shows the youthful Morgan already in full possession of the literary powers that would distinguish the great books of his maturity: a bright wit, lively writing, a passion for factual accuracy, and mastery of an enormous body of primary and secondary writings. If one can make allowances for the fact that it is now over a half century old, it is still the best single book available about the lake, and two university presses—Nebraska and Utah—have subsequently paid tribute to that excellence by issuing paperback reprint editions with no revisions whatever.

Bringing this selection from Morgan's book up to date requires only a few comments. For one thing, Morgan's geological discussions are limited by his amateur knowledge of the field and also by the lack of good scientific knowledge in his day. We now know, for example, that the Oquirrh Mountains and the islands of the lake, although they are lined up in the same direction, are unrelated geologically. And we also know that the rising levels of Lake Bonneville were more related to larger global climatic and volcanic events than Morgan realized.

Since Morgan's day, the lake has experienced both its lowest and highest recorded levels. From an elevation of about 4197.5 when Morgan wrote, the lake dropped in the early 1960s to 4191.3. Since the early 1980s the level has been relatively high, and reached an elevation of 4212 in April 1987, at which point huge pumps installed the previous year on the western shore began pumping water out into the west desert in order to save Interstate 80 and the Southern Pacific railway from inundation (the lake will drain naturally into that western basin at an elevation of 4217, but at that point both of those transportation routes and the Salt Lake International Airport would be under water).

The grand vista of the lake available from Highway 89 is still available as Morgan described it, and readers of this anthology are enthusiastically encouraged to seek it out. Most traffic today, though, follows the Interstate 15 freeway at a much lower elevation that offers intermittent but mundane glimpses of the lake.

The Lucin Cutoff pilings became too rickety to be safe under heavy loads, even with a speed limit for trains of only twenty miles per hour, so much of it was replaced with solid fill in 1959. Most railroad traffic, though, now takes the route along the south shore originally built, as Morgan says, by the Denver & Rio Grande Western but now owned by the Southern Pacific, and the little community of Kelton described by Morgan is today a ghost town. Although a culvert system through the railroad causeway allows exchange of water between the north and south arms, little flow in fact occurs, and the north arm has consequently become much more salty than the south arm. The sluggish Bear River is the north arm's only major tributary, while the south arm is fed by, among others, the Weber and Jordan Rivers, both major sources of fresh water. Since Morgan's time, population expansion throughout Salt Lake Valley has shifted land use from agricultural to residential, and the Jordan River has gradually recovered its status as the lake's biggest tributary, far eclipsing the flow of the Bear River. The discussion Morgan reports regarding construction of a north-south dike to create a freshwater recreational facility on the eastern shore has completely died, but many currently advocate a greater breaching of the causeway to even out the lake's salinity in the interests of its magnificent population of shorebirds and other wildlife.

Antelope Island is now a state park, accessible by means of a paved causeway to its north end. It is one of the most opportune vantage points for observing the lake at close hand. Bridger Bay provides the lake's only appealing beach that is readily accessible for swimming and sunbathing, a small marina offers a few slips for sail-boats (though most sailors use the much larger and better equipped marina on the lake's southeast shore), and a concession stand and a network of bicycle and hiking trails are available.

Motorboats are rarely seen on the lake these days, with the exception of two large commercial tour boats operating between the Antelope Island and south shore marinas, and the State Park Service rescue boat. The extreme salinity of the water makes waterskiing unappealing, and the lake has no fish, so most motor-boaters prefer to seek out the state's many freshwater lakes and reservoirs where watersports and fishing are available, and avoid exposing their engines to the cor-rosive lake water. The techniques Morgan describes for surviving rough weather on the lake are still valid, but today's sailors almost universally add to Morgan's rec-ommendation of a good anchor a recommendation of an electronic depth sounder to avoid running aground along the shallow shorelines of the lake and the islands and a ship-to-shore radio to summon help from other boats or from the prompt and well-trained personnel at the marina or sheriff's office.

Finally, Morgan was no sailor, and only inexperienced or foolhardy ones today adopt the rather cavalier attitude he seems to have held regarding the perils of plying the lake's waters. Storms can roll in with amazing rapidity, and those sailors who venture more than a few miles from the marina feel confident only when they have some rough weather experience and a fast boat in which to run for a sheltered anchorage ahead of an approaching front.

Suggestions for further reading

All study of the Great Salt Lake must begin with Morgan's book from which this selection is drawn. As indicated in the introduction, it is fortunately in print again in a paperback edition (Salt Lake City: University of Utah Press, 1995). A full-scale biography of Morgan is urgently needed, but in the meantime two excellent intro-ductions to his life and writings are available in John Philip Walker, ed., *Dale Morgan on Early Mormonism: Correspondence and a New History* (Salt Lake City: Signature Books, 1986), and Harold Schindler's introduction to the reprint edition cited above. While Morgan's book remains unsurpassed as a history of the lake, the scientific aspects which Morgan only covers superficially are dealt with in consid-erable depth in J. Wallace Gwynn, ed., *Great Salt Lake: A Scientific, Historical and*

Economic Overview (Salt Lake City: Utah Geological and Mineralogical Survey Bulletin 116, 1980), an anthology of articles by various scientific specialists. A new edition is being prepared at this writing. Peter Czerny's *The Great Great Salt Lake* (Provo, Utah: Brigham Young University Press, 1976) is out of print, but well worth seeking out for its splendid photographs and comprehensive text.

THE MOUNTAIN SEA
Dale L. Morgan

Great Salt Lake is unique among the great American lakes, arresting in its name, yet least known. Its name itself has an aura of the strange and the mysterious, but it resists those who would know it. Lake of paradoxes, in a country where water is life itself and land has little value without it, Great Salt Lake is an ironical joke of nature—water that is itself more desert than a desert.

Moody and withdrawn, the lake unites a haunting loveliness to a raw desolateness. Not many have achieved a sense of intimacy with it. It is intolerant of men and reluctant in submission to their uses. Defending itself with its own shallows, the lake is almost impossible of access except at its southeastern shore. Men have attempted to force it into the servitude of navigation; recalcitrantly it has withdrawn from their piers, leaving them high and dry, or has risen to inundate them entirely. Men have mined its waters of its salts; indifferently the lake has replaced the salts from its affluent waters and has remained unchanged.

The pervasive mystery clinging to the lake has found expression in a bizarre folklore. Gigantic Indians riding on elephants have lived upon its islands, and the mysterious white Indians, the Munchies, once dwelt there, too. Maelstroms have ravaged its surface, great vents have opened in its bottom to drain its water horribly into the bowels of the earth, and of course it was connected to the Pacific Ocean by subterranean passage. Appalling monsters have bellowed in its shallows and made forays upon its shores. Noxious vapors rising from its surface have brought instant death to birds flying above it, and its corrosive salts have burned the skin from swimmers rash enough to risk themselves in its waters.

All these tales one believes or not, at his pleasure. But other ideas about the lake are widely held. In the years of the "ox-team telegraph" rumors periodically swept the East that the lake had left its bed and sunk Great Salt Lake City in fifty feet of water. There still exists a tendency to wonder whether the Mormon country can be quite safe from a lake so strangely removed from common experience. Such fears are hardly

Reprinted with permission of Simon & Schuster, Inc., from *The Great Salt Lake* by Dale L. Morgan. Copyright © 1947 by Dale L. Morgan; copyright renewed © 1975 by James S. Morgan. Pp. 17–41.

shared by those who dwell in its immense valley, but even they look upon the lake a little askance. It is regarded as given to irrational moods of violence, its navigation attended by unusual hazards. Its strangling brine is feared unreasonably, and swimmers are carefully indoctrinated in the technique of caring for themselves should the stinging salt splash into their eyes—suck a finger clean and wash the eyes with saliva.

Wholly apart from the folklore, the lake has an obstinate and fascinating identity of its own. It has its own history, a startling history. But also in three centuries it has been a part of the written history of men. Spaniards and mountain men sought it out; the Mormons fled to it for a promised land. Its salt waters and the blazing deserts of its making, lying athwart the American westering, forced trails and roads and railroads north and south around it. A barrier sea, fascinating and strange, implacable and wayward!

Visitors have called its waters bright emerald, grayish green and leaden gray; they have called them sapphire and turquoise and cobalt—and they have all been right. Its color varies with the time of day, the state of the weather, the season of the year, the vantage point from which it is seen. It can lie immobile in its mountain setting like a vast, green, light-filled mirror, or, lashed by a sudden storm, rise wrathful in its bed to assault boats and its shoreline with smashing four-foot waves. The wind is its only master. The wind drives it contemptuously about from one part to another of its shallow basin, piling up the water here, exposing the naked lake floor there, as if the basin itself were twisted and tilted under the surging green brine.

It lies at the bottom of three great north-south depressions which together comprise the valley of the Great Salt Lake. East of the lake the mighty rampart of the Wasatch Mountains, rising as high as eleven and twelve thousand feet above sea level, exacts from the prevailing westerly winds a tribute of rain and snow which created the lake and has maintained it. West of the Wasatch rises a lesser, parallel range, the Oquirrh, which dips beneath the lake at its southeastern shore to create its only good beaches. Farther north, this range rises intermittently as Antelope Island and the speck called Egg Island, then again as Frémont Island, and emerges finally as that long, rocky spine, the Promontory Mountains. A third parallel range, the Stansbury Mountains, falls off to a sand bar at the lake shore, lifts to create Stansbury Island and finally subsides into the water as two rocky crests called Carrington and Hat Islands. Along its west shore the lake is contained for much of its length by the Lakeside Mountains and Strongs Knob but then breaks free to the west for a few more miles to wash against the eastern base of the Terrace and Hog Mountains.

The lake is deepest in the sunken valley lying between the two island chains. In 1850 Captain Howard Stansbury found depths up to 36 feet between Carrington and Antelope Islands, as against an average depth of 13 feet. The depth is less today, for the lake in 1947 was approximately 4 feet lower than in Stansbury's time.

Roughly Great Salt Lake is 75 miles long by 50 wide, but its dimensions can rarely be stated with any precision. All its shores slope so gently that its shore line is subject to extraordinary fluctuation. A rise of a few feet in the lake level may change its contours amazingly and add hundreds of square miles to its surface area.

The shallowness of the lake's basin has been its primary defense against intruders. Save only for the southeastern beaches at the base of the Oquirrhs, it is everywhere bulwarked with mud morasses and salt marshes which have made it nearly inaccessible and have done much to preserve its atmosphere of desolate strangeness. From all but a very few it has withheld itself. There have been those who have gone out upon its waters to find it possessed of an unimaginable glory, a true splendor. But intimacy with the lake for most has been of a more remote kind.

Since 1903 the fills and trestles of the Lucin Cutoff have hurtled trains east and west across the lake, and the Southern Pacific's passengers have come to know something of its character. But a Pullman is insulated from reality. Carefully groomed upholstery, starched white pillows, obsequious porters and unwearying air conditioning do violence to the very nature of the lake.

Walk the salt-encrusted beaches of the southeastern shore and savor the sour, strange odor, half-stench yet alive and individual, that rises from the drying salt flats. Watch the heavy, unquiet water seeking the beach, while with harsh, untiring outcries the gray-and-white winged gulls wheel above you. This is a holiday hour; children play along the beaches; an old man floats on his back before you, gently rising and falling in six inches of brine transparent above the rippling lake floor; girls sun themselves on the sand; and a boat with tall white sails is making for the boat harbor. But listen to the gulls and stare out over the water. Behind you is the shoulder of the smoky Oquirrhs, burnt umber and ocherous gray; in front of you, far out, is deepening green water intercepted by a band of deep, dark blue in which is set the low-lying gold-and-amethyst bulk of Antelope Island. To the west the high, bare silhouette of Stansbury Island awaits the descending sun. The sunlight plays magically with the water, spilling quicksilver on it the while it prepares the stain of scarlet and gold which must see the sun to its setting. The feel of the sun and the salt on your skin, the wide sweep of the open sapphire sky, the strangely scented wind raucous with the screaming of the gulls, the intermingled beauty and stripped ugliness of lake and shore . . . in all these things is something of the experience of Great Salt Lake.

There are other, more distant intuitions. Take US 89, the mountain highway, south from Ogden, follow it around the hillsides to the mouth of the Weber, above the green-and-gold cove of Uintah, then drive on around the shoulder of the Wasatch south toward Salt Lake City. The highway climbs a long hill and curves gently amid the Orchards from which come Utah's surpassing peaches. All at once the land to the west falls away and the Great Salt Lake spreads far in the plain before you. There is the wide silver ribbon of beach beyond the green valley farmlands, the concentrate blue line of the lake, and the warm-hued mass of Antelope hugging the dark band of water. The lake lies immaculately alone under your sight—withdrawn and desolate, yet touched with a strange, compelling beauty.

Similarly, it is worth bumping and bouncing over the old road to Promontory to go on a few miles beyond the gray, pyramidal Golden Spike monument and experience the sudden shouting presence of the northwestern arm of the lake. Except for the twisting, rutted road and the unsteady line of dusty telephone poles, this is the lake of history that lies abruptly under sight. The gray-green sage and greasewood seem withdrawn and unfriendly, the darkly green blotches of juniper immensely unrelated to human existence, the far curve of lake shore new and undiscovered; you know that this is how it always was, back to the time when the first immigrant company to California went this way.

This experience may be constantly repeated. The lake is too difficult to approach to be taken for granted; the tang of surprise and the shock of recognition are a part of its character.

Men have made themselves at home only along the southern and eastern shores of the lake. Except along the old route of the Central Pacific over the Promontory summit and around the north shore, which was finally abandoned in 1942, and along the Lucin Cutoff, with its service points and sidings, the northern and western shores of the lake are almost completely uninhabited. Kelton, the jumping off spot for the Oregon and Idaho stages until a railroad was built to the Northwest, is the sole metropolis of all this vast area. It consists today of a single store, a red warehouse and a few buildings constructed of railroad ties, its sole reason for survival some outlying sheep and cattle ranches.

At the south shore of the lake small Mormon towns with their green farmlands and smoke-encrusted smelters give an accent of life to Tooele Valley, rimmed by the Oquirrh and Stansbury Mountains. But the Great Salt Lake country, expressed in terms of the people who live there, is the sloping plain stretching for over a hundred miles along the west face of the Wasatch Mountains and curving southward to include, by courtesy, Utah Valley.

This long, narrow strip of land, only 20 or 30 miles wide, has been called the Wasatch Oasis and comprises most of Utah's five richest and most populous counties—Utah, Salt Lake, Davis, Weber and Box Elder. Seven-tenths of the population of the entire state lives in this green oasis. Provo, (18,071 population) in Utah Valley is surrounded by a cluster of vigorous small towns. Salt Lake City (149,934 population), the state capital, wholly dominates Salt Lake Valley and is a regional metropolis as well, profoundly influencing life for hundreds of miles in all directions. The Davis Valley is a continuous wealth of green farms broken up into a succession of small towns. In the Weber Valley is Ogden (43,688 population), Utah's second largest city, and its chief rail center. Northernmost of these prosperous towns is Brigham City (5,641 population), at the head of Bear River Bay. Though the Wasatch Oasis is regarded as extending northeasterly into Cache Valley, where Logan (11,868 population) is Utah's fourth city, this area is more remote from the lake shores.

For all these cities the distance to salt water varies from five to twenty miles. Land adjacent to the lake is generally poor, alkaline and badly drained; the benchlands lying close under the mountains not only have richer soil but may be more readily irrigated by diversion canals which bring the waters of the canyon creeks to the land. The population has naturally concentrated itself on a higher land.

The lake has three great affluents—Bear River in the north, emptying into Bear River Bay; Weber River, with its delta some miles to the south; and Jordan River, emptying into the lake several miles northwest of Salt Lake City. Both the Bear and the Weber rise in the high Uinta Mountains 80 miles to the east, and after long and tortuous courses break through the Wasatch mountain wall to reach the lake. The Jordan drains fresh-water Utah Lake, which itself is principally fed by the Provo River, a stream rising within a few miles of the Weber and the Bear. Among Great Salt Lake's three primary affluents, the Bear is by far the most important, the waters of the Weber and the Jordan to a large extent having been diverted for irrigation purposes.

Great Salt Lake itself is the remnant of a vast inland sea which once rolled over most of western Utah and small areas of eastern Nevada and southern Idaho. Called Lake Bonneville, that prehistoric fresh-water lake was almost as big as Lake Michigan and far deeper. For a time it spilled over the rim of the Great Basin, north into the Snake, but as the climate changed, it shrank upon itself, breaking up into half a dozen smaller lakes. Great Salt Lake, Utah Lake, Rush Lake, Sevier Lake, and Little Salt Lake, far south in Utah, are all remnants of the ancient sea.

Through thousands of dry years, perhaps fluctuating widely in that time but in the long run receding, Great Salt Lake withdrew toward its present lake bed. Evaporation of its waters during all these years created a higher and higher concentration of the mineral salts its tributary waters had poured into its depths, and the withdrawal from the Pilot Range, at the Nevada border, formed a vast, level, salt-strewn desert like nothing else under the American sun, a poisoned earth where the old idea of the Great American Desert has taken final refuge.

The lake has been many times given up to death since men came to its shores. In the 80's the great geologist, Grove Karl Gilbert, predicted its early disappearance. Increasing diversion of its affluent waters for purposes of irrigation could have no other outcome, he reasoned. Antelope and Stansbury Islands would become permanently united with the mainland; the greater part of Bear River Bay and Farmington Bay would become dry; the deltas of the Bear and the Weber would join near Frémont Island, and the lake would make its last stand in the central depression west of Antelope Island.

Gilbert's reasoning was impeccable, but the lake has shown a great obstinacy in the matter. Although its level has exhibited a general downward trend, from time to time the lake has embarked on astonishing adventures.

Exact data have been kept on its fluctuations since 1874, and traditional data have been correlated for the quarter-century before that time to give a precise picture of its fluctuations. The lake level is calculated with reference to an arbitrary elevation designated as the "zero level." The present zero, on the Saltair gage, is at an elevation of 4,196.85 feet above sea level. This is used as the convenient standard of comparison, although there is another gage at Boat Harbor with the zero mark 10 feet lower. At the time of the Stansbury Survey in 1850 the lake was 4,201 feet above sea level. In the next 5 years it rose almost 4 feet higher, but at the end of the decade fell 5 feet. In 1862 it began a sudden, sharp climb, by 1868 rising nearly 12 feet, and in 1872 and 1873 rising 6 inches to its highest recorded mark. After 1875, however, it began to plummet, falling more than 10 feet in 9 years, and persuading Gilbert that it would soon dry up entirely. It rallied briefly in 1884–1885, rising to 4,207.5 feet., but it fell yearly thereafter until in 1905 it plumbed a depth almost a foot below zero on the Saltair gage. Gilbert's prophecies seemed on their way to rapid fulfillment when, under the stimulus of a succession of wet years, the lake started climbing again; in four years it climbed 8 feet, to a level 3 feet above Stansbury's mark of 1850. For 15 years the lake level remained fairly stable, but trending slightly upward until it reached the 4,205 mark. Then again, however, it dropped clear out of sight. In 1934 it struck zero on the Saltair gage, and kept going right on down, in 1935 reaching a low of 3.1 feet below zero.

However, the lake level promptly rose 2.5 feet, but drought in 1940 brought it down again to an all-time low, 3.2 feet below the zero level, or 4,193.55 feet above sea level. At this point stubbornly the lake again began to struggle upward, and in April 1946 for the first time since 1934 it rose above the zero level, climbing as high as .3 feet into the plus zone (4,197.15 feet) before relaxing back below the zero line, in the usual late summer fluctuation.

The lake fluctuates from month to month as from year to year. The level is always highest in the late spring, when the lake has been swelled by the spring runoff, and usually lowest in late November and December, when evaporation has got in its deadly work; this fluctuation during the year normally approximates about one foot, though in 1907 the lake actually gained about 3.5 feet, losing only about a foot of that amount during the months of adversity.

These fluctuations in the lake level directly follow upon conditions of precipitation. A series of wet or dry years will be followed by a corresponding increase or decrease in the size of the lake. It is said that the effect of wet or dry years in the lake's watershed is felt with diminishing effect for seven years.

Though irrigation has cut down the inflow of water, the lake has been more intimately responsive to general conditions of precipitation than to diversion by irrigation projects, and here rests the lake's case for survival: it cannot dry up until all its affluent waters have dried up, until a far-reaching climatic change has come about. And there may be as much reason to anticipate a cycle of wet years as of dry. So, far from disappearing, the lake may become as obnoxious a neighbor as it showed itself to be in 1924–1925, when it threatened to put the Lucin Cutoff out of business and flood the highway along its south shore. Or it may behave as it did in the 70's, when it flooded vast areas of low-lying meadowland and induced the Salt Lake County Commission to send out an exploring expedition to learn whether the rising waters could not be diverted westward to expend themselves in again flooding the long-dry Salt Desert.

This continuous fluctuation of the lake level has given the Great Salt Lake islands an adventurous history. Depending on the stage of the water, there are as many as 13 islands. In low water some are joined to the mainland or each other, and in high water some are inundated in whole or in part.

Antelope, the largest of the islands, is 15½ miles long by 5½ miles wide with an area of 23,175 acres. It rises abruptly from the water on its western shore but slopes gently toward the brine on its eastern side. Alone among the lake islands, it has been continuously inhabited since 1848, used for the grazing of sheep, cattle and horses. Antelope disappeared from it in the 70's, but a small herd of buffalo has been maintained there since the early 90's. In time of low water it is connected to the mainland by a sand bar over which cars may be driven, but visitors, whether by land or by water, are not encouraged by the owners, for fear of such fires as in 1945 destroyed thousands of acres of valuable grass.

Frémont Island, north of Antelope, is 5 miles long and 2 miles wide with an area of 2,945 acres. Though Frémont in 1843 described it as "simply a rocky hill, on which is neither water nor trees of any kind," there is a seepage of brackish water near the waterline on the north coast, and two artesian wells provide an additional supply for the sheep which are pastured on the island.

Stansbury Island, west of Antelope, is usually a peninsula connected with the mainland, 11½ miles long and 5½ miles wide, with an area of 22,314 acres. Mountains rising 3,000 feet above the lake make it the most rugged of the islands. Like Antelope and Frémont, it is privately owned and used for grazing purposes.

Carrington Island, north of Stansbury, is a circular islet slightly more than 2 miles in diameter with an area of 1,767 acres. Although good roofing slate was early found on it, the island was never utilized until it was homesteaded by sheepmen in 1927.

Gunnison Island, the other principal island, in the northwestern part of the lake, is less than a mile long and has an area of only 155.06 acres. Like Bird (or Hat) Island, a 22-acre pile of granitic conglomerate, it is held under mineral patent for its guano deposits and is the largest of the 4 islands harboring bird rookeries.

Egg Island and White Rock, lying off the west coast of Antelope, are tiny islets also occupied by waterfowl, and like Dolphin and Cub Islands in the northwestern part of the lake, still public domain.

Mud Island, off the mouth of the Weber, is actually a 600-acre sandbar exposed only when the lake is low; another such sandbar is Badger Island, between Stansbury and Carrington islands. Strongs Knob on the west shore with an area of 703 acres is normally a part of Strongsknob Mountain, severed from it only when the water is very high.

Although an island at no stage of the water, Promontory (almost unversally miscalled Promontory Point), with its long, mountainous finger probing the heart of the lake, is a feature of the shore line as important as any of the islands; it, too, is privately owned in large part and is used as a range for livestock.

The Pacific Railroad in 1868 was tantalized by the idea of driving directly west across the lake but had to settle for a circuitous course to the north, and the Golden Spike was driven at the wind-blown summit of the Promontory Range on May 10, 1869. In 1902–1903, when the Union Pacific and its affiliated lines were engaged in straightening their routes, the opportunity was seized to build west across the lake during a time of low water, and the Lucin Cutoff resulted, slashing the distance to Lucin, far west in the Salt Desert, by 44 miles and eliminating the heavy grades over the Promontory.

The Cutoff drove a final spike into the hopes Salt Lake City had never been able to abandon, that it would get on the main line of the Union Pacific by adoption of "the only logical route" to the Pacific, around the south shore of the lake; the city was not entirely reconciled to the Cutoff until railroad lines down into the heart of Utah were completed to Los Angeles in 1905, giving Salt Lake City arterial connection with the Pacific Coast. In 1908 the old dream of a railroad around the south shore of the lake was finally realized when the Western Pacific was completed, giving the Denver & Rio Grande Western an outlet to San Francisco.

To construct the 102-mile Lucin Cutoff 3,000 men worked a year and a half. The cost was in excess of $8,000,000, and the job required hundreds of trainloads of rock and the timber from 38,000 trees. The arm across Bear River Bay to Promontory Point is 9 miles long, all of it rock fill except for 600 feet of pile trestle midway its length. From Promontory Point to Lakeside on the west shore of the lake is 20 miles. There are 4 miles of rock fill, then 20 miles of wooden trestle work, and a final 6 miles of fill at the west shore.

The salt water seems to preserve and harden the 100-foot pilings, but the Southern Pacific, the modern incarnation of the Central Pacific, must maintain a safety patrol at Saline, on the west shore of Promontory, to keep the rock fill under constant inspection, for storm waves exert an inconceivable battering force against the fill. For boatmen the Cutoff presents some problems, for clearance between bents of the trestles is not great, and passage is difficult if not impossible when waves are high. Moreover, when the lake level is high, vertical clearance is limited, and sailboats must dismast.

Like the railroad, the airlines chose the direct course westward. A flashing series of beacons guides planes east and west from the Salt Lake Airport across the low-lying salt water. The lake has never been hospitable to commercial boats, so its history is almost barren of dramatic shipwrecks, but since 1935 airplanes have periodically crashed in the heavy brine to provide the lake with derelicts of a different kind.

Most memorable of these crashes was the first, a two-motored Standard Oil Company of California plane on October 6, 1935. Three men lost their lives, and it required four months of intensive work to locate the plane; the oil company brought in Coast and Geodetic Survey officers familiar with hydrographic work, outfitted four search boats and carried on full scale surveying and dragging operations. Headlines were also made by the crash of an Army plane on August 31, 1937. One flier made the long swim to the highway west of Black Rock, frightening motorists with the specter of "a naked maniac" waving his arms at them, but his companion, after electing to stay with the ship in the stormy seas, swam for it too late. Search parties found his body two days later. On April 25, 1943, a B-25 bomber flying out of Sacramento crashed in the northwestern part of the lake, five men losing their lives, and a P-47 ship was wrecked off the west coast of Antelope on August 7, 1944, the pilot being killed. Early in May, 1946, a student pilot, stunting just off Black Rock, dipped his wing too low and paid with his life for his foolhardiness, plunging into the lake within 50 feet of two bathers.

More headlines have been made by crashing planes and by marooned boating parties than by drownings. Because the lake is feared for its strangeness and regarded as dangerous to swimmers and boatmen, its safety record is probably unapproached by any American lake of remotely comparable size. Among the few drownings perhaps the most celebrated was that of the Salt Lake merchant, J. D. Farmer, on August 6, 1882. His "semipetrified" body was not found till October 11, 1886.

Boating activity has periodically been attended by fatal mishaps; the earliest, perhaps, was that of three young men sailing out of Hooper in mid-June 1889. In general, however, boatmen are not flattered by the hue and cry that goes up in the newspapers when a boat does not get back to the boat harbor on schedule. The salt water sometimes splashes on the engines of outboard craft, putting them out of commission, and the high waves kicked up by storms are always regarded with respect, but a boat can ride out almost any storm if it is equipped with an anchor and scope of line and a means of bailing the boat. With a proper anchor overboard and the motor off or the sails furled, the bow of a boat will stay in the wind and withstand wind and waves. In fact, a boat with an anchor can come home safely without any other means of propulsion, simply by anchoring when the wind is unfavorable and lifting the anchor to drift with the wind when it is favorable. The prevailing winds, being westerly, will soon drift the boat to the inhabited eastern or southeastern shores of the lake, for in only a moderate wind a boat will drift a mile an hour.

During the 1930's more attention was attracted to the salt flats west of the lake than to Great Salt Lake itself, when the possibilities of the salt beds for racing automobiles were first fully realized. As early as 1911 W. D. Rishel had taken a big Packard to the salt to "open 'er up" to the terrific speed of 50 miles an hour. Thoroughly sold on the vast, salt plain as a speed course, Rishel three years later induced the speed demon, Teddy Tetzlaff, to take his Blitzen Benz to the salt flats. Tetzlaff broke all records with a mark of 141.73 miles an hour, but the American Automobile Association and the Automobile Club of America declined to recognize the feat.

The salt flats then lapsed back into oblivion, but after the Salt Lake daredevil, Ab Jenkins, became acquainted with the salt flats in 1925 by winning a race with an excursion train from Salt Lake City to Wendover, in which he traveled the newly completed Victory highway, he conceived the idea of turning the level expanse of salt to serious purposes of speed demonstration. In case of mishap a driver had plenty of room to fight his car. The concretelike salt also had a cooling effect on tires, and its hardness insured that in case of a blowout the rim of the wheel would not dig into soft sand, as it had been known to do at Daytona Beach, Florida, hurling car and driver end over end. The only disadvantage was that the salt, always a little moist from the effect of solar evaporation upon the mud and water underlying it, furnished slightly less traction than a dry dirt, board or concrete track.

Jenkins made a 24-hour run on the salt beds in 1932, driving the entire time himself at an average 112.935 miles an hour, but he could get no official recognition, and it was a week before the Salt Lake City newspapers would condescend to notice the "stunt." The race course, a 10-mile circle, had been marked out by the Utah State Road Commission, with 4-foot stakes, placed every 100 feet in holes made by driving a steel wedge into the salt. Jenkins says that the surface was so hard that at times the steel wedges bent like wax while they were being driven in. Twenty small oil flares lighted the course at night.

In 1933 AAA sanction was finally obtained, and in his 12-cylinder Pierce-Arrow Jenkins averaged 117.77 miles an hour for 24 hours and covered 3,000 miles in 25 hours, 30 minutes and 36.62 seconds. This was far in advance of anything it had been possible to do on European tracks and immediately attracted the attention of British drivers. When Jenkins' runs of 1934 shoved the 24-hour average to 127.229 miles an hour, these drivers began making preparations to try their own luck on the Salt Desert.

For some time Sir Malcolm Campbell had been trying for a new record at Daytona Beach in his *Bluebird,* and in August 1935 he brought his car to the salt flats. His first trial, on September 3, brought him his coveted record of 301.13 miles an hour for the measured mile. Before Campbell's arrival, his fellow countryman, John Cobb, pushed Jenkins' 24-hour mark up to 134.85 miles an hour, though the Utah-born driver alone made a specialty of driving the entire run himself. Jenkins regained the record at 135.58 later in the summer, but the following year the English drivers, Cobb and George E. T. Eyston, returned to the competition. A summer of racing left the record in Jenkins' possession, but the 24-hour mark had been pushed up to 153.823 miles an hour. Under stress of competition, all the cars were now being powered by airplane engines.

In 1937 Jenkins advanced his record for 24 hours to 157.27 miles per hour, and in 1939 he boosted it to a still higher figure, 161.18 miles per hour. Campbell retired from racing after his triumph in 1935, but his countrymen, Cobb and Eyston, embarked upon a competition between themselves for the one-mile record. In November 1937 Eyston covered the distance in his *Thunderbolt* at the speed of

311.42 miles an hour, and the next summer he shoved the record up to 347.49 miles. Cobb streaked over the course at a 350.25 pace, but this record lasted for just one day as Eyston promptly regained supremacy with a 357.5 figure. Cobb, however, had the last word. He returned to the Bonneville Salt Flats, as they had now been named, just before war broke out in the summer of 1939, and set the record, 368.9 miles an hour, which has since stood.

The rigorous testing given the British engines and the engineering genius that went into them bore rich dividends during the war when the gallant few of the RAF had to fight the Battle of Britain. It is the 24-hour endurance runs that primarily contribute to automotive engineering advances. The salt beds are a unique testing ground, a "speed laboratory," for making cars safer and better.

In this contrary fashion, by sharing its bed with a few lusty engineers and racing drivers, Great Salt Lake contrives a certain utility. But it seems more in character in other situations. In May 1939 it inveigled off course an Ogden resident herding sheep on Frémont Island. He had started for the mainland with horses and a two wheeled cart along a narrow sand bar eight inches under water spanning island and shore. Though the way was marked at quarter-mile intervals with stakes, the herdsman, unused to "horse and wagon seamanship," wandered off his course and lost his horses in quicksand. He had to hike the six miles to shore and arrived in no very happy frame of mind.

That is rather more like the Great Salt Lake to which history has always had to accommodate itself. Always it has defied those who would use it. The most ambitious project of all, to dike it along its chain of islands—from the south shore to Antelope, from Antelope to Frémont, and from Frémont to Promontory, shutting the saltwater into its western half and creating of its eastern reaches a freshwater lake to provide industrial water—has threatened the very existence of the obstinate mountain sea. But even though the great French engineer, De Lesseps, builder of the Suez Canal, is said to have urged the practicability of the idea, and though intensive studies were made in 1935–1936 establishing its feasibility, the lake has a way of wriggling out of all such tight spots. Dr. Thomas C. Adams, who directed the engineering investigation, says that present public attitudes trend toward the feeling that it would be better to reserve such a development until other developments are made at higher levels on the affluent streams, where the water would be fresher and might be more economically developed.

Although there are a few scattered salt and sodium product refineries along its shores, and although potash has been mined from its Salt Desert, the mountain sea manages to maintain itself aloof from easy money-making. In the end you must take the lake on its own terms—refractory, obstinate, not to everyone's taste. Self-preoccupied, often sullen of mood, yet on occasion yielding itself up with an abandoned beauty that only the desert knows, it is a fit lake for a desert land.

II

NATIVES AND NEWCOMERS

Prehistoric Indians

Viewed from a distant vantage point, like Highway 89 near Kaysville, or even from certain closer perspectives like the cockpit of a sailboat, the Great Salt Lake has a beauty that defies the writer, the painter, and even the photographer. Traveling along its shore on Interstate 80 and out across the Great Salt Lake Desert, however, the observer is perhaps less impressed by the beauty than by what appears to be a largely sterile terrain that seems forbidding to most human uses. How surprising it is, then, to learn from the following article not only that human beings have inhabited the desert longer than any other part of Utah, but that they found, throughout most of that period of habitation, much more plentiful food sources in marshes surrounding the lake and on the Great Salt Lake Desert than in the surrounding mountains. Perhaps nowhere on the face of the earth do we modern, civilized people have to face more dramatically the degree to which we egregiously underestimate the capacities and resourcefulness of early peoples. That modern naiveté, which has elsewhere led to such fanciful explanations of the Easter Island statues, the Egyptian pyramids, or Stonehenge as the work of visitors from outer space, causes us to lift our eyebrows when confronted with evidence that similarly ancient peoples could not only live, but in fact live in abundance, in such an apparently unpromising environment as the Great Salt Lake Desert.

To read this article is to enter into another world, a world lived in the most profound harmony with nature and in tune with nature's rhythms, both seasonally and in larger geological cycles. While we moderns, in our industrial might and arrogance, violently wrest from nature those commodities we think we need (and sometimes suffering unforeseen consequences from the resulting imbalances in nature), peoples such as those discussed here exhibit a sophistication unbelievable to us in their ability to understand nature's resources and to adapt to their use. Looking at ourselves from their perspective ought to be a humbling experience, and it surely offers many lessons if we have the wisdom to learn them.

David B. Madsen, formerly state archaeologist of Utah, is presently employed by the Utah Geological and Mineralogical Survey, which published the anthology from which the article is taken. Madsen is one of the most highly respected students of Great Basin prehistory, perhaps most noted for his development of techniques for studying ancient food forms through analysis of pollen types found in prehistoric sites. He has also made repeated archaeological expeditions to China, where he has brought his expertise in Great Basin prehistory to bear in analyzing ancient Chinese sites.

Suggestions for further reading

A groundbreaking article like this one largely supersedes previous literature and much of it is based, as one can see from the accompanying bibliography, on technical scientific studies that can be forbidding to the general reader. Madsen's more recent study, *Exploring the Fremont* (Salt Lake City: University of Utah Press, 1989), updates some of the data reported in this article. Helen Z. Papanikolas, ed., *The Peoples of Utah* (Salt Lake City: Utah State Historical Society, 1976), begins with a section on prehistoric and historic Indians in Utah, including the Great Basin. Jesse D. Jennings, *Accidental Archaeologist* (Salt Lake City: University of Utah Press, 1994), is the autobiography of one of the pioneers of Great Basin archaeology, though it contains less discussion of the subject than one might wish. Some of the Jennings titles in the bibliography to the present article are accessible to the general reader. No one should miss the somewhat tongue-in-cheek article by Madsen and his father, historian Brigham D. Madsen, "One Man's Meat Is Another Man's Poison: A Revisionist View of the Seagull 'Miracle,'" *Nevada Historical Society Quarterly* 30 (fall 1987): 165–81, conveniently anthologized in John S. McCormick and John R. Sillito, *A World We Thought We Knew: Readings in Utah History* (Salt Lake City: University of Utah Press, 1995), 55–67, which contrasts the attitudes of primitive and modern people toward food sources. Finally, Forrest S. Cuch, ed., *A History of Utah's American Indians* (Salt Lake City: Utah Division of Indian Affairs and the Utah Division of State History, 2000), contains chapters on the Great Basin Indians of northern Utah.

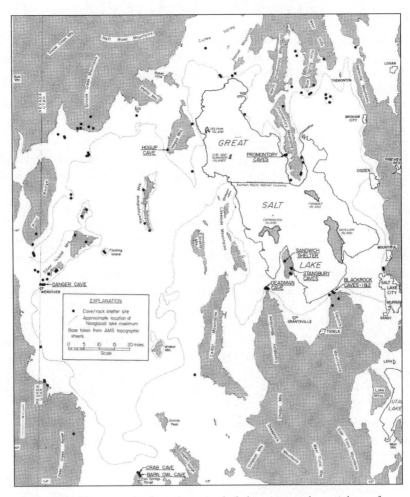

Map: Plot of known archeological cave/rock shelter sites on the periphery of the Great Salt Lake. Outer line is the approximate location of Neoglacial lake maximum.

The Human Prehistory of the Great Salt Lake Region
David B. Madsen

Abstract

Until about 600 years ago, the marsh and lake edge resources were of primary importance in the subsistence economies of local prehistoric peoples. Fluctuations in the level of the Great Salt Lake greatly affected the availability of these resources; changes in population density and settlement patterns can be attributed in part to changes in the lake. The area was probably initially occupied about 10,000 years ago by Paleo-Indians who relied on a mix of big-game hunting and collecting of lake margin resources. By about 8,500 years ago, relatively sedentary Archaic peoples occupied cave/rockshelters on the lake edge. Mid-Holocene desiccation of the lake 5,500 to 3,500 years ago resulted in a shift to a more nomadic lifestyle and to a reliance on upland as well as lake margin resources. Flooding of lake periphery resources resulted in the abandonment of lake margin sites and a subsistence economy based on upland flora and fauna. By about 2,500 years ago the area had been virtually abandoned. A Formative Stage Culture, characterized by small villages, domesticated plants, and pottery, occupied the lake margin and marsh areas between about 1,500 and 600 years ago. Their subsistence economy was very similar to that of previous area occupants; corn was not a dominant resource and was apparently of minor importance. By 500 years ago these people had been replaced by Shoshonians moving in from the southwestern Great Basin. The Shoshonian groups differed from earlier inhabitants in that they relied more on upland resources, such as pinyon nuts, rather than lake shore resources.

David B. Madsen, "The Human Prehistory of the Great Salt Lake Region," from *Great Salt Lake: A Scientific, Historical, and Economic Overview*, ed. J. Wallace Gwynn, Utah Geological and Mineralogical Survey Bulletin 116 (Salt Lake City: 1980), 19–31.

Introduction

The "prehistory" of the area immediately adjacent to the Great Salt Lake is ordinarily limited to placing pre-Columbian aboriginal groups in spatial and chronological perspective. However, this approach is primarily descriptive and does not reveal the changing patterns of human adaptation which occur in response to fluctuating environmental conditions. Generally speaking, the size and complexity of a culture is a product of environmental conditions (that is, the type and amount of resources available to the culture) and its technological capabilities (that is, the tools and labor organizations used to transform those resources into usable forms). As a result, the examination of cultural change in an area of marked environmental instability, such as the area around the Great Salt Lake, can provide a clearer insight into the processes of cultural evolution. The alternate flooding and desiccation of the lake and of spring and river-fed marshes on its periphery can be shown to have greatly affected the history of pre-historic human adaptation in the region throughout the ten thousand plus years of occupation. The examination of the relationships between these environmental changes and the corollary cultural changes is fascinating and rewarding in terms of understanding the nature of the culture. In addition to discussing the area's prehistory, focus will be on changes in the environmental conditions in and around the lake; the effects these chances had on adaptation and settlement patterns, and the processes through which these changes occurred.

A word of caution must be offered about the interpretations which follow. The archeology of the eastern Great Basin and western Colorado Plateau is currently in a state of flux. Between 1975 and the present, a number of new hypotheses have been offered that radically conflict with previous widely accepted interpretations. That these hypotheses are partially contradictory is due primarily to the lack of an adequate data base. As a result, the discussion which follows is only my current interpretation of the prehistory of the Great Salt Lake area; subsequent modifications are bound to occur.

Environments and Resources of the Great Salt Lake

The initial impression of the lake and the Great Salt Lake desert today is usually one of stark desolation. The barren salt flats and low-elevation fault-block mountains appear to have insufficient flora and fauna to support more than an extremely sparse population. This is simply not the case, however; and this impression can probably be attributed to the cultural biases of modern civilization. We tend to see only those resources we are accustomed to using. Therefore, clarification of the nature of the resources available to the prehistoric inhabitants of the area is a necessity. Specific environmental data from the Great Salt Lake area cannot be given here.

The first and probably most important resource areas are the extensive marshes which surround the lake and the Great Salt Lake desert. The most obvious of these are the large Farmington Bay and Bear River Bay marshes. In addition, a number of springs found on the periphery of the Great Salt Lake desert, such as Fish Springs in western Juab County, still support relatively large marsh areas. Other spring supported marshes, such as those at Wendover, Utah, have been modified to the extent that it is presently difficult to conceive of the size of the marshes they once supported. Extensive marsh areas are also found along the Bear River which drains into the Salt Lake basin. The area's riverine marshes have been greatly reduced by present day water control which has altered the environment to one more appropriate for European types of resource utilization (Nielson, 1978).

Marshes are the single richest ecosystem yet defined in terms of available energy, even when compared with most types of intensive farming (Odum, 1963). The number of types of edible flora and fauna, as well as the amount of each type, far exceeds that found in other terrestrial ecosystems. As a single example, an acre of cattails (*Typha sp.*) produces up to 4,896 kg (10,792 lbs) of harvestable roots and tubers which can be reduced to 2,494 kg (5,500 lbs) of edible flour (Claassen, 1919). This flour is equal to or exceeds rice, wheat, and corn in nutritive value. Even more important is that cattails grow rapidly throughout most of the year and can rapidly replace those harvested (Niering, 1966: Reimold and Queen, 1974).

Prior to the nineteenth century these extensive and extremely productive marsh areas were the focus of human subsistence and habitation. In one relatively small (50 mile) stretch of the central Sevier Valley, for instance, there were more than an estimated 10,000 acres of cattail/bulrush marshlands which surrounded Utah and Great Salt lakes prior to water control have never been made.

The second area of resources is the margin of the salt flats. These margin areas ring the entire Great Salt Lake basin between the foothills of the fault-block ranges and the true salt flats. They are flat to slightly sloping areas of highly saline soils that support large populations of salt-loving halophytic plants. Although the variety of plants is limited, the distribution of the few edible species is extensive. For example, pickleweed (*Allenrolfia sp.*) is a low ground cover herb which is a prolific producer of small edible seeds. These seeds, readily collected and stored, are known to have served as one of the basic dietary, staples of prehistoric human inhabitants (Aikens, 1970). Many of the spring marshes are immediately adjacent to extensive halophytic-dominated flats, and the utilization of both resource zones was a relatively simple matter.

The third and relatively minor area of resource utilization is in the mountains which surround the lake basin. A variety of ecological zones are found on the Wasatch Range to the east of the lake; on the Raft River Mountains to the north, and the Pilot and Deep Creek ranges to the west. These zones range from pinyon-juniper forests which produce large quantities of the edible plant resources and were used primarily as a source of game. The exception is the pinyon forests which produce large quantities of edible nuts. However, until the advent of protohistoric Shoshonian groups, there is little evidence that pinyon nuts were used as a basic staple, if at all.

The pattern of utilization of the various resource zones is readily apparent form the distribution of the more than 500 archeological sites that have been identified in the area (Madsen and Berry, 1974, 1975). Less than 5% are at elevations above 1,850 m (6,070 feet). By far the large majority of the remaining sites are either in or adjacent to marsh areas at elevations of 1,275 to 1,375 m (4,200 to 4,500 feet). This limited distribution is critical to understanding the impact of the lake on prehistoric groups, and should be kept in mind in the discussion which follows (map).

Pre-projectile Point (Early Man) Cultures(40,000 to 12,000 B.P.)

The presence of man in the New World prior to the close of the last glacial stade has been one of the more controversial topics in American archeology. Unfortunately, no sites clearly substantiate the presence of human groups in North America prior to ca. 20,000 years ago. In every case there are questions as to whether or not the artifacts are really of human origin or whether or not the geological units are accurately dated.

In the area of the Great Salt Lake, the single purportedly Early Man site is questionable, but it is a good example of the type of evidence usually marshalled in support of these claims. The site, possibly 40,000 years old, is located on the highest (1,610 m) (5,280 feet) Lake Bonneville terrace near Lehi, Utah (map) and has been described by Clark (1975). It consists of two small apparently wave-cut caves on the beach terrace. Flakes and bifacially retouched stone tools were found associated with fire hearths in the caves and on the slope above the beach terrace. The human origin of the artifacts and their association with the cave deposit appears to be relatively well-established. However, the estimated age of the site is based on some unfounded assumptions. The first of these, that the beach is about 40,000 years old, is based on the assumption that dates on carbonates, taken from cores in the Great Salt Lake, date the lake when it was at the 1,610 in level. This has yet to be adequately demonstrated, and work by others (e.g., Morrison. 1966, Currey in this volume) suggests the lake was at or about this level about 18,000 years ago and again about 14,000 years ago. The second assumption is that since the artifacts are on top of the beach, they are the same age as the beach. Obviously, the artifacts could have been deposited anytime after the caves were cut and the water receded. In other words, they could be any age from 0 to 14,000 years old, but probably not 40,000 years old.

Paleo-Indian/Big Game Hunters (ca. 12,000 to 9,000 B.P.)

The earliest widespread, well-recognized cultural stage in North America has been variously termed "Big Game Hunting" or "Paleo-Indian". Information concerning the technology and subsistence adaptation of these peoples is extremely sparse. Little is known about these groups except that they were adapted to the hunting of large Pleistocene mammals such as the mammoth and camel, and that they used well-made "fluted" projectile points to procure them. Most information concerning these cultures comes from excavated "kill sites" in the Southwest and High Plains areas. Dating of those sites suggests that reliance on the killing of large herbivores persisted from around 13,000 to 8,500 years ago. The sites can only be classed together because of demonstrated reliance on Pleistocene megafauna, but the large majority of the sites give little or no indication of the overall subsistence adaptation or settlement pattern. The fluted projectile points associated with the kill sites are quite distinctive. The best known and most widely distributed of these points are the Clovis and Folsom fluted points. Surface finds of these points in the vicinity of the Great Salt Lake suggest that Paleo-Indian groups may well have inhabited the region.

In the immediate vicinity of the lake, the surface finds are from the Curlew Valley north of the lake (Butler, 1973), the Sevier Desert area near Delta, Utah, (Madsen, Currey, and Madsen, 1976), and the Deep Creek mountain area southwest of the lake (Lindsay and Sargent, 1977). Locations are shown in figure 2. Both Clovis and Folsom varieties of points have been found, as well as a possible later Paleo-Indian biface known as a Cody Knife. The presence of all three types suggest occupation of the area throughout the entire Paleo-Indian period.

Several sites on the western periphery of the lake contain basal cultural deposits which date prior to 10,000 years ago. Danger Cave (Jennings, 1957), Deer Creek Cave (Shutler and Shutler, 1963), and Smith Creek Cave (Bryan, 1972) all contain dated cultural materials of a nondiagnostic nature. These early occupations have been attributed to later Archaic groups because of the presence of overlying, readily identified Archaic diagnostics (e.g., Fry, 1976), and because of the assumed absence of large Pleistocene mammals (e.g., Jennings, 1966, 1978). However, neither of these assumptions is valid, and in light of numerous finds of megafauna which postdate the earliest cultural sites, the sites may well represent Paleo-Indian occupations.

One of these fossil sites is of particular importance since it occurs near a recessional beach of Lake Bonneville. This site, in the Draper Formation near Sandy, Utah, contained a mammoth dated from 6,000 to 8,800 years ago (Madsen, Currey, and Madsen, 1976).

The probability of such contemporaneity is strengthened by the association of Pleistocene mammals and cultural materials at several sites in relative proximity to the Great Salt Lake. At the Pine Springs site (Sharrock, 1966) in southwestern Wyoming, bison and camel bones, found in association with Paleo-Indian materials, were dated to ca. 9,750 years ago. At the Wasden site in south central Idaho, fluted points were found associated with mammoth remains (Miller and Dort, 1978). This important kill site has been radiocarbon dated to 11,000 to 12,00 years ago.

Another rarely used source of data is rock art. Several rock art sites in Utah contain elements which seem clearly to be representations of proboscideans (Stokes, 1972; Madsen, Currey, and Madsen, 1976), and the existence of these sites gives ancillary support to the probable co-occurrence of these animals and man in the region. However, since rock art cannot be dated and because it is rarely associated with cultural materials, the art should only be used to support more concrete sources of information.

In summary, several lines of evidence support the presence of Paleo-Indians of the shores of Great Salt Lake between 9,000 and 1,000 years ago. Although most of the evidence for the Paleo-Indian culture is derived from kill sites which give little indication of the overall subsistence strategy, recently completed surveys and excavations in the Great Basin area indicate that Paleo-Indian groups were primarily adapted to lake, spring, and river peripheries and were probably adapted as well to the collection of marsh resources (e.g., Davis, 1976; Thomas, 1978). This means that Paleo-Indian groups probably did not differ greatly from the later Archaic cultures, and their adaptation to marsh environments, such as that found around the Great Salt Lake, is a pattern which has remained basically stable for the last 10,000 to 12,000 years. Therefore, it may well be that what changes did occur during Paleo-Indian times and during the transition to the Archaic were the result of lake level changes and the concomitant effect on the availability of periphery marsh resources.

Archaic Stage (8,500 to 2,500 B.P.)

The Archaic Stage in North America is defined as a broadly based subsistence adaptation, with subsistence varying "from season to season as it focused first on one species or community of species and then on another a fundamental lifeway, not created to any one ecosystem" (Jennings, 1974: 110–111).

Unfortunately, the term "Archaic", based as it is on a subsistence adaptation definition, is something of a misnomer. In actual use, Archaic cultures have come to be defined on the basis of technological and chronological criteria. That is, cultures are assigned to the Archaic Stage because they follow big game hunters and precede agriculturalists; because they use tools such as the atlatl (spear-thrower); grinding stones, stone vessels, basketry, and skin robes; and because they lack other tools such as fluted points, pottery, and the bow-and-arrow. This confusion is due to the ambiguous definition of the stage originally provided by Willey and Phillips (1955, 1958). They defined the stage as a "migratory hunting and gathering" type of subsistence adaptation, but the criteria they used to distinguish this stage from others are primarily technological, not economic/environmental. This confusion has led to the classification of both sedentary collectors and big game hunters as Archaic Stage cultures. The problem is much the same when dealing with the "Archaic" cultures of the Great Salt Lake area. In terms of subsistence adaptation these groups cannot readily be distinguished from preceding and following groups, and technological and chronological criteria must be used.

These criteria indicate that Archaic peoples appeared in the Great Salt Lake area about 8,500 to 9,000 years ago, and occupied the area continuously until about

2,500 years ago. Whether or not they occupied the area continuously until the introduction of agriculture about A.D. 400 is presently a subject of contention.

Between 9,000 and about 5,500 years ago, the focus of Archaic subsistence adaptation was the marsh/salt flat ecosystem that surrounds the lake. During this period Archaic peoples lived in cave/rockshelters adjacent to the fresh-water springs on the lake periphery.

Simms (1977) suggests that during this period the population around the lake was gradually increasing. This hypothesis is based on the gradual increase with time in the number of sites occupied on the lake periphery. Only two sites, Danger Cave (Jennings, 1957) and Hogup Cave (Aikens, 1970), date to the earliest period of Archaic occupation. Basal dates suggested by Simms (1977) for other sites are Sandwich Shelter (ca. 7,000 B.P.), Stansbury Caves I and II (ca. 7,000 to 5,000 B.P.) Promontory Cave No. 2 (ca. 7,000 to 5,000 B.P.), Deadman Cave (ca. 7,000 to 5,000 B.P.), and Fremont Island (ca. 550 B.P.) (See figure 2 for locations). All these sites were continously occupied, so the apparent increase in the number of sites cannot be attributed simply to a shift of a group from one site to another. Some evidence that entirely different groups of people occupied the different sites (Fry and Adovasio, 1970), implies that the number of groups as well as group size was increasing.

This increase in population appears to be tied directly to changes in the level of the lake. Throughout the early Archaic period the people lived almost entirely on lake edge resources such as pickleweed, sedge, rodents, and marsh birds. There is evidence that they used some upland game, such as sheep and deer, and that some of their tools were made of upland plant species. However, there are no known upland sites occupied during this early era; at best, these areas were supplemental. It presently appears that these Archaic peoples were relatively sedentary, and that the resources on the periphery of the lake were sufficient to support a growing population.

The size of this lake edge ecosystem and the amount of available resources are inversely tied to lake level fluctuations. As the lake level fell from its Pleistocene high, due to reduced precipitation or higher temperatures, it gradually exposed fresh-water springs, more extensive marsh habitats, and larger areas of halophytic plant dominance. The amount of available resources was actually increased. This increase in resources resulted in a larger human population that was largely dependent on the productivity of the lake periphery ecosystem.

This relationship between decreasing lake levels and increasing resources is not continuous, however. As the lake is reduced in size, a point of diminishing returns is reached when the water table can no longer support fresh-water flow in several of the springs, and flow is much reduced or becomes brackish in many of the others. Simms (1977) suggests that this point occurs at around 1,280 m (4,200 feet), and that the decrease in lake size had reached this point by 5,500 years ago. This is in accord with general estimates for a mid post-Pleistocene warm period (e.g. Antevs, 1955), and time estimates of mid-Holocene desiccation of the lake (Eardley et. al., 1957).

It is not surprising then, that around 5,500 years ago sites in upland areas began to be occupied, probably the result of the combined pressure of increased population and decreased lake margin resources. Lake edge sites continued to be occupied, but apparently in a less sedentary fashion. Subsistence adaption was more of a classic "Archaic" type, in that it consisted of a migratory shift from site to site, from one ecosystem to another, as resources became available in differing areas.

Excavated upland sites are found in the fault-block mountains west and south of the lake (Gruhn, 1972; Sargent, 1978; Fowler, 1968; Heizer, Baumhoff, and Clewlow, 1968; Shutler and Shutler, 1963); in the Grouse Creek and Raft River Mountain area northwest of the lake (Dalley, 1976); and in the Wasatch Range southeast of the lake (Mock, 1971). They are situated in pinyon/juniper zones in locations that would allow access to sage/grass communities and higher montane resources. These upland sites apparently were used primarily as hunting camps, although grasses such as Indian ricegrass *(Oryzopsis hymenoides)*, were also collected. The preferred (or perhaps the most abundant or the most readily procured) faunal resource was mountain sheep. Deer and rabbit remains are also abundant, and bison remains are occasionally recovered. Evidence from these sites (e.g., Dalley, 1976) indicates occupation by "family groups" rather than small male hunting parties. This strengthens the probability that these sites are related to the lake edge sites through an occupational pattern often referred to as a "seasonal" or annual round. This Archaic pattern of group movement from lake edge to foothills to lake edge apparently continued from ca. 5,500 to 3,000 years ago until another change, again probably caused by a lake level fluctuation, occurred.

Between 3,500 and 2,200 years ago a period of increased effective moisture known as the Neoglacial period resulted in rising lake levels that reached 1,298 in (4,260 feet) in elevation (Mehringer, 1977). At this level, the high water essentially eliminated the majority of marsh areas and halophytic-dominated salt flat margins and flooded a majority of the peripheral fresh-water springs. Resources around such lake edge sites as Hogup Cave (Aikens, 1970) were eliminated, and there is evidence that these sites were abandoned at this time (Madsen and Berry, 1975). However, Archaic occupation of the upland sites continued, and in all probability the carrying capacity of these upland areas was somewhat enhanced by the increased effective moisture. However, there is presently no evidence of an increase in the number of upland sites during this period, and a population decline of unknown magnitude probably occurred in the Great Salt Lake area. This scenario is strongly supported by a recent study of projectile point densities in lake periphery sites (Holmer, 1978).

At the end of the Neoglacial period, Archaic occupation of the Great Salt Lake area apparently ended. Why the region was abandoned is not clear at present, but of the 25 to 30 excavated Archaic sites in the general area, none give an unequivocal indication of occupation between ca. 2,500 and 1,500 years ago. The cause is most probably a combination of cultural and environmental factors. The carrying capacity of the upland areas was again reduced: and while lake edge resources were again available, after a thousand or more years of upland occupance, these groups were probably not familiar with or adapted to lakeside ecosystems and hence, could not and did not use them. The probability of an occupational hiatus or of cultural continuity is presently a matter of contention (e.g., Madsen and Berry, 1975; Aikens 1976), but whichever case is ultimately supported it seems clear that the population density of the area was markedly reduced after 2,500 years ago.

In summary, Archaic occupation of the Great Salt Lake area began about 8,500 years ago and continued to about 2,500 years ago (possibly later). Change in the number and location of sites in and around the lake suggests an increasing population until about 5,500 years ago, then a reduction in population, a moderate regrowth, finally followed by a marked reduction in population. The subsistence adaptation, settlement pattern, and indeed the life-style of these Archaic groups were intimately tied to the lake and the effect its level had on lake edge resources. Initially these groups were basically sedentary and shifted to a pattern of seasonal mobility only when the lake was reduced beyond a point where it would not support a stable existence. With the subsequent flooding of the lake edge resources, a radical change to primary dependence on upland ecosystems occurred. When these resources were in turn reduced, Archaic groups essentially abandoned the region.

Formative Stage, Sevier Culture (1,500 to 500 B.P)

In North America (north of Mexico) post-Archaic cultures are grouped together into what has been defined as the "Formative Stage" (Willey and Phillips, 1958). This stage is characterized by the advent of agriculture (principally corn, beans, and squash), pottery, bow-and-arrow, and settled villages. Due to the definitional confusion which surrounds the Archaic, the transition between the two stages is rather ambiguous. Fortunately, this problem does not exist in the eastern Great Basin. The apparent Archaic abandonment (or, at the very least, markedly reduced occupation) of the area makes it easy to separate the Formative Stage culture found around the Great Salt Lake from the preceding Archaic Stage.

The Formative Stage culture in the eastern Great Basin has been defined as the Sevier Culture (Madsen and Lindsay, 1977), and represents a redefinition of cultural variants once classed with the Fremont Culture (Marwitt, 1970). The following is modified from Madsen and Lindsay's (1977) definition: Settlement pattern is characterized by villages located on alluvial fans in intermontane valleys adjacent to marsh or riverine ecosystems and by temporary encampments spread throughout other environmental zones surrounding these centrally located villages. The ratio of temporary camps to villages is roughly ten to one. Subsistence economy is based on collecting wild flora and fauna, primarily from marsh environments, and is supplemented by corn agriculture. Given the type of settlement pattern and the lack of restrictions imposed by the seasonality of agriculture, the social organization probably consisted of loosely confederated family aggregates. Architecture is characterized by semisubterranean dwellings and rectangular adobe surface storage units. Masonry is extremely rare. With the exception of some variation in pottery types, the artifact inventory is fairly consistent in all areas where the culture is found, and is characterized by plain and decorated varieties of coil-made gray ware, corner- and side-notched arrow points, trough metates, one-rod-and-bundle basketry, and a variety of bone implements and ornaments. The Sevier Culture can be identified as a distinct entity from about 1,300 to 650 B.P.

In the specific area of the Great Salt Lake, significant variations in artifacts, architecture, and adaptation have suggested a larger degree of interaction with the Plains area and possibly even an origin in that region (Aikens, 1966; Madsen and Lindsay, 1977). Distinctive features include paddle-and-anvil pottery, shallow basin-shaped dwelling structures, and an adaptation to bison hunting. Prior to the definition of the Sevier Culture, post-Archaic groups in the Great Salt Lake area were described as the Great Salt Lake Variant of the Fremont Culture (Marwitt, 1970; Fry, 1970). This variant was divided into two temporal phases which are characterized primarily by slight differences in architecture, projectile points, and pottery. Two phases, the Bear River Phase (A.D. 400 to 1,000) and the Levee Phase (A.D. 1,000 to 1,350+), have been identified (Fry and Dalley, 1973). The earlier Bear River Phase is more characteristic of the Plains, and the later phase is characterized by features more closely resembling southern areas of the Sevier Culture. The differences between the two phases may be due to shift in interaction with the Plains area to interaction with the southeastern Great Basin.

The subsistence adaptation of these Sevier groups greatly resembles that of the preceding Archaic peoples. With the exception of a single site, all of the village sites are located in marsh areas on saline soils which preclude agriculture (e. g., Aikens, 1966, 1967; Fry and Dalley, 1973). The majority of these are on the 1,283 m (4,209 feet) contour (indicating the lake was probably slightly below this level) in the Bear River Bay and Farmington Bay areas of the east side of the lake. Protein resources were primarily bison and large waterfowl such as the Canada goose. Plants known to be collected were bulrush (*Scirpus* sp.) and goosefoot (*Chenopodiaceae sp.*). Other, more perishable and/or less readily identified plant types, such as cattails (*Typha* sp.) were also probably collected. The exceptional site at Willard, Utah (Judd, 1926), contains adobe storage structures and charred corncobs. This site suggests some reliance on agriculture, but corn appears to represent a minor portion of the overall subsistence economy. Other possible agricultural sites in the Grantsville/Tooele area, may be related to those on the eastern side of the lake and further research in these areas may demonstrate a heavier reliance on agriculture than is presently indicated.

The cave/rockshelter sites around the lake and in the upland areas, such as Swallow Shelter (Dalley, 1976) and Hogup Cave (Aikens, 1970) (map), were occupied by Sevier peoples and appeared to have been used as temporary base camps with hunting as the primary focus. Depending on the location of the site, the primary game sought was either mountain sheep, deer, antelope, or bison. Grasses and other plants were also collected at these sites, but they appear to have been of minor importance. These temporary hunting camps appear to be related to the marsh village sites in the overall subsistence economy. At Crab Cave, in the Fish Springs marsh area, there is evidence suggesting that hunting and pinyon nut collecting occurred in the fall and that the marsh areas were subsequently occupied during the late fall and winter (Madsen, 1979). At present, the pattern appears to have been one of a relatively sedentary existence in and around the marsh areas, with occasional movement into other environmental areas to procure meat and wild plants. This relatively settled condition, supported by marsh collecting and hunting, has occurred throughout the entire time-span of human occupation in the area. The high degree of similarity between the Archaic and Sevier subsistence economies argues for some sort of cultural continuity between the two groups.

After about 600 years ago the Sevier Culture can no longer be recognized in the eastern Great Basin. At present there is no clear evidence why these people disappeared, or indeed, what happened to them. There is some speculation that they reverted to a nomadic way of life due to environmental pressures, and may be recognized as the protohistoric Shoshonian groups (Gunnerson, 1969). However, current evidence suggests instead a wholesale replacement of the Sevier peoples by Shoshonian groups (e.g., Aikens, 1970). The Sevier peoples may have emigrated to other areas, or simply died out. An examination of the unique basketry styles (Adovasio, 1978, personal communication) supports the latter theory.

In summary, the Formative Stage in the eastern Great Basin is represented by the Sevier Culture. Settled village life was supported by the collection of marsh resources and hunting, supplemented by agriculture. The culture can first be recognized about 1,500 years ago. and may have either developed *in situ* from an older Archaic culture or may have resulted from an influx of people from the Plains area and/or the Southwest. By 500–600 years ago the culture had disappeared and had been replaced by the protohistoric Shoshonians.

Protohistoric Shoshonians (550 B.P. to present)

The best current evidence suggests that the predecessors of the historic aboriginal groups in the Great Salt Lake region arrived in the area about 500–600 years ago. The Shoshonian peoples speak dialects of the Numic branch of the Uto-Aztecan language family. Linguistic analysis of the Numic languages suggests that they diverged from a common language about 1,000 years ago, and that at that time, Numic-speaking peoples lived in the southwestern Great Basin (Lamb, 1958; Miller et. al., 1971; Fowler, 1972). This linguistic hypothesis is supported by dates on distinctive Shoshonian pottery which indicate the Numic-speaking peoples began to move north and east from their homeland 900 to 1,000 years ago (Madsen, 1975).

In the Great Salt Lake area, Shoshonian pottery first occurs about 600 to 700 years ago (e.g., Aikens, 1970).

Distinctive Paiute/Shoshoni artifacts, such as pottery, have been found in association with Sevier Culture materials at a number of sites, suggesting that the two groups co-existed in the region for a period of several hundred years (Madsen, 1975). Although the two cultures seem to have had somewhat different types of subsistence systems, the large number of sites with both Sevier and Paiute/Shoshoni artifacts suggests a relatively large degree of interaction. In the absence of any indications of warfare or other violence, we assume that this interaction was amicable.

The subsistence adaptation of historic Shoshonian groups has been described in detail by Steward (1938), and was probably very similar during the prehistoric period. Briefly, subsistence was based on a mixture of collecting wild flora and hunting. It was based on the movement of small groups from one area to another as differing resources became available. Occasionally, when local resources were particularly abundant, these small groups came together to participate in a variety of social activities. However, Shoshonian subsistence and settlement patterns were highly variable and substantial modifications of this generall pattern occurred. The Shoshoni seem to have relied less on lake, river, and spring edge resources than did previous groups, but there were exceptions, such as the virtually sedentary Shoshonian groups on the shores of Utah Lake.

The small, mobile groups of Shoshoni differed from previous occupants of the region in their heavy reliance on pinyon nuts. These nuts were extensively collected in the fall and served as the winter staple. The entire seasonal round revolved around the quantity of nuts collected, and years of feast or famine depended on variations in the yearly productivity of the pinyon.

Following years of poor pinyon nut production, the Shoshonian groups relied on ephemeral grasses, such as Indian ricegrass, during the late spring. Since the productivity of these grasses is based largely on highly variable precipitation, reliance on these resources rather than the more permanent and more reliable marsh resources necessitated a smaller group size and a more migratory type of existence.

In summary, Shoshoni groups appeared in the Great Salt Lake area about 500–600 years ago and replaced or displaced Sevier peoples. Their subsistence adaptation generally differed from previous cultures, and was not particularly well adapted to the lake and its spring and river tributaries.

Summary and Discussion

The human prehistory of the Great Salt Lake area can be summarized as follows:

1. Brief Paleo-Indian occupation (ca. 12,000 to 9,000 B.P.); evidence of type of subsistence limited, but probably combination of hunting Pleistocene megafauna and collecting lake periphery resources.

2. Early Archaic (ca. 8,500 to 5,500 B.P.); basically sedentary on lake periphery with subsistence focused on marsh and lake-edge resources; growth of population.
3. Mid-Archaic (ca. 5,500 to 3,500 B.P.); migratory hunting and gathering based on both upland and lake edge resources; population reduction.
4. Late Archaic (3,500 to 2,500 B.P.); upland hunting and gathering subsistence and occupation; little evidence of lake margin habitation or use; population markedly reduced or regional abandonment.
5. Sevier (1,500 to 500 B.P.); sedentary village life based on collecting of marsh resources and agriculture: supplemented by seasonal procurement of animals.
6. Proto-Shoshoni (550 B.P. to Present); migratory hunting and gathering: the degree of sedentarism was variable and dependent on local resources.

Throughout this prehistoric period, the Great Salt Lake and the resources which surround it have been a primary factor in the development of local cultures. The only real exception to the lake/river margin adaptation pattern was the Shoshoni subsistence system, which may have been modified by displacement of the Indians by European settlers. In a way it is unfortunate that the Shoshoni groups were the only occupants of the area when historic contact was made. They had arrived not long before the arrival of groups of European origin and maintained a subsistence economy that was in many ways as dissimilar from previous cultures as the European subsistence economy was dissimilar. Archeologists with a European cultural background, knowing only the historic record of Shoshonian subsistence economies, presented a somewhat biased view of prehistoric cultures in the area. Past cultures are most often viewed as "Desert Dwellers with Few Resources" (Jennings, 1978) and statements such as the following are common:

> "The Basin had long been an inhospitable land. To those who lived here on the edge of subsistence, the slightest change, an unusually dry period, for example, could mean disaster. More than once, groups must have moved out of this area, not knowing what lay before them, but well aware that death lay behind them (Wormington 1955).

Such images are poetic but misleading. Throughout most of the prehistory of the Great Salt Lake area, people appear to have led life-styles that were not nearly so marginal. While they were surrounded by desert environments, they were not wholly adapted to them. They lived by collecting lake river spring flora and fauna and by hunting upland game animals. They were not adapted to desert ecosystems and it is something of a misnomer to refer to them as desert dwellers. It is also misleading to conceive of these groups as having few resources, and, by implication, of living hand-to-mouth existence. The carrying capacity of the area was much larger than the surrounding deserts, and it is evident that at times in the past the region supported a large and relatively stable population.

More importantly, the conception of "desert" oriented groups precludes an understanding of the importance the Great Salt Lake had in the subsistence economy of past cultures. and the impact lake level fluctuations had on the development of culture in the area. It has been argued here that many of the changes which occurred in the region were a direct result of increasing and decreasing resource availability, and that the quantity of these resources was a direct result of the size of the lake. Only by focusing on prehistoric subsistence adaptations (and on the environments to which these adaptations were made) will we fully understand the lifeways of prehistoric man in the region.

References

Adovasio, J. M., et. al., 1978, Meadowcroft Rockshelter: *in* Alan L. Bryan (ed.), Early Man in America from a Circum-Pacific Perspective, p. 140–180, Occasional Papers no. 1, Department of Anthropology, University of Alberta, Edmonton.

Aikens, C. M., 1966, Fremont-Promontory-Plains relationships in northern Utah: University of Utah Anthropological Papers, no. 82, Salt Lake City.

Aikens, C. M., 1967, Excavations at Snake Rock Village and the Bear River No. 2 Site: University of Utah Anthropological Papers, no. 87, Salt Lake City.

Aikens, C. M., 1970, Hogup Cave: University of Utah Anthropological Papers, no. 87, Salt Lake City.

Aikens, C. M., 1976, Cultural Hiatus in the Eastern Great Basin?: American Antiquity, v. 41, no. 4, p. 543–550, Salt Lake City.

Antevs, E., 1955, Geologic-Climatic dating in the west, American Antiquity, v. 20, no. 4, p. 317–335. Salt Lake City.

Berry, M. S., The Evans Site, A Special Report, Department of Anthropology, University of Utah, Salt Lake City.

Bryan, A. L., 1972, Summary of the Archeology of Smith Creek and Council Hall Caves, White Pine County, Nevada, 1971: Nevada Archeological Reporter, v. 6, no. 1, Reno.

Butler, B. R., 1973, Folsom and Plano points from the peripheries of the Upper Snake County: Tebiwa, v. 16, no. 1, p. 69–72, Pocatello.

Claassen, P. W., 1919, A possible new source of food supply (cat-tail flour): Scientific Monthly, v. 9, p. 179–185, New York.

Clark, L. L., 1975, A 40,000 year-old stone industry on Lake Bonneville's Alpine Beach: Proceedings of the Utah Academy of Sciences, Arts, and Letters, v. 52, pt. 1. p. 44–49, Salt Lake City.

Dalley, G. F., 1976, Swallow Shelter and associated sites: University of Utah Anthropological Papers, no. 96, Salt Lake City.

Davis. E. L., 1976, Paleo-Americans, extinct animals and a possible shelter at China Lake: Paper delivered at 1976 Great Basin Anthropological Conference, Las Vegas.

Eardley, A. J., V. Gvosdetsky, and R. E. Marsel, 1957, Hydrology of Lake Bonneville and sediments and soils of its basin (Utah): Geological Society of America Bulletin, v. 68, no. 9, p. 1141–1202.

Fowler, D. D., 1968, The Archeology of Newark Cave, White Pine County, Nevada: Desert Research Institute Social Sciences and Humanities Publication, no. 3, Reno.

Fowler, C. S., 1972, Ecological clues to Proto-Numic homelands, *in* Great Basin Cultural Ecology: A Symposium, edited by D. D. Fowler, Desert Research Institute Publications in the Social Sciences, no. 8, Reno.

Fry, G. F., 1970, "Salt Lake Fremont": Paper presented at the Fremont Culture Symposium, 35th Annual meeting of the Society for American Archeology, April 30–May 2, 1970, Mexico City, D. F., Mexico.

Fry, G. F., 1976, Analysis of prehistoric coprolites from Utah: University of Utah Anthropological Papers, no. 97, Salt Lake City.

Fry, G. F., and J. M. Adovasio, 1970, Population differentiation in Hogup and Danger Caves, two Archaic Sites in the Eastern Great Basin: Nevada State Museum Anthropological Papers, no. 15, p. 207–215, Carson City.

Fry, G. F., and G. F. Dalley, 1973, The Levee and Knoll Sites: University of Utah Anthropological Papers, no. 98, Salt Lake City.

Gruhn, R., 1972, Summary report on field work at Amy's Shelter, Smith Creek Canyon, White Pine County, Nevada, 1971: Nevada Archeological Survey Reporter, v. 6, no. 1, p. 3–5, Reno.

Gunnerson, J. H., 1969, The Fremont Culture, a study in culture dynamics on the Northern Anasazi Frontier: Papers of the Peabody Museum of Archeology and Ethnology, Harvard University, v. 59, no. 2, Cambridge.

Heizer, R. F., M. A. Baumhoff, and C. W. Clewlow, Jr., 1968, Archeology of South Folk Shelter (NV-EL-11), Elko County, Nevada: University of California Archeological Survey, Reports 7:1–58.

Holmer, R. N., 1978, A mathematical typology for Archaic projectile points of the Eastern Great Basin: Ph.D. dissertation, Department of Anthropology, University of Utah, Salt Lake City.

Jennings, J. D., 1957, Danger Cave: University of Utah Anthropological Papers, no. 27, Salt Lake City.

Jennings, J. D., 1966, Early man in the Desert West: Quaternaria, v. 8, p. 81–89, Rome.

Jennings, J. D., 1974, The Prehistory of North America, 2nd edition, McGraw-Hill, New York.

Jennings, J. D., 1978, Prehistory of Utah and the Eastern Great Basin, A Review 1968–1976: University of Utah Anthropological Papers, no. 98, Salt Lake City.

Judd, N. M., 1926, Archeological observations north of the Rio Colorado: Bureau of American Ethnology Bulletin no. 82, Washington.

Lamb, S. M., 1958, Linguistic prehistory in the Great Basin: International Journal of American Linguistics, 24 (2):95–100, Baltimore.

Lindsay, L. W., and K. Sargent, 1977, An Archeological survey of the Deep Creek Mountain area, Juab County, Utah: MS on file, Antiquities Section, Utah State Historical Society, Salt Lake City.

Madsen, D. B., 1975, Dating Paiute-Shoshoni expansion in the Great Basin: American Antiquity, v. 40, no. 1, Washington.

Madsen, D. B. and M. S. Berry, 1974, Box Elder County Archeological Summary: MS on file, Antiquities Section, Utah State Historical Society, Salt Lake City.

Madsen, D. B., and M. S. Berry, 1975, A reassessment of Northeastern Great Basin prehistory: American Antiquity, v. 40, no. 4, p. 391–405.

Madsen, D. B., D. R. Currey, and J. H. Madsen, 1976, Man, mammoth, and lake fluctuations in Utah: Antiquities Section Selected Papers, v. 2. no. 5, Salt Lake City.

Madsen, D. B., and L. W. Lindsay, 1977, Backhoe Village: Antiquities Section Selected Papers. v. 4, no. 12, Salt Lake City.

Marshall, S. B., 1978, The Paleo-Indian component Shawnee-Minisink Site, Eastern Pennsylvania: Paper delivered at the 43rd Annual Meeting, Society for American Archeology, Tucson.

Marwitt, J. B., 1970, Median Village and Fremont culture regional variation: University of Utah Anthropological Papers, no. 95, Salt Lake City.

Mehringer, P. J., Jr., 1977, Great Basin Late Quaternary environments and Chronology; in Models and Great Basin Prehistory, A Symposium, D. D. Fowler (ed.): Desert Research Institute Publications in the Social Sciences, no. 12, Reno.

Miller, S. J., and W. Dort, Jr., 1978, Early man at Owl Cave, current investigations at the Wasden Site, Eastern Snake River Plain, Idaho: in Alan L. Bryan (ed.), Early Man in America from a Circum-Pacific Perspective, Occasional Papers no. 1, Department of Anthropology, University of Alberta, Edmonton.

Miller, W. R., J. L. Tanner, and L. P. Foley, 1971, A Lexicostatistic Study of Shoshoni Dialects: Anthropological Linguistics 13 (4): 142–164.

Mock, J. M., 1971, The Archeology of Spotten Cave, Utah County, central Utah: M.A. thesis, Department of Anthropology and Archeology, Brigham Young University, Provo.

Morrison, R. B., 1966, Predecessors of Great Salt Lake: Guidebook to the Geology of Utah, no. 20, p. 77–104, Utah Geological Society, Salt Lake City.

Nielson, A. S., 1978, Proposed subsistence models for the Sevier Culture, Sevier River drainage, west central Utah: M.A. thesis, Department of Anthropology, Brigham Young University, Provo.

Niering, W., 1966, The life of the marsh, The North American wetlands, New York.

Odum. E. P., 1963, Ecology, Modern Biology Series: Holt, Rinehart, and Winston, New York.

Reimold, R. J., and W. H. Queen, 1974, Ecology of Halophytes: Academic Press.

Sargent, K., 1978, Deep Creek Mountains test excavations, Juab County, Utah: MS on file, Antiquities Section, Utah Division of State History, Salt Lake City.

Sharrock, F. W., 1966, Prehistoric occupation patterns in southwestern Wyoming and cultural relationships with the Great Basin and Plains culture areas: University of Utah Anthropological Papers, no. 77, Salt Lake City.

Shutler, M. E., and R. Shutler, Jr., 1963, Deer Creek Cave, Elko County, Nevada: Nevada State Museum Anthropological Papers, no. 11, Carson City.

Simms, S. R., 1977, A Mid-archaic subsistence and settlement shift in the Northeastern Great Basin, in Models and Great Basin Prehistory: A Symposium edited by D. D. Fowler, Desert Research Institute Publications in the Social Science, no. 12, p. 195–210, Reno.

Steward. J. H., 1938, Basin-Plateau aboriginal socio-political groups: Bureau of American Ethnology, Bulletin 120, Washington.

Stokes, W. L., 1972, Probable proboscidian petroglyphs of southeastern Utah: Utah Academy of Sciences, Arts, and Letters Proceedings, v. 49, pt. 2, p. 84–85, Salt Lake City.

Thomas, D. H., 1978, A preliminary report on Paleo-Indian settlement patterns at Pleistocene Lake Tonapah: Paper delivered at the 43rd Annual Meeting, Society for American Archeology, Tucson.

Willey, G. R., and P. Phillips, 1955, Method and theory in American archeology: Historical-development interpretation, American Antiquity, v. 57, no. 4, p. 723–819, Menasha.

Willey, G. R., and P. Phillips, 1958, Method and theory in American Archeology: University of Chicago Press, Chicago.

Wormington, H. M., 1955, A reappraisal of the Fremont culture: Denver Museum of Natural History, Popular Series 1: 1–129, Denver.

Mountain Men

W hen the Spanish Franciscan friars Dominguez and Escalante reached Utah
Lake in the summer of 1776 in their attempt to find an overland route from
Santa Fe to Monterrey, California, they could have helped historians avoid what
has become an ongoing debate about who the first European was to see the Great
Salt Lake. Alas, the stories told them by Indians in Utah Valley did not tempt them
sufficiently to make the side trip to view the great natural phenomenon. Thus it
was not until 1824 that the American fur trapper James Bridger made the first
recorded sighting of the lake. But was he actually the first? The French trapper
Etienne Provost, operating out of Taos, New Mexico, was also in the area that
spring and may have beaten Bridger to it. On the other hand, Provost neither
recorded nor told anyone of such a sighting, and it cannot be proven that he ever
saw it at all. Such are the little gnat-bites of history that disturb historians' sleep.

The first Europeans to *explore* the lake were the mountain men, fur trappers mainly
of French, British, or American extraction who first arrived in the region in the 1820s
in search primarily of beaver. The lucrative beaver trade could bring one a fortune, as
it did William H. Ashley, in as little as three years. Or if one ventured into the rich
beaver streams jealously guarded by the Blackfoot Indians, for example, one could
even more quickly lose life itself. So it was a risky business, but the profits, the freedom, and the adventure it held out were irresistible temptations to many young men.

Among the mountain men who visited the lake were Jedediah Smith and
Osborne Russell, whose narratives of their experiences are given below. The careers
of Smith and Russell bracket the heyday of the fur trade, 1822–1840, for Smith was
a member of the first party of trappers sent up the Missouri and into the mountains by St. Louis entrepreneur and politician William H. Ashley and his partner
Andrew Henry in 1822, and Russell first reached the mountains as a member of
Nathaniel Wyeth's second expedition in 1834. The two never met, for Smith sold
his share in the partnership Smith, Jackson, and Sublette in 1830, left the mountains, and was killed by Commanches near the Cimarron River in 1831.

A sketch of Jedediah Smith reportedly drawn by a
friend after Smith's death in 1831. Used by permission,
Utah State Historical Society, all rights reserved.

Many of the mountain men, like Provost, were illiterate, and few of those who
could write, wrote very much, no doubt because life in the mountains offered little
time for literary projects. Thus these narratives by Smith and Russell are quite brief,
though both are part of much longer works.

Jedediah Smith was the most intrepid explorer among the mountain men. Co-
discoverer of South Pass, which became the great passageway across the
Continental Divide for overland travelers, survivor of the three greatest Indian bat-
tles in the history of the fur trade, and proprietor of one of the great fur companies, Smith's biography is full of drama. Not the least dramatic of his adventures is
the story included here of the first crossing of the Great Basin by a European on
the return leg of his epic journey to California in 1826–1827. With a party of either
thirteen or eighteen men (the records are conflicting), Smith left the great annual
trappers' rendezvous on the Green River and proceeded along the eastern shore of
the Great Salt Lake to the Old Spanish Trail in central Utah, which he followed to
southern California. Leaving most of his party to winter there, Smith took Robert
Evans and Silas Goble with him on a return trip to the summer rendezvous in

northern Utah, during which they became the first white men to cross the Sierra Nevada and the Great Basin. It is the portion of his journey over the Salt Lake Desert from about the modern Utah-Nevada border to the Great Salt Lake that is included here. During the heyday of the California Trail in the 1840s and 1850s, travelers crossed the Great Basin at a slightly more northern latitude to take advantage of the water of the Humboldt River, which they followed across most of modern Nevada. Smith, who was not aware of the existence of the river, almost perished for that lack of knowledge, as this excerpt from his account dramatically tells.

Osborne Russell, who was operating out of Fort Hall, the Hudson's Bay Company trading post in modern Idaho, spent the winter of 1841–1842 in the Wasatch Mountains near present-day Ogden, Utah, and visited the vicinity of the Great Salt Lake at that time. His narrative is important not only because it is one of the first descriptions of the lake and the Indians who lived on its shores from the pen of a white man, but also because Russell was one of the last of the mountain men, and his journal records a way of life that was rapidly disappearing. The last of the famous summer rendevous of trappers—proverbial blowouts of drinking and brawling during which the mountain men traded their furs for supplies for the following season—had taken place in 1840, and the remaining trappers like Russell were now trading with fixed establishments like Fort Hall. Fort Hall was also soon to become important as a supply point on the Oregon Trail, for the first wagon party of Oregon emigrants, the Elijah White company, opened that trail in 1842, the very year of Russell's journal, and mountain men like Russell eventually found better employment as emigrant guides than trappers.

Suggestions for further reading

The Southwest Expedition of Jedediah S. Smith has been reprinted in paperback (Lincoln: University of Nebraska Press, 1989), as has *Journal of a Trapper* (Lincoln: University of Nebraska Press, 1965, and other editions). Not surprisingly, the colorful mountain men have attracted a lot of attention from historians. The best recent general history of the fur trade, which focuses on the mountain men as explorers and also provides an excellent guide to the historical literature, is Robert M. Utley, *A Life Wild and Perilous: Mountain Men and the Paths to the Pacific* (New York: Henry Holt, 1997). Dale L. Morgan's *Jedediah Smith and the Opening of the West* (Indianapolis: Bobbs-Merrill, 1953) is a classic of western history. John R. Alley Jr.'s "Prelude to Dispossession: The Fur Trade's Significance for the Northern Utes and Southern Paiutes," *Utah Historical Quarterly* 50 (spring 1982): 104–23, conveniently reprinted in John S. McCormick and John R. Sillito, *A World We Thought We Knew: Readings in Utah History* (Salt Lake City: University of Utah Press, 1995): 18–33, examines the darker side of the relationship between mountain men and Indians in northern Utah, which is recorded both in Russell's journal and in an earlier portion of Smith's journal not reprinted here.

The Southwest Expedition of Jedediah S. Smith: His Personal Account of the Journey to California, 1826–1827
Jedediah S. Smith

22nd June 1827[1] North 25 Miles. My course was parrallel with a chain of hills on the west on the tops of which was some snow and from which ran a creek to the north east. On this creek I encamped. The Country in the vicinity so much resembled that on the south side of the Salt Lake that for a while I was induced to believe that I was near that place. During the day I saw a good many Antelope but could not kill any. I however killed 2 hares which when cooked at night we found much better than horse meat.[2]

June 23d NE 35 Miles, Moving on in the morning I kept down the creek on which we had encamped until it was lost in a small Lake. We then filled our horns and continued on our course, passing some brackish as well as some verry salt springs and leaving on the north of the latter part of the days travel a considerable Salt Plain. Just before night I found water that was drinkable but continued on in hopes of find better and was obliged to encamp without any.[3]

June 24th N E 40 Miles I started verry early in hopes of soon finding water. But ascending a high point of a hill I could discover nothing but sandy plains or dry Rocky hills with the Exception of a snowy mountain off to the N E at the distance of 50 or 60 Miles. When I came down I durst not tell my men of the desolate prospect ahead. but framed my story so as to discourage them as little as possible. I told them I saw something black at a distance near which no doubt we would find water. While I had been up on the one of the horses gave out and had been left a short distance behind. I sent the men back to take the best of his flesh for our supply

From George S. Brooks, ed., *The Southwest Expedition of Jedediah S. Smith: His Personal Account of the Journey to California, 1826–1827* (Glendale, California: Arthur H. Clark, 1977), 186–97. Annotation by George S. Brooks reprinted by permission of the publishers, The Arthur H. Clark Company.

was again nearly exhausted whilst I would push forward in search of water. I went on a short distance and waited until they came up. They were much discouraged with the gloomy prospect but I said all I could to enliven their hopes and told them in all probability we would soon find water. But the view ahead was almost hopeless. With our best exertion we pushed forward walking as we had been for a long time over the soft sand. That kind of traveling is verry tiresome to men in good health who can eat when and what they choose and drink as often as they desire. and to us worn down with hunger and fatigue and burning with thirst increased by the blazing sands it was almost insurportable. At about 4 O Clock we were obliged to stop on the side of a sand hill under the shade of a small Cedar. We dug holes in the sand and laid down in them for the purpose of cooling our heated bodies. After resting about an hour we resumed our wearysome journey and traveled until 10 O Clock at night when we laid down to take a little repose. Previous to this and a short time after sun down I saw several turtle doves and as I did not recollect of ever having seen them more than 2 or 3 miles from water I spent more than a hour in looking for water but it was in vain. Our sleep was not repose for tormented nature made us dream of things we had not and for the want of which it then seemed possible and even probable we might perish in the desert unheard of and unpitied. In those moments how trifling were all those things that hold such an absolute sway over the busy and the prosperous world. My dreams were not of Gold or ambitious honors but of my distant quiet home of murmuring brooks of cooling cascades. After a short rest we continued our march and traveled all night. The murmur of falling waters still sounding in our ears and the apprehension that we might never live to hear that sound in reality weighed heavily uppon us.[4]

June 25th When morning came it saw us in the same unhappy situation pursuing our journey over the desolate waste now gleming in the sun and more insuportably tormenting than it had been during the night. At 10 O Clock Robert Evans laid down in the plain under the shade of a small cedar being able to proceed no further. The Mountain of which I have before spoken was apparently not far off and we left him and proceeded onward in the hope of finding water in time to return with some in season to save his life. After traveling about three Miles we came to the foot of the Mt and then to our inexpressible joy we found water. Goble plunged into it at once and I could hardly wait to bath my burning forehead before I was pouring it down regardless of the consequences. Just before we arrived at the spring I saw two indians traveling in the direction in which Evans was left and soon after the report of two guns was heard in quick succession. This considerably increased our apprehension for his safety but shortly after a smoke was seen back on the trail and I took a small kettle of water and some meat and going back found him safe He had not seen the indians and had discharged his gun to direct me where he lay and for the same purpose had raised a smoke. He was indeed far gone being scarcely able to speak. When I came the first question he asked me was have you any water! I told him I had plenty and handed the kettle which would hold 6 or 7 quarts in which there was some meat mixed with the water. O says he why did you bring the meat and putting the kettle to his mouth he did not take it away untile he had drank all the water of which there was at least 4 or 5 quarts and then asked me why I had not brought more. This however revived him so much that he was able to go on to the spring. I cut the horse meat and spread it out to dry and determined to remain for the rest of the day that we might repose our wearied and emaciated bodies. I have at different times suffered all the extremes of hunger and thirst. Hard as it is to bear for succesive days the knawings of hunger yet it is light in comparison to the agony of burning thirst, and [o]n the other hand I have observed that a man reduced by hunger is some days in recovering his strength. A man equally reduced by thirst seems renovated almost instantaneneously. Hunger can be endured more than twice as long as thirst. To some it may appear surprising that a man who has been for several days without eating has a most incessant desire to drink and although he can drink but a little at a time yet he wants it much oftener than in ordinary circumstances. In the course of the day several indians showed themselves on the high points of the hills but would not come to my camp.[5]

26th June N 10 miles along a valley and encamped at some brackish water having passed during the day several salt springs and one Indian Lodge. The lodge was occupied by 2 indians one squaw and 2 children. They were somewhat alarmed but friendly and when we made signs to them of being hungry they cheerfully divided with us some antelope meat. They spoke like the snake Indians and by enquiry I found they were Panakhies from Lewis's River. They had some pieces of Buffalo Robes and told me that a few days travel to the North E. Buffalo were plenty. Although they knew the shoshones I could not learn any thing from them in relation to the Salt Lake. In the evening I discovered from a high piece of ground what appeared to be a large body of water.[6]

June 27th North 10 Miles along a valley in which were many salt springs. Coming to the point of the ridge which formed the Eastern boundary of the valley I saw an expanse of water Extending far to the North and East. The Salt Lake a joyful sight was spread before us. Is it possible said the companions of my sufferings that we are so near the end of our troubles. For myself I durst scarcely believe that it was really the Big Salt Lake that I saw. It was indeed a most cheering view for although we were some distance from the depo yet we knew we would soon be in a country where we would find game and water which were to us objects of the greatest importance and those which would contribute more than any others to our comfort and happiness. Those who may chance to read this at a distance from the scene may perhaps be surprised that the sight of this lake surrounded by a wilderness of more than 2000 miles diameter excited in me these feelings known to the traveler who after long and perilous journeying comes again in view of his home. But so it was with me for I had traveled so much in the vicinity of the Salt Lake that it had become my home of the wilderness. After coming in view of the lake I traveled East keeping nearly paralel with the shore of the lake. At about 25 miles from my last encampment I found a spring of fresh water and encamped. The water during the day had been generally Salt. I saw several antelope but could not get a shot at them.[7]

28th East 20 Miles   traveling nearly parallel with the shore of the Lake. When I got within a mile of the outlet of the Uta Lake which comes in from the south East I found the ground which is thick covered with flags and Bulrushes overflowed to a considerable distance from the channel and before I got to the current the water had increased to between 2 & 3 feet and the cain grass and Bulrushes were extremely thick. The channel was deep and as the river was high was of course rapid and about 60 yards wide. As I would have to wade a long distance should I attempt to return before I would find dry land I determined to make a raft and for this purpose cut a quantity of Cain Grass for of this material there was no want. The grass I tied into Bundles and attaching them together soon formed a raft sufficiently strong to bear my things. In the first place I swam and lead my horse over the mule following to the opposite bank which was also overflowed. I then returned and attaching a cord to the raft and holding the end in my mouth I swam before the raft while the two men swam behind. Unfortunately neither of my men were good swimmers and the current being strong we were swept down a considerable distance and it was with great difficulty that I was enabled to reach the shore as I was verry much strangled. When I got to the shore I put my things on the mule and horse and endeavored to go out to dry land but the animals mired and I was obliged to leave my things in the water for the night and wade out to the dry land. We made a fire of sedge and after eating a little horse flesh we laid down to rest.[8]

29th 15 Miles North   Early in the morning I brought my things out from the water and spread them out to dry. We were verry weak and worn down with suffering and fatigue but we thought ourselves near the termination of our troubles for it was not more than four days travel to the place where we expected to find my partners. At 10 O Clock we moved onward and after traveling 15 miles encamped. Just before encamping I got a shot at a Bear and wounded him badly but did not kill him. At supper we ate the last of our horse meat and talked a little of the probability of our suffering being soon at an end. I say we talked a little for men suffering from hunger never talk much but rather bear their sorrows in moody silence which is much preferable to fruitless compaint.[9]

30th North 15 miles. I Started early and as Deer were tolerably plenty I went on ahead and about 8 O Clock got a shot at a Deer. he ran off I followed him and found a good deal of blood and told the men to stop while I should look for him. I soon found him laying in a thicket. As he appeared nearly dead I went up to him took hold of his horns when he sprang up and ran off. I was vexed at myself for not shooting him again when it was in my power and my men were quite discouraged. However I followed on and in a short time found him again. I then made sure of him by cutting his ham strings It was a fine fat Buck and it was not long before we struck up a fire and had some of his meat cooking. We then employed ourselves most pleasantly in eating for about two hours and for the time being forgot that we were not the happiest people in the world or at least thought but of our feast that was eaten with a relish unknown to a palace. So much do we make our estimation of happiness by a contrast with our situation that we were as much pleased and as well satisfied with our fat venison on the bank of the Salt Lake as we would have been in the possession of all the Luxuries and enjoyments of civilized life in other circumstances. These things may perhaps appear trifling to most readers but let any one of them travel over the same plain as I did and they will consider the killing of a buck a great achievement and certainly a verry useful one. After finishing our repast the meat of the Deer was cut and dried over the fire.

July 1st 25 miles North along the shore of the Lake. Nothing material occured.

2nd 20 Miles North East made our way to the Cache. But just before arriving there I saw some indians on the opposite side of a creek. It was hardly worth while as I thought to be any wise careful so I went directly to them and found as near as I could judge by what I knew of the language to be a band of the snakes. I learned from them that the whites as they term our parties were all assembled at the little Lake a distance of about 25 miles. There was in this camp about 200 Lodges of indians and as the[y] were on their way to the rendezvous I encamped with them.[10]

3d I hired a horse and a guide and at three O Clock arrived at the rendezvous My arrival caused a considerable bustle in camp for myself and party had been given up as lost. A small Cannon brought up from St Louis was loaded and fired for a salute.[11]

Notes

1. The text for the balance of the trip back to the Rendezvous is from the section of Smith's journal discovered and published by Maurice Sullivan in his *The Travels of Jedediah Smith* in 1934 on pages 19–26. It is here reproduced through the kind permission of the present owner of the manuscript: The Jennewein Western Collection, Dakota Wesleyan University, Mitchell, S.D.

   The present version of the text was made from a microfilm in the possession of the Missouri Historical Society. For Dale Morgan's interpretation of Smith's route through Utah—one which seems perfectly valid—see Morgan, *Jedediah Smith and the Opening of the West*, 211–15. With some slight modifications, it is essentially the itinerary offered here.

2. Keeping the Deep Creek Mountains, which now replace the Snake Range on their left the group moves north to camp on Thomas Creek, which runs northeast from the mountains (see Sullivan, *Travels*, 165 n. 37).

3. Thomas Creek today is considerably less impressive than in Smith's time and the small lake has disappeared. The trio, however, moves northeast past the northern tip of the Fish Springs Range, passes the brackish salt springs near present Wilson Health Springs (or perhaps the Fish Springs themselves), and then enters the southern tip of the Great Salt Lake Desert, the present Wendover Bombing and Gunnry Range. They make camp at some unspecified point west and south of the Dugway Range.

4. Tired as the men are, the party now embarks on some of the most difficult and discouraging travel of the entire expedition. Moving up to pass between the Dugway Range on the south and Granite Peak on the north, Smith ascends a hill (possibly either

the Dugways or Sapphire Mountain) and is presented with the bleak view across what is now the Dugway Proving Grounds. The only relief is the sight of the Stansbury Range (and perhaps some of the Onaqui Mountains) far off in the distance.

After passing Granite Peak, Smith journeys among the sand dunes in the approximate direction of what is now the Stark Road. Someplace in that desert, he and his men rest briefly and see the doves. Charles Kelly in his *Salt Desert Trails*, 25, mentions that there is a spring at Granite Peak, which Smith misses, or perhaps the doves found their water on Government Creek to the east. Certainly it would appear that the party camps someplace along the southern end of the Cedar Mountains (near either Little Dove or Little Granite mountains), somewhere west of present Dugway. There is nothing to indicate that they get as far as Skull Valley itself, as Morgan suggests (Morgan, *Smith*, 418 n. 42).

5. From the very general description given, it would appear that Robert Evans gave out near the entrance to Skull Valley, perhaps not far from present Dugway. Smith and Gobel then continue their march to an undetermined spring at the foot of the Stansbury or Onaqui mountains where they find the water which averts tragedy. Morgan offers that the water was found at Spring Creek, just inside the present Skull Valley Indians Reservation (Morgan, *Smith*, 418 n. 43), which is also a strong possibility.

The group seems to have advanced some distance up the valley, and probably stops in the vicinity of the Indian reservation. Sullivan, *Travels*, 166 n. 42, relates that "Charles Kelly . . . tells me that Moodywoc, an ancient Goshute Indian, recalls hearing his grandmother say that in her girlhood three starving men, the first whites she had ever seen, emerged from the Salt Desert." Kelly in his *Salt Desert Trails*, 25, has another variant, which he quotes from Isaac K. Russell's, *Hidden Heroes of the Rockies:* "For years after Smith's journey the Piute Indians of Skull Valley, Utah, repeated the tradition that the first white men they ever saw were three who staggered, almost naked, in from the western desert, and were half crazy from breathing alkali dust."

6. Travel ten miles north from their camp of June 25 would put Smith and his party in the general vicinity of Horseshoe Springs. Sullivan, *Travels*, 166 n. 41 correctly identifies the Indians as Bannocks, a Shoshonean tribe from the Snake River.

7. On this encouraging day, Smith travels to the northern tip of the Stansbury Mountains from which spot he catches sight of his "home in the wilderness," the Great Salt Lake. The party then continues eastwardly along the shore to camp near present Marshall in the Tooele Valley.

8. Smith's course around the southern shore of the lake eventually brings him to another familiar landmark, the Jordan River, which in its swollen condition offers a considerable challenge.

9. The group now moves north along the route they had used coming south in the previous August. In three days (June 29, 30, and July 1) they cross the Weber River (although Smith does not mention it) and come to the site of present Brigham City, at the mouth of Box Elder Creek.

10. . . . There seems no reason to doubt that Smith returns to the cache on Blacksmith Creek in Cache Valley by reversing the route he used in leaving, going up Box Elder Canyon and then through Sardine Canyon. At the cache, Smith learns that the Rendezvous is assembled at Bear Lake.

11. Apparently leaving the cache by way of Blacksmith Creek Canyon, Smith and his Indian guide move on east to the Rendezvous at the southern end of Bear Lake near present Laketown (Morgan, *Smith*, 215, 228).

Journal of a Trapper or Nine Years Residence among the Rocky Mountains
Osborne Russell

I arrived at the Fort on the Fort on the 23rd of Novr. when after getting such articles for trade as I wished and my personal supplies for the winter I returned to Cache Valley accompanied by a halfbreed On arriving at the Village I found several Frenchmen and half breed trappers encamped with the Snakes One Frenchman having an Indian wife and child invited me to pass the winter in his lodge and as he had a small family and large lodge I accepted the invitation. And had my baggage taken into his lodge and neatly arranged by his wife who was a flathead but the neat manner in which her lodge and furniture was kept would have done honor to a large portion of the "pale faced" fair sex in the civilized world. We staid in this valley until the 15th of Decr. when it was unanimously agreed on to go to the Salt lake and there spend the remainder of the winter The next day we travelled accross the Valley in a SW direction Then took into a narrow defile which led us thro. the mountain in to the valley on the East borders of the lake. The day following we moved along the Valley in a South direction and encamped on a small branch close by the foot of the mountain. The ground was still bare and the Autumnal growth of grass was the best I ever saw at this season of the year 18th I arose about an hour before daylight took my rifle and ascended the Mountain on foot to hunt sheep The weather was clear and cold but the Mountain being steep and rugged and my rifle heavy the exercise Soon put me in a perspiration. After Climbing about half a mile I sat down on a rock to wait for daylight and when it came I discovered a band of about 100 rams within about 80 yds of me I shot and killed one the others ran about 50 yds further and stopped. Whilst I was reloading my rifle one of them ascended a high pinnacle of rock which jutted over a precipice there were others nearer to me but I wished to fetch this proud animal from his elevated position. I brought my rifle to my face the [ball] whistled thro. his heart and he fell headlong

---

From Aubrey L. Haines, ed., *Journal of a Trapper* [Osborne Russell] (Portland: Oregon Historical Society, 1955), 113–22.

over the precipice I followed the band at some distance among the crags and killed two more butched them then returned and butchered the two I had first killed and returned to camp—and sent some men with horses to get the Meat. 20th Decr. we moved along the borders of the Lake about 10 Mls. and encamped on a considerable stream running into it called "Weaver's river" At this place the Valley is about 10 Mls wide intersected with numerous Springs of salt and fresh hot and cold water which rise at the foot of the Mountain and run thro. the Valley into the river and Lake—Weavers river is well timbered along its banks principally with Cottonwood and box elder—there are also large groves of sugar maple pine and some oak growing in the ravines about the Mountain—We also found large numbers of Elk which had left the Mountain to winter among the thickets of wood and brush along the river. Decr. 25th It was agreed on by the party to prepare a Christmas dinner but I shall first endeavor to describe the party and then the dinner. I have already said the man who was the proprietor of the lodge in which I staid was a French man with a flat head wife and one child The inmates of the next lodge was a half breed Iowa a Nez percey wife and two children his wifes brother and another half breed next lodge was a half breed Cree his wife a Nex percey 2 children and a Snake Indian The inmates of the 3d lodge was a half breed Snake his wife (a Nez percey and two children). The remainder was 15 lodges of Snake Indians Three of the party spoke English but very broken therefore that language was made but little use of as I was familiar with the Canadian French and Indian tongue. About I oclk we sat down to dinner in the lodge where I staid which was the most spacious being about 36 ft. in circumference at the base with a fire built in the center around this sat on clean Epishemores all who claimed kin to the white man (or to use their own expression all that were gens d'esprit) with their legs crossed in true Turkish style—and now for the dinner The first dish that came on was a large tin pan 18 inches in diameter rounding full of Stewed Elk meat The next dish was similar to the first heaped up with boiled Deer meat (or as the whites would call it Venison a term not used in the Mountains) The 3d and 4th dishes were equal in size to the first containing a boiled flour pudding prepared with dried fruit accompanied by 4 quarts of sauce made of the juice of sour berries and sugar Then came the cakes followed by about six gallons of strong Coffee already sweetened with tin cups and pans to drink out of large chips or pieces of Bark Supplying the places of plates. on being ready the butcher knives were drawn and the eating commenced at the word given by the landlady as all dinners are accompanied with conversation this was not deficient in that respect The principal topic which was discussed was the political affairs of the Rocky Mountains The state of governments among the different tribes, the personal characters of the most distinguished warriors Chiefs etc One remarked that the Snake *Chief Pah da-hewak um da* was becoming very unpopular and it was the opinion of the Snakes in general that *Moh woom hah* his brother would be at the head of affairs before 12 mos as his village already amounted to more than 300 lodges and moreover he was supported by the bravest men in the

Nation among whom were *Ink a tush e poh Fibe bo un to wat su* and *Who sha kik* who were the pillars of the Nation and at whose names the Blackfeet quaked with fear. In like manner were the characters of the principal Chiefs of the Bonnak Nez percey Flathead and Crow Nations and the policy of their respective governments commented upon by these descendants of Shem and Japhet with as much affected dignity as if they could have read their own names when written or distinguish the letter B from a Bulls foot. Dinner being over the tobacco pipes were filled and lighted while the Squaws and children cleared away the remains of the feast to one side of the lodge where they held a Sociable tite a tite over the fragments. After the pipes were extinguished all agreed to have a frolic shooting at a mark which occupied the remainder of the day. Jany. 1st The ground was still bare but the weather cold and the fresh water streams shut up with ice On the 3d we moved Camp up the stream to the foot of the mountain where the stream forks The right is called Weavers fork and the left Ogden's both coming thro. the mountain in a deep narrow cut The mountain is very high steep and rugged which rises abruptly from the plain about the foot of it are small rolling hills abounding with springs of fresh water. The land bordering on the river and along the Stream is a rich black alluvial deposite but the high land is gravelly and covered with wild sage with here and there a grove of scubby oaks and red cedars On the 10th I started to hunt Elk by myself intending to stop out 2 or 3 nights I travelled up Weavers fork in a SE direction thro the mountains The route was very difficult and in many places difficult travelling over high points of rocks and around huge precipices on a trail just wide enough for a single horse to walk in, in about 10 Mls I came into a smooth plain 5 or 6 Mls in circumference just as the Sun was setting here I stopped for the night the snow being about 5 inches deep and the weather cold I made a large fire—As I had not Killed any game during the day I had no supper at night but I had a blanket horse to ride and a good rifle with a plenty of Amunition I was not in much danger of Suffering by hunger cold or fatigue So I wrapped myself in my blanket and laid down on some dry grass I had collected before the fire. About an hour after dark it clouded up and began to snow but as I was under some large trees it did not trouble me much and I soon fell asleep at daylight it was still snowing very fast and had [?] about 8 inches during the night—I saddled my horse and started in a North direction over high rolling hills covered with Scrubby oaks quaking asp and maples for about 10 Mls where I came into a smooth valley about 20 Mls in circumference called "Ogdens hole" with the fork of the same name running thro. it. Here the snow was about 15 inches deep on a level. Towards night the weather cleared up and I discovered a band of about 100 Elk on the hill among the Shrubbery. I approached and killed a very fat old doe which I butcherd and packed the meat and skin on my horse to an open spring about a quarter of a mile distant where I found plenty of dry wood and stopped for the night. I had now a good appetite for supper which after eating I scraped away the Snow on one side of the fire spread down the raw Elk hide and laid down covering myself with my blanket. In the morning when

I awoke it was still snowing and after eating breakfast I packed the Meat on my horse and started on foot leading him by the bridle Knowing it was impossible to follow down this Stream with a horse to the plains I kept along the foot of the Mountain in a Nth. direction for about 2 Mls then turning to the left into a steep ravine began to ascend winding my way up thro. the snow which grew deeper as I ascended I reached the Summit in about 3 hours in many places I was obliged to break a trail for my horse to walk in I descended the mountain West to the plains with comparative ease and reached the Camp about dark On arriving at the lodge I entered and sat down before a large blazing fire My landlady soon unloaded my horse and turned him loose and then prepared supper with a good dish of Coffee whilst I as a matter of course related the particulars of the hunt. We staid at this place during the remainder of January The weather was very cold and the snow about 12 inches deep but I passed the time very agreeably hunting Elk among the timber in fair weather and amusing myself with books in foul The 3d day of Feby. I took a trip up the mountain to hunt Sheep I ascended a spur with my horse some- times riding and then walking until near the top where I found a level bench where the wind had blown the snow off. I fastened my horse with a long cord and took along the side of the mountain among the broken crags to see what the chance was for supper just as the sun was sinking below the dark green waters of the Salt Lake I had not rambled far before I discovered 3 rams about 300 ft perpendicular below me I shot and killed one of them but it being so late and the precipice so bad I con- cluded to sleep without supper rather than to go after it I returned to my horse and built a large fire with fragments of dry sugar maple which I found scattered about on the Mountain having for a shelter from the wind a huge piece of Coarse Sandstone of which the mountain was composed the air was calm serene and cold and the stars shone with an uncommon brightness after sleeping till about Midnight I arose and renewed the fire My horse was continually walking backwards and forwards to keep from freezing I was upwards of 6,000 ft above the level of the lake, below me was a dark abyss silent as the night of Death I set and smoked my pipe for about an hour and then laid down and slept until near daylight—My Chief object in Sleeping at this place was to take a view of the lake when the Sun arose in the Morning. This range of mountains lies nearly Nth & South and approaches the Lake irregularly within from 3 to 10 Mls. About 8 Mls from the SE shore stands an Island about 25 Mls long and six wide having the appearance of a low Mountain extending Nth & South and rising 3 or 400 ft Above the water To the Nth [W] of this about 8 Mls. rises another Island apparently half the size of the first. Nth of these about six Mls. and about half way between rises another about 6 Mls. in circumference which appears to be a mass of basaltic rock with a few scrubby Cedars Standing about in the Cliffs the others appear to be clothed with grass and wild Sage but no wood except a few bushes near to the western horizon arose a small white peak just appearing above the water. which I supposed to be the mountain near the west Shore. On the Nth. side a high Promontory about Six Mls

wide and 10 long projects into the lake covered with grass and scattering Cedars On
the South Shore rises a vast pile of huge rough mountains; which I could faintly
discern thro. the dense blue atmosphere The water of the lake is too much impregnated with Salt to freeze any even about the shores. About sun an hour high I commenced hunting among the rocks in search of Sheep but did not get a chance to
shoot at any till middle of the afternoon when crawling cautiously over some shelving cliffs I discovered 10 or 12 Ewes feeding some distance below me I shot and
wounded one reloaded my rifle and crept down to the place where I last saw her
when I discovered two standing on the side of a precipice Shot one thro the head
and she fell dead on the cliff where she stood. I then went above and fastened a cord
(which I carried for the purpose) to some bushes which overhung the rocks by this
means I descended and rolled her off the cliff where she had caught when she fell
upwards of 100 ft. I then pulled myself up by the cord and went round the rock
down to where she fell butcherd her hung the meat on a tree then pursued and
killed the other After butchering the last I took some of the [meat] for my supper
and started up the mountain and arrived at the place where I had slept about an
hour after dark I soon had a fire blazing and a side of ribs roasting and procured
water by heating Stones and melting snow in a piece of skin by the time supper was
over it was late in the night And I lay down and slept till morning At sun rise I
started on foot to get my meat and left my rifle about half way down the Mountain
when I came to where the first sheep had been hung in a tree I discovered a large
Wolverine sitting at the foot of it I then regretted leaving my rifle but it was too
late he saw me and took to his heels as well he might for he had left nothing behind
worth stopping for All the traces I could find of the sheep were some tufts of hair
scattered about on the snow. I hunted around for sometime but to no purpose. In
the meantime the cautious thief was sitting on the snow at some distance watching
my movements as if he was confident I had no gun and could not find his meat.
and wished to agravate me by his antic gestures he had made roads in every direction from the root of the tree dug holes in a 100 places in the snow apparently to
decieve me but I soon got over my ill humour and gave it up that a Wolverine had
fooled a Yankee. I went to the other Sheep and found all safe carried the meat to
my horse mounted and went to Camp. Feby 15 the weather began to moderate and
rain and on the 23d the ground was bare about the Mountain Feby 24th I left the
Camp with a determination to go to the Eutaw Village at the SE extremity of the
Lake to trade furs I travelled along the foot of the Mountain about 10 Mls when I
stopped and deposited in the ground such articles as I did not wish to take with me
The next day I travelled along the foot of the Mountain South about 30 Mls and
encamped on a small spring branch which runs in a distance of 4 Mls from the
mountain to the lake. This is a beautiful and fertile Valley intersected by large
numbers of fine springs which flow from the mountain to the Lake and could with
little labour and expense [be] made to irrigate the whole Valley. The following day
I travelled about 15 Mls along the lake when a valley opened to my view stretching

to the SE about 40 Mls and upwards of 15 Mls wide At the farther extremity of this valley lies Trimpannah or Eutaw lake composed of fresh water about 60 Mls in circumference The outlet of it is a stream about 30 Yds wide which, after cutting this valley thro the middle empties into the Salt Lake. I left the Lake and travelled up this Valley over smooth ground which the snow had long since deserted and the green grass and herbage were fast supplying its place After crossing several small streams which intersected this vale I arrived at the Village rode up to a lodge and asked of a young Indian who met me where Want a Sheep's lodge was but before he could reply a tall Indian very dark complected with a thin visage and a keen piercing eye having his Buffaloe robe thrown carelessly over his left shoulder gathered in folds around his waist and loosely held by his left hand stepped forth and answered in the Snake tongue "I am Want a Sheep", follow me' at the same time turning round and directing his course to a large white lodge. I rode to the door dismounted and followed him in he immediately ordered my horses to be unsaddled and turned loose to feed whilst their loads were carefully arranged in the lodge After the big pipe had gone round several times in silence he then began the conversation—I was asked the news, where travelling for what whom and how I replied to these several inquiries in the Snake tongue which was understood by all in the lodge. He then gave me an extract of all he had seen heard and done for 10 years past He had two Sons and one daughter grown to man and womanhood I and the same number of less size his oldest son was married to a Snake Squaw and his daughter to a man of the Same nation The others yet remained single. After supper was over the females retired from the lodge and the principal men assembled to smoke and hear the news which occupied the time till near midnight when the assembly broke up the men retiring to their respective lodges and the women returned. I passed the time as pleasantly at this place as ever I did among Indians in the daytime I rode about the Valley hunting water fowl who rend the air at this season of the year with their cries and at night the Old Chief would amuse me with traditionary tales mixed with the grossest superstition some of which were not unlike the manners of Ancient Israelites. There seems to be a happiness in ignorance which knowledge and Science destroys here is a nation of people contented and happy they have fine horses and lodges and are very partial to the rifles of the white man If a Eutaw has 8 or 10 good horses a rifle and ammunition he is contented if he fetches a deer at night from the hunt joy beams in the faces of his wife and children and if he returns empty a frown is not seen in the countenances of his companions. The Buffaloe have long since left the shores of these Lakes and the hostile blackfeet have not left a footprint here for many years. During my stay with these Indians I tried to gain some information respecting the southern limits of the Salt Lake but all that I could learn was that it was a sterile barren mountainous Country inhabited by a race of depraved and hostile savages who poisoned their arrows and hindered the exploring of the country. The Chiefs son informed me he had come from the largest Island in the lake a few days previous having passed the winter upon it with his family which he had conveyed backwards and forth on a raft of bulrushes about 12 ft square. He said there was large numbers of antelope on the Island and as there was no wood he had used wild Sage for fuel. The Old Chief told me he could recollect the time when the Buffaloe passed from the main land to the island without swimming and that the depth of the waters was yearly increasing. After obtaining all the furs I could from the Eutaws I started towards Fort Hall on the 27th of March and travelled along the borders of the Lake about 25 Mls. The fire had run over this part of the country the previous autumn and consumed the dry grass The new had sprung up to the height of 6 inches intermingled with various kinds of flowers in full Bloom. The shore of the Lake was swarming with waterfowls of every species that inhabits inland lakes. The next day I went on to Weavers river April 1st I left Wavers river and travelled along the [shore] to the NE extremity of the lake about 25 Mls. The next day I went on to Bear river and struck it about 15 Mls below Cache Valley and twelve Mls from the mouth There I found my winter Comrades and staid one night and then pursued my journey towards Fort Hall where I arrived on the 7th of April

III

EXPLORERS AND
EMIGRANTS

Exploring Fremont Island

Each age seems to generate its own types of heroes, and in our day when people mostly focus their interest on entertainment and athletic figures, it is hard to comprehend the adulation inspired in the nineteenth century by a western explorer, John C. Frémont (1813–1890). He did look the part—that much we can grasp: his dark, wavy hair featured just the right tousle to suggest a character in a Byronic poem, and his large, dark eyes carried a hint of the vulnerability that set female pulses racing. His published reports, while laden with scientific detail, were dramatically and yet clearly written, and accessible to a vast public whose interest in the West in the 1840s had become an obsession. Bookstores could not keep them in stock, and even libraries could not prevent theft of their precious copies as eastern Americans planned (or at least fantasized) their own way West in response to the divine call of Manifest Destiny—the idea that God had foreordained a transcontinental American empire.

Earlier generations of historians have found it possible to dismiss Frémont as a romantic, egotistical, posturing nonentity whose career was made possible by his marriage to the daughter of powerful Missouri senator Thomas Hart Benton and through self-creation of his own romantic persona. Instead of the "Pathmarker of the West," as biographer Allan Nevins considered him, they called him at best the "path *follower* of the West" for his reliance on mountain men like Kit Carson, Basil LeJeunesse, and Bill Williams as guides, and for following trails developed by Indians and on information gleaned from them directly. At worst they called him, for his posturing, "Major Jinks of the Horse Marines," Bernard DeVoto's allusion to the Gilbert and Sullivan character.

The skeptics have a point, for Frémont's explorations did indeed mostly follow routes previously identified by others, and his famous reports are marred by geographical errors and motivated by self-promotion. But there is much more to be said of Frémont than those critical comments.

For one thing, as historian Robert Utley points out, the seasoned mountain men who served with him admired him and went back into the mountains with him repeatedly. Frémont "never considered himself to be" a pathfinder, biographer Ferol Egan adds, and depended upon the knowledge of the mountain men for the success of his expeditions. "He recognized his own limitations," Egan continues, "and knew that a dependable guide" was a necessity. Also, even if Frémont's reports publicized no new discoveries, they popularized current knowledge of, for example, the Oregon Trail, which was of great interest among eastern Americans, and provided them with highly accurate information on what they would face if they decided to move west. Finally, through his own comprehension of western geography and the maps and illustrations of his cartographer and artist Charles Preuss, Frémont was the first to pose the conception of the Great Basin as a separate western geophysical province. One could easily defend such a record as an impressive achievement in western exploration.

The selection from his 1843 report presented here represents Frémont at his best, in the geographical accuracy of his detailed field notes, his courageous willingness to venture out upon unknown terrain, which undoubtedly endeared him to the mountain men who accompanied him, and his resourcefulness in meeting unexpected obstacles, which surely characterizes great explorers.

The Oregon Trail was relatively crowded in 1843. Frémont's party followed it roughly, at least as far as the Continental Divide, but crossed through the Great Divide Basin instead of South Pass, which most wagon trains followed. Upon reaching Soda Springs, on the Bear River, Frémont decided to follow that meandering and sluggish stream down to the Great Salt Lake instead of immediately proceeding farther along the Oregon Trail (a course he resumed after his exploration of the lake). At the point where he turned south along the Bear, he dispatched his head guide, Kit Carson, to Fort Hall, Nathaniel Wyeth's Oregon Trail supply point by now in the hands of the Hudson's Bay Company, to seek replenishment of their stores. This narrative begins on September 1, 1843, and recounts Carson's rendezvous with the party on September 4 with the disappointing news that overland emigration had largely depleted Fort Hall's inventory, and that the Frémont party would have to make do with limited provisions. It recounts the party's frustrations in finding a navigable route to the lake down the shallow Bear River, their determination to abandon that idea and to seek another way to the lake via another drainage of the Wasatch Mountains, and their eventual arrival at the Weber River, which led them onto the lake and their exploration of what came to be known as Fremont Island.

Frémont is important, at the very least, as a pioneer in modern river running, for he was the first to navigate western rivers on both sides of the Continental Divide in inflatable boats, which are almost universally used by modern river runners. In 1842 he ferried most of his supplies across the unexpectedly swollen Kansas River on a twenty-foot inflatable boat, but the venture ended in tragedy on the last voyage when an inexperienced and terrified helmsman (according to Frémont) capsized the boat, losing both it and the supplies of one of his exploring brigades. On

Christopher "Kit" Carson, the legendary mountain man who accompanied most of John C. Frémont's expeditions. Carson inscribed a cross on a rock on Fremont Island which is still visible today. Used by permission, Utah State Historical Society, all rights reserved.

John C. Frémont, the western explorer as romantic hero. Frémont's reports provided detailed and accurate information for prospective western emigrants.

the 1843 expedition narrated here, Frémont carried an eighteen-foot inflatable boat. The voyage to Fremont Island almost ended in a tragedy similar to the 1842 trip, for the boat's glued (instead of sewn) seams began to come apart under the stress of the Great Salt Lake's waves, and only the intrepid paddling and bailing of the crew (including the strong swimmer Basil LeJeunesse, who had managed the Kansas River crossings of the 1842 expedition prior to the upset) got the party back to the mainland without mishap.

One important event not mentioned in this narrative is the inscription of a cross by Kit Carson at the highest point on the island. It is an attractive point of interest to modern sailors who land there (with special permission of the owners, for Fremont Island today is private property). Carson was a recent—and sincere—convert to Roman Catholic Christianity, as required of residents of New Mexico, which was not yet American property. Many mountain men and other American immigrants made their conversions as a nominal compliance with the requirement for Mexican citizenship, but Carson, who had recently married a Mexican Catholic woman, was one who took his conversion seriously, and evidently signified that fact by inscribing the cross on the rock. Frémont was either unaware of Carson's inscription or regarded it as insignificant, for he fails to mention it in this report, and historians can ascribe it to Carson only through the mountain man's autobiography.

Another event that has piqued subsequent interest in Fremont Island and the Frémont visit was the fact that Frémont discovered upon his departure that he had left a telescope lens cap behind. Later explorers of the island have looked in vain for the Frémont artifact, for history discloses that the lens cap was found in the 1860s by Jacob Miller, whose family was among the early livestock grazers on Fremont and Antelope Islands.

Suggestions for further reading

A relatively recent edition of Frémont's report is *The Exploring Expedition to the Rocky Mountains*, with an introduction by Herman J. Viola and Ralph E. Ehrenberg (Washington, D. C.: Smithsonian Institution Press, 1988). Two early Frémont biographies, Frederick S. Dellenbaugh, *Fremont and '49* (New York: G. P. Putnam's Sons, 1914), and Allan Nevins, *Fremont: Pathmarker of the West* (New York: Longmans, Green & Co., 1939 and 1955), were themselves pathmarking ventures, but based only on the few sources available at the time. Both have been superseded by Ferol Egan, *Fremont: Explorer for a Restless Nation* (New York: Doubleday & Co, 1977). Robert M. Utley's *A Life Wild and Perilous: Mountain Men and the Paths to the Pacific* (New York: Henry Holt & Co., 1997) is a lively recounting of the expanding geographic knowledge accumulated by the mountain men's travels, and gives Frémont's expeditions ample space and credit. No one interested in western exploration should deny themselves the pleasure of the outspoken and controversial Bernard DeVoto's *Year of Decision, 1846* (Boston: Houghton Mifflin, 1942), which dwells entertainingly on Frémont's less admirable attributes. Harvey L. Carter, ed., *"Dear Old Kit": The Historical Christopher Carson* (Norman: University of Oklahoma Press, 1968), is the best edition of Carson's memoirs, and Carter and Thelma S. Guild's *Kit Carson: A Pattern for Heroes* (Lincoln: University of Nebraska Press, 1984) is a recent and definitive biography. David Roberts, *A Newer World: Kit Carson, John C. Fremont, and the Claiming of the American West* (New York: Simon & Schuster, 2000), is a good study of the two men's collaboration.

A Report of the Exploring Expedition to Oregon and North California in the years 1843–44
John C. Frémont

We had been detained so long at the village, that in the afternoon we made only five miles, and encamped on the same river after a day's journey of 19 miles. The Indians informed us that we should reach the big salt water after having slept twice and travelling in a south direction. The stream had here entered at nearly level plain or valley, of good soil, eight or ten miles broad, to which no termination was to be seen, and lying between ranges of mountains which, on the right, were grassy and smooth, unbroken by rock, and lower than on the left, where they were rocky and bald, increasing in height to the southward. On the creek were fringes of young willows, older trees being rarely found on the plains, where the Indians burned the surface to produce better grass. Several magpies *(pica Hudsonica)* were seen on the creek this afternoon; and a rattlesnake was killed here, the first which had been seen since leaving the eastern plains. Our camp to night had such a hungry appearance, that I suffered the little cow to be killed, and divided the roots and berries among the people. A number of Indians from the village encamped near.

The weather the next morning was clear, the thermometer at sunrise at 44°.5, and, continuing down the valley, in about five miles we followed the little creek of our encampment to its junction with a larger stream, called *Roseaux,* or Reed river. Immediately opposite, on the right, the range was gathered into its highest peak, sloping gradually low, and running off to a point apparently some forty or fifty miles below. Between this (now become the valley stream) and the foot of the mountains, we journeyed along a handsome sloping level, which frequent springs from the hills made occasionally miry, and halted to noon at a swampy spring, where there were good grass and abundant rushes. Here the river was forty feet wide, with a considerable current; and the valley a mile and a half in breadth; the

From John C. Frémont, *Report of the Exploring Expedition to the Rocky Mountains in the Year 1842 and to Oregon and North California in the Years 1843–44*, U.S. 28th Cong., 2nd sess., Senate Exec. Doc. 174 (Washington, D.C.: Blair and Rives, printers, 1845), 146–60.

soil being generally good, of a dark color, and apparently well adapted to cultivation. The day had become bright and with the thermometer at 71°. By observation, our latitude was 41° 59' 31", and the elevation above the sea 4,670 feet. On our left, this afternoon, the range at long intervals formed itself into peaks, appearing to terminate, about forty miles below, in a rocky cape; beyond which, several others were faintly visible; and we were disappointed when at every little rise we did not see the lake. Towards evening, our way was somewhat obstructed by fields of *artemisia,* which began to make their appearance here, and we encamped on the Roseaux, the water of which had acquired a decidedly salt taste, nearly opposite to a cañon gap in the mountains, through which the Bear river enters this valley. As we encamped, the night set in dark and cold, with heavy rain; and the artemisia, which was here our only wood, was so wet that it would not burn. A poor, nearly starved dog, with a wound in his side from a ball, came to the camp, and remained with us until the winter, when he met a very unexpected fate.

September 1.—The morning was squally and cold; the sky scattered over with clouds; and the night had been so uncomfortable, that we were not on the road until 8 o'clock. Travelling between Roseaux and Bear rivers, we continued to descend the valley, which gradually expanded, as we advanced, into a level plain of good soil, about 25 miles in breadth, between mountains 3,000 and 4,000 feet high, rising suddenly to the clouds, which all day rested upon the peaks. These gleamed out in the occasional sunlight, mantled with the snow which had fallen upon them, while it rained on us in the valley below, of which the elevation here was about 4,500 feet above the sea. The country before us plainly indicated that we were approaching the lake, though, as the ground where we were travelling afforded no elevated point, nothing of it as yet could be seen; and at a great distance ahead were several isolated mountains, resembling islands, which they were afterwards found to be. On this upper plain the grass was everywhere dead; and among the shrubs with which it was almost exclusively occupied, (artemisia being the most abundant,) frequently occurred handsome clusters of several species of *dieteria* in bloom. *Purshia tridentata* was among the the frequent shrubs. Descending to the bottoms of Bear river, we found good grass for the animals, and encamped about 300 yards above the month of Roseaux, which here makes its junction, without communicating any of its salty taste to the main stream, of which the water remains perfectly pure. On the river are only willow thickets (*salix longifolia,*) and in the bottoms the abundant plants are canes, solidago, and helianthi, and along the banks of Rosentix are fields of *malva rotundifolia.* At sunset the thermometer was at 54°.5, and the evening clear and calm; but I deferred making any use of it until 1 o'clock in the morning, when I endeavored to obtain an emersion of the first satellite; but it was lost in a bank of clouds, which also rendered our usual observations indifferent.

Among the useful things which formed a portion of our equipage, was an India-rubber boat, 18 feet long, made somewhat in the form of a bark canoe of the northern lakes. The sides were formed by two air-tight cylinders, eighteen inches in diameter, connected with others forming the bow and stern. To lessen the danger from accidents to the boat, these were divided into four different compartments, and the interior space was sufficiently large to contain five or six persons, and a considerable weight of baggage. The Roseaux being too deep to be forded, our boat was filled with air, and in about one hour all the equipage of the camp, carriage and gun included, ferried across. Thinking that perhaps in the course of the day we might reach the outlet at the lake, I got into the boat with Basil Lajeunesse, and paddled down Bear river, intending at night to rejoin the party, which in the mean time proceeded on its way. The river was from sixty to one hundred yards broad, and the water so deep, that even on the comparatively shallow points we could not reach the bottom with 15 feet. On either side were alternately low bottoms and willow points, with an occasional high prairie; and for five or six hours we followed slowly the winding course of the river, which crept along with a sluggish current among frequent *détours* several miles around, sometimes running for a considerable distance directly up the valley. As we were stealing quietly down the stream, trying in vain to get a shot at a strange, large bird, that was numerous among the willows, but very shy, we came unexpectedly upon several families of *Root Diggers*, who were encamped among the rushes on the shore, and appeared very busy about several weirs or nets which had been rudely made of canes and rushes for the purpose of catching fish. They were very much startled at our appearance, but we soon established an acquaintance; and finding that they had some roots, I promised to send some men with goods to trade with them. They had the usual very large heads, remarkable among the Digger tribe, with matted hair, and were almost entirely naked, looking very poor and miserable, as if their lives had been spent in the rushes where they were, beyond which they seemed to have very little knowledge of anything. From the few words we could comprehend, their language was that of the Snake Indians.

Our boat moved so heavily, that we had made very little progress; and, finding that it would be impossible to overtake the camp, as soon as we were sufficiently far below the Indians, we put to the shore near a high prairie bank, hauled up the boat, and *cached* our effects in the willows. Ascending the bank, we found that our desultory labor had brought us only a few miles in a direct line; and, going out into the prairie, after a search we found the trail of the camp, which was now nowhere in sight, but had followed the general course of the river in a large circular sweep which it makes at this place. The sun was about three hours high when we found the trail; and as our people had passed early in the day, we had the prospect of a vigorous walk before us. Immediately where we landed, the high arable plain on which we had been travelling for several days past, terminated in extensive low flats, very generally occupied by salt marshes, or beds of shallow lakes, whence the water had in most places evaporated, leaving their hard surface encrusted with a shining white residuum, and absolutely covered with very small *univalve* shells. As we advanced, the whole country around us assumed this appearance; and there was no other vegetation than the shrubby chenopodiaceous and other apparently saline plants, which were confined to the rising grounds. Here and there on the river bank, which was raised like a levee above the flats through which it ran, was a narrow border of grass, and short, black-burnt willows; the stream being very deep and sluggish, and sometimes 600 to 800 feet wide. After a rapid walk of about 15 miles, we caught sight of the camp-fires among clumps of willows just as the sun had sunk behind the mountains on the west side of the valley, filling the clear sky with a golden yellow. These last rays, to us so precious, could not have revealed a more welcome sight. To the traveller, and the hunter, a camp-fire in the lonely wilderness is always cheering; and to ourselves, in our present situation, after a hard march in a region of novelty, approaching the *debouches* of a river, in a lake of almost fabulous reputation, it was doubly so. A plentiful supper of aquatic birds, and the interest of the scene, soon dissipated fatigue; and I obtained during the night emersions of the second, third, and fourth satellites of Jupiter, with observations for time and latitude.

September 3.—The morning was clear, with a light air from the north, and the thermometer at sunrise at 45°.5. At 3 in the morning, Basil was sent back with several men and horses for the boat, which, in a direct course across the flats, was not 10 miles distant; and in the mean time there was a pretty spot of grass here for the animals. The ground was so low that we could not get high enough to see across the river, on account of the willows; but we were evidently in the vicinity of the lake, and the water-fowl made this morning a noise like thunder. A pelican (*pelecanus oncrotalus*) was killed as he passed by, and many geese and ducks flew over the camp. On the dry salt marsh here, is scarce any other plant than *salicarnia herbacea.*

In the afternoon the men returned with the boat, bringing with them a small quantity of roots, and some meat, which the Indians had told them was bear meat.

Descending the river for about three miles in the afternoon, we found a bar to any further travelling in that direction—the stream being spread out in several branches, and covering the low grounds with water, where the miry nature of the bottom did not permit any further advance. We were evidently on the border of the lake, although the rushes and canes which covered the marshes prevented any view; and we accordingly encamped at the little *delta* which forms the month of Bear river; a long arm of the lake stretching up to the north between us and the opposite mountains. The river was bordered with a fringe of willows and canes, among which were interspersed a few plants; and scattered about on the marsh was a species of *uniola,* closely allied to *U. spicata* of our sea-coast. The whole morass was animated with multitudes of water-fowl, which appeared to be very wild—rising for the space of a mile round about at the sound of a gun, with a noise like distant thunder. Several of the people waded out into the marshes, and we had to-night a delicious supper of ducks, geese, and plover.

Although the moon was bright, the night was otherwise favorable; and I obtained this evening an emersion of the first satellite, with the usual observations. A mean result, depending on various observations made during our stay in the neighborhood, places the mouth of the river in longitude 112° 19'30" west from

Greenwich; latitude 41° 30'22"; and, according to the barometer, in elevation 4,200 feet above the gulf of Mexico. The night was clear, with considerable dew, which I had remarked every night since the first of September. The next morning, while we were preparing to start, Carson rode into the camp with flour and a few other articles of light provision, sufficient for two or three days—a scanty but very acceptable supply. Mr. Fitzpatrick had not yet arrived, and provisions were very scarce and difficult to be had at Fort Hall, which had been entirely exhausted by the necessities of the emigrants. He brought me also a letter from Mr. Dwight, who, in company with several emigrants, had reached that place in advance of Mr. Fitzpatrick, and was about continuing his journey to Vancouver.

Returning about five miles up the river, we were occupied until nearly sunset in crossing to the left bank; the stream, which in the last five or six miles of its course, is very much narrower than above, being very deep immediately at the banks; and we had great difficulty in getting our animals over. The people with the baggage were easily crossed in the boat, and we encamped on the left bank where we crossed the river. At sunset the thermometer was at 75°, and there was some rain during the night, with a thunder-storm at a distance.

September 5.—Before us was evidently the bed of the lake, being a great salt marsh perfectly level and bare, whitened in places by saline efflorescences, with here and there a pool of water, and having the appearance of a very level sea-shore at low tide. Immediately along the river was a very narrow strip of vegetation, consisting of willows, helianthi, roses, flowering vines, and grass; bordered on the verge of the great marsh by a fringe of singular plants which appear to be a shrubby salicornia, or a genus allied to it.

About 12 miles to the southward was one of those isolated mountains, now appearing to be a kind of peninsula; and towards this we accordingly directed our course, as it probably afforded a good view of the lake; but the deepening mud as we advanced forced us to return toward the river, and gain the higher ground at the foot of the eastern mountains. Here we halted for a few minutes at noon, on a beautiful little stream of pure and remarkably clear water, with a bed of rock *in situ*, on which was an abundant water-plant with a white blossom. There was good grass in the bottoms; and, amidst a rather luxuriant growth, its banks were bordered with a large showy plant (*eupatorium purpureum,*) which I here saw for the first time. We named the stream *Clear creek.*

We continued out way along the mountain, having found here a broad plainly beaten trail, over what was apparently the shore of the lake in the spring; the ground being high and firm, and the soil excellent and covered with vegetation, among which a leguminous plant (*glycyrrhiza lepidota*) was a characteristic plant. The ridge here rises abruptly to the height of about 4,000 feet; its face being very prominently marked with a massive stratum of rose-colored granular quartz, which is evidently an altered sedimentary rock; the lines of deposition being very distinct. It is rocky and steep; divided into several mountains; and the rain in the valley appears to be always snow on their summits at this season. Near a remarkable rocky point of the mountain, at a large spring of pure water, were several hackberry trees, (*celtis,*) probably a new species, the berries still green; and a short distance rather, thickets of sumach (*rhus.*)

On the plain here I noticed blackbirds and grouse. In about seven miles from Clear creek, the trail brought us to a place at the foot of the mountain where there issued with considerable force ten or twelve hot springs, highly impregnated with salt. In one of these, the thermometer stood at 136°, and in another at 132°.5; and the water, which spread in pools over the low ground, was colored red.

An analysis of the red earthy matter deposited in the bed of the stream from the springs, gives the following result:

Peroxide of iron	-	-	-	33.50
Carbonate of magnesia	-	-	-	2.40
Carbonate of lime	-	-	-	50.43
Sulphate of lime	-	-	-	2.00
Chloride of sodium	-	-	-	3.45
Silica and alumina	-	-	-	3.00
Water and loss	-	-	-	5.22
				100.00

At this place the trail we had been following turned to the left, apparently with the view of entering a gorge in the mountain, from which issued the principal fork of a large and comparatively well timbered stream, called Weber's fork. We accordingly turned off towards the lake, and encamped on this river, which was 100 to 150 feet wide, with high banks, and very clear pure water, without the slightest indication of salt.

September 6.—Leaving the encampment early, we again directed our course for the peninsular *butte,* across a low shrubby plain, crossing in the way a slough-like creek with miry banks, and wooded with thickets of thorn (*cratægus)* which were loaded with berries. This time we reached the butte without any difficulty, and, ascending to the summit, immediately at our feet, beheld the object of our anxious search—the waters of the Inland Sea, stretching in still and solitary grandeur far beyond the limit of our vision. It was one of the great points of the exploration; and as we looked eagerly over the lake in the first emotions of excited pleasure, I am doubtful if the followers of Balboa felt more enthusiasm when, from the heights of the Andes, they saw for the first time the great Western Ocean. It was certainly a magnificent object, and a noble *terminus* to this part of our expedition; and to travellers so long shut up among mountain ranges, a sudden view over the expanse of silent waters had in it something sublime. Several large islands raised their high rocky heads out of the waves; but whether or not they were timbered, was still left to our imagination, as the distance was too great to determine if the dark hues upon them were woodland or naked rock. During the day the clouds had been gathering black over the mountains to the westward, and, while we were looking, a storm burst down with sudden fury upon the lake, and entirely hid the islands from our view. So far as we could see, along the shores there was not a solitary tree, and but little appearance of grass; and on Weber's fork, a few miles below our last encampment, the timber was gathered into groves, and then disappeared entirely. As this appeared to be the nearest point to the lake where a suitable camp could be found, we directed our course to one of the groves, where we found a handsome encampment, with good grass and an abundance of rushes, (*equisetum hyemale.*) At sunset, the thermometer was at 55°; the evening clear and calm, with some cumuli.

September 7.—The morning was calm and clear, with a temperature at sunrise of 39°.5. The day was spent in active preparation for our intended voyage on the lake. On the edge of the stream a favorable spot was selected in a grove, and, felling the timber, we made a trade a strong *corál,* or horse-pen, for the animals, and a little fort for the people who were to remain. We were now probably in the country of the Utah Indians, though none reside upon the lake. The India-rubber boat was repaired with prepared cloth and gum, and filled with air, in readiness for the next day.

The provisions which Carson had brought with him being now exhausted, and our stock reduced to a small quantity of roots, I determined to retain with me only a sufficient number of men for the execution of our design; and accordingly seven were sent back to Fort Hall, under the guidance of François Lajeunesse, who, having been for many years a trapper in the country, was considered an experienced mountaineer. Though they were provided with good horses, and the road was a remarkably plain one of only four days' journey for a horseman, they became bewildered, (as we afterwards learned,) and, losing their way, wondered about the country in parties of one or two, reaching the fort about a week afterwards. Some straggled in of themselves, and the others were brought in by Indians who had picked them up on Snake river, about sixty miles below the fort, travelling along the emigrant road in full march for the Lower Columbia. The leader of this adventurous party was François.

Hourly barometrical observations were made during the day, and, after departure of the party for Fort Hall, we occupied ourselves in continuing our little preparations, and in becoming acquainted with the country in the vicinity. The bottoms along the river were timbered with several kinds of willow, hawthorn, and fine cottonwood trees (*populus canadensis*) with remarkably large leaves, and sixty feet in height by measurement.

We formed now but a small family. With Mr. Preuss and myself, Carson, Bernier, and Basil Lajeunesse had been selected for the boat expedition—the first ever attempted on this interior sea; and Badeau, with Derosier, and Jacob, (the colored man,) were to be left in charge of the camp. We were favored with most delightful weather. To-night there was a brilliant sunset of golden orange and green, which left the western sky clear and beautifully pure; but clouds in the east made me lose an occulation. The summer frogs were singing around us, and the evening was very pleasant, with a temperature of 60°—a night of a more southern autumn. For our supper we had *yampah,* the most agreeably flavored of the roots, seasoned by a small fat duck, which had come in the way of Jacob's rifle. Around our fire to-night were many speculations on what to-morrow would bring forth, and in our busy conjectures we fancied that we should find every one of the large islands a tangled wilderness of trees and shrubbery, teeming with game of every description that the neighboring region afforded, and which the foot of a white man or Indian had never violated. Frequently, during the day, clouds had rested on the summits of their lofty mountains, and we believed that we should find clear streams and springs of fresh water; and we indulged in anticipations of the luxurious repasts with which we were to indemnify ourselves for past privations. Neither, in our discussions, were the whirlpool and other mysterious dangers forgotten, which Indian and hunter's stories attributed to this unexplored lake. The men had discovered that, instead of being strongly sewed, (like that of the preceding year, which had so triumphantly rode the cañons of the Upper Great Platte,) our present boat was only pasted together in a very insecure manner, the maker having been allowed so little time in the construction, that he was obliged to crowd the labor of two months into several days. The insecurity of the boat was sensibly felt by us; and, mingled with the enthusiasm and excitement that we all felt at the prospect of an undertaking which had never before been accomplished, was a certain impression of danger, sufficient to give a serious character to our conversation. The momentary view which had been had of the lake the day before, its great extent and rugged islands, dimly seen amidst the dark waters in the obscurity of the sudden storm, were well calculated to heighten the idea of undefined danger with which the lake was generally associated.

September 8.—A calm, clear day, with a sunrise temperature of 41°. In view of our present enterprise, apart of the equipment of the boat bad been made to consist in three air-tight bags, about three feet long, and capable each of containing five gallons. These had been filled with water the night before, and were now placed in the boat, with our blankets and instruments, consisting of a sextant, telescope, spyglass, thermometer, and barometer.

We left the camp at sunrise, and had a very pleasant voyage down the river, in which there was generally eight or ten feet of water, deepening as we neared the mouth in the latter part of the day. In the course of the morning we discovered that two of the cylinders leaked so much as to require one man constantly at the bellows, to keep them sufficiently full of air to support the boat. Although we had made a very early start, we loitered so much on the way—stopping every now and then, and floating silently along, to get a shot at a goose or a duck—that it was late in the day when we reached the outlet. The river here divided into several branches, filled with fluvials, and so very shallow that it was with difficulty we could get the boat along, being obliged to get out and wade. We encamped on a point among rushes and young willows, where. there was a quantity of driftwood, which served for our fires. The evening was mild and clear; we made a pleasant bed of the young willows; and geese and ducks enough had been killed for an abundant supper at night, and for breakfast next morning. The stillness of the night was enlivened by millions of water-fowl. Latitude (by observation) 41° 11' 26"; and longitude 112° 11' 30".

September 9.—The day was clear and calm; the thermometer at sunrise at 49°. As is usual with the trappers on the eve of any enterprise, our people had made dreams, and theirs happened to be a bad one—one which always preceded evil—and consequently they looked very gloomy this morning; but we hurried through our breakfast, in order to make an early start, and have all the day before our adventure. The channel in a short distance became so shallow that our navigation was at an end, being merely a sheet of soft mud, with a few inches of water, and sometimes none at all, forming the low-water shore of the lake. All this place was absolutely covered with flocks of screaming plover. We took off our clothes, and, getting overboard, commenced dragging the boat—making, by this operation, a very curious trail, and a very disagreeable smell in stirring up the mud, as we sank above the knee at every step. The water here was still fresh, with only an insipid and disagreeable taste, probably derived from the bed of fetid mud. After proceeding in this way about a mile, we came to a small black ridge on the bottom, beyond which the water became suddenly salt, beginning gradually to deepen, and the bottom was sandy and firm. It was a remarkable division, separating the fresh water of the rivers from the briny water of the lake, which was entirely *saturated* with common salt. Pushing our little vessel across the narrow boundary, we sprang on board, and at length were afloat on the waters of the unknown sea.

We did not steer for the mountainous islands, but directed our course towards a lower one, which it had been decided we should first visit, the summit of which was formed like the crater at the upper end of Bear river valley. So long as we could touch the bottom with our paddles, we were very gay; but gradually, as the water deepened, we became more still in our frail batteau of gum cloth distended with air, and with pasted seams. Although the day was very calm, there was a considerable swell on the lake; and there were white patches of foam on the surface, which were slowly moving to the southward, indicating the set of a current in that direction, and recalling the recollection of the whirlpool stories. The water continued to deepen as we advanced; the lake becoming almost transparently clear, of an extremely beautiful bright-green color; and the spray, which was thrown into the boat and over our clothes, was directly converted into a crust of common salt, which covered also our hands and arms. "Captain," said Carson, who for some time had been looking suspiciously at some whitening appearances outside the nearest islands, "what are those yonder?—won't you just take a look with the glass?" We ceased paddling for a moment, and found them to be the caps of the waves that were beginning to break under the force of a strong breeze that was coming up the lake. The form of the boat seemed to be an admirable one, and it rode on the waves like a water bird; but, at the same time, it was extremely slow in its progress. When we were a little more than half-way across the reach, two of the divisions between the cylinders gave way, and it required the constant use of the bellows to keep in a sufficient quantity of air. For a long time we scarcely seemed to approach our island, but gradually we worked across the rougher sea of the open channel, into the smoother water under the lee of the island; and began to discover that what we took for a long row of pelicans ranged on the beach, were only low cliffs whitened with salt by the spray of the waves and about noon we reached the shore, and transparency of the water enabling us to se the bottom at a considerable depth.

It was a handsome broad beach where we landed, behind which the hill, into which the island was gathered, rose somewhat abruptly; and a point of rock at one end enclosed it in a sheltering way; and as there was an abundance of drift-wood along the shore, it offered us a pleasant encampment.

We did not suffer our fragile boat to touch the sharp rocks; but, getting overboard, discharged the baggage, and, lifting it gently out of the water, carried it to the upper part of the beach, which was composed of very small fragments of rock.

Among the successive banks of the beach, formed by the action of the waves, our attention, as we approached the island, had been attracted by one 10 to 20 feet in breath, of a dark-brown color. Being more closely examined, this was found to be composed, to the depth of seven or eight, and twelve inches, entirely of the *larvæ* of insects, or, in common language, of the skins of worms, about the size of a grain of oats, which had been washed up by the waters of the lake.

Alluding to this subject some months afterwards, when travelling through a more southern portion of this region, in company with Mr. Joseph Walker, an old hunter, I was informed by him, that, wandering with a party of men in a mountain country east of the great Californian range, he surprised a party of several Indian families encamped near a small salt lake, who abandoned their lodges at his approach, leaving everything behind them. Being in a starving condition, they were delighted to find in the abandoned lodges a number of skin bags, containing a quantity of what appeared to be fish, dried and pounded. On this they made a hearty supper; and were gathering around an abundant breakfast the next morning, when Mr. Walker discovered that it was with these, or a similar worm, that the bags had been filled. The stomachs of the stout trappers were not proof against their prejudices, and the repulsive food was suddenly rejected. Mr. Walker had further opportunities of seeing these worms used as an article of food; and I am inclined to think they are the same as those we saw, and appear to be a product of the salt lakes. It may be well to recall to your mind that Mr. Walker was associated with Captain Bonneville in his expedition to the Rocky mountains; and has since that time remained in the country, generally residing in some one of the Snake villages, when not engaged in one of his numerous trapping expeditions, in which he is celebrated as one of the best and bravest leaders who have ever been in the country.

The cliffs and masses of rock along the shore were whitened by an incrustation of salt where the waves dashed up against them; and the evaporating water, which had been left in holes and hollows on the surface of the rocks, was covered with a crust of salt about one-eighth of an inch in thickness. It appeared strange that, in the

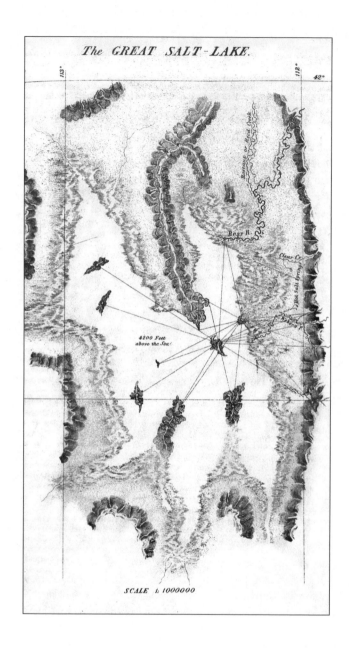

The GREAT SALT-LAKE.

SCALE 1: 1000000

midst of this grand reservoir, one of our greatest wants lately had been salt. Exposed to be more perfectly dried in the sun, this became very white and fine, having the usual flavor of very excellent common salt without any foreign taste; but only a little was collected for present use, as there was in it a number of small black insects.

Carrying with us the barometer and other instruments, in the afternoon we ascended to the highest point of the island—a bare rocky peak, 800 feet above the lake. Standing on the summit, we enjoyed the extended view of the lake, enclosed in a basin of rugged mountains, which sometimes left marshy flats and extensive bottoms between them and the shore, and in other places came directly down into the water with bold and precipitous bluffs. Following with our glasses the irregular shores, we searched for some indications of a communication with other bodies of water, or the entrance of other rivers; but the distance was so great, that we could make out nothing with certainty. To the southward, several peninsular mountains 3,000 or 4,000 feet high entered the lake, appearing, so far as the distance and our position enabled us to determine, to be connected by flats and low ridges, with the mountains in the rear. Although these are probably the islands usually indicated on maps of this region as entirely detached from the shore, we have preferred to represent them in the small map on the preceding page, precisely as we were enabled to sketch them on the ground, leaving their more complete delineation for a future survey. The sketch, of which the scale is nearly sixteen miles to an inch, is introduced only to show clearly the extent of our operations, which, it will be remembered, were made when the waters were at their lowest stage. At the season of high waters in the spring, it is probable that all the marshes and low grounds are overflowed, and the surface of the lake considerably greater. In several places (which will be indicated to you in the sketch, by the absence of the bordering mountains) the view was of unlimited extent—here and there a rocky islet appearing above the water at a great distance; and beyond, everything was vague and undefined. As we looked over the vast expanse of water spread out beneath us, and strained our eyes along the silent shores over which hung so much doubt and uncertainty, and which were so full of interest to us, I could hardly repress the almost irresistible desire to continue our exploration; but the lengthening snow on the mountains was a plain indication of the advancing season, and our frail linen boat appeared so insecure that I was unwilling to trust our lives to the uncertainties of the lake. I therefore unwillingly resolved to terminate our survey here, and remain satisfied for the present with what we had been able to add to the unknown geography of the region. We felt pleasure also in remembering that we were the first who, in the traditionary annals of the country, had visited the islands, and broken, with the cheerful sound of human voices, the long solitude of the place. From the point where we were standing, the ground fell off on every side to the water, giving us a perfect view of the island, which is twelve or thirteen miles in circumference, being simply a rocky hill, on which there is neither water nor trees of any kind; although the *Fremontia vermicularis,* which was in great abundance, might easily be mistaken for a timber at a distance. The plant seemed here to delight in a congenial air, growing in extraordinary luxuriance seven to eight feet high, and was very abundant on the upper parts of the island, where it was almost the only plant. This is eminently a saline shrub; its leaves have a very salt taste; and it luxuriates in saline soils, where it is usually a characteristic. It is widely diffused over all this country. A chenopodiaceous shrub, which is a new species of OBIONE, (O. Rigida, *Torr. & Frem.*) was equally characteristic of the lower parts of the island. These two are the striking plants on the island, and belong to a class of plants which form a prominent feature in the vegetation of this country. On the lower parts of the island also a prickly pear of very large size was frequent. On the shore, near the water, was a wooly species of *phaca*; and a new species of umbelliferous plant (leptotæmia) was scattered about in very considerable abundance. These constituted all the vegetation that now appeared upon the island.

I accidentally left on the summit the brass cover to the object end of my spyglass; and as it will probably remain there undisturbed by Indians, it will furnish matter of speculation to some future traveller. In our excursions about the island, we did not meet with any kind of animal; a magpie, and another larger bird, probably attracted by the smoke of our fire, paid us a visit from the shore, and were the only living things seen during our stay. The rock constituting the cliff along the shore where we were encamped, is a talcous rock, or stealite, with brown spar.

At sunset, the temperature was 70°. We had arrived just in time to obtain a meridian attitude of the sun, and other observations were obtained this evening, which place our camp in latitude, 41° 10' 42", and longitude 112° 21' 05" from Greenwich. From a discussion of the barometrical observations made during our stay on the shores of the lake, we have adopted 4,200 feet for its elevation above the gulf of Mexico. In the first disappointment we felt from the dissipation of our dream of the fertile islands, I called this *Disappointment island.*

Out of the driftwood, we made ourselves pleasant little lodges, open to the water, and, after having kindled large fires to excite the wonder of any straggling savage on the lake shores, lay down, for the first time in a long journey, in perfect security; no one thinking about his arms. The evening was extremely bright and pleasant; but the wind rose during the night, and the waves began to break heavily on the shore, making our island tremble. I had not expected in our island journey to hear the roar of an ocean surf; and the strangeness of our situation, and the excitement we felt in the associated interests of the place, made this one of the most interesting nights I remember during our long expedition.

In the morning, the surf was breaking heavily on the shore, and we were up early. The lake was dark and agitated, and we hurried through our scanty breakfast, and embarked—having first filled one of the buckets with water from the lake, of which it was intended to make salt. The sun had risen by the time we were ready to start; and it was blowing a strong gale of wind, almost directly off the shore, and raising a considerable sea, in which our boat strained very much.

It roughened as we got away from the island, and it required all the efforts of the men to make any head against the wind and sea; the gale rising with the sun, and there was danger of being blown into one of the open reaches beyond the island. At the distance of half a mile from the beach, the depth of water was 16 feet, with a clay bottom; but, as the working of the boat was very severe labor, and during the operation of rounding it was necessary to cease paddling, during which the boat lost considerable way, I was unwilling to discourage the men, and reluctantly gave up my intention of ascertaining the depth, and the character of the bed. There was a general shout in the boat when we found ourselves in one fathom, and we soon after landed on a low point of mud, immediately under the *butte* of the peninsula, where we unloaded the boat, and carried the baggage about a quarter of a mile to firmer ground. We arrived just in time for meridian observation, and carried the barometer to the summit of the butte, which is 500 feet above the lake. Mr. Preuss set off on foot for the camp, which was about nine miles distant; Basil accompanying him, to bring back horses for the boat and baggage.

The rude-looking shelter we raised on the shore, our scattered baggage, and boat lying on the beach, made quite a picture; and we called this the *Fisherman's camp*. *Lynosiris graveolens,* and another new species of OBIONE, (O. Confertifolia—*Torr. & Frem.*) were growing on the low grounds, with interspersed spots of an unwholesome salt grass, on a saline clay soil, with a few other plants.

The horses arrived late in the afternoon, by which time the gale had increased to such a height that a man could scarcely stand before it; and we were obliged to pack our baggage hastily, as the rising water of the lake had already reached the point where we were halted. Looking back as we rode off, we found the place of recent encampment entirely covered. The low plain through which we rode to the camp was covered with a compact growth of shrubs of extraordinary size and luxuriance. The soil was sandy and saline; flat places, resembling the beds of ponds, that were bare of vegetation, and covered with a powdery white salts, being interspersed among the shrubs. Artemisia tridentata was very abundant, but the plants were principally saline; a large and vigorous chenopodiaceous shrub, five to eight feet high, being characteristic, with Fremontia vermicularis, and a shrubby plant which seems to be a new *salicornia*. We reached the camp in time to escape a thunder-storm which blackened the sky, and were received with a discharge of the howitzer by the people, who, having been unable to see anything of us on the lake, had begun to feel some uneasiness.

September 11.—To day we remained at this camp, in order to obtain some further observations, and to boil down the water which had been brought from the lake, for a supply or salt. Roughly evaporated over the fire, the five gallons of water yielded fourteen pints of very fine-grained and very white salt, of which the whole lake may be regarded as a saturated solution. A portion of the salt thus obtained has been subjected to analysis—giving, in 100 parts, the following proportions:

Analysis of the salt

Chloride of sodium, (common salt)	-	-	-	97.80
Chloride of calcium	-	-	-	0.61
Chloride of magnesium	-	-	-	0.24
Sulphate of soda	-	-	-	0.23
Sulphate of lime	-	-	-	1.12
				100.00

Glancing your eye along the map, you will see a small stream entering the *Utah lake*, south of the Spanish fork, and the first waters of that lake which our road of 1844 crosses in coming up from the southward. When I was on this stream with Mr. Walker in that year, he informed me that on the upper part of the river are immense beds of rock salt of very great thickness, which he had frequently visited. Farther to the southward, the rivers which are affluent to the Colorado, such as the Rio Virgen, and Gila river, near their mouths are impregnated with salt by the cliffs of rock salt between which they pass. These mines occur in the same ridge in which, about 120 miles to the northward, and subsequently in their more immediate neighborhood, we discovered the fossils belonging to the oolitic period, and they are probably connected with that formation, and are the deposite from which the Great Lake obtains its salt. Had we remained longer, we should have found them in its bed, and in the mountains around its shores.

By observation, the latitude of this camp is 41° 15' 50", and longitude 112° 06' 43".

The observations made during our stay give for the rate of the chronometer 31".72, corresponding almost exactly with the rate obtained at St. Vrain's fort. Barometrical observations were made hourly during the day. This morning we breakfasted on yampah, and had only kamás for supper; but a cup of good coffee still distinguishes us from our *digger* acquaintances.

September 12.—The morning was clear and calm, with a temperature at sunrise of 33°. We resumed our journey late in the day, returning by nearly the same route which we had travelled in coming to the lake; and, avoiding the passage of Hawthorn creek, struck the hills a little below the hot salt springs. The flat plain we had here passed over consisted alternately of tolerably good sandy soil and of saline plats. We encamped early on Clear creek, at the foot of the high ridge; one of peaks of which we ascertained by measurement to be 4,210 feet above the lake, or about 8,400 feet above the sea. Behind these front peaks the ridge rises towards the Bear river mountains, which are probably as high as the Wind river chain. This creek is here unusually well timbered with a variety of trees. Among them were birch (*betula,*)the narrow-leaved poplar (*populus angustifolia,*) several kinds of willow, (*salix,*) hawthorn, (*cratægus,*) alder, (*alnus viridis,*) and *cerasus*, with an oak allied to *quercus alba*, but very distinct from that or any other species in the United States.

We had to-night a supper of sea-gulls, which Carson killed near the lake. Although cool, the thermometer standing at 47°, musquitoes were sufficiently numerous to be troublesome this evening.

September 13.—Continuing up the river valley, we crossed several small streams; the mountains on the right appearing to consist of the blue limestone, which we had observed in the same ridge to the northward, alternating here with a granular quartz already mentioned. One of these streams, which forms a smaller lake near the river, was broken up into several channels; and the irrigated bottom of fertile soil was covered with innumerable flowers, among which were purple fields of *eupatorium purpureum*, with helianthi, a handsome solidago (*S. canadensis*) and a variety of other plants in bloom. Continuing along the foot of the hills, in the afternoon we found five or six hot spring gushing out together, beneath a conglemerate, consisting principally of fragments of a grayish-blue limestone, efflorescing a salt upon the surface. The temperature of these springs was 134°, and the rocks in the bed were colored with a red deposite, and there was common salt crystallized on the margin. There was also a white incrustation upon leaves and roots, consisting principally of carbonate of lime. There were rushes seen along the road this afternoon, and the soil under the hills was very black, and apparently very good; but at this time the grass is entirely dried up. We encamped on Bear river, immediately below a cut-off, the cañon by which the river enters this valley bearing north by compass. The night was mild, with a very clear sky; and I obtained a very excellent observation of anoccultation of Tau' Arietis, with other observations, the longitude is 112° 05' 12", and the latitude 41° 42' 43". All the longitudes on the line of our outward journey between St. Vrain's fort and the Dalles of the Columbia, which were not directly determined by satellites, have been chronometrically referred to this place.

The people to-day were rather low-spirited, hunger making them very quiet and peaceable; and there was rarely an oath to be heard in the camp—not even a solitary *enfant de garce*. It was time for the men with an expected supply of provisions from Fitzpatrick to be in the neighborhood; and the gun was fired at evening to give them notice of our locality, but met with no response.

September 14.—About four miles from this encampment, the trail led us down to the river, where we unexpectedly found an excellent ford—the stream being widened by an island, and not yet disengaged from the hills at the foot of the range. We encamped on a little creek where we had made a noon halt in descending the river. The night was very clear and pleasant, the sunset temperature being 67°.

The people this evening looked so forlorn, that I gave them permission to kill a fat young horse which I had purchased with goods from the Snake Indians, and they were very soon restored to gayety and good humor. Mr. Preuss and myself could not yet overcome some remains of civilized prejudices, and preferred to starve a little longer; feeling as much saddened as if a crime had been committed.

The next day we continued up the valley, the soil being sometimes very black and good, occasionally gravelly, and occasionally a kind of naked salt plains. We found on the way this morning a small encampment of two families of Snake Indians, from whom we purchased a small quantity of *kooyah*. They had piles of seeds, of three different kinds, spread out upon pieces of buffalo robe; and the squaws had just gathered about a bushel of the roots of a thistle, (*circium Virginianum.*) They were about the ordinary size of carrots, and, as I have previously mentioned, are sweet and well flavored, requiring only a long preparation. They had a band of twelve or fifteen horses, and appeared to be growing in the sunshine with about as little labor as the plants they were eating.

Shortly afterwards we met an Indian on horseback who had killed an antelope, which we purchased from him for a little powder and some balls. We crossed the Roseaux, and encamped on the left bank; halting early from the pleasure of enjoying a wholesome and abundant supper, and were pleasantly engaged in protracting our unusual comfort, when Tabeau galloped into the camp with news that Mr. Fitzpatrick was encamped close by us wit a good supply of provisions—flour, rice, and dried meat, and even a little butter. Excitement to-night made us all wakeful; and after a breakfast before sunrise the next morning, we were again on the road, and, continuing up the valley, crossed some high pints of hills, and halted to noon on the same stream, near several lodges of Snake indians, from whom we purchased about a bushel of service berries, partially dried. By the gift of a knife, I prevailed upon a little boy to show me the *kooyah* plant, which proved to be *valeriana edulis.* The root, which constitutes the *kooyah*, is large, of a very bright yellow color, with the characteristic odor, but not so fully developed as in the prepared substance. It loves the rich moist soil of river bottoms, which was the locality in which I always afterwards found it. It was now entirely out of bloom; according to my observation, flowering in the months of May and June. In the afternoon we entered a long ravine leading to a pass in the dividing ridge between the waters of Bear river and the Snake river, or Lewis's fork of the Columbia; our way being very much impeded, and almost entirely blocked up, by compact fields of luxuriant artemisia. Taking leave at this point of the waters of Bear river, and of the geographical basin which encloses the system of rivers and creeks which belong to the Great Salt Lake, and which so richly deserves a future detailed and ample exploration, I can say of it, in general terms, that the bottoms of the river, (Bear,) and of some of the creeks which I saw, form a natural resting and recruiting station for travellers, now, and in all time to come. The bottoms are extensive; water excellent; timber sufficient; the soil good, and well adapted to the grains and grasses suited to such an elevated region. A military post, and a civilized settlement, would be of great value here; and cattle and horses would do well where grass and salt so much abound. The lake will furnish exhaustless supplies of salt. All the mountain sides here are covered with a valuable nutritious grass, call bunch grass, from the form in which it grows, which has a second growth in the fall. The beasts of the Indians were fat upon it: our own found it a good subsistence; and its quantity will sustain any amount of cattle, and make this truly a bucolic region.

Surveying the Lake

C aptain Howard W. Stansbury's narrative of his exploration and survey of the Great Salt Lake in the spring of 1850 is the longest selection in this anthology. It is also perhaps the most exciting and entertaining, in the vivid immediacy of his description of the adventures and tribulations of coping with the lake's forbidding topography and weather. Stansbury's map, his field notes, and the book which they support (excerpted here) are among the most important documents in Utah history. During 1849–1850 Stansbury's crew of U.S. Army Corps of Topographical Engineers, aided by members recruited among the local Mormon population, prepared the first instrument survey of the lake, drew the first accurate map of the valley of the Great Salt Lake, recorded or assigned most of the modern place-names on the lake, and wrote one of the first accurate and objective descriptions of Mormon ideas and institutions by an outsider.

The immediate and ostensible purpose of the Stansbury survey was to begin collecting scientific information on the vast new territory acquired through the Mexican War of 1846–1848, the largest single territorial acquisition in American history. Even before the California gold rush of 1849 began, it was apparent that United States settlers were going to be looking for routes across the new territory and eventually occupy it, both of which could be facilitated by prior scientific survey. A less apparent goal of Stansbury's expedition, however, was to collect information on the Mormons, whose migrations across the Midwest and eventually to the Great Basin since the church's founding in 1830 had been dogged by rumors of exotic economic, political, and social practices and accusations of disloyalty.

It would take a man with a special blend of scientific and personal capabilities to accomplish such diverse ends, but Colonel John J. Abert found such a man among his topographical engineers in the person of Captain Howard Stansbury. Trained as a civil engineer, Stansbury had worked for the army in a civilian capacity on projects on the Great Lakes, in Virginia, and various midwestern locales before being offered a commission in the Corps of Topographical Engineers when it was founded in 1838. Among the eventually seventy-two officers who comprised the corps, Stansbury and John C. Frémont were two of only eight without a West Point background. What Stansbury lacked in military spit and polish, he made up for in scientific skill and personal diplomacy, both of which he found much more useful in coping with the challenges of the Great Salt Lake and the Mormon society of Brigham Young.

Stansbury's primary assistant, Lieutenant John Williams Gunnison, was an equally fortunate choice. A West Point man, he could claim scientific abilities equal to Stansbury's. Personally, too, he proved to possess patience and diplomacy. In spite of frail health, Gunnison endured the rough terrain and rough weather of the lake survey with little complaint. A devout Episcopalian, he found Mormonism exotic, but studied it dispassionately and wrote his own book about the Saints that they embraced as fair and accurate. Much of the value of both Stansbury's and Gunnison's reports on the Mormons derives from the fact that they spent an entire winter in Salt Lake City and observed the Mormons extensively, whereas most other nineteenth century accounts are superficial descriptions of travelers who spent a few days at most among the Saints.

Two other crew members deserve mention. John Hudson, an English artist on his way to the California gold fields, had fallen ill in Salt Lake City and converted to Mormonism during his convalescence. Stansbury hired him to make the artistic renderings that illustrate the book. And finally, Albert Carrington, a Mormon official with a Dartmouth degree, became a valuable crew member and liaison with the Mormon community.

Beyond these, Stansbury tells us little about the other crew members, who in any event came and went as time passed. Although Stansbury had little regard for military red tape and protocol, he did have an officer's aristocratic aloofness from his crew members and rarely communicated with any but the aforementioned leaders. Thus it was the leaders who experienced most of the joys of scientific discovery, while to the men the survey meant little more than hard work in a harsh environment. Even at that, they had little cause for complaint, for Stansbury saw that they were fed and equipped as well as he had it in his power to do.

For the most part, Stansbury's careful narrative speaks for itself, but the reader may find a few minor preliminary comments useful. For one thing, he dispenses information about his boats only gradually, and one eventually learns that he was using an ideal combination of a yawl, a small two-masted sailboat, as his primary craft supported by a skiff, a flat-bottomed rowboat necessary for making landings along the lake's shallow shoreline. Even with access to the skiff, Stansbury tended to sail the yawl in too close, and on at least a couple of occasions his crew found themselves having to push laboriously to get the larger boat off a mud grounding and into deeper water.

Some of his place-names, too, may require some comment. His "Tuilla Valley" is of course his phonetic rendering of a common local pronunciation of Tooele

Valley. Mud Island was evidently a shallow protuberance at the edge of Bear Lake Bay, and has not survived either as a place-name or a feature. Others, like "Cloth Cap" and "Flat-rock Point," designate minor features whose locations are adequately indicated in the narrative.

Suggestions for further reading

A more recent edition of Stansbury's narrative is *Exploration of the Valley of the Great Salt Lake*, with and introduction by Don D. Fowler (Washington, D.C.: Smithsonian Institution Press, 1988). Brigham D. Madsen, professor emeritus of history at the University of Utah, is virtually a one-man industry of publication about the Stansbury survey. One could begin with his introductory article, "Stansbury's Expedition to the Great Salt Lake, 1849–50," *Utah Historical Quarterly* 56 (spring 1988): 148–59, and from there move on to his massive and definitive edition of Stansbury's field notes, *Exploring the Great Salt Lake: The Stansbury Expedition of 1849–50* (Salt Lake City: University of Utah Press, 1989). Madsen also edited the John Hudson documents, *A Forty-niner in Utah with the Stansbury Exploration of Great Salt Lake: Letters and Journal of John Hudson, 1848–50* (Salt Lake City: University of Utah Press, 1981). Lieutenant John Williams Gunnison's book is *The Mormons* (Philadelphia: J. B. Lippincott, 1860), also available in reprint editions. Information on the background and work of the Army Corps of Topographical Engineers may be found in William H. Goetzmann, *Army Exploration in the American West, 1803–1863* (New Haven, Yale University Press, 1959).

Reconnoissance of the Deserts Around the Western Shores of the Great Salt Lake

Howard W. Stansbury

The two following days were busily occupied in making preparation for an exploration around the western shore of the lake, which I desired to complete previous to
entering upon a more minute survey of its waters. The expedition was deemed necessary, to enable me as well to ascertain its general features as to gain some knowledge
of the means and appliances necessary to carry on the survey with safety and expedition. By the old mountain-men such a reconnoissance was considered not only hazardous in the highest degree, but absolutely impracticable, especially at so late a
season of the year. In this opinion they were confirmed by the representations of the
Indians, who represented water to be extremely scarce and the country destitute of
game. It was affirmed that the contemplated circuit had been repeatedly attempted
by old and experienced trappers, in search of beaver, but always without success; the
adventurers being invariably obliged to return with the loss of most of their animals.
This was discouraging; but in addition to these objections, it was known that mortal
offence had been taken by the Shoshonee or Snake Indians, (through whose country
we would be obliged to pass,) arising from a gross and wanton outrage which had
been a short time before inflicted upon them by a company of unprincipled emigrants, by whom their women had been most brutally treated, and their friends mur-
dered while attempting to defend them. Fears were entertained lest, in the wilds of
this inhospitable region, where foot of white man had never trod, we should fall a sacrifice to the just vengeance of those infuriated savages.

Having determined, however, that the examination was necessary to enable me
to carry out the instructions of the department, I resolved to proceed, or at least to
make the attempt. My preparations were simply to kill a beef and dry as much of

From Howard W. Stansbury, *An Expedition to the Valley of the Great Salt Lake* (Philadelphia:
Lippincott, Grambo., 1852), 97–119.

the flesh as we could carry upon our pack-mules; Since it would have been unsafe to risk the existence of the party upon the chances of killing game by the way. We also provided ourselves with three India-rubber bags, of the capacity of five gallons each, and a small keg, for transporting water across the desert; some sacks of flour, a small tent without poles, a tent-fly, and a blanket to each man. In addition, each person carried a few pounds of fresh beef attached to his saddle, which might be used before resorting to our store of dried meat. Thus equipped and well armed, we set out on the afternoon of the 19th of October, the little party numbering five men and sixteen mules. The provision-train for the surveying party was sent forward by the emigrant road, on the east side of the lake, under Lieutenant Howland, with orders to report to Lieutenant Gunnison at Salt Lake City. Colonel Porter had left us the day previous, on his return to Cantonment Loring.

From the ford of Bear River we followed the emigrant road westward for about four miles, which brought us to the Malade River. The crossing here was very difficult, and we found it impossible to get our animals over with their packs on, because of the depth of water; they were accordingly unloaded and dragged or driven over, one at a time, and some of them came near being swamped in the soft, Sticky mud composing the bottom. The men were obliged to strip, and carry the packs over on their heads, the lighter articles being thrown across. Wood was very scarce: we had but artemisia-bushes and a few charred sticks found amid the ashes of the extinguished fires left by the emigrants. These were, however, sufficient for cooking purposes. Grass there was none; and we began already to have some foretaste of the hardships to which our poor animals were about to be exposed. The night was cold; thermometer 22°. As wood could not be obtained even for tent-poles, we contented ourselves with stretching our weary bodies upon the ground, and, wrapped in our blankets, slept soundly till the morning.

The bottoms of Bear River and the Malade are composed of white clay, in which no trace of organic remains was discovered. The current of the Malade is here slow, and the water brackish and nauseous.

Saturday, October 20.—Ther. at daylight, 26°. Continued on the emigrant road about four miles, when we left it and turned more to the southward, with the intention of doubling a lofty promontory that puts into the lake from the north, and forms the western boundary of the Malade valley. In about a mile we came upon three or four beautiful springs of clear, bright water: they were gushing out from a rocky point, (of dark limestone and coarse argillaceous sandstone, with a dip of about 20° to the east,) and unite to form a branch which runs southward some miles, and then sinks in the sand, before reaching the lake. The water was, however, warm, brackish, and entirely unfit for drinking. Following down this stream for several miles, we struck on a succession of bare, level plains, composed of white clay and mud, with occasionally pieces of limestone and obsidian scattered on the surface. These dreary plains were occasionally separated from each other, by patches of salt grass and scattered clumps of artemisia. They had apparently formed, at some remote period, a part of the lake, and it is probable were partially covered during the freshet months. Some portions of the ground were still moist, and too soft to admit the passage of our mules without danger of miring. Where dry, the surface was hard and smooth.

In the afternoon, as I felt apprehensive of being overtaken by night without water for our animals, we turned more to the westward, and directed our steps toward the promontory range previously mentioned. Before reaching it, however, we came upon a small stream, fifteen feet wide and a foot deep, but it was quite salt, and almost unfit to drink; yet, as we had no prospect of finding better, we were fain to bivouac on its bank for the night. Artemisia was abundant, furnishing plenty of excellent fuel, although it reminded me somewhat of the scriptural phrase, "crackling of thorns under a pot," so constantly did the fire require replenishing. Day's travel, twenty-two miles.

Sunday, October 21.—Ther. at daybreak, 27°. There being neither grass nor water at this point, we left it early, and made in a south-west direction for the foot of the mountain, travelling over a hard, even surface of dry mud, as level as a floor and without a particle of vegetation of any kind. Before reaching the base of the hills, we descried some Indians at a distance, who, as soon as they discovered us, commenced a most rapid and precipitate flight. As they were on foot, I despatched the guide after them at full gallop to bring them to a parley, being desirous of obtaining from them some information, and if possible, to prevail upon some of them to act as guides through the unknown regions before us. The man overtook them at the foot of the mountain, when several of them, finding their retreat about to be cut off, halted, and advanced upon him with their guns presented, but were restrained from firing by an old Indian, who seemed to act as their chief. As soon as they perceived the rest of our party moving toward them from the plain, the whole band, consisting of some six or eight men and half a dozen squaws, retreated incontinently up the mountain, and in a few minutes totally disappeared, nor did we see them again. As we continued to advance, we passed through their encampment, which they had abandoned in such haste that they left every thing as it was at the moment of their flight—the kettle was boiling over the fire, and a good gun rested against a bush. We left all untouched, and did not even dismount as we knew they were watching us from behind the rocks, and I was desirous of convincing them of our peaceable disposition.

Following down the eastern base of the promontory for about two miles, we encamped on a small spring-branch, coming down from the mountains, furnishing very tolerable water and plenty of grass—refreshment most welcome to our jaded and famished animals, which had not had a full meal for nearly two days. At the Indian camp there was a spring, but the water, although abundant, was salt and unfit for use. Temperature of the spring, 84°. The mountain or main promontory seemed to be composed of limestone, altered shales, and sandstones: it rises from fifteen hundred to two thousand feet.

Monday, October 22.—Ther. at sunrise 25°. Morning clear and calm. The Salt Lake, which lay about half a mile to the eastward, was covered by immense flocks of wild geese and ducks, among which many swans were seen, being distinguishable by their size and the whiteness of their plumage. I had seen large flocks of these birds before, in various parts of our country, and especially upon the Potomac, but never did I behold any thing like the immense numbers here congregated together. Thousands of acres, as far as the eye could reach, seemed literally covered with them, presenting a scene of busy, animated cheerfulness, in most graceful contrast with the dreary, silent solitude by which we were immediately surrounded.

Our course until noon was south, along the base of the high promontory which puts into the lake from the north. On our left, for about three miles from our encampment, was an isolated knob or hill, separated from the main range by a grassy plain. It consisted of limestone and slaty shales, in the former of which were some small caves. The rocks were thrown up at a very high angle, and in some places were perpendicular, and rested, as far as could be ascertained, on a primitive formation below. Toward the southern end of the promontory the limestones disappeared, and the surface rock was formed of conglomerate composed chiefly of the older sedimentary rocks, and some boulders of serpentine and porphyry. Upon examining several isolated masses of this, it was found that each stone (principally rounded pebbles of quartz) was surrounded by a crystalline layer of satin spar, as if it had formed a nucleus around which the lime had crystallized. In about ten miles we reached the southern extremity of this high rocky range, where it juts into the lake. Within this distance we passed five or six springs, some of them with very good water, bursting from the foot of the mountain. Innumerable salt and sulphur springs break out of the bank all along, but are soon lost in the broad sand and mud flat which lies between the banks and the water. This flat is about two miles broad, entirely without vegetation, and has, I think, been slightly covered by the lake in the spring and summer. Both yesterday and to-day, considerable quantities of small drift-wood was seen lying on the sands—a fact which favours this opinion.

The mirage along the lake shore, and above the moist, oozy plains, has been, for the last two days, very great, giving rise to optical illusions the most grotesque and fantastic, and rendering all estimate of the distance or form of objects vague and uncertain. Two miles farther we reached a small rill of brackish, indifferent water, upon which we bivouacked, fearing to go on, lest we should be left without any.

The evening was mild and bland, and the scene around us one of exciting interest. At our feet and on each side lay the waters of the Great Salt Lake, which we had so long and so ardently desired to see. They were clear and calm, and stretched far to the south and west. Directly before us, and distant only a few miles, an island rose from eight hundred to one thousand feet in height, while in the distance other and larger ones shot up from the bosom of the waters, their summits appearing to reach the clouds. On the west appeared several dark spots, resembling other islands, but the dreamy haze hovering over this still and solitary sea threw its dim, uncertain veil over the more distant features of the landscape, preventing the eye from discerning any one object with distinctness, while it half revealed the whole, leaving ample scope for the imagination of the beholder. The stillness of the grave seemed to pervade both air and water; and, excepting here and there a solitary wild-duck floating motionless on the bosom of the lake, not a living thing was to be seen. The night proved perfectly serene, and a young moon shed its tremulous light upon a sea of profound, unbroken silence. I was surprised to find, although so near a body of the saltest water, none of that feeling of invigorating freshness which is always experienced when in the vicinity of the ocean. The bleak and naked shores, without a single tree to relieve the eye, presented a scene so different from what I had pictured in my imagination of the beauties of this far-famed spot, that my disappointment was extreme.

Tuesday, October 23.—Ther. at daylight, 37°. Morning clear and calm; the lake and mountains to the eastward yet wrapped in mist. The west side of the extremity of the promontory is composed of porphyry, interspersed with seams of white quartz, which veined it in the most beautiful manner. The quartz veins in some instances were several feet thick. These rocks, evidently in place, rose boldly, forming escarpments looking to the south-west, with a dip, apparently to the north, of about 50°. Decomposed limestone, containing organic remains, and also trap rock, were here observed. The ground near our encampment was covered with a species of *Astragalus,* the seed-pods of which were covered by a substance resembling cotton, and presented the appearance of oval white balls, about the size of a robin's egg. I afterward found this plant upon most of the islands of the lake.

Rounding the point of the promontory, the shore of the lake trends off to the northward, forming several picturesque little bays with bold rocky headlands. After travelling about nine miles, we came to several springs of good and most welcome water, and we stopped to refresh our animals and to noon. The finding of this water was entirely unexpected, as, from the representations of an old Shoshonee Indian, made to us before leaving Bear River, I did not look for any for two days, and had in consequence dismounted one of the men to enable us to carry the more vessels, all of which had been filled before leaving our camp in the morning. I went down to the shore of the lake to taste of the water: it was as salt as very strong brine, and clear and transparent as diamond. A large flock of gulls was swimming about near the shore. After feasting our animals upon the grass that grew among the tall rushes and canes around the spring, we continued along the shore of the lake for about nine miles farther, and succeeded in discovering three springs within that distance, at the last of which we halted for the night.

After doubling the southern end of the promontory, the broad flats, which had characterized the shore at its eastern base, entirely disappeared, and the water, although apparently shallow, came nearly up to the base of the hills. Near the margin of the lake it is not safe in all places for animals to pass, as the almost constant exudations of salt water from the edge of the grass, undermine the surface, rendering the narrow intervening beach treacherous and miry. The water to the westward appears bold and deep; and enough has been seen to convince me that a large sail-boat will be absolutely indispensable in the contemplated survey, for the supply of the different parties with provisions and water. Wood there is none. Fuel for cooking, can, however, be generally obtained from the artemisia which abounds almost everywhere; but timber for the construction of the triangulation stations, will, in most instances, have to be transported by water, or hauled down from the cañons of the mountains.

The rocks observed were porphyry, gneiss, dark slaty shales, and metamorphic sandstone, dipping to the north-east. After proceeding some miles to the north, dark limestones with white marble veins occurred, alternating with clayey shales. The rocks on this side of the promontory are much more rugged than on the other, or eastern slope, presenting numerous lofty escarpments where they crop out, the dip being to the east. A cactus, with very long prickles, was observed near our morning camp; and at the spring where we nooned, a small jointed cane trailed on the ground, in some instances to a distance of more than thirty feet. The men made excellent pipe-stems of this material. The spring where we encamped for the night was an oval hole or pit, with perpendicular sides, about fifteen feet long, six broad, and four deep. The water was tolerably good: a small spring, rising at the base of the hill, ran into the lake close by. These springs afterward afforded us nearly all the water used upon the survey of the west shore of the lake; but a voyage of fifty miles was frequently necessary to obtain a supply even for a few days.

Wednesday, October 24.—Clear and calm. Ther. at daylight, 19°; sunrise, 24°. Continuing our journey up the lake-shore, we shortly came to a brackish spring, where there had been a camp of Indians the night before. We had thought last night that we saw their fires, but they had fled, alarmed probably by the report of some guns that had been discharged in our camp. A quantity of some species of seeds they had been beating out lay in small heaps around, and I found an old water-bottle they had left in their haste. It was ingeniously woven of a sort of sedge-grass, coated inside with the gum of the mountain pine, by which it was rendered perfectly water-tight. I afterward saw some similarly shaped vessels, and made of the same material, that would hold nearly two gallons.

As nothing was to be gained by rigidly following the lake-shore, I determined to cut across the projecting points, keeping the general features of the lake in view. At this point we came upon a low range of basaltic hills, extending some miles west of the mountains which continued to the northward, and presenting a steep escarp-ment on the lake, where we again struck it. This lower series of hills extended also to the north, and we followed along their base for many miles, the range gradually falling off to the east as we advanced. The general soil was white clay, formed from the decomposition of the rocks. At three o'clock, having travelled eighteen miles without water, we halted, removed the packs from the backs of our weary beasts, and served out from our scanty store a pint of water to each mule, which the famished creatures eagerly drank from a tin pan. We remained here a couple of hours, to allow them to graze on some tolerably good bunch-grass, when we again saddled up at sundown, and continued our journey, determined to go on till water should be found, or at least as long as the animals could travel. At ten o'clock we reached a small sluggish stream, containing some water entirely too salt for our use, but which the poor animals drank with great avidity, having been without for more than twelve hours. Here we lay down for the night, both man and beast much fatigued with the day's march.

The country passed over to-day has been barren, desolate, and forlorn to the last degree. Artemisia has prevailed to the exclusion of all other vegetation. Not the note of a bird nor the chirp of an insect was to be heard. A solitary crow and one grasshopper were the only living things seen during the whole day's march.

Thursday, October 25.—Ther. at sunrise, 24°. We had an opportunity this morning of seeing fully the ground over which we had passed the night previous. It consisted of an oval flat of clay and sand, some four or five miles broad from east to west, and extending double that distance toward the north; bounded on both sides by lofty hills, with high mountains in the background. North of the flat the ridge was much lower, and it appeared as if there were a pass or depression through it, leading to another valley or plain beyond. Three streams came down from this low ridge, and, flowing to the southward, either sank into the sand or discharged themselves into the lake, which we now judged to be some six or eight miles to the southward, the flat extending in that direction to the water's edge. Two of these streams (all of which were salt) we crossed without much difficulty; but the third, on the western side of the flat, was impassable, and we had to ascend it for three miles before we could obtain a crossing. On the west side of this latter branch comes in a small tributary, in the bed of which, near its source, a beautiful spring, ten feet wide, bubbles up from the bottom, with a column of water rising in its centre six inches in diameter. The water was clear as crystal, but salt and sulphurous, which latter quality might account for the numerous tracks of the antelope around its margin, as that animal is known to delight in waters of this character.

This extensive flat appears to have formed, at one time, the northern portion of the lake, for it is, now but slightly above its present level. Upon the slope of a ridge connected with this plain, thirteen distinct successive benches, or water-marks, were counted, which had evidently, at one time, been washed by the lake, and must have been the result of its action continued for some time at each level. The highest of these is now about two hundred feet above the valley, which has itself been left by the lake, owing probably to gradual elevation occasioned by subterraneous causes. If this supposition be correct, and all appearances conspire to support it, there must have been here at some former period a vast *inland* sea, extending for hundreds of miles; and the isolated mountains which now tower from the flats, forming its western and south-western shores, were doubtless huge islands, similar to those which now rise from the diminished waters of the lake.

In passing over this mud-plain, the glare from the oozy substance of which it is composed was extremely painful to the eyes. Leaving it behind us, we ascended a ridge to the west of it, two or three miles broad, passing over some remains of shales and altered limestone with conglomerate, the crest being composed of porous trap, underlying the sedementary rocks, and cropping out to the west. It may be remarked here, that the general direction of all the ridges noticed in this region is north and south, and they terminate most frequently in sharp, bold promontories, to the south. A herd of antelope was seen on this ridge, numbering about a hundred, but too wild to be approached.

Descending its western slope, we came into another plain, somewhat similar to the last in form, but much more extensive in all directions, and densely covered with artemisia. Over this desolate, barren waste, we travelled until nearly dark, when we reached a rocky promontory, constituting the southern point of a low ridge of hills jutting into the plain from the north. The rock was porous trap, in which no stratification could be made out. The mules having been without water or grass the whole day, and our stock of the former being insufficient to give them even their stinted allowance of one poor pint, we halted for a couple of hours, and drove them upon the side of the mountain to pick what they could get from the scanty supply of dry bunch-grass that grew in tufts upon its side. The prospect of water now began to be rather gloomy; and I was obliged to put the party upon allowance, lest we should be left entirely destitute. At eight o'clock we replaced the packs upon our mules, all of which began to show the effects of their unusual abstinence, and rode on till near midnight by the light of the moon, in a south-westerly direction, over a country similar to that we had traversed during the day; when, finding the indications of water growing less and less promising, and that our animals were nearly worn out, we halted, and, covered with our blankets, we lay down on the ground till morning, regardless of a heavy shower that fell during the night.

Friday, October 26.—The poor animals presented this morning a forlorn appearance, having been now without a drop of water for more than twenty-four hours, during eighteen of which they had been under the saddle, with scarcely any thing to eat. I now began to feel somewhat anxious. Should our mules give out before we could reach the mountains west of us, to which I had determined to direct our course as speedily as possible, we must all perish in the wilderness. Sweeping the horizon with a telescope, I thought I discovered something that looked like willows to the north-west, distant about four or five miles. Reanimated by this gleam of hope, we saddled up quickly and turned our steps in that direction. We soon had the lively satisfaction of finding our expectations confirmed; for, arriving at the spot, we found, after some search, a small spring welling out from the bottom of a little ravine, which having with some labour been cleaned out, we soon enjoyed a plentiful, most needed, and most welcome supply of excellent water for all.

The whole party being much exhausted from their long abstinence and unceasing exertions, we halted here for the day, to afford opportunity for our animals to recruit their wasted strength upon the plentiful supply of grass which grew all around us. Old decayed wigwams, constructed of willows, indicated that this spot had long been a favourite place of resort for the Indians, for the same reason, doubtless, which rendered it so welcome to ourselves.

On the summit of a ridge south-west of our halting-place, large masses of magnetic iron ore were discovered, some of which were partially encased in basaltic rock. In the ravine whence the spring broke out, were found pebbles of alabaster, obsidian, and other rocks, apparently the result of the disintegration of beds of conglomerate, none of which, however, was seen in place.

Saturday, October 27.—Ther. at sunrise, 35°. Resuming our journey, we took a course south by east, which led us past the ridge upon which we had halted two nights before. The formation was porous trap, and the direction of the ridge north by west and south by east. We then passed along, the base of a range of low hills, composed apparently of trap and basalt. After travelling ten miles, we came to a range of higher hills extending north-west and south-east. Here the dark limestone was again observed, but the stratification could not be ascertained. We then passed, in a southerly direction, through deep sand, along what at one time had been the beach of the lake, as drift-wood was frequently seen lying on the sands that stretch out to the eastward for many miles. In one instance a drifted cotton-wood log was seen, lying near what had evidently been the water-line of the lake, as thick as the body of a man. On our right was a high ridge or promontory, with a narrow bottom sloping down to the edge of the flat.

The soil here was not so clayey as heretofore, being composed in many places of calcareous sand and decomposed conglomerate. Some masses of the latter were seen, resembling exactly that met with on the eastern side of the promontory range putting out into the lake. The country to-day has been similar to that passed over previously—dry, barren, and entirely destitute of water. We dug a well some five feet deep on the edge of the flat, which soon filled with water. The mules crowded around the hole, and seemed to watch the process of our labour, as if sensible of the object of our exertions, but upon tasting the water, refused to drink, although they had been travelling the whole day without a drop. Day's march, about sixteen miles.

Sunday, October 28.—Our little stock of water had become so reduced that we were compelled to forego our coffee this morning, and the most rigid economy in the use of the former was strictly enforced. We were on the road very early, and followed for several miles, down the edge of the sand at the foot of the range of hills on our right, when we ascended it, taking a course south-west by west, and passing over beds of conglomerate, which presented a stratification almost horizontal. The ridge was about five miles wide, stretching off to the southward, and about five hundred feet above the level of the beach. The soil consisted of decomposed conglomerate, and was much cut up by deep ravines. On the west side, volcanic rock was again met with.

Leaving the ridge, we entered upon a plain or sort of bay, partly covered with artemisia, and partly (to the westward) with mud and salt. It appeared to be bounded on the west, about thirty miles distant, by a high mountain-range, extending far to the northward, upon an eastern spur of which I judged we had encamped on Friday. The plain contained several island mountains, rising from it as from the water. To one of these, distant about twelve miles south-west by west, we directed our course and reached it about an hour before sunset. Here we stopped for a short time to prepare our scanty supper, and to give the mules a chance to pick a little grass, which was scarce and dried up. Not a drop of water had we met with the whole day; but at noon I had ordered a pint to be served out to each animal. Before arriving at this spot, one of the poor creatures "gave out," and we thought we should have to leave him to the wolves, but he afterward partially recovered, and another pint of water being given him, he went on. The rocky island, at the north end of which we halted, extended many miles to the southward, and was apparently surrounded on all sides by the mud-plain. One of the party ascended it, but could see nothing of the lake, nor any appearance of water in any direction. The rocks were formed of altered clayey and sandy shales, and strata of conglomerate, all of which had been much contorted, but evidently at different periods, as they were not conformable.

It now became a matter of serious importance to find water for the mules, as they had been without for nearly forty hours, most of the time under the saddle, and almost without food. Nothing, therefore, remained but to go on as far as possible during the night, so as to reach the western ridge bounding this basin as early the following day as practicable. We accordingly saddled up about dark and proceeded on the same course, directing our steps toward another island in the plain, which appeared to be about fifteen miles distant. The night was quite cold, and the moon shone as bright as day. Our course lay over a flat of damp clay and salt mud, in many places soft and deep, which made the travelling slow and laborious. All trace of vegetation had vanished, and even the unfailing artemisia had disappeared. The animals were so tired and weak that the whole party was on foot, driving our herd before us. The mule which had given out in the afternoon was now unable to proceed, and had to be abandoned in the midst of the plain, where it no doubt perished. Many others showed symptoms of extreme exhaustion, so that their packs had to be shifted and lightened repeatedly. I began to entertain serious fears that I should not be able to reach the mountain with them: nor was I certain that when we did reach it we should be able to find water in time to save their lives. The night was consequently passed in a state of great anxiety. We continued on until after midnight, crossing occasionally some little drains of salt water coming from the north, when we reached a small isolated butte, which was only a pile of barren rocks, with scarce a blade of grass upon it. Wood or water there was none; so, although the night was quite cold, we laid ourselves down, fireless and supperless, upon the sand, wearied to exhaustion by a continuous march of eighteen hours.

The only sign of vegetable life to be seen here was a small chenopodeaceous plant without leaves, but having long prickles. The artemisia had entirely disappeared. On each side of us, to the north and the south, was a rocky island or butte, similar in character to the one near which we had halted, but much larger.

Monday, October 29.—On awaking early, we found the mules gathered around us looking very dejected and miserable. They had searched in vain for food, and were now in nearly a starving condition. Before us, indeed, lay the mountain, where we hoped to find both food and water for them, but between lay a mud-plain fifteen or twenty miles in extent, which must be crossed before we could reach it. I was much afraid the animals were too weak to succeed in the attempt, but it was our only hope. We set out, the whole party on foot, pursuing the same general course of south-west by west that we had followed yesterday.

The island, at the foot of which we had slept last night, presented sections of sandstones and shales, which appeared to be of comparatively recent origin. They had evidently been somewhat altered by heat, but not to any great extent. At the north-east point of the island on our left, the strata were inclined at an angle of 70° to north-east. No fossils were found in them. Near the western side of this rocky protrusion, I observed what appeared to have been an ancient crater, forming three-fourths of an inverted cone, open to the north-west, around which were sections of shales and sandstones, very much contorted, and dipping in opposite directions on opposite sides. The lower part of the cone was filled with claystone. No volcanic rocks were found at the point where we crossed these islands, but decomposed conglomerate and alabaster occurred in considerable quantities.

The first part of the plain consisted simply of dried mud, with small crystals of salt scattered thickly over the surface. Crossing this, we came upon another portion of it, three miles in width, where the ground was entirely covered with a thin layer of salt in a state of deliquesencce, and of so soft a consistence that the feet of our mules sank at every step into the mud beneath. But we soon came upon a portion of the plain where the salt lay in a solid state, in one unbroken sheet, extending apparently to its western border. So firm and strong was this unique and snowy floor, that it sustained the weight of our entire train, without in the least giving way or cracking beneath the pressure. Our mules walked upon it as upon a sheet of solid ice. The whole field was crossed by a network of little ridges, projecting about half an inch, as if the salt had expanded in the process of crystallization. I estimated this field to be at least seven miles wide and ten miles in length. How much farther it extended northward I could not tell; but if it covered the plain in that direction as it did where we crossed, its extent must have been very much greater. The salt, which was very pure and white, averaged from one-half to three-fourths of an inch in thickness, and was equal in all respects to our finest specimens for table use. Assuming these data, the quantity that here lay upon the ground in one body, exclusive of that in a deliquescent state, amounted to over four and a-half millions of cubic yards, or about one hundred millions of bushels.

At two o'clock in the afternoon we reached the western edge of the plain, when to our infinite joy we beheld a small prairie or meadow, covered with a profusion of good green grass, through which meandered a small stream of pure fresh running water, among clumps of willows and wild roses, artemisia and rushes. It was a most timely and welcome relief to our poor famished animals, who had now been deprived of almost all sustenance for more than sixty hours, during the greater part of which time they had been in constant motion. It was, indeed, nearly as great a relief to me as to them, for I had been doubtful whether even the best mule we had could have gone more than half a dozen miles farther. Several of them had given out in crossing the last plain, and we had to leave them and the baggage behind, and to return for it afterward. Another day without water and the whole train must have inevitably perished. Both man and beast being completely exhausted, I remained here three days for refreshment and rest. Moreover, we were now to prepare for crossing another desert of seventy miles, which, as my guide informed me, still lay between us and the southern end of the lake. He had passed over it in 1845, with Frémont, who had lost ten mules and several horses in effecting the passage, having afterward encamped on the same ground now occupied by our little party.

During our stay here, it rained almost every day and night. The salt plain, which before had glistened in the sunlight like a sheet of molten silver, now became black and sombre; the salt, over which we had passed with so much ease, dissolved, and the flat, in places, became almost impassable. We had encamped at the eastern base of a range of high mountains, stretching a great distance to the north, and terminated, three miles below, in an abrupt escarpment, called Pilot Peak: upon the lofty summit of which rested a dark cloud during the whole of our stay. For three miles from the base the ascent is gradual, the surface being covered with gravel and boulders of granite, féldspathic rock, and metamorphic sandstones, all evidently waterworn. Higher up the mountain, the only stratified rocks seen were micaceous; schists and slaty shales, intersected in various directions by veins of quartz, and very much displaced. The general dip was north by east from 70° to 80°. Proceeding south a few miles along the mountain, the same stratified rocks were again noticed, evidently much altered by heat, being interspersed with veins of granite and quartz. Dwarf cedar was growing here, and, higher up the mountain, dwarf pine; in the bottom, white and red willow, and *Equisetum*.

In a nook of the mountain, some Indian lodges were seen, which had apparently been finished but a short time. They were constructed in the usual conical form, of cedar poles and logs of a considerable size, thatched with bark and branches, and were quite warm and comfortable. The odour of the cedar was sweet and refreshing. These lodges had been put up, no doubt, by the Shoshonee Indians for their permanent winter-quarters, but had not yet been occupied. The savages had been in the neighbourhood to collect the nuts of the pine-tree, called here piñon, for food, but what they left had been destroyed by insects. While at this camp, one of our best mules was stolen. A couple of men, whom I had sent back across the plain to search for a revolver that had been lost in our last night march, reported, on their return to the camp, that they had discovered the tracks of two Indians on our trail, and had seen their fires in the mountains. These stealthy depredators must have followed us at a distance and watched their opportunity to plunder. The only wonder is that they did not steal more than a single mule; for the country was so utterly desolate, that we never once thought that any human being would ever be found where we had passed, except from absolute necessity, and consequently the vigilance of our night-guard was relaxed. Snow fell the night before we left this camp, and covered the ridge about halfway down from its summit.

Friday, November 2.—Ther. at sunrise, 19°. As we were aware that immediately before us lay another desert plain, without wood, water, or grass, for seventy miles, some little preparation was necessary before undertaking to cross it. This consisted simply in baking bread and cooking meat enough to last us through, and in packing upon our mules as much grass as they could carry which we had out, a handful at a time, with our hunting-knives. We had only vessels sufficient to carry twenty gallons of water—a small supply for so many men and animals. The mules, however, were now much recruited by their rest, and we started in good spirits. Following the western edge of the mud-plain at the foot of the range for three miles, we came to the southern point of the mountain, where there had been an encampment of emigrants, who had taken this route from Salt Lake City in 1848. There were here several large springs of excellent water, and the encampment had apparently been quite a large one. The usual destruction of property had taken place. Clothes, books, cases of medicine, wagonwheels, tools, &c., lay. strewn about, abandoned by their owners, who had laboriously brought them two thousand miles only to throw them away.

The route from the Salt Lake to this point was first taken by Colonel Frémont, in 1845. A year afterward, it was followed by a party of emigrants under a Mr. Hastings, whence its present name of " Hastings's Cut-off." A portion of his company, which had followed at some distance behind him, becoming belated in crossing the Sierra Nevada Mountains, a number of them perished, and the remainder were reduced to the revolting necessity of living upon the bodies of their dead comrades, until they were rescued by relief from Sutter's Fort.

The road to California from this point follows around the southern end of the ridge, passes to the north of another high mountain, and thence on to the head of Humboldt's or Mary's River.

Leaving the springs, we crossed, once more, though in an opposite direction, the same mud-plain over which we had been obliged to pass in order to reach the mountain. It was twelve miles in width; and now, in consequence of the recent rains, was soft and slippery—all the salt having disappeared, except a few crystals left in some old wagon-tracks. The travelling was in consequence heavy and laborious. After crossing, we passed, by a gentle ascent, over a neck of land which connected the high ridge on our left, at the north end of which we I had bivouacked on the 29th, with another and broader one to the south, and which latter turned off considerably to the south-west. Here we halted for a short time, to give our mules their last chance to pick a little bunch-grass which grew in thin scattered tufts on the mountain-side.

The strata, at this point, were very much contorted, as at the northern end of the same protruded ridge, inclining in all directions. The higher hills were composed of dark limestone, traversed in various directions by veins of white marble, some of which were of considerable thickness. The dip was to the north-west, 65°. Over the limestone were beds of conglomerate, not conformable; the lower layers of which, or those in immediate contact with the limestone, consisted of portions of the rock that had not been waterworn. Lower down, near the base of the hill, was found a coarse, imperfect oolitic limestone, dipping about 50° to north-west, and under these some sandstone, not conformable, and imperfect.

After halting an hour, we pursued our journey along the eastern base of this isolated mountain or butte, where the dark limestone was again seen, with gypsum, conformable and at right angles with the strata. Some six miles farther on, we passed another isolated butte, upheaved through the level mud-plain, containing what appeared to be another crater, analogous to that seen on the northern end of the ridge, open to the eastward, with the strata dipping in every direction. The main butte appeared to be, at this end, about ten miles wide from east to west, and had manifestly been very much disturbed.

From this point we travelled on until past midnight, over a level mud-plain, lighted by the rays of the moon, which struggled through a mass, of dark and threatening clouds. The wind was fresh and cold, and the mud soft and tenacious, making the travelling very slow and fatiguing. During the night, we passed five wagons and one cart, which had stuck fast in the mud, And been necessarily left by their owners, who, from appearances, had abandoned every thing, fearful of perishing themselves in this inhospitable desert. Great quantities of excellent clothing, tool-chests, trunks, scientific books, and, in fact, almost every thing, both useless and necessary on a journey of this kind, had been here left strewn over the plain. Many articles had not even been removed from the wagons. The carcasses of several oxen lying about on the ground satisfactorily explained the whole matter. In attempting to cross the plain, the animals had died from exhaustion and want of water, and the wagons and their contents had of course to be abandoned.

About one o'clock in the morning, we halted in the midst of the plain, enticed by the sight of a broken ox-yoke, the remains of a barrel, and part of an old wagon-bed, which served for fuel sufficient to boil a little coffee, of which all hands stood very much in need. The mud was ankle-deep; and the only place upon which we could spread down a blanket to sleep was around some scattering bushes of artemisia, where the wind had collected a little sand, presenting a spot rather higher and not so wet as the mud-flat around. The whole scene was as barren, dreary, and desolate as could be well imagined. We gave the mules a portion of the grass that had been packed upon them in the morning, and two pint-cups of water each—the only liquid they had tasted during the day. We then fastened them up as well as we could to the artemisia-bushes, and, wrapping ourselves in our blankets, lay down to wait for the morning. The night was windy and quite cold, and the poor mules kept up such a pitiful and mournful cry, that we were but little recruited by our night's rest.

It may well be supposed that there were few attractions to detain us long on this spot. We had exhausted our fuel last night, and there was nothing with which to cook breakfast; so we started quite early, without any, pursuing the same general course through the heavy mud. The wind, uninterrupted by any obstacle, blew hard over the level plain; and although the thermometer stood at only 47°, yet it was very cold, and brought into requisition all appliances for preventing the escape of animal heat. In the course of the morning, we passed a spot where some emigrants had made a large "cache" of such things as they could not carry. But it had been constructed in such a bungling manner, that it had easily been discovered and robbed: twelve ox-yokes remained in a heap on the ground. After travelling until noon, we came to a low ridge of hills running nearly north and south. We sheltered ourselves behind it, and finding plenty of artemisia, kindled a fire, and boiled our coffee, which, with a piece of bread and cold bacon, constituted our first and only meal for the day.

Our poor animals looked wretchedly, and two of them giving out before reaching the ridge, were with great difficulty driven up. As they had been without water for twenty-four hours, except the cupful which had been served out to them last night, after filling a few canteens for our own use, the remainder of our little stock was divided among them.

The ridge was composed of porous trap. The hills were higher toward the north, where they were connected with a range which seemed to form a spur from the mountains east of us. They gradually diminished to the south, not extending more than a mile or two in that direction.

Before us, distant about twelve miles, was a high mountain-range, on the eastern side of which, the guide informed me, there was a spring with plenty of water. I had hoped to be able to cross it today, but the state of our animals was such that it proved impracticable, since it was dark before we reached its western base. I the less regretted this, as in the course of the afternoon we had found several little pools of rain-water, from which the mules drank with great avidity and to repletion. The ascent to the range was gentle, and we encamped at the mouth of a narrow, winding pass through it, amid plenty of large cedar-trees and very large artemisia—a welcome sight, as the day had been cold and blustering, and there was every prospect of a heavy storm. Large fires were soon blazing, and every one was tired enough at once to seek his blanket, without going to the trouble of preparing the evening meal. Indeed, there was little or nothing to prepare; our bread was all gone, and there was not water enough either to make bread or coffee, and none could be sought for in the dark. The two mules that had failed in the morning, again gave out before reaching the mountain, and had finally to be abandoned.

Sunday, November 4.—Ther. 33°. Upon rising we found it snowing hard, and the ground covered to the depth of two inches. It soon ceased, however, and before night had melted in the plain, although the neighbouring mountains continued all whitened by it. After much search, water was found in a deep ravine near by; and grass was tolerably abundant, though dry and hard. As the mules were nearly exhausted and much stiffened by their journey across the deep mud-plains, I determined to remain here for the day, to recruit them. A couple of men were sent back afoot, to try and recover those left yesterday: they returned, after dark bringing with them one only; the other had strayed from the road, and all efforts to recover it were vain. It was the third lost on this trip.

A deep ravine at the foot of the mountain presented sections of the strata. The lowest exposed was dark limestone with white veins, inclined to the south-east, at an angle of 85°; in fact, almost vertical. Ascending the ravine, the limestone was found to be overlaid by red sandstone, and this again by clayey shales. All these rocks had been altered by heat. No organic remains were found in the sandstones or shales, but some corals were seen in the limestone. The rocks were all veined with white marble. Large crystalline nodules of this substance were found, which assumed the form of *arragonite.* Some specimens of iron ore were also found, apparently a carbonate, but not in place. Ther. at noon, 37°; sunset, 31°.

Monday, November 5.—Ther. 23°. Morning clear and quite cold. Crossed the mountain through the pass. The snow was about two inches deep and the ground frozen hard. Followed down the eastern slope for about two miles, when we came to a spring-branch issuing from a gorge of the mountains where there was plenty of green grass—the first full supply our animals had enjoyed for several days.

The only rocks observed in crossing the mountain were limestones, containing remains of encrinites and corals. A wide dike of trap formed the crest; and, on the eastern side, another dike was seen running north by east, and south by west, forming the summit of a lower ridge. The limestones were tilted up almost vertically, but as the surface of the ground was covered with snow, the nature of the strata and their direction could not be very accurately ascertained. A piece of altered coal was found at the eastern base of the mountain, but not in place. The lower hills were covered with conglomerate not conformable.

Leaving the spring, our true course lay about east, to strike the southern point of another range ten miles distant, and forming the eastern boundary of a broad, green, intervening valley, which extended northward to the southern shore of the Great Salt Lake, and was covered with grass, the first we had seen since leaving Pilot Peak. It was shut in toward the south by a range of comparatively low hills, connecting the two mountain ranges that formed its eastern and western boundaries. A direct course could not be taken for this point, owing to numerous springs, which rendered the valley in that direction marshy and wholly impassable. We were consequently forced many miles to the southward, and obliged to make a circuit of more than a semicircle to gain the opposite side. We followed down the western base of the mountain for two or three miles, passing a fine spring, with good grass, near which we encamped for the night, among some dwarf cedars, that both furnished us with fuel and afforded a protection against the wind, which blew fresh and cold from the north-west. Ther. at sunset, 43°.

Tuesday, November 6.—Ther. at sunrise, 30°. Continued our journey in a northerly direction, along the western base of the mountain, for twelve miles, when we reached its northern extremity, which was about a mile and a-half wide, and terminated in bold escarpments five or six hundred feet high. One of these resembled, in a remarkable manner, a huge castle, the vertical walls of which were not less than three hundred feet in height.

Before reaching this point of the mountains, I remarked, on our left, in the middle of the valley, a curious, isolated mass of rocks, resembling a small fortification or redoubt: it was surrounded by marshy meadow-land, and could, in case of need, be defended by a small force against almost any number of Indians. Numerous springs broke out from the mountain and at the edge of the prairie; but they were all saline, with a temperature of 74°, and totally unfit to drink. To this place we gave the name of "Spring Valley." Near the point of the mountain was a very large spring, which discharged its waters northward into the lake. The water was very salt, nauseous, and bitter, with a temperature of 70°; notwithstanding which it swarmed with innumerable small fish, and seemed to be a favourite resort for pelicans and gulls.

In a shallow ravine near our morning camp, limestone was found cropping out, with a dip of 80° to the north-west. This rock was seen as we followed the range, appearing at the spurs; and dikes of trap were observed, forming peaks farther back up the mountainside. The ridge gradually became less elevated as we proceeded toward the point, where the stratified rocks (limestone and shales) were found in a horizontal position. Along the northern termination of the range, the strata were again found to be much displaced and almost vertical. They were composed of limestone and shales, overlaid in some places by conglomerate. Salt springs were very numerous in this locality.

After doubling the point, we came upon another valley, similar to the one through which we had just passed, and from which it was divided by the ridge or mountain just described. Our true course here, also, was to cross this valley in an easterly direction, and strike the northern point of another range where it terminates immediately on the southern shore of the Salt Lake, now plainly visible; but the numerous salt springs, as in the case of that passed yesterday, rendered a straight course impracticable. Consequently, after following the eastern base of the ridge about six miles to the south, we began gradually to diverge from it to the eastward, and at dark encamped in the prairie, near a noble spring of fresh, cold water, with abundance of excellent grass, and an extensive grove of large willows for fuel. A fierce gale sprang up from the south-east, which kept us in a constant state of alarm during the night, lest we should be burned in our beds from the tall dry grass taking fire. It had in fact kindled several times, and the flame was extinguished with some difficulty, rendering a strict watch necessary until morning. This valley is called "Tuilla Valley" by the Mormons, and forms an excellent pasturage for numerous herds of cattle, wintered here by them under the charge of keepers. The grass is very abundant, and numerous springs are found on both sides of it.

On the eastern side of the mountain, which divides it from Spring Valley, the same geological appearances occur as were seen yesterday at the point of the range and on its western side. The limestones were thrown up at a very great angle, and in some places the strata were perpendicular.

Another mule gave out to-day, and was necessarily abandoned. Ther. at sunset, 43°.

Wednesday, November 7.—Ther. at sunrise, 47°. Starting early in the morning, we crossed to the eastern side of the valley, followed the base of the mountain to its northern extremity, and reached the shores of the Great Salt Lake near Black Rock, whence we crossed the valley of the Jordan, over sterile artemisia plains, and reached the city in the afternoon—being the first party of white men that ever succeeded in making the entire circuit of the lake by land. Attempts had, in early times, been made to circumnavigate it in canoes, by some trappers in search of beaver; but they all proved unsuccessful, from want of fresh water.

The examination just completed proves that the whole western shore of the lake is bounded by an immense level plain, consisting of soft mud, frequently traversed by small, meandering rills of salt and sulphurous water, with occasional springs of fresh, all of which sink before reaching the lake. These streams seem to imbue and saturate the whole soil, so as to render it throughout miry and treacherous. For a few months, in midsummer, the sun has sufficient influence to render some portions of the plain, for a short time, dry and hard: in these intervals the travelling over it is excellent; but one heavy shower is sufficient to reconvert the hardened day into soft, tenacious mud, rendering the passage of teams over it toilsome, and frequently quite hazardous.

These plains are but little elevated above the present level of the lake, and have, beyond question, at one time formed a part of it. It is manifest to every observer, that an elevation of but a few feet above the present level of the lake would flood this entire flat to a great distance north and south, and wash the base of the Pilot Peak range of mountains, which constitute its western boundary; thus converting what is now a comparatively small and insignificant lake into a vast inland sea. This extensive area is, for the most part, entirely denuded of vegetation, excepting occasional patches of artemisia and greasewood. The minute crystals of salt which cover the surface of the moist, oozy mud, glisten brilliantly in the sunlight, and present the appearance of a large sheet of water so perfectly, that it is difficult, at times, for one to persuade himself that he is not standing on the shore of the lake itself. High rocky ridges protrude above the level plain, and resemble great islands rising above the bosom of this desert sea.

The mirage, which frequently occurs, is greater here than I ever witnessed elsewhere, distorting objects in the most grotesque manner, defying all calculation as to their size, shape, or distances, and giving rise to optical illusions almost beyond belief. With the exception of the two valleys lying at the south end of the lake, the country is, as a place of human habitation, entirely worthless. There is, however, one valuable use to which it may and perhaps will be applied: its extent, and perfectly level surface, would furnish a desirable space on which to measure a degree of the meridian.

The Infamous Hastings Cutoff

The extreme shallowness of the basin in which Great Salt Lake is situated means that even minor fluctuations in the lake level have dramatic effects on its shoreline, exposing or submerging vast tracts of land. And as previous selections in this anthology have mentioned, the lake level does fluctuate drastically, not so much seasonally as over longer, multi-year cycles. The resulting shoreline shifts have been frustrating to human utilization of the lake, which often depends on geographically fixed facilities: the extremely low lake levels of the early 1930s, for example, left the Saltair recreational facility so far from the water that a special railroad was built to transport swimmers between the dressing rooms and the water. In contrast, the high levels of the mid-1980s submerged so much of the reconstructed Saltair that it was unusable.

By 1986 the lake had risen so high that special dikes had to be built to keep the water off of the Southern Pacific tracks and Interstate 80 as they round the south end of the lake. Anticipating even higher levels, Governor Norman H. Bangerter secured funds from the Utah State Legislature to purchase and install huge pumps on the west shore to lower the lake level by pumping water into a vast, shallow catchment basin created by low dikes on the salt flats to the west. The lake level did recede, whether through the pumping or the return of drier weather, or both. The lake level since the late 1980s has never again been so high, but the pumps remain in place to recreate what was popularly known as "Lake Bangerter" if necessary at some future time.

The article reprinted here was written as partial compliance with various environmental laws that require either protection or "mitigation" of any historical sites that would be affected by such topographical alterations as "Lake Bangerter." "Mitigation" means that if a historic site must be destroyed, exhaustive research must be conducted to preserve, through such means as photographs, documentary research, oral history interviews, and even archaeological excavation if necessary, as much of the informational value of the site as possible. Historians had long been aware that a shortcut on the California Trail called the Hastings Cutoff crossed the area to be submerged, and that in fact there were several mounds within the area that had been formed by sand that had blown around discarded cargo left by the tragic Donner-Reed party of 1846 and subsequent explorers and emigrants. Those mounds had to be researched and excavated.

The project was placed under the general direction of David B. Madsen, Utah state archaeologist at the time, who was already involved in an ongoing investigation of various prehistoric sites west of the salt flats. I was employed at the Utah State Historical Society, where the State Archaeologist's office was located, and I was asked to contribute to the project by preparing a general background history of the Hastings Cutoff and then to participate in excavation of the mounds. The full text of my history appeared in the final report of the project, and an abridged version reprinted here appeared in the *Utah Historical Quarterly.*

Reprinting the article here allows the opportunity to correct an egregious factual error that somehow crept in during the abridgment process. Even the most casual historian will know that the Louisiana Purchase extended only from the Mississippi River to the Continental Divide, not all the way to the Pacific as I say in the first paragraph. It did, of course, fuel Americans' interest in exploration beyond the Rockies to the Pacific, where Lewis and Clark arrived in 1805, and eventually to overland emigration and possession.

Suggestions for further reading

The full report on the archaeological project that gave rise to this article, including the longer text from which this article was abridged, may be found in Bruce R. Hawkins and David B. Madsen, *Excavation of the Donner-Reed Wagons: Historic Archaeology along the Hastings Cutoff* (Salt Lake City: University of Utah Press, 1990). It also includes a comprehensive bibliography of the literature on the Hastings Cutoff. Since that time, several additional notable works have appeared. Rush Spedden, "The Hastings Cutoff," in Peter H. DeLafosse, *Trailing the Pioneers: A Guide to Utah's Emigrant Trails, 1829–1869* (Logan: Utah State University Press, 1994), 73–92, is an accurate guide to retracing the trail. Kristin Johnson, "*Unfortunate Emigrants*": *Narratives of the Donner Party* (Logan: Utah State University Press, 1996), supplements the narratives in J. Roderick Korns, *West from Fort Bridger*, reissued with updated editorial apparatus by Will Bagley and Harold Schindler (Logan: Utah State University Press, 1994). Joseph A. King, *Winter of Entrapment: A New Look at the Donner Party* (Toronto: P. D. Meany, 1992; revised ed., Walnut Creek, California: K & K, 1994), offers new research on Patrick Breen's background in Ireland and emigration to California.

Overland Emigration, the California Trail, and the Hastings Cutoff
Gary Topping

By the 1840s California had begun to exert something of the same fascination for the American imagination that it does today. Its reputation had been created by infrequent reports from the mountain men, by promoters like Dr. John B. Marsh and Johann Sutter, and by sailors engaged in the hide and tallow trade such as Richard Henry Dana, whose *Two Years Before the Mast* told of a tropical climate and an easy, laid-back tenor of life known today through Hollywood and the Beach Boys. After the Louisiana Purchase of 1803 brought Americans uncontested title to a vast land empire extending to the Pacific Ocean, it was perhaps understandable that the resulting continental vision would cause them to cast their eyes to the hospitable valleys of California as well.

Getting there was the problem. At the beginning of the 1840s Americans who wished to settle in California could choose either a long and perilous sea voyage around the Horn or attempt to develop a road based on sketchy accounts of possible trails across the Great Basin and Sierra Nevada passed along by mountain men, none of whom had found a route suitable for wagons.

Development of a wagon road to California was first attempted in 1841 by the Bartleson-Bidwell party. We are fortunate to have both first-hand and reminiscent accounts of the trip from the pen of one of the principals, John Bidwell, in whose lighthearted prose much of the humor, the frustration, and the improbable spirit of the venture memorably comes alive.[1] Although even more poorly equipped and otherwise unprepared for arduous overland travel then the Donner-Reed party five years later, the Bartleson-Bidwell emigrants somehow succeeded in their journey, becoming the first overland party of settlers to reach California and including the first woman settler to cross the Sierra, Nancy Kelsey.

Gary Topping, "Overland Emigration, the California Trail, and the Hastings Cutoff," *Utah Historical Quarterly* 56 (spring 1988): 109–27.

The story begins with the young man John Bidwell who, at twenty years of age, was suddenly possessed of a desire to see the West. He left his home in western Ohio to catch a boat at Cincinnati for St. Louis and the Missouri frontier with an outfit that was simplicity itself: about seventy-five dollars, a few extra clothes in a knapsack, and formidable armament in the form of a pocketknife.

On the Missouri frontier Bidwell heard glowing reports of California from a mountain man, and since his prospects in Missouri were dim he formed a group called the Western Emigration Society with the purpose of traveling together to California in the spring of 1841.

It was an improbable group indeed that assembled for the journey. "Our ignorance of the route was complete," Bidwell admitted. "We knew that California lay west, and that was the extent of our knowledge." A map from one of Bidwell's friends had depicted two large rivers emerging from the Great Salt Lake, both larger that the Mississippi. His friend advised him to plan on building canoes at that point and floating all the way to California.

Their individual equipment for the journey was quite unequal in quality and effectiveness. It would become important later on, for one thing, that some brought mules and horses and others brought oxen, which would mean that the rate of travel would vary considerably between the two groups. All were relatively impoverished: "I doubt whether there was one hundred dollars in money in the whole party," Bidwell recalled, "but all were enthusiastic and anxious to go." Bidwell's partner, who was to provide the horses to pull Bidwell's wagon, backed out at the last moment. Bidwell must have been a persuasive salesman though, for he talked another man into throwing in with him and allowing Bidwell to trade a nice black horse he had for a yoke of oxen to draw the wagon and a one-eyed mule for him to ride.

The Bartleson-Bidwell party enjoyed their first great stroke of good luck in being allowed to begin the journey with a party of three Jesuits under Father Pierre Jean DeSmet who were on their way to Fort Hall and beyond to work among the Flathead Indians and were guided by the celebrated mountain man Thomas Fitzpatrick.[2] So they were assured of being in good hands for the first long leg of the journey. Fitzpatrick knew the way and the Indians, and the genial and courageous DeSmet was, by Bidwell's account, a constant inspiring example of meeting inevitable difficulties with good humor.

Such good fortune was destined to end, though, at Soda Springs, which Fitzpatrick informed the California contingent would be a good separation point for their divergent destinations. The information they got from others on the trail was neither very specific nor very encouraging: "They brought the information that we must strike out west of Salt Lake . . . being careful not to go too far south, lest we should get into a waterless country without grass. They also said we must be careful not to go too far north, lest we should get into a broken country and steep canons, and wander about, as trapping parties had been known to do, and become bewildered and perish." Following directions like those was not easy, and accordingly the party wandered around in the salt desert to the north and west of the Great Salt Lake for some days with no good idea of what they were trying to accomplish and gradually running out of water and provisions.

At the foot of the Pequops in Nevada they finally made the fortunate decision that the wagons were too poorly suited for travel on that terrain and should be abandoned in favor of packing what possessions they could on the animals. The emigrants were almost totally ignorant of packing techniques, but thy had observed the pack saddles of mountain men at Green River, and imitated them as best they could with parts fashioned from the wagons. The results, according to Bidwell, were quite inept and humorous, primarily because even the oxen had to carry pack saddles, and their backs were not as suited to them as the horses': "It was but a few minutes before the packs began to turn, horses became scared, mules kicked, oxen jumped and bellowed, and articles were scattered in all directions. We took more pains, fixed things, made a new start, and did better, though packs continued occasionally to fall off and delay us."

It was a comical and clumsy way to travel, but it brought them down the Humboldt River, which they followed because of its mediocre supply of water for the animals and its apparently correct direction of flow toward their destination. At the expense of considerable difficulty, indeed suffering, the Bartleson-Bidwell party continued south along the Sierra and up the Walker River to an arduous crossing of the mountains to the headwaters of the Stanislaus River and thence down into the San Joaquin Valley to the ranch of Dr. John B. Marsh on November 4, 1841. Although they had succeeded in their quest, their route was not again followed closely across the northern part of the Great Salt Lake Desert nor across the Sierra. But they had proven that wagons could be taken at least most of the way to California, and perhaps with more exploration a route could be worked out the rest of the way.

In 1843 Joseph B. Chiles, who had been a member of the Bartleson-Bidwell party, returned to the East and organized another wagon train of emigrants bound for California.[3] Aware of the obvious fact that the Bartleson-Bidwell route could be improved upon, he enlisted the services of the mountain man Joseph Reddeford Walker, who had discovered the pass through the Sierra that bears his name and thought that wagons could be taken through it.

Chiles's first innovation was to avoid the salt flats north of the Great Salt Lake that had so taxed and bewildered the Bartleson-Bidwell party. Instead, he continued along the Oregon Trail to Fort Boise where the party divided. Chiles, with a party of one hundred horsemen, ascended the Malheur River and crossed into the upper Sacramento River Valley. The wagon contingent, under Walker, reached the Humboldt, followed it to the Sierra, then turned southward all the way to Owens Valley, where he relocated Walker Pass. They were forced to abandon their wagons in the mountains, however, which proved to be a good move anyway after they reached the San Joaquin Valley and had a struggle though miles of choking alkaline dust before they finally arrived at Sutter's Fort.

By the beginning of the 1844 emigration season, then, two prominent facts characterized the California Trail: it was obvious in the first place that the Humboldt River was indeed, as Dale Morgan has called it, the "highroad of the West." Though it was the most hated of all western rivers, Morgan continued, because of the hostile Indians and risk of cholera, it was also the most necessary, for it pointed the way most directly to the only practical passes over the Sierra.[4] The other prominent fact was that only pack animals so far had been taken over those mountains, and a wagon road was necessary to sustain any large emigration.

It was the Stevens-Townsend-Murphy party of 1844 that first crossed what became more or less the standard California Trail and located a pass suitable for wagons through the Sierra. The party is named for the three captains of the eleven wagons, but credit for the route goes largely to the guiding skills of the old mountain man Caleb Greenwood, who was eighty years old when he left Missouri in March at the head of the emigrant train.[5]

Among Greenwood's accomplishments as guide on that trip was the successful first attempt of the sixty-mile dry shortcut between South Pass and the Green River that became known as the Greenwood Cutoff. From Fort Hall, Greenwood chose an almost direct southwesterly course to the Humboldt, a route that had not been used before. How Greenwood knew of the route it uncertain. He claimed to have been in California eighteen years before, and perhaps it was on that trip that he had discovered what turned out to be the most practical wagon route from Fort Hall to the Humboldt. Whatever his previous experience, it is clear that he knew what he was doing. During the subsequent history of the California Trail only two significant revisions of Greenwood's route through the Great Basin were ever used: the Hastings Cutoff across the salt flats to the south and west of the Great Salt Lake and the Salt Lake Cutoff, which allowed emigrants to use Salt Lake City as a way station, then skirt the Great Salt Lake to the north, passing near present-day Snowville and west to the City of Rocks, where it joined the Greenwood route.

Upon reaching the Humboldt Sink, however, Old Greenwood's knowledge ran out. If he had crossed the mountains before, he had not done so by means of a route that would admit wagons, and so a quest for such a route began. He was fortunate at that time to encounter a Piute Indian named Truckee who told him that a river (which now bears the Indian's name) directly to the west of their camp would lead them to a pass that wagons could negotiate. It proved to be a rough pass, but the Indian was right, though the party barely beat the early snows to reach Sacramento. The California Trail had been established, the first wagons had reached Sutter's Fort, and the way was now prepared for emigrants. All that remained was the need for a good propagandist to advertise the new route and the glories of California.

Lansford W. Hastings is so deeply rooted in the historiography of the California Trail as the villain in the Donner tragedy that some space needs to be devoted to the exact nature of his role in luring the Donners to the West and then to the trail that caused their demise.[6] There is no question that Hastings's *Emigrants' Guide* is as much an advertising tract as a geographical treatise, nor did Hastings deny the fact. The California one finds in its pages is a paradise in which "December is a pleasant as May," where disease is virtually unknown, where meat can be cured in its pure atmosphere for weeks without rotting, where wild oats with stalks suitable for walking sticks can be cultivated merely by fencing off a field of them to keep the animals out.[7] And so on.

For the politically ambitious, Hastings indicated that California was ripe for the picking. The Mexicans and Indians who made up the bulk of the population were almost equally ignorant and degraded, and governed despotically by priests and dictators. " A Mexican always pursues that method of doing things which requires the least physical or mental exorcise [sic]," Hastings alleged, "unless it involves some danger, in which case, he always adopts some other method." The purpose of the Catholic church in California, he continued, was "not only to enslave and oppress, thousands of these timid and unsuspecting aborigines, but also to reduce all of the common, and lower orders, of the people, to a most abject state of vassalage, and to stamp indellible [sic] ignorance and superstition, upon their imbecile and uncultivated minds." Militarily, California was a pushover: it was defended by soldiers who

> are mere Indians, many of whom, are as perfectly wild and untutored, as the most barbarous savages of the forest; yet it is with these wild, shirtless, earless and heartless creatures, headed by a few timid, soulless, brainless officers, that these semi-barbarians, intend to hold this delightful region, as against the civilized world.[8]

In evaluating Hastings's experience as a guide and knowledge of the overland routes one must recognize that he was in fact a man of considerable outdoor skill, experience, and leadership ability who was able to communicate those qualities to those whom he proposed to guide and, as it turned out, was able to deliver upon his promises. Hastings's overland experience began in 1842 when he joined, and eventually took over leadership of, the Oregon-bound train of Elijah White. After Dr. John McLoughlin, the Hudson's Bay Company factor at Fort Vancouver, discouraged Hastings from settling there and luring even more Americans to follow him, he led another party of equally disgruntled emigrants down the coast to Sacramento. From there he crossed the Sierra twice, perhaps foolishly, in adverse weather and crossed on horseback the cutoff he proposed to lead wagons over in 1846.

With regard to this proposed cutoff, which left the main trail at Fort Bridger, crossed the Wasatch Mountains, passed to the south of the Great Salt Lake and over the salt flats to rejoin the California Trail at the Humboldt River, it is vital to note that Hastings's book did not advocate use of that route. It is presented, as Hastings's biographer points out, in an offhand manner as a geographical observation rather than a suggestion:

Lansford Warren Hastings, author of the
trail guide recommending the "Hastings
Cutoff" across the Great Basin. Used by permission, Utah State Historical Society, all
rights reserved.

The most direct route, for the California emigrants, would be to leave
the Oregon route, about two hundred miles east from Fort Hall; thence
bearing west southwest, to the Salt Lake; and thence continuing down to
the bay of San Francisco, by the route just described. The emigrants, up
to this time, however, have traveled together, as far as Fort hall, because
of this being the only settlement, in that vicinity, at which they are
enabled to procure horses, and provisions.[9]

It was only after Hastings had passed across the cutoff himself that he proposed to
lead others across it. Indeed, it proved to be an extremely difficult route, much
more difficult than Hastings had imagined, but he successfully led a wagon train
over it in 1846, and it was used repeatedly through 1850. Many who used the route
seem to have considered its mileage saving as of Pyhrric value, given the toll it
exacted on people, animals, and equipment, but the Donners, with one exception,
were the only ones to lose lives because of it.

Hastings himself certainly did not regard the cryptic reference to the cutoff in
his *Guide* as sufficient information for emigrants. In fact he and his partner, the
mountain man James Hudspeth, proceeded eastward from Fort Bridger in the

summer of 1846 with the specific purpose of meeting the emigrant parties and offering to guide them through the new route.[10]

The first party to take advantage of Hastings's offer was the Bryant-Russell group who were traveling somewhat in advance of the others because they were on muleback. Edwin Bryant's journal of the trip, published later as *What I Saw in California*, is one of the classics of western narrative.[11] A medical doctor who chose a career in journalism, Bryant was on his way from Kentucky to California primarily to write a book about his experiences rather than to settle in the promised land. His partner was William H. Russell, a Kentucky colonel who started out as leader of the party but proved unequal to the task and was replaced. At that point, Bryant, Russell, and seven others opted to sell their wagons and buy mules.

While Hastings decided at Fort Bridger to take charge of the slower wagon parties, the Bryant-Russell group pushed on under the leadership of Hudspeth, who promised to accompany them as far as the salt flats, at which point he intended to leave them to engage in further exploration. Although the Bryant-Russell party left Fort Bridger on July 20, the same day as the polyglot wagon party known as the Harlan-Young group, which was under Hastings's leadership, they soon moved far in advance. Hudspeth elected to lead them across the Wasatch through Weber Canyon, which was a narrow gorge that required frequent riding through the stream but was otherwise not a difficult passage for animals. The rest of the journey, until they parted company with Hudspeth, presented no difficulties either. That parting occurred at the summit of Hastings Pass through the Cedar Mountains, from which a long view of the salt flats confronted them. At that point, Bryant reported, Hudspeth gave his final instructions:

> standing on one of the peaks, he stretched out his long arms, and with a voice and gestured as loud and impressive as he could make them, he called to us and exclaimed—"Now, boys, put spurs on your mules and ride like h____!" The hint was timely given and well meant, but scarcely necessary, as we all had a pretty just appreciation of the trails and hardships before us.[12]

Although Bryant made a fairly forlorn assessment of their prospects at that point, emphasizing the fact that they would have no guide until they struck the California Trail some two hundred miles to the west, they actually were in fairly good condition to meet the challenges of that difficult passage. Bryant's account of their crossing of the salt flats is memorable. Not only did their animals sink at times clear to their bellies in the soft ground, but mirages repeatedly plagued their riders with visions of ethereal cities "with countless columned edifices of marble whiteness, and studded with domes, spires, and turreted towers, [which] would rise upon the horizon of the plain, astonishing us with its stupendous grandeur and sublime magnificence [*sic*]." Even with those problems, which sometimes forces the riders to dismount, the party eventually reached the springs at Pilot Peak late at night; they had crossed the entire eighty-mile expanse in one long day.

The crossing of the salt flats was the only real adventure for the Bryant-Russell party. They had little difficulty in reaching the main California Trail at the Humboldt and followed the route of the Stevens-Townsend-Murphy group through the Sierra, though they seem to have been unaware of their predecessors' identity or history.

In terms of overland emigration, the Bryant-Russell party was relatively insignificant, since of its innovations, the route down the Weber as yet disclosed none of the difficulties it would present to wagons, and the Great Salt Lake Desert had been crossed on horseback several times before. It was the Harlan-Young party which followed hard on the heels of the Bryant-Russell group that put the Hastings Cutoff to its first real test.

The Harlan-Young party was a loosely affiliated group of forty wagons that did not really exist as a unit until it left Fort Bridger. Originally a part of the Bryant-Russell party, the Harlan-Young contingent split off when the party was first being organized, giving reasons of compactness and efficiency as their motives. Eventually the party grew to about fifty-seven wagons, as latecomers joined between Fort Bridger and the valley of the Great Salt Lake.

The Weber Canyon route was the choice of Hudspeth not Hastings. Hudspeth rode back from the Bryant-Russell camp at the mouth of the canyon to convince the Harlan-Young party to follow them down to the Weber. Hastings was not with the Harlan-Young group at the time, having ridden back to look after stragglers. By the time he rejoined the party they were already well into Weber Canyon. The upper part of the canyon was not bad, but the lower reaches presented serious difficulties, necessitating the use of winches for both animals and wagons at some points. It was thus quite probable, in Hastings's mind, that a better route could be found, perhaps present-day Parley's Canyon, which Hastings and Clyman had used to get out of the Salt Lake Valley on their earlier trip, and which he probably had intended to try before Hudspeth persuaded the emigrants to try the Weber.

Having crossed the Wasatch, the first great obstacle of the Hastings Cutoff, the emigrants then faced the Great Salt Lake Desert, the other great obstacle. They were not, as we have seen, the first wagon train to have crossed that desert, but they were the first to attempt a crossing to the south of the Great Salt Lake. The crossing took three days, August 16–18, and was extremely trying. Heinrich Lienhard's detachment was the only wagon party to have crossed the Hastings Cutoff through 1850 without having to abandon wagons or animals, but even he complained of great tribulation: "Our oxen all appeared to be suffering; the whole of their bowels appeared to cry out, and incessant rumbling which broke out from all; they were hollow-eyed, and it was most distressing to see the poor animals suffer thus." Lienhard also related a pathetic story of the oxen pulling his personal wagon, which was second in line. His animals, he said were in constant danger of breaking off their horns because they were desperate to get too close to the wheels of the first wagon in order to stand briefly in its shade. The other detachments of the Harlan-Young party were less fortunate than Lienhard and his companions: before reaching Pilot Peak, Lienhard counted no less than twenty-four abandoned wagons (about one-third of their total vehicles) on the salt flats.[13] The Harlan-Young party lost a number of animals but abandoned none of the wagons permanently, for they were able to return with freshly fed and watered animals to pick up the equipment they had left behind.

The Hastings Cutoff, then, was a usable route but not a very desirable one. It required light wagons lightly loaded, fresh strong animals, and a great deal of man power for hacking trails and winching gear over precipices. The Harlan-Young party made the journey but at the expense of considerable hardship and only barely even at that. The Donners were not so fortunate.

If ever a group was doomed at the beginning it was the Donners.[14] The party consisted of eighty-seven people in twenty wagons. Of their total number only twenty-nine were men fifteen years of age or older who could be expected to perform the hard work of road building in rough country; the rest were women, children, or elderly men. Their equipment was equally inadequate for the purpose, primarily because of James Frazier Reed's "Pioneer Palace" wagon, a two-story behemoth of far too great size and weight, which Reed obstinately refused to abandon until the party reached the Humboldt River. Furthermore, they were intellectually and psychologically unprepared for the trials they would face. They were Illinois farmers who had never seen a mountain or a desert and had no idea how to cope with either except for what they had read in Hastings's *Guide*, and that they had partly ignored. They were personally incompatible, so that rivalries and hostilities were a constant fact of their social life: Reed and Keseberg feuded; Reed and Snyder fought, resulting in Snyder's murder; Breen refused food to the destitute Eddy family; old man Hardcoop was abandoned to die of exposure— and so on. Finally, they decided for some unknown reason very early on that they would attempt the Hastings Cutoff, even before Hastings himself recommended it as a practical route. James Clyman met Reed as far east as Fort Laramie and reported Reed's intention already to follow the "nigher route" described in Hastings's *Guide*. Unfortunately, they were too late on the trail and too slow to make up the difference, so they deprived themselves of the immediate guide services of Hastings himself, perhaps the one man on the trail at that time who could have brought them through, and of the added manpower available in the Harlan-Young party.

If history does not disclose its alternatives, still it is difficult to avoid asking what might have happened if Hudspeth had taken the Harlan-Young party through Parley's Canyon instead of the Weber which Hastings recognized the Donners simply could not have negotiated with their limited manpower. A usable road would already have existed for the Donners, thus eliminating the need for the extremely taxing and time-consuming trail-hacking through Emigration Canyon. Or what if Reed had been induced to abandon his Pioneer Palace early in the mountains, and the others had been able to catch up with the Harlan-Young party and gone down the Weber with them instead?

The Donner-Reed party arrived in Fort Bridger on July 27, 1846 only a week after the Bryant-Russell and Harlan-Young parties have left, but they had been driving their animals so hard to get there that they stayed four more days to allow them to rest and recuperate. By the time they left, on July 31, they were eleven days behind the others and out of reach of any real assistance. The gap widened as the summer and fall continued, and the weather in the Sierra would not wait.

The Donner wagons had no trouble following their predecessors to the head of Weber Canyon, but when they got there, they found a note from Hastings advising against that route and offering to return to help them find another if they would send a messenger ahead to get him. Unfortunately, by the time Reed and two others could get to Hastings, he was already at Adobe Rock in Tooele Valley and was no longer in position to guide them personally through the Wasatch. Instead, he returned with Reed to the summit of Big Mountain where he pointed out an alternative route which the Donner-Reed party then followed.[15] The alternative was arduous in the extreme, indeed almost beyond the ability of the party, but at least it was passable to them which the Weber was not.

The delay in getting through the Wasatch was great, as was its toll on their animals. For many days in getting through East Canyon and over to Mountain Dell, they made only two or tree miles, hacking every inch of the way through the tangled brush, and double- and triple-teaming their wagons over the hills. Where the Harlan-Young party had taken eighteen days to get from Fort Bridger to the valley of the Great Salt Lake (July 20–August 7), it took the Donners twenty-six days (July 27–August 22). Even more to the point, perhaps, is the fact that on August 22, when the Donners emerged from Emigration Canyon, the Harlan-Young party were resting their animals at Pilot Spring, having crossed the last of the unknown and formidable obstacles of the Hastings Cutoff.

It took the Donner-Reed party three days, August 31 to September 2, to cross the salt flats, and the effect of the crossing on their animals, equipment, and morale was devastating. The Donner animals were much less prepared for the arduous crossing than the Harlan-Young animals, so it is no wonder that they, too, began to fail long before the passage was completed. Many of their animals simply died on the spot before water could be brought back for them or wandered off to die or possibly to fall into the hands of Indians. Two of Reed's three wagons had to be abandoned on the salt flats, as did one of George Donner's and one of Keseberg's.[16]

It was the beginning of the end for the Donner-Reed party. Seeing one's worldly goods simply abandoned to the elements had a psychological effect that one can only imagine, though its manifestations in terms of increased selfishness and bickering through the rest of the trip are well documented. Such animals as remained were exhausted beyond complete recovery, and the pace of the party, which needed to increase now that they had gained solid terrain, had to continue slowly. Some members of the party, in particular the Eddy family, were reduced to destitution, and few of the others still had an inclination to share their meager resources.

The remainder of the tragic story is too familiar to need retelling here except in summary. Progress toward and along the Humbolt River was slow, and seething resentments flared up: Reed and Snyder fought, resulting in Snyder's death and Reed's banishment from the company; Breen and Eddy fought, in Eddy's extremity, over food and water; and old man Hardcoop fell behind and was left to die in the cold. When they reached the mountains, their daily progress, because of the emaciated and exhausted animals and people, could often be measured in feet as easily as in miles. At last, time ran out and the snow came, trapping them not far below the summit where roughly half of them died of starvation, exposure, and perhaps even of murder by cannibalistic companions.

As one might expect, news of the Donner tragedy had a discouraging effect on wagon travel over the Hastings Cutoff.[17] During the next two years, 1847 and 1848, no wagon parties used the route, and only three horseback parties are known to have crossed it, all eastbound travelers from California. It should not be surprising that the gold rush which began in 1849 and caused men to throw caution to the wind in so many other ways should also revive use of that reckless trail, the Hastings Cutoff. Even so, most of those who reached California by the overland route in that year use the Salt Lake Cutoff to the north of the Great Salt Lake, which was becoming known as a better, if less direct, route. Though some are known to have used the Hastings Cutoff, there are no surviving diaries, and their experiences are known to us only through references in diaries of others who took the Salt Lake Cutoff and met them elsewhere on the trail. At that, no more than two or three groups probably chose the more direct crossing of the salt flats. Capt. Howard Stansbury's survey party of that year accomplished the best-documented crossing of the Hastings trail, and an account of his experiences is contained elsewhere in this volume.

The overland travel to California in 1850 dramatically exceeded even that of 1849, which had been by far the largest to date, and though most continued to use the Salt Lake Cutoff, others who thought they could steal a march on the rest of the mob spilled over onto the Hastings Cutoff. The term "Hastings Cutoff," incidentally, by 1850 meant only that part of the route to the south of the Great Salt Lake and across the salt flats. Travel over the eastern part of the old Hastings Cutoff had been greatly improved by development of Parley Pratt's "Golden Pass" road down the canyon that today bears his name, so that reaching Salt Lake City was no longer difficult. And reaching Salt Lake City had became largely a necessity in 1850, since the trail was so clogged with gold rushers that the small supply posts like Forts Laramie, Bridger, and Hall were simply swamped with customers. So the detour to Salt Lake City became a common practice.

Although overland emigration to California continued in unabated numbers through the 1850s, the gold rushers of 1850 were the last travelers of whom we have record who used the Hastings Cutoff. The sudden abandonment of the route is interesting and not entirely explicable, though one suspects that travelers that year had sufficient opportunity to compare notes with those who had used the Salt Lake

Mound of abandoned pioneer material and animal bones on the Hastings Cutoff. Used by permission, Utah State Historical Society, all rights reserved.

Cutoff and learned that the southern route's supposed advantages were illusory. Virtually every journal of the Hastings Cutoff is replete with stories of suffering and delays to salvage wagons and recuperate animals, and it seems a reasonable assumption that the trail's bad reputation had become widely enough circulated that after 1850 no one any longer saw good reason to attempt it.

Given the famously tragic end of the Donner party, it is not surprising that historians have told its story in the most minute detail and popular interest in it has always been high. It is also perhaps not surprising that knowledge of its abandoned equipment on the salt flats has led to a large number of impromptu salvage efforts. By the time professional archaeologists directed their attention to the Donner site in the fall of 1986, no fewer that thirteen recorded salvage expeditions had preceded them, as well as untold unrecorded ones, particular since the development of all-terrain vehicles which make travel on the boggy surface of the salt flats safe and easy. Much of the material removed had wound up in the hands of souvenir hunters, and even those placed in museums had been excavated in an unprofessional manner and virtually all of its archaeological context destroyed.

The 1986 expedition was made possible by the West Desert Pumping Project to lower the level of the record-high Great Salt Lake by pumping some of its water into large evaporation ponds to the west of the lake. Since the project required flooding the Donner sites, which were protected by the National Historic Preservation Act of 1966 as well as other legislation, the state was required to remove all historic material before the project could begin.[18]

Pioneer wagon tracks still visible in the salt flats on the Hastings Cutoff. Used by permission, Utah State Historical Society, all rights reserved.

Abandoned wagon wheel at a water hole on Hastings Cutoff. Used by permission, Utah State Historical Society, all rights reserved.

Previous salvage efforts had disturbed the sites so completely that mere identification of the sites was something of a problem in a couple of cases. In all, five sites which it was assumed corresponded to the four wagons and one small cart reported by the Stansbury survey of 1849 were discovered and excavated, though only three still contained significant artifacts. Although none of the artifacts appear to offer the possiblility of major historical reinterpretation, some did provide minor insights that add to our understanding of the Donner tragedy.

Perhaps the most interesting discovery was the three sets of wagon ruts that cut through the sites. The wagon wheels sunk several inches below the surface of the ground and created a permanent disturbance that remains visible even 140 years later. Two sets of tracks measured fifty-eight and fifty-nine inches apart, center to center, and showed a tire width of four inches at the bottom of the rut. These dimensions correspond closely to those of other wagons of the period found in museums. The other set, however, measured no less than eighty-six inches apart and showed a tire width of ten inches at the bottom of the rut. It is difficult to escape the conclusion that these are the tracks of James Reed's gigantic Pioneer Palace wagon, the Winnebago of its day, whose luxury came at the expense of the laborious progress that cost the Donner party valuable days, then weeks, then finally death in the snow. This is the first knowledge we have had of any of the dimensions of the wagon, and it adds considerably to our understanding of the reasons for the tragedy. It also helps us understand why, when Reed broke an axle on the wagon crossing the Wasatch, he had to travel fifteen miles to find a suitable replacement.[19]

Another significant feature had little to do with the Donners. At one site, a large blackened area was discovered, several feet in average diameter. Since most of the ammunition specimens, the military buttons, and geological samples were found at the same site, the evidence suggests that this was the site of the camp of the Stansbury survey party which spent a cold night near one of the Donner wagons in the fall of 1849 and used boards from the wagon for firewood. The geological specimens are a type of quartz that is found most closely in the mountains to the north and west of the lake where the party had just passed.

The nature of the ammunition itself, though, is cause for some uncertainty in making that conclusion. The nine balls and shot found came from no fewer than seven different calibers of weapon and thus suggest civilian equipment rather than regular military issue. The great majority of animal remains—bones, hide, and manure—are at that site, which might suggest that some of the ammunition was used by the Donners in dispatching exhausted animals, except for the fact that no spent bullets were found to correspond to the fired percussion caps. So a theory explaining all of those artifacts still eludes us.

The supposed Stansbury site also contained specimens of leather strap and buckles which were probably harnesses. It is unlikely, though, that those items are associated with either the Donner or Stansbury parties, since the former used oxen exclusively and ox riggings do not require leather straps or buckles, and the

Stansbury party were mounted on horses and mules. It is thus possible that some other party, perhaps the large one of 1850 led by Auguste Archambault, included an outfit with horse or mule-drawn wagon and that it abandoned some of its gear along with a dead animal at that point. Overland emigrants in 1846 were already learning that the slower pace of oxen was a fair price to pay for their greater strength and their lesser attraction than horses or mules for Indians.

Otherwise, the artifacts recovered from the Donner sites were about what one might expect an emigrant party in trouble to discard: hardware from wagons' ceramic specimens, both bottles and dishes; leather and hardware from luggage; and tools, including auger bits, a grass-hook, a plane handle, and a hay fork. All of those were reasonable selections to include in one's wagon on a trip to start a new life in California, but they were also reasonable ones to discard when circumstances became desperate. The Donners would have to make their way in California the best they could without them, for the mere goal of getting there had now became the central problem.

Notes

1. John Bidwell, "The First Emigrant Train to California," *Century* 41 (1890): 106–30. Since the present article offers little original research or interpretation before its discussion of the 1986 archaeological project, only the basic sources and literature are supplied for each expedition discussed.
2. In two letters to his superior DeSmet offers interesting and humorous sidelights on his relations with the emigrants, especially theological discussions with Bartleson and a Methodist minister. Reuben Gold Thwaites, *Early Western Travels* (Cleveland: Arthur H. Clark Co., 1906), vol. 27, pp. 190, 236–38.
3. George R. Stewart, *The California Trail* (New York, 1962), pp. 203–7.
4. Dale L. Morgan, *The Humboldt: Highroad of the West* (New York, 1943), p. 5.
5. Charles Kelly, *Old Greenwood* (Salt Lake City, 1936), pp. 50–80.
6. There is an older, negative literature on Hastings, exemplified by such works as Bernard DeVoto, *1846: The Year of Decision* (Boston, 1943); George R. Stewart, *Ordeal By Hunger* (New your, 1936); and Charles Kelly, *Salt Desert Trails* (Salt Lake City, 1930). The interpretation presented here, however, follows Thomas F. Andrews, "The Controversial Career of Lansford Warren Hastings: Pioneer California Promoter and Emigrant Guide" (Ph.D. diss., University of Southern California, 1970); and "Lansford W. Hastings and the Promotion of the Salt Lake Desert Cutoff: A Reappraisal," *Western Historical Quarterly* 4 (1973): 133–50.
7. Lansdord W. Hastings, *The Emigrants' Guide to Oregon and California* (Cincinnati, 1845), pp. 83, 87.
8. Ibid., pp. 93–94, 105, 122
9. Ibid., pp. 137–38.
10. J. Roderick Korn, "West from Fort Bridger," *Utah Historical Quarterly* 19 (1951), is a collection of most of the primary sources of the emigration of 1846, but see also Dale L. Morgan, *Overland in 1846* (Georgetown, Calif., 1963).
11. Edwin Bryant, *What I Saw in California* (New York, 1848)

12. Ibid., p. 172.
13. Korns, "West from Fort Bridger," pp. 148–52.
14. The diary of James Frazier Reed, the only primary source within the Donner party for the Utah portion of the trip, is in Korns, "West from Fort Bridger," pp. 195–221: see also Stewart, *Ordeal by Hunger.*
15. It is the contention of J. Roderick Korns that Hastings returned with Reed as far back on the trail as Big Mountain, which is the only place along the route where the vista described by Reed can be achieved. If so, Hastings's assistance to the Donner-Reed party was not as desultory as the old literature indicates, for from that vantage point he could have given Reed a very good idea indeed of the best route. Korns, "West from Fort Bridger," pp. 198–99, n. 16.
16. It might be well to point out here that in spite of the after-the fact recollections of the child Virginia Reed, whom many have chosen to believe over the first-hand diary of her father, Reed's Pioneer Palace wagon was not one of those abandoned on the salt flats. Its ultimate fate is unknown; Stewart believes it was abandoned somewhere along the Humboldt after Reed's banishment following his murder of Snyder. Stewart, *Ordeal By Hunger,* p. 67; Virginia Reed Murphy, "Across the Plains in the Donner Party (1846)," *Century,* July 1891, p. 417. Compare with Virginia Reed's letter to Mary C. Keyes, May 16, 1847 (much closer in date to the actual events), in which she mentions abandoning wagons on the salt flats, but does not name the Pioneer Palace and also mentions abandoning their last wagon on the Humboldt after Snyder's murder. The letter is published in Morgan, *Overland in 1846,* vol. 1, p. 282.
17. Charles Kelly, "Gold Seekers on the Hasting Cutoff," *Utah Historical Quarterly* 20 (1952): 330; "The Journal of Robert Chalmers," *Utah Historical Quarterly* 20 (1952): 30–55
18. Records kept and artifacts recovered by the project are being preserved by the Antiquities Section, Utah State Historical Society.
19. Korns, "West from Fort Bridger," p. 203 n. 25.

IV

SETTLERS

Corinne: The Gentile Capital of Utah

When one thinks of the West, sooner or later one thinks of ghost towns. The headlong rush to riches that fueled so much of the westward movement ended in failure more often than in success, and even success, where it did occur, was often short-lived. Thus the western landscape is strewn with ghost towns, the sun-bleached, broken down material remains of failed dreams. Utah has its share of such places, most often defunct mining communities where the ore veins finally gave out and the people moved on. Corinne, however, was an industrial and commercial center just north of the Great Salt Lake that made a desperate bid in 1869–1870 to break the economic back of Salt Lake City and even to supersede its political dominance. Although it failed to attain either of those goals, it was a rip-roaring center of Gentile ambition for a brief period and is one of Utah history's more colorful episodes. And unlike most such failed enterprises, Corinne is not dead even today, though as a tiny Mormon farming village it bears few outward signs of its former greatness.

As the transcontinental railroad neared completion in the spring of 1869, it was apparent to all that it would bring vast changes to Utah. It would, in the first place, end the isolation upon which the Mormon experiment in creating a self-sufficient religious utopia depended. For the Gentiles in Utah, who were largely engaged in businesses and mining, the railroad would open access to distant markets and sources of goods and link the territory, to put it concisely, to the larger world of capitalism. A group of Gentile entrepreneurs seized upon the idea of building a city near the point where the railroad would cross the Bear River. They would use the Great Salt Lake to link them with the mining communities in the Oquirrh Mountains and use the railroad to ship ore out and supplies in, both for those mines and others to the north in Idaho and Montana. Salt Lake City, they hoped, would be isolated and would quickly decline. Corinne, Utah, grew up suddenly, like other such towns in the West. Its enterprising citizens built a boat, the *City of Corinne*, to ply the Great Salt Lake, and opened a great overland freight road to the

Idaho and Montana mines. Like most such boomtowns, its economic virtues were offset by the vices of its social life, which stood in stark contrast to the sober Mormon farming communities of northern Utah. Eventually, though, it was the Mormons who won out, under the leadership of the wily Brigham Young, by fighting fire with fire, linking northern Utah with Idaho and Montana by building the Utah Northern Railroad and driving the less efficient Gentile freighters out of business. Even nature seemed to conspire against Corinne, as the silty channel of the sluggish Bear River became unnavigable.

Wallace Stegner, author of the following lively narrative of the rise and fall of Corinne, spent his high school and college years in Salt Lake City before moving east to develop his literary career. As an instructor at Harvard in the early 1940s, he found himself homesick for his native West and wrote *Mormon Country*—from which this selection is taken—partly as a remedy. There had been other books about Utah, but none exhibiting the literary genius that would make Stegner one of the West's greatest writers. A unique feature of the book in the context of Utah literature of its day is that it divides its attention roughly equally between the Mormon and Gentile ways of life, this selection coming, of course, from the latter category.

Suggestions for further reading

For almost forty years, Stegner's little essay reprinted here was virtually the only historical narrative of Corinne available, and it still ranks as one of the most entertaining and accurate. In 1980, the attention of the prolific historian Brigham D. Madsen turned to the neglected Montana Trail which began at Corinne, and with his wife Betty M. Madsen he published *North to Montana: Jehus, Bullwhackers, and Mule Skinners on the Montana Trail* (Salt Lake City: University of Utah Press, 1980; reprinted, Logan: Utah State University Press, 1998). Two articles of his developed the Corinne story further: "Corinne, the Fair: Gateway to Montana Mines," *Utah Historical Quarterly* 37 (winter 1969): 102–24 (with Betty M. Madsen); and "Frolics and Free Schools for the Youthful Gentiles of Corinne," *Utah Historical Quarterly* 48 (summer 1980): 220–34. Madsen's study of Corinne culminated in *Corinne: The Gentile Capital of Utah* (Salt Lake City: Utah State Historical Society, 1980).

The Burg on the Bear . . .
Wallace Stegner

In 1869 the Gentiles dreamed a dream. They had for years fought unsuccessfully against the stranglehold that the Church had on political and economic and social affairs. They were few compared with the Saints, and though they had friends in Washington, Washington was a long way off and federal edicts had a way of never coming to anything. Brigham Young, seated solidly in the Lion House, with the wires of the Deseret Telegraph at his finger tips and his whole empire within immediate call, calmly nullified all the strenuous efforts of outsiders to establish themselves or their ideas. He ruled the roost, and if the few Gentiles perched on it and squawking annoyed him, he shouldered them off. That was what brought about the Gentile dream, actually. The anti-Gentile boycott drove most of Salt Lake's unblessed merchants out of business, and as a last resort they gravitated to the railroad, just coming through from east and west. They induced the Union Pacific, for a consideration of every other house-lot, to survey a town on the main line, and they moved in en masse, determined to make a Gentile capital that would outshine Salt Lake City and be a haven for all the democratic ideas unpopular around the Lion House.

That town, Corinne, was on Bear River Bay at the north end of Great Salt Lake. Within two weeks of its location there were fifteen hundred people and three hundred buildings in the place. Lots sold for anything from three hundred to a thousand dollars. The boom was on, even before the Union Pacific and Central Pacific met at Promontory, a few miles west. When that historic junction took place, Corinne was the second largest city in the territory, and by all odds the busiest.

Transportation, the thing that the Mormons both welcomed and dreaded, because cheap freight rates and easy access were bound to be accompanied by a flood of unwelcome men, and because the fostered isolation of the region was sure to be broken down, was the backbone of Corinne's prosperity. By rail, by wagon, by boat, the Gentiles attempted to get control of all the hauling in the territory, and

Wallace Stegner, "The Burg on the Bear . . ." from *Mormon Country* (New York: Duell, Sloan & Pearce, 1942), 251–58.

for a while they almost did. The rich mines of Idaho and Montana, cut off from the world, needed supplies, needed an outlet for their high-grade ores. Corinne took the situation in hand. One company alone, the Diamond R, had four hundred mules and eighty wagons constantly on the road, going and coming. Then, because refined ore was easier and cheaper to ship than raw ore, they built a smelter in Corinne. Slag piles mounted on the banks of the Bear, and bullion went eastward and westward by rail. The rutted streets were choked with wagons. Crews from "Hell's Half Acre," a construction camp up the line, flocked back to cavort in Corinne's twenty-nine saloons and two dance halls, or gamble their pay in the immense gambling tent that had followed the steel all the way from Omaha. Ladies came in to supply the feminine touch, and found so warm a welcome that John Hanson Beadle, the town's first editor, counted eighty soiled doves at one time in Corinne's sinful cote.

The Gentiles of Corinne were energetic people. Enterprise piled on enterprise. A slaughterhouse and meat packing plant, designed to provide beef for railroad camps and the mines, rose like an exhalation. Warehouses groaned with good Mormon produce going east or west along the main line. When the silver mines of the Oquirrh range, worked inadequately until transportation came, opened into big production, the citizens of Corinne chipped in four thousand dollars to build a boat for bringing the ores to the new smelter. Here was none of the hand-whittled, home-made industry of Mormondom. Engines from Chicago, redwood from California, were rushed in. The *City of Corinne* was launched and for a time carried ore mountain-high on her three decks. Other boats came out of the local navy yard: the *Kate Connor*, the *Rosie Brown*, the *Pluribustah*. Transport was going four ways from the Gentile stronghold, and the dreams blossomed. It became obvious that the Chicago of Utah Territory would have to become the heart of a great political movement destined to overthrow the priestly nabobs in Salt Lake.

They had their political caucus, organized the Liberal Party on strictly anti-Mormon lines, Republican and Democrat uniting against the theocracy. They put up a candidate for Congress who got votes by tens where his Mormon opponent of the "People's Party" got them by thousands, but they were not dismayed. The future was bright. Preparing their town against that future, they drew up a set of laws for Corinne as strict in its legal way as the regulations of a Mormon town were in their theological way. Unfortunately, Corinne didn't have quite the same population as a Mormon town, and the laws had little effect on the toughs and rowdies and *nymphs du pave*.

They went beyond politics, opened their arms and welcomed to the town's soiled but motherly breast all the non-Mormon denominations they could lure in. The first Methodist church, the first Presbyterian church, and the first Episcopalian church in Utah were in the Burg on the Bear. True, they did not have many communicants. Captain Codman, visiting the place in 1874, found one church with two members, one with one, and the third with eleven, and felt a twinge of pity for the lonely pastor he discovered playing the organ to himself in his deserted cathedral. The reminiscences of Alexander Toponce, a salty old reprobate who made a good deal of money freighting, staging, and furnishing beef all along the Union Pacific right of way, mention one minister who, for lack of anything better to do with his time, resorted to prospecting and reducing the samples to powder with a mortar and pestle. On one Sunday the minister and a vestryman were the only attendants at worship. Dunn, the minister, sat and talked prospects with his one customer until it was clear that no one else was coming. "Well, Brother Stein," he said, "what shall we do, preach or pound quartz?" They decided to pound quartz, and a little later, when Dunn in a rage ran a claim-jumper off Antelope Island with a shotgun, Bishop Tuttle gave him the opportunity to resign. He wound up as a mining promoter in Bonanza, Idaho.

Something similar happened to everything that Corinne did. It started as one thing and wound up as something else. In spite of its zeal and enterprise, the fortress of the embattled Gentiles dwindled. Even so good a business, so fool-proof a business, as that of Johnson and Underdunk fell away and gave up. Johnson and Underdunk were lawyers. Taking their part in the blaze of energy that dazzled the town, they got up a scheme for granting mail order divorces. For a price of two dollars and a half, they would separate anyone from the bosom of his family. The petitioner didn't have to be present, and he could even get alimony if he wanted it. I have never been able to lay hands on one of those divorce decrees, but tradition says that they were completely official, ribbons and wax and the court seal and all. Either Johnson and Underdunk were skilled forgers, or they had a pipeline to the judge. Tradition also says that for ten years United States courts were unraveling the divorces that Johnson and Underdunk distributed with so lavish a hand. However that may be, it is rather charming to see all this going on practically next door to Brigham City, one of the strongest United Order towns in Mormondom, and jammed with polygamous wives. Johnson and Underdunk were in the main Corinne tradition: they helped along the faith that Corinne was destined to reverse everything that the Saints stood for.

But Corinne's road, after the first years, was down, and the Mormons delighted in contributing grease for the slide. Brigham Young built a railroad, the Utah and Northern, linking Salt Lake and the Idaho mines and virtually destroying the steamer traffic on the lake. Ogden, not Corinne, was finally established as the division point on the Union Pacific. The boats which had been launched with such exuberant ceremony went out of commission one after another. The *City of Corinne*, unable to dock at her home port because the river filled with bars, ended her days as an excursion boat off Black Rock, and finally burned with the Garfield Beach pavilion. Her hulk is supposed to lie somewhere in a swamp below the smelter town of Garfield. The *Kate Connor* sank with a full load of ore in the deep part of the river. The others are gone, no one knows where—*Rosie Brown, Pluribustah*, symbols of Corinne's enterprising dream, addresses unknown.

Transportation made Corinne, and transportation killed it. When the Utah and Northern was made standard gauge up to Silver Bow, Montana, the freighting business was gone. Ogden stole most of the railroad and shipping business, and other smelters closer to the mines reduced the flow of ores into the mouth of Bear River. The smelter closed down. Corinne couldn't have had worse luck if the Mormons' pious curses had been effective. For witness the outcome of the smelting business: Slag from the mountainous dumps had been piled behind the abutments of the Bear River Bridge and had been used to pave the streets, originally ankle-deep in dust or mud. In the waning days of the Burg on the Bear mining men came poking around, knocked off hunks of slag from the abandoned dumps, and ended by buying the works. The slag which Corinne's heedless citizenry had ground into the alkali with their heels, or dumped into Bear River, ran twenty dollars to the ton in gold when re-smelted.

The weak-spirited left early, but the die-hards clung. They even aspired to challenge the Mormons in their own field, agriculture. If Corinne's boom days as a transportation town were over, it could at least be a farming community. In 1890 the Bear Lake and River Water and Irrigation Company put in a dam and diversion canal in Bear River Canyon and opened ten thousand acres to irrigation. At first the land produced heavily; within a year or two the alkali and salts, leached to the surface by the irrigation water, turned the fields into worthless swamps.

But if it couldn't be a farming community, it might be a health center. Henry House, son of one of the founders, dreamed of a spa at the sulphur springs which bubbled from the base of the hills west of Corinne, and went so far as to evaporate the water and sell the resulting salts as a cure-all. Texas has no monopoly on fizz-powders and Alka-Seltzers. But House's plans for the health resort also died on the vine. The final blow came in 1903, when the Lucin Cutoff was built across forty miles of Great Salt Lake and Corinne was left stranded on a branch line.

The town was virtually ghost. The buildings were burned or torn down, the politicos were gone, the merchants had moved to Ogden, the warehouses were empty and falling apart, the railroad ran around the dead walls of the Gentile stronghold.

But now the metamorphosis, the ironic twist. Corinne is not dead as of 1942. It is not as big as it once was, and its twenty-nine saloons and two dancehalls and gambling tent and ladies of pleasure are gone, and the biggest of its saloons now languishes under the title of Dewdrop Inn. Two of the three Protestant churches are vanished and the other can scarcely be said to be in use. The Bear River has shrunk to half its former width, because of the canal which takes out the irrigation water, and everything that made Corinne a place of importance in the eighteen seventies is no longer there. But Corinne is no ghost. There is an L.D.S. Ward House in Corinne; there are two or three hundred farmers living in and around Corinne; the land which the first irrigation spoiled has been drained and reclaimed, and the Bear River Canal furnishes plenty of water. There are wells of marsh gas from which the farmers get heat and power. The alfalfa and beets raised in the valley have a ready market—and the bulk of the population is Mormon.

Quietly, without fuss, the Mormons waited until the Burg on the Bear burnt itself out. They disliked it, they did their best to boycott and ruin it, but they never made active war on it. But when the debacle came, when the quick money was no longer available and the hordes of the infidels had departed, the Saints moved quietly in and took over, transforming Corinne into a sleepy Mormon village.

And there, at least for the time and in that locality, Mormon society showed itself the more stable and lasting one. The might of the Gentile, unsmote by the sword, had melted like snow. The reason is plain enough. The thing the Gentiles were chasing was clearly no longer available in Corinne. But the thing the Mormons were after still was.

On other fronts the Gentiles did not succumb so easily.

Grazing and Living on Antelope Island

Viewed from a distance—say, from the mouth of Emigration Canyon where Brigham Young got his first view of Great Salt Lake—the lake's two largest islands, Stansbury and Antelope, appear to be mountain ranges flanking the water. Stansbury, in fact, is just that, for it would take an extremely high lake level to cover the base of the peninsula it normally is, and to turn it into the "island" of its misleading name. But it would take a correspondingly extreme low lake level to expose dry land between Antelope Island and the eastern lake shore, though historically there have been times when one could ride a horse to the island without swimming. The mountain range appearance of the island effectively indicates its immense size, and closer examination discloses a correspondingly diverse terrain that hosts an equally diverse wildlife population. It is little wonder, then, that Antelope Island has seen more historical activity than any other island, particularly grazing, as the following selection narrates, nor that it is today a state park unto itself with commercial concessionaires, interpretive facilities, a marina, a swimming beach, and miles of hiking and bicycling trails, all accessible by means of a paved causeway.

Marlin Stum, a freelance writer and journalist now residing in Salt Lake City, bases his expertise on exhaustive archival and library research and interviews with pioneers, as well as thirty years' experience in exploring the island by boat and by boot. Dan Miller, a friend of Stum's since boyhood, was in fact a full collaborator in the research and exploration rather than just the contributor of a collection of memorable color and black and white photographs that make the book a visual as well as an intellectual and literary delight. Their book, which the reader of the following selection will see is written from an outspoken environmentalist point of view, belongs on the shelf of every Great Salt Lake aficionado, both for the depth and accuracy of its research and for its coverage of current political and scientific issues involving the island and the lake.

This selection is largely self-contained and self-explanatory, and only a few minor editorial comments seem useful. One is to explain a bit further, to the reader unfamiliar with Mormon history and institutions, the central importance of the Perpetual Emigrating Fund, of which the livestock herds on both Antelope and Stansbury Islands were a foundation stone. Mormonism, born during the era of utopian communitarian experiments in early nineteenth century America, possesses a group ethos lacking in most other religions. As a part of its first foreign missionary endeavors in England and Scandinavia in the early 1850s, converts were encouraged to emigrate to Utah to form a centralized Mormon community. As most of their converts at the time were coming from Europe's impoverished masses, some means of marshaling resources to help them meet the expenses of the journey was necessary. Thus a church corporation was established in which individuals and the church itself could invest, to create a revolving loan fund. As Stum indicates, most emigrants chose to repay their loans in kind rather than in cash, so the livestock herd on Antelope Island became a sort of bank with hooves. Lasting until the late 1880s, the fund was an immense success, helping to bring some ten thousand poor Mormon converts to Utah.

The reader unfamiliar with American Indian mythology may not understand Stum's brief allusion toward the end of the selection to Coyote, a character common to many Indian cultures, who is both a trickster and a creator. Stum uses Coyote as an underlying literary device in the book, symbolizing Antelope Island's natural wildness and its function as a sanctuary for animals. In addition to the herd of some five hundred bison mentioned in this selection, Stum elsewhere discusses the state park's reintroduction in recent years of previously indigenous pronghorn antelope and bighorn sheep, which, with the bison and mule deer, provide a diverse population of large quadrupeds that give visitors some sense of the island's original condition.

Suggestions for further reading

The bibliography and notes in Stum's book are highly recommended. Prominent among his sources are A. M. Cutler, *Fielding Garr and His Family: Early Mormon Pioneers on Antelope Island* (n.p.: The Ralph Cutler Family Organization, 1991); and Max R. Harward, *Where the Buffalo Roam: Life on Antelope Island* (n.p.: by author, 1996). The larger history of the Perpetual Emigrating Fund and the importance of the Antelope Island livestock herd is given in Leonard J. Arrington, *Great Basin Kingdom: An Economic History of the Latter-day Saints, 1830–1900* (Cambridge: Harvard University Press, 1958). The story of the Frarys' sojourn on the island is told in Dale Morgan, *The Great Salt Lake*, 326–29; that of the Wenner family appears in the same book, 329–37, and in David E. Miller, ed., "A Great Adventure on Great Salt Lake: A True Story by Kate Y. Noble," *Utah Historical Quarterly* 33 (summer 1965): 218–36.

BUILDING A HOME IN THE WILDERNESS
Marlin Stum

"There was so much to do, so much to think about in this new life away from the world, the only family on the Island. I began to feel much of my life would have been wasted living in the outside world imitating fashions, wondering about neighbors' affairs, worrying about my children's companions. We learned to know ourselves, enjoy ourselves, children and books."
—Kate Wenner in Dale L. Morgan, *The Great Salt Lake*

In 1981, the Fielding Garr Ranch house—an adobe home nestled in a grove of trees two-thirds of the way down the east side of Antelope Island—was the oldest continually occupied residence in the state of Utah. I had never seen it. For five years, I tried to wheedle and cajole a glimpse of the ranch—the very cornerstone of island history—but to no avail. Anschutz Corporation (doing business as Anschutz Oil and Cattle Company) owned all of the island except a 2,300-acre state toehold on the north end, and company representatives refused to even discuss a visit. They ignored phone calls from both Dan Miller and me, signed for our certified letters then forgot them.

Anschutz cattle peacefully grazed along the lower slopes during all but the hottest months of the year. A lone manager and a few ranch hands watched over the stock. Corporate executives occasionally visited to hunt trophy mule deer in nearby canyons during which time the spartan ranch house served as a primitive vacation resort for the cattle and oil moguls. Except for these few, seemingly innocuous intrusions, the island remained inviolate and off limits.

Trespassers did so at their own peril. The angry and bored ranch manager shot at the few duck hunters who surreptitiously boated onto the shore. Hikers risked receiving a fine from state parks personnel or a load of buckshot in their breeches.

Local and state government officials continually pressured Anschutz to sell the rest of the island to the state, but the Denver-based corporation steadfastly spurned giving up its private paradise. In light of the stalemate, the last thing Anschutz officials

Marlin Stum (with photographs by Dan Miller), "Building a Home in the Wilderness," from *Visions of Antelope Island and Great Salt Lake* (Logan: Utah State University Press, 1999), 73–89.

wanted was a writer and photographer publicizing their retreat and further agitating Davis County residents who were chomping at the bit to gain a look at the island. The small state park on the north end of Antelope was but a tasty hors d'oeuvre doled out to a famished public yearning to ingest the island's history and natural nourishment.

Utah finally succeeded in acquiring the entire island. A few months later, state park manager Mitch Larsson agreed to give Dan and me a tour of the ranch. We were working for a small weekly newspaper in Layton, the *Lakeside Review,* and proposed a feature article on the island. After half a decade of knocking, the gate to the "private island" swung open to us on August 23, 1981. We felt like commoners with keys to the palace.

The island interior appears pristine and rugged as we get our first look at it. Rolling eastern grasslands, tanned to earth tones by the August sun, rise out of an indigo lake and sweep up past scattered verdant springs. The slopes skip across ancient shorelines of Lake Bonneville, then steepen into parallel canyons that climb a mountainous ridge. Like a chiseled, stone-age tool, this ridgeline splits the atmosphere two thousand feet above the brine.

I ride with Mitch in his pickup and Dan follows in his car. As we drive along a rough dirt road contouring the eastern shore, fifty bison—about a quarter of the island's free-roaming herd—graze undisturbed above one of the springs. We stop to shoot a few photos, then continue up across a rib leading to Beacon Knob, our vehicles urging the bison into a trot. We head them off at the high point of the road, where Mitch and I sit in the truck while Dan quickly sets up his camera behind a boulder. I envision him as a young frontier scout kneeling for a shot and imagine the bark of a .50 Hawkin as he extends the legs of his tripod. The herd thunders past so close the truck shakes with the earth's vibration.

"This is a part of the wild West that is still untouched," Mitch says excitedly as the dust swirls around Dan. "It is the same here today as it was when Frémont and Kit Carson were here."

Dan staggers out of the dust cloud, his eyes wide with disbelief. In less than a minute, the bison easily run two miles west, down into the expansive White Rock Bay.

As we continue along the twelve-mile drive to the ranch, a short-eared owl *(Asio flammeus)* wafts by in a floppy flight. He often sees them during the day, says Mitch. Several mourning doves *(Zenaidura macroura)* greet us with plaintive cooing along the way. A hawk that none of us can identify is sighted. A fat, male ring-necked pheasant *(Phasianus colchicus)* adds a stroke of color to the earthtone movements.

The shoreline edges east toward a muddy protuberance called Sea Gull Point. Mitch motions toward an old lane leading up a canyon in the opposite direction. It puts my gaze up toward Frary Peak, 6,596 feet, the high point on the island. Like the ranch, the peak is a long-coveted goal that intrigues me more, at the time, than Mitch's discourse about the man who left his name there.

Mitch spouts a fountain of information as we bounce down the road. My mind stretches like a water bag filled to its bursting point. I try to soak up his anecdotes while scribbling frantic notes and gawking at a landscape that is at once new and ageless.

I wonder whether Brigham Young was similarly overwhelmed when he read John C. Frémont's published expedition reports in the 1840s. They helped convince Young that northern Utah was the place to build his Zion and to settle his Mormon emigrants who were fleeing religious persecution in the Midwest. Just past the Continental Divide on his maiden trek west, Young met mountain men Moses "Black" Harris and Jim Bridger. Bridger told the Mormon leader that the whole of the West was excellent, that there was nowhere a better place in the world. The mountain men confirmed Frémont's description of Great Salt Lake Valley and described even better country farther south.

Brigham and some men rode their horses across the shallows to investigate Antelope Island shortly after the pioneers arrived in the valley in 1847. Young recognized the island's grazing potential immediately. He commissioned Fielding Garr, a big, square-shouldered man of 225 pounds, to build a house on the island and to manage the church's livestock there. Garr, a bonded herdsman licensed to receive stock and insure their safe return by giving bonds to the owner, was also an experienced mason

An old mountain man and bear hunter known as Daddy Stump was already living on the island, reportedly at the head of a small open canyon under a steep ridge. He built a crude cabin of juniper posts with a dirt roof and remained on the island for several years after the Mormons came. Credited with planting Utah's first peach trees on the island, Stump is a missing piece of the historical puzzle. His full name, his background, exactly where he built his cabin, and what ultimately became of him remain unknown. Fielding Garr family records note that Stump left the island around 1855, apparently feeling that civilization was encroaching, and moved his cattle and horses to a secluded spot in Cache Valley. After the severe winter of 1855–56, one of Fielding's sons, Abel, and friend William Ashby went looking for Stump, who could not be found. A story circulated that some starving Utes during the hard winter implored the old mountain man to share his beef, and when he would not, an Indian woman slit his throat. Antelope Island's long, high backbone is named after him: Daddy Stump Ridge.

Mitch, Dan, and I round a bend in the road and a lush, green oasis bursts like a pheasant out of the otherwise brown and stark scenery. It is immediately obvious why this ranch became such a favorite haunt of Brigham Young's. It looks out over marshland to a placid lake and beyond to the violet rim of the Great Basin—the Wasatch Mountains—fifteen miles away. Huge trees, an anomaly on the island, caress the corners of a green lawn and the single-story house. Mature cottonwoods, willows, Russian olives, and poplars—many planted by the pioneers—draw moisture from the high water table and lend shade to the idyllic site. Several stout honey locusts push skyward on the east side of the home; although leisure was a rarity for ranch hands, George Frary reportedly whiled away hot, torpid afternoons like this one in his hammock tied to the honey locusts. According to Mitch, Brigham and his friends sometimes held wrestling matches on the lawn. Being Mormon Church president and the father of Salt Lake City were busy and demanding tasks for Young. Although a public and sociable man, he too, at times, required recreation and solitude for introspection and rejuvenation. Antelope Island became his retreat.

I could live here a while, I think. Watch the sun rise over the lake. Listen to the meadowlarks singing, to breezes whispering their wisdom through the trees. But the quiet scene belies the hardships endured by the pioneers.

During the spring of 1848, pioneers throughout the valley found their gardens and fields in pitiful shape. A series of late frosts had badly damaged the first-year crop of beans and cucumbers, pumpkins, melons, and squash. Then hoards of black crickets began devouring the heads off the corn and wheat as fast as they sprouted, portending the pilgrims' starvation. Building a promised land out of the wilderness seemed doomed to failure. In June, however, flocks of gulls from the lake's islands swarmed into Salt Lake City and began gorging themselves on the insects. The gulls flew off and regurgitated their meals before returning to eat more. The miracle saved the pioneers' crops and earned for the California guff *(Larus californicus)* the esteemed status of state bird. When Brigham launched a forty five-foot, livestock-hauling sailboat on the lake in 1854, he christened it the *Timely Gull*.

Cattle ranching on the island began in the fall of 1848. Daddy Stump and Benjamin Ashby, assisted by two teenage boys—Fielding's son Abe and Thomas Thurston's son, George—drove the cattle to the island. Ashby wrote that the drive took three days, culminating in them getting stuck in the mud close to the island. The herders camped in the snow that night. Fielding and the others built a small hut at the ranch site and left the two teenagers to guard the stock that winter.

The next spring, while their sons looked after the livestock, Fielding Garr, Joseph B. Noble, and Thomas Thurston began building the Antelope Island house. Because trees and money were scarce in the valley and clay was readily available, adobe was the preferred construction material for many pioneer homes; a log house cost twice as much to build. Garr and Noble were already experienced adobe masons when they erected this modest, five-room house. I try to envision the three men laboring here alongside the freshwater spring in 1849, mixing the straw and island clay, forming the mixture into bricks, and baking them in the sun. Could they have imagined that their simple, earthy building would withstand the ravages of decades, be expanded several times, and be lived in continuously for the next 132 years?

"A new cedar shake roof was just installed," says Mitch, sounding like a proud father as we walk around the house before going in.

"Who did that?" I ask, remembering the newspaper article I still had to write.

"About 120 Youth Conservation Corps workers," he replies. "They helped us clean up the place, repaint some of the buildings."

I walk gingerly up onto the old porch. The original, storm-beaten bricks are gray as rain clouds. Bits of straw used to help bind the clay peek through the gray strata.

The home's first renovation (thirty years later) is marked by hurried mortar work and a ragged brick seam to the right of the main door. I open the door, half expecting the frail-looking wall to collapse into dust like a painting on a mirror that shatters. Instead, a cool, refreshing draft greets me through the doorway. These walls are a foot thick, providing ample insulation against the searing August heat. The cool, damp air invigorates my skin, and I shiver at the sudden temperature change.

"I have an identity of my own," the house seems to say. "Try to get to know me."

The air is somewhat stale, thick with a century and a third of deep and subtle secrets. My eyes slowly readjust to a dark but sizable front living space. There are two of these rooms backed by three tiny bedrooms—all part of the original building. Two large brick hearths, charred black as a raven and mantled with rough-hewn timbers, hold memories of hearty, one-pot meals, and hot baths. Except for a few rusted tools and old, colored bottles on the windowsills, the clean rooms are empty. They feel peaceful, but lonely. I walk into a large kitchen, the 1880 addition, and peek into another bedroom and storeroom added in the mid-twentieth century. In the kitchen, worn, multiple layers of linoleum lie cracked and peeling on the floor, burdened with an aura of hard labor.

Garr's wife, Paulina, died just before the family came west and the eldest daughter remained in Indiana. His second daughter, Nancy—already married and with a little girl of her own—selflessly filled the role of mother to her seven brothers and sisters. She was twenty-six years old when they entered the valley. Garr moved his family to the island in late fall or early winter, 1849; Brigham had already ordered the church livestock taken there. In 1850, U.S. Army captain and topographical engineer Howard Stansbury, who was completing a thorough survey of the lake, moved his stock to the island as well. Garr, his sons, and his daughters had their days filled with much responsibility.

The Garr children were hearty, God-fearing pioneers from eldest to youngest. Nancy became a devoted surrogate mother to them all. With long hair and a beard, John reportedly lived on his horse and was a cowboy par excellence. He later married a Shoshone woman and was one of the first settlers in Cache Valley. William also herded cattle on the island and he too settled in Cache Valley. Son Abel's responsibilities included looking after the herds that first winter. Caroline, Fielding's third daughter, did most of the cooking for the family and ranch hands on Antelope Island. Living her later childhood and early teens there, Garr's fourth daughter, Sarah, received only one year of formal schooling because of the ranch's isolation. It tested the mettle of Mary too, who was only nine years old. There were chickens to tend, clothes to wash and mend, butter to churn, and countless other chores. She found no girls her age, played little and worked hard, but did meet a young boy there, Nathaniel Ashby, who grew up to be her husband. Benjamin, the baby of the family, was only six when the Garrs moved into the adobe ranch house.[1]

In September 1850, legislation designated Antelope and Stansbury Islands for the sole use of Perpetual Emigration Company stock. The Mormons created the

Perpetual Emigrating Fund to aid poor converts who wished to relocate in Salt Lake Valley. Once here, they paid their debt back to the fund. Cash was often wanting, so repayments and donations were mostly of the four-legged kind. Cattle and horses were the day's exchange currency and became the Mormons' primary export commodity. While the Garrs were there, six hundred church-owned stallions and brood mares were turned loose on the island.

Grasslands were lush in parts of the valley; pioneer diaries noted that cows were sometimes lost in fields of grass that grew over their heads. The island provided natural pastures and fresh water, and the lake was a secure barrier for wandering herds. Cattle, horses, and sheep grazed on east slopes in summer and on sunny western slopes in winter. During dry years, when the south end of the island connected to the mainland via the Antelope Island bar, livestock was easily herded through the shallows. When precipitation increased and the lake deepened, a boat was required.

Garr was skilled and trustworthy. He kept watch over the island herds for seven years, dying in June 1855. His children left the island soon after, and Heber C. Kimball hired a young Dane, Peter O. Hansen, to take over as ranch manager. Upon his arrival, Hansen described the twenty-five-acre ranch complex: There was the small log shack and the adobe home, a cattle corral large enough to hold one thousand head, a sheep corral, various fences, pens for hogs and chickens, a boat wharf in front of the house, the large spring, a garden, and young fruit trees. The ranch grew over the next century.

As we walk around the grounds, I also notice a large barn and several more outbuildings, including a three-sided cattle shed opening into a nearby corral. The original part of this structure, on the north end, is made of stone. Adjacent to it is a section built of adobe, and attached to the adobe wall is an extension of galvanized steel. A small stack of unused adobe bricks lies nearby. There is also a two-story blacksmith shop with upstairs sleeping quarters for hired help. Another two-story building built just east of the house in the latter nineteenth century has a rubble stone foundation and adobe upper level now covered with cinder blocks. Initially, flour, smoked meat, and dried fruit were stored upstairs, and the stone cellar, reached by an outside stairwell, kept vegetables and apples over the winter. As more hired hands came to work on the island in the 1880s, the second floor of the building became a bunkhouse. Mitch tells us that cowboys rested their weary bones here on bunks stacked three high. A low stone building straddles the spring pond, now a haven for mosquitoes.

Numerous antiques lie scattered around the grounds. The blacksmith shop contains old tools of the trade and we find horse tack in a shed. An unusual "rocking antelope" lies broken in several pieces on the lawn. Carved of stone, this rocking horse-like child's toy later disappeared without a trace. Mitch is amenable to the utmost, careful not to rush Dan's photographs, thoughtfully answering my inquiries. But he never leaves us out of his sight for more than a few seconds at a time to insure that we aren't swept by a devilish temptation to pocket some artifact.

The Fielding Garr ranch house on Antelope Island, built in 1849, was until 1981 the oldest continually occupied residence in Utah. Photo by Dan Miller.

With integrity and dedication equal to Fielding Garr's, Briant Stringham took over as ranch manager in July 1856. When Nancy Garr's husband, Rodney Badger, drowned trying to rescue a family whose wagon came apart crossing the Weber River, Nancy returned to the island soaked in grief. Briant later made her one of his wives.

Stringham corralled every horse at least once a year so he could handle and brand them and look them over to insure their good health. The island horses were esteemed as some of the most prized in all the Utah Territory. Solomon Kimball wrote that they grew "nimble, wiry and sure-footed" rambling the broken terrain of the island.

> It became second nature to them to climb over the rugged mountain-sides, and to jump up and down precipitous places four or five feet high. The speed which they could make while traveling over such places was simply marvelous. They neither stumbled nor fell, no matter how rough the country nor how fast they went. They were naturally of a kind disposition, and as gentle as lambs, after having been handled a few times. But with all of their perfections they had a weakness that made many a man's face turn red with anger; they loved their island home, and it was hard to wean them from it. When a favorable opportunity presented itself, during the summer months, they would take the nearest cut to the island, swimming the lake wherever they happened to come to it, and keep going until they reached their destination. Lot Smith's favorite saddle horse played this trick on him several times, even taking the saddle with him on one occasion.[2]

In July 1871, the lake was high enough that sheep being transported to the south shore were loaded on several boats for the trip to Black Rock. A fierce windstorm caught Briant and his co-workers on the lake, drenching them all. Stringham developed severe congestion in his lungs, and he died on August 4.

The land already showed signs of being overgrazed by too many animals before he took over as manager, and with Stringham's passing, the care of Antelope Island spiraled downward. Church cattle had been relocated to Cache Valley. For four years, the horses on Antelope Island ran wild and unchecked. When several men were hired to remove them, the horses became ingeniously elusive of their would-be captors. Discouraged, the men finally gave up. The horses were no longer wanted. By 1875, Kaysville residents stocked the island with thousands of sheep; their habit of cropping plants down to the very roots as they fed quickly decimated the grasslands. The remaining horses—once the envy of the Territory—began to starve, and the last few prize mounts were shot with rifles.

Ranching, nonetheless, continued, and for those whose spirits were free as a wild horse, Antelope Island provided solitude and a simple life. George Isaac Frary, who learned to sail as a boy on Lake Superior, fell in love with Great Salt Lake after moving west. When he took a job herding cattle on Antelope Island in the latter nineteenth century, the labor demanded as much seafaring as ranching skill. Stocky and strong, George piloted a clumsy sloop that held forty head; when he wasn't working, he often sailed the boat alone around the lake. In 1891, George and his wife Alice homesteaded 160 acres north of Fielding Garr Ranch, near the mouth of a gulch leading to the peak which now bears their name.

Alice, a thin, frail schoolteacher who suffered from asthma, tended their garden and guided their children's home studies. After six years of homesteading, she became quite ill, and George sailed to Syracuse and then traveled to Ogden to get her medication. Returning to Syracuse, he spotted three fires burning on the island—a distress signal—and he hurried to cross the lake. Before he reached land, wind-whipped waves capsized his boat and he nearly drowned, losing Alice's medicine. Clinging to his vessel, he finally dragged himself onto the beach. His wife died that afternoon.

A chilly north breeze blows on a sunny afternoon in early December 1997, when Dan Miller and I visit the Frary homestead. The view of the lake from here is marvelous. The slope sweeps gently down through patches of yellow grass and chocolate-brown mullein stalks to the Fielding Garr Ranch road a mile and a half away. Beyond the shore, deep blue water stretches toward the snowy Wasatch. Not much remains of the homestead. Stones pressed into the grass outline the foundation of the one-room log house and a kitchen and bedroom added later. We find twisted, blanched wood pieces the size of a strong man's upper arm lying about where an orchard once grew. A shallow creek still runs down the ravine past stone wall of two small stock-holding pens. The dry channel of an irrigation ditch, which brought water to the garden and orchard, is visible. A recent bronze plaque names George, Alice, and their seven children and tries to tell their story in a few words. Alice's grave is fenced off and marked with a small chunk of pink quartzite. Her spirit, if it resides here, has company; nearby, several dozen bison beds dot the grassy hillside.

Alice Frary lived on Antelope Island with her husband George and their children for six years. She died and was buried here, at the family's homestead site. Photo by Dan Miller.

Equally enamored with the lakescape was Judge U. J. Wenner who, in 1886, moved with his young wife Kate to Fremont Island. Two friends helped the Wenners construct a stone house; like the Frary home, the foundation is all that remains of that house a century later.

Kate loved living on the island—she said it made her feel like a real pioneer woman. While friends and relatives insisted that they return to civilization, Kate and the judge savored their pastoral ranching lifestyle. They raised chickens and ducks, turkeys and sheep. They rode horses all around the island, reread Frémont's first accounts of their homeland, recited poetry, and basked in the company of their three children. When she was eighty-five years old, Kate penned her memoirs of those joyous days.

"There was so much to do, so much to think about in this new life away from the world, the only family on the Island," she wrote. "I began to feel much of my life would have been wasted living in the outside world imitating fashions, wondering about neighbors' affairs, worrying about my children's companions. We learned to know ourselves, enjoy ourselves, children and books."[3]

For half a decade in the clear air and sunshine on Fremont Island, Judge Wenner fled his tuberculosis, but it pursued him. On September 16, 1891, it caught him in its talons and tore him apart. His lungs hemorrhaged. The bleeding was stopped, and his pain relieved, but three days later he died in Kate's arms. She buried her husband on the island that had been their dear home. Perhaps she sensed that other people, centuries earlier, had lived and died on this island. Did she and her children step over the Fremonts' stone bowls while collecting colored pebbles from the beach, pebbles they used to spell "LOVE" over her husband's grave?

Alfred Lambourne, an artist and writer who was independent of mind, mood, and taste, was a man who could appreciate both solitude and a ride on a good horse through the open hills of Antelope Island. Born in Queen Victoria's England in 1850, Alfred moved to Salt Lake City when he was sixteen. His parents were Mormons, but Lambourne later in life affiliated himself with Unitarian beliefs. In the early 1880s, after Adam Patterson delivered him to Antelope Island in Patterson's yacht, the *Maud,* Lambourne rode one of the fine island mounts along the western highlands. Traversing the undulating folds and mesmerizing curves of that incomparable landscape, Lambourne grew enthralled with the island's sensuous beauty. The expansive lake enticed him to sail its body and sketch its protean scenes.

Lambourne did just that. The attraction that sparked while riding that day blazed into desire. He made innumerable cruises with his friend David L. Davis on the yachtsman's catamaran, the *Cambria,* and Lambourne's passion for the lake led him to a solitary pilgrimage on Gunnison Island. He first set foot on Gunnison in 1887, and in 1895 friends helped him built a crude stone hut there. Its furnishings included a mahogany piano, an artist's easel, and copies of *Don Quixote* and Walt Whitman's *Leaves Of Grass.* For decades he cruised the lake and haunted the islands with pen and sketchpad, producing several fine volumes. His writings were ebullient and descriptive, at times caustic as salt in a cut, and sometimes melancholy. Often they were jubilant. In 1902, the *Deseret News* in Salt Lake City published his book, *Pictures of an Inland Sea,* in which he wrote:

> From the affluence of the heavens there comes a transfiguration. Always, there are the same great stretches of water, always the same monotonous and dreary hills, ever the same strange walls of the far-off desert, and ever the same clustered multitude of mountain peaks. But how the seasons and the great sun play with them! They are ever the same, yet never the same, eternal yet evanescent, playmates with time and with the elements. (p. 94)
>
> My island is but a vast, natural sun-dial, a horologe set in this sea to measure the flight of time. Its mighty gnomon is the northern cliff, and its circling shadow has crept thus far how many years? The sky sometimes appears black—that is, at noonday when it is clear and the near snow fields rise against it. Black with a thin scumbling of atmospheric cobalt. (pp. 25–26)
>
> A thrilling spectacle! Just now—at twilight—the Inland Sea rages beneath a storm of the Vernal equinox. March brings in the spring and it comes in a fierce disorder . . . Hurrying from windward (N. W.) the waves in thick-set ranks, sweep past the cliff-head, and wildly burst on the island sands. Huge foam-globes, formed by the beating of the briny waves among the rocks, are cast adrift, and sent seawards by the changing wind. In this swift transition and extreme of effect, who would think that this island, knew such winter storms? In some respects it might be likened to an outlying fragment of "sea-beat Hebrides," but now with the distant shining of snow-covered peaks and the gleaming waters, it more closely resembles some lonely rock of Azores. (pp. 45–46)

While Lambourne lived alone with the gulls, pelicans, and scorpions, struggling to grow a small vineyard on Gunnison Island, Utah gained formal statehood. It was a fact that mattered little to the ascetic in his remote corner of the world. Except for the temporary summer arrival of bird-guano gatherers, Lambourne's isolation was complete.

Guano became a hot commodity as fertilizer for crops, however, and the collectors persisted, even turning up an Indian grave in the course of their digging. After fourteen months on the small island northwest of Antelope, Lambourne had friends pluck him back to the city. There, under the Homestead Act, he filed in February of 1897 for 78.35 acres on Gunnison Island, approximately half its surface, hoping to secure his solitude. But industrious local citizens and guano sellers, who were calling the island a *mineral* deposit, finally forced the artist to withdraw his homesteading application and abandon his retreat. He did not forsake his beloved lake, though. He published *Pictures of an Inland Sea* and later expanded it into the lyrical *Our Inland Sea.*

Like the mountain men who preceded them, the Garr family, Frarys, Wenners, and Lambourne all escaped the trappings of civilization, sacrificing comfort and sometimes safety for heartfelt values. They all found a particular affinity for Great Salt Lake. Time slowed. Without electricity, stores, and other amenities, life on the islands was out of synch with the rest of the region. The same lake that provided solitude and sanctuary, even as the wilderness diminished, could at times be irascible and unforgiving. Eventually, even the lake could not thwart "progress," and commerce brought its own values to the islands.

Mormon occupation and caretaking of Antelope Island lasted only twenty-six years. In 1884, prominent banker and land developer John F. Dooly Sr. and his partner Frederick Meyer gained ownership of most of the island and formed the Island Improvement Company. In only a few short years, as its gentle stewards died, Antelope Island ranching slid from sensitive husbandry helping to sustain new settlers in a strange land into several decades of greedy shepherding from which the island has yet to recover.

Around 1911, Island Improvement Company built a sheep-shearing barn at the ranch. In this giant tin-roofed structure, as many as a dozen sheep at a time could be trimmed of their wool. From high in the air, its shiny roof still flashes sunlight like a shard of broken glass. The facility was considered one of the most modern of its day. In the 1920s and 30s, up to ten thousand sheep ravaged the island, champing the native grasses down to the dust. The island was quickly overgrazed and denuded while its owners boasted the largest sheep-shearing operation west of the Mississippi.

Large flocks of domestic sheep disgust me. I loathe their innate habits of fouling springs and stripping grass from the land. Although it is an important part of the island's ranching history, my first look inside this building in 1981 turns my stomach. As Mitch Larsson notes a pair of antique hand shears hanging on the wall and nifty tool drawers trimmed with handles crafted of bent horseshoes, I can hardly control my profound disdain. This is nothing more than a solemn monument to overgrazing, I think, an ironic counterpoint to the rustic integrity of the adobe house. Then Mitch points to a rusted barrel on a dark and dusty window shelf in a back corner of the barn.

"That's full of black powder," he declares with an edge to his voice. "We don't know how long it's been there or how unstable it is." It is one of the reasons the public is not yet allowed to visit the ranch, he explains, adding that National Guardsmen are supposed to come and remove the volatile material. For a moment, I indulge a sardonic fantasy: sneaking back to the ranch later and igniting the powder keg, leveling this tin, mutton-glutton mausoleum. Unaware of my terrorist thoughts, Mitch casually picks up a small pail of grain, strolls outside, and tosses a few handfuls on the ground for the pheasants.

Too many sheep and cattle and their greedy owners were not the only ones to blame for the ruination of Coyote's wildlife sanctuary. A herd of nearly four hundred bison thrived from 1921 to 1926, but a "Big Buffalo Hunt" in 1926 all but eliminated the animals. Then the starvation death of Antelope Island's last pronghorn in 1933 came as a missive from the overgrazed land. Livestock numbers were reduced to about four hundred cattle and eight thousand sheep, but degradation of this once prime rangeland continued.

Although unchecked overgrazing seems the result of venal men, I now realize that it came at a time when Americans battled for their very survival. By 1935, Utah and the rest of the nation struggled through a profound depression from which Franklin D. Roosevelt's New Deal economics had not fully relieved them. That same year, Italy marched into Ethiopia. Germany—shocked by defeat in the First World War—let its chancellor, Adolph Hitler, purge his political opponents and order compulsory military training. Like a leaden, July thunderstorm darkening the skies over Great Salt Lake, World War II loomed on the horizon.

Max Harward came to the island as a young boy with his parents in 1938. Max's father, Jabez Broadhead (J. B.) Harward, had landed the job of ranch foreman. It was a godsend for the family, providing room, board, a salary, and plenty of hard work at the tail end of the Great Depression. In 1942, J. B. was promoted to general foreman of Island Improvement Company ranching, a title he held until his death in 1950. Max grew up on the island, learning the benefits of close family, hard work, and fresh air, and he eventually earned a Ph.D. in environmental biology. In 1996, he published a small book detailing his experiences on Antelope Island.[4]

In *Where the Buffalo Roam: Life on Antelope Island,* Harward notes the proliferation of June grass, sage, stork's bill, and other plants indicative of overgrazed land. His background as a long-time rancher and his later training in biology give him a rounded perspective of the problems of ranching—the low stock prices, encroaching development, and land-grabbing faced by ranchers, as well as the overgrazing and range abuse that help to destroy their way of life.

"The Island Ranching Co. reduced the number of livestock, reseeded the ranges and in general, tried very hard to preserve what we had," he wrote (p. 79). Nonetheless, Harward said he is glad that the state acquired the island. "Perhaps it can now rest and recover from nearly 150 years of grazing" (p. 82).

In 1935, Max's oldest sister Ida and her husband Arnold Haskell gave birth to a baby girl that they named Wanda. After Max's father was promoted to general foreman, Arnold Haskell became the ranch foreman and moved to the island. Wanda grew up attending school in Payson and fondly remembers her twelve summers—from 1943 to 1955—on Antelope Island. After she married Duane C. Naylor, the couple spent several summers together on the island. Just after my first visit to Fielding Garr Ranch, I met Wanda Naylor and interviewed her at her home in Kaysville.

When the Haskells first moved to the island there was no running water at the ranch, she told me. Later, cold water was piped in for washing via a hydraulic ram pump, but the excellent spring water for drinking and cooking was hauled by hand. There was no electricity, so perishable food was dried, canned, or refrigerated in the springhouse.

The spring was a boggy, mosquito-infested area off limits to the children, she noted.

Raising sheep, horses, cattle, and pigs were dominant activities on the island when Wanda and Max were growing up there. Wild grasses and sedges along the lake shores were harvested as hay for the livestock, and wheat fields were planted north and south of the ranch. Sheep shearing happened in early May, when workers would do up to one hundred sheep each day. Wanda recalled that her uncle Orren Hale could shear a lamb in no time flat, but what she remembered most about the sheep-shearing barn was that scorpions and tarantulas lived there.

Wanda helped her mother cook for up to thirty-five hired hands living at the ranch during the summer. Each morning, they baked twenty-one loaves of bread for the hungry workmen. When Wanda and her sister cleared the table after a meal, if one of the men didn't clean off his own plate, he always tipped the girls a few cents.

Many of the ranch hands were drifters after seasonal labor. Some of them were alcoholics, sent to the "dry" island to work and recover, while others worked a month or two, then went to town to get drunk and blow some money. In his book, Max Harward recollects frequent trips to the mainland to bail men out of jail or pick them up off the streets. For one employee, the daunting prospect of life without liquor was too much; he sneaked off and drank a gallon of vanilla extract he found at the ranch, dying on the way to a Salt Lake City hospital.

Wanda's ranch chores were many and sometimes dangerous. Once, while feeding a big old sow, she noticed the pig lying on one of her piglets. Wanda poked the mother with a stick to move her. The agitated sow jumped up and crashed through the side of the pen, chasing the young girl into a corral. As Wanda scampered up onto the fence, the pig tried to crawl up after her. "I thought I was a goner!" she said. Another time, while fetching a sledgehammer from the back of a wagon during a thunderstorm, Wanda was hit by lightning and knocked unconscious.

From age eight to twenty, Wanda managed plenty of time to play and explore the island. She could drive a truck when she was ten years old and learned to ride a horse even earlier. There were a few fruitless, abandoned silver mines that she and her brother investigated, although they would never admit it to their parents. On hot, lazy afternoons, the children would ride to White Rock Bay and float out to the big, blanched rock that gave it that name. If it was mid-summer, they might stop for a cool dip in one of the springs, where they also picked mulberries in season. Flocks of geese fed in the wheat fields in the fall, and hunting them was how Wanda learned to shoot a rifle.

A serious illness kept Wanda out of school and living with her parents on the island through the winter of 1945. Rheumatism struck her idyllic existence as summer's play gave in to an icy, insufferable winter. Snow piled unusually deep at the ranch, she recalled, and her father labored to haul hay to the livestock.

Wanda's memories of an otherwise happy and adventurous childhood and adolescence center on the island. Her youth and the lake's geography isolated her from the realities of World War II, though the war's effects were being felt all around her. The prolific lake resort trade that sprang up over several decades was hampered as tires and gasoline were rationed and railroad lines were requisitioned for use by the government. The state's deflated economy, however, was bolstered as Geneva Steel, Hill Field (now Hill Air Force Base), and Ogden Naval Supply Depot were built to support the war effort. To this day, Utah's economy remains dependent on national defense and war-preparation dollars. During the 1990s, F16 Fighting Falcon jets scream from Hill Air Force Base and regularly fly over Antelope's ridge on their way to gunnery and bombing practice beyond the lake's western shore.

More than 1,800 Utahns were killed in World War II, but for a country girl with more than 23,000 acres of island terrain to explore, there was no war. The closest the conflict came was one night when a military plane on maneuvers passed low over the house before it crashed on the ridge near Molly's Nipple. Investigating authorities arrived quickly thereafter, but found no one alive at the burning plane and presumed the two pilots dead. Actually, they bailed out over the lake, swam to shore, and bivouacked. The next day, they found a road and hiked to the ranch, where they knocked on the door of an incredulous family. Wanda remembers a groundswell of joy as the airmen called their loved ones on the two-way ranch radio.

Years later with a family of her own, Wanda Naylor's most vivid recollections of childhood were of sunny, carefree days riding horses on Antelope Island. Her warm eyes sparkled when she tried to remember being so young that she *couldn't* ride a horse. When she was very small, she would climb the corral fence like a tree to reach the horse's head and bridle the animal, she told me. Then, after saddling the large beast, she climbed the fence a second time to mount the horse. She stayed in the saddle—sometimes riding for hours through fields and canyons—until she rode back to that fence.

"I didn't get off once I was on," she laughed. She was talking about her horse, but she might just as well have been referring to the island.

Notes

1. For more history on the Garrs, see A. M. Cutler, *Fielding Garr and His Family: Early Mormon Pioneers on Antelope Island.*
2. Morgan, *The Great Salt Lake*, p. 256.
3. Ibid., p. 331.
4. Max Harward's book chronicles his life as a boy and young man on the island. His narrative is engaging, informative, and spiced with his special humor.

Artist and Gunnison Island resident Alfred
Lambourne as he appeared later in life. Used
by permission, Utah State Historical Society,
all rights reserved.

The Thoreau of Gunnison Island

The suitability of the islands of the Great Salt Lake for bird and animal life is beyond question, for most of the smaller islands sustain rookeries where thousands of shore birds breed and rear their young, and the larger islands like Fremont and Antelope have supported flourishing herds of domestic livestock and communities of undomesticated rodents and carnivores as well as Antelope Island's well known bison population. The possibility of *human* habitation, though, even on the larger islands, is much less obvious, for their terrain appears arid, rocky, and exposed. Nevertheless, resourceful and adventuresome humans have found the islands not so forbidding after all, and there is evidence of at least sporadic human habitation on some of the islands from prehistoric times. Even during the historic period civilized people, who are supposedly much less adaptable to apparently stark natural conditions than their primitive ancestors, have found themselves drawn to the islands' serene beauty and solitude as a refuge from the sterile imperatives of modern urban life. Island dwellers like George Frary on Antelope, Charles Stoddard on Carrington, Judge U. J. Wenner and his family on Fremont, and Alfred Lambourne on Gunnison discovered that not only was life possible on the islands, but the good life as well. "Conflict makes news, and news makes history," the historian Dale Morgan observes, "yet men live rich and quiet lives outside the boiling currents of their times, and who shall say whether the thousand existences in quiet do not more nearly express the shape of human experience than the fiercely spotlighted existence that survives as history?"

Almost by definition, one who would choose to live in such a place must be an interesting individualist (or a misanthrope, which none of these people were), so the story of the island settlers inevitably is an interesting theme in the history of the lake. Of those, the story of the artist Alfred Lambourne, who spent fourteen months during the 1890s in almost total solitude on Gunnison Island with his dogs, his piano, his books, his paints, and his paintings, is one of the most colorful.

Born in England in 1850, Lambourne emigrated to America with his parents and lived for a time in St. Louis before setting out for Utah with an ox team in 1866.

Although his parents were Mormon converts and members of that church until death, Lambourne remained aloof. Only late in life did he make a religious profession, finding a home in creedless Unitarianism. In place of religious inspiration, his fourteen books are scattered with quotations gleaned from his broad reading in the romantic and Victorian authors of his own day, and the literature of classical antiquity. Instead of Mormonism, it was the cultural life of rapidly developing Salt Lake City that engaged his passion, as well as the city's close proximity to unspoiled nature to which he felt drawn by a Byronic romanticism.

Even as a youth, Lambourne displayed major artistic talent. While others toiled with the mundane aspects of ox-skinning on the overland trail, he filled his sketchbooks with drawings of the ever changing grand vistas of plains and mountains. As he entered Salt Lake City, one of the first buildings that struck his eye was the magnificent Greek revival architecture of the Salt Lake Theater, designed in 1862 under Brigham Young's direction by William H. Folsom. It was the cultural center of the Mormon Zion, an ideal showcase for both local talent and visiting luminaries, who performed everything from Shakespeare to lowbrow musical comedy. Lambourne's demonstrated skill at landscape art soon led to his employment as one of the theater's landscape painters, bringing him both fame and a handsome income.

Lambourne's love of nature led him first to the Wasatch Mountains, then to the great national parks of southern Utah, which he was among the first to paint. By the late 1880s, he had made friends with yachtsmen who plied the waters of the Great Salt Lake, and it was there that Lambourne found his hunger for contact with wild nature most fully satisfied. Particularly in David L. Davis's catamaran, the *Cambria*, Lambourne enjoyed many cruises on the lake in which they fully circumnavigated the great body of water from north to south and east to west, visiting each of the islands and shores. Lambourne and Davis had the full run of the lake in those days before the construction of the Lucin Cutoff in the early twentieth century, and the later railroad causeway that cuts modern boaters off from the northern part of the lake.

It was in that northwestern arm of the lake in the summer of 1895 that Lambourne visited Gunnison Island and immediately fell in love with its grand vistas and potential as an isolated hideaway for a solitary thinker and painter. Although he was at that time forty-five years old and a married man with four children, he conceived the idea of filing a claim to part of the island under the Homestead Act. That law required a five year continuous residency (though brief visits to the mainland were permissible), development of a water supply, construction of a house, and in general, evidence of intention of permanent habitation. There were other terms under the act whereby the homesteader could acquire title before the five-year residency was over by completing certain development requirements and purchasing the property at a reduced price, and that is what Lambourne planned to do. His intention was to live on the island for fourteen months while cultivating a vineyard, then buy out the claim.

Lambourne began his Gunnison Island residency in November 1895. The selection which follows, from his book *Our Inland Sea*, describes the humble but cozy stone house he built with the help of his friends, with its immense fireplace fed with driftwood logs, its furnishings (including even a piano), and his library. Some of his experiences and reflections on life on the island are included, and something on his competition with the "guano sifters," fertilizer merchants who intruded upon his solitude to harvest the island's plentiful bird manure.

In the end, Lambourne's homestead venture came to grief. When, after his fourteen months' residency, he returned to Salt Lake City to file his homestead application, he found that the fertilizer entrepreneurs had beaten him by securing classification of the island as a mineral reserve rather than an agricultural site. Lambourne's vineyard had not prospered, so he had little to offer in rebuttal, and he became a city dweller again until his death in 1926. He visited the island only once again, in 1908 after the Lucin Cutoff had drastically changed both the view from the island and its accessibility, and he departed without regrets in the realization that his island idyll would have been short-lived even if his homestead claim had succeeded.

As an evocation of nature's complex personality and the equally diverse responses of a human being experiencing that nature directly, *Our Inland Sea* compares favorably with classics like *Robinson Crusoe* or *Walden*, as well as most modern nature writings. What it lacks is the critical edge honed into those great classics by authors who used the device of man thrust into unspoiled nature as a vantage point from which to castigate civilization's dehumanizing tendencies, for Lambourne's eye is turned back toward life in the city less frequently, though he does emphasize the quiet solitude of his island homestead as a relief from the pressures of civilization.

Suggestions for further reading

Beginning in the 1890s Alfred Lambourne increasingly turned from the paintbrush to the pen as his favored means of expression. It was a fortunate choice, for he was as good a writer as artist. His many books may be found in any library with a strong section on Utah literature. The Great Salt Lake was the subject of several of those books, including *A Glimpse of the Great Salt Lake* (n.p., but evidently published by the Union Pacific Railroad as an advertising brochure); *Pictures of an Inland Sea* (Salt Lake City: Deseret News Publishers, 1902); and of course *Our Inland Sea*, from which the selection presented here is taken. An engaging biographical sketch of Lambourne is in Dale L. Morgan's *The Great Salt Lake*. The other lake dwellers are briefly dealt with in Morgan's book as well as in David E. Miller's *Great Salt Lake Past and Present* (Salt Lake City: Publishers Press, 1997). Miller edited the reminiscences of Kate Wenner's days on Fremont Island in "A Great Adventure on Great Salt Lake: A True Story by Kate Y. Noble," *Utah Historical Quarterly* 33 (summer 1965): 218–36.

Our Inland Sea:
The Story of a Homestead
Alfred Lambourne

I. Gunnison Island in Winter.

GHOSTLY, wrapped in its shroud of snow, my island stands white above the blackness of unfreezing waters.

What have I done? Although I had lived these days by anticipation, no sooner had the sails of the departing yacht vanished below the watery horizon, and left me with my thoughts alone, than I realized at once, and with a strange sinking of the heart, how more intense, indeed, how deeper than all imagining, is the wildness and desolation of the savage poem around me.

Clearly I have committed an error! In winter this comfortless place might be some lonely spot of the Arctics. Often on still nights the snow around my dwelling is illumined by the boreal light. Through the hours, at times of tempest, is heard the grinding of boulders, as they are lifted by the heavy brine and then let fall again to pound great holes in the outlying strata, or the roar of the breakers as they hurl briny foam far up the face of the Northern Cliff.

"A man," says Alger, "may keep by himself because he is either a knave or a fool," and Bacon, in writing "Of Friendship," has put in italics this quoted sentence from Aristotle, "*Whosoever is delighted in solitude is either a wild beast or a god.*" "Now I am not a knave, and there are good reasons, I hope, why I should not consider myself a fool. Neither am I a wild beast, nor may I arrogate unto myself the belief that I am a god. Yet for the time being, I have chosen to be alone.

"What a man has in himself," writes Schopenhauer, "is the chief element in his happiness." This, however, the sage makes haste to define as— "apart from health and beauty—the power to observe and commune." "The proper study of mankind is man." We must allow that dictum. Nature is secondary. The alleys in the wood or forest of Windsor or Arden were but backgrounds in the mind of Shakespeare— stage-settings for the actors in the human drama.

From Alfred Lambourne, *Our Inland Sea: The Story of a Homestead* (Salt Lake City: Deseret News Publishers, 1909), 19–27, 34–9, 43–9, 119–28, 231–38.

Here is the digest of the thought I follow: *"If the seeking of isolation proceed not out of a mere love of solitude, but out of a love and desire to sequester a man's self for a higher conversation, then, indeed,"* writes Veralum, *"one may feel the god-like within us."* And in this benefit I hope to share. Saying unto my soul: *From out the wildness of this desert solitude, I desire to extract the beautiful and the good, and to be taught, too, by the voices that dwell therein, I plead NOT GUILTY to the charges of moroseness, and also to those equal follies against which the master last quoted has warned us—"a too great admiration of antiquity and a love of novelty."*

Is this the North Cape? Dreary is the land and dreary is the sea. My hut, massive though small, its low, thick walls, built of rough, untrimmed slabs of stone, taken from the cliff by which they stand, its roof, earth-covered, its chimney starting from the ground, and almost as big as the hut itself—might be that of some hardy Lofoten fisherman. By the distant islands, that on winter days appear like mighty bergs, by the tongues of land, resembling snow-covered floes, by the brine, more like a plain of ice than water, and by the midnight moon, with a lonely storm-ring round it, the northern feeling is further supplied. I rise late. Oil and drift-wood are not so plentiful that one should use unseemly hours for their burning. Slowly, O slowly, the hours creep by!

More trying are the silent, implacable days than are the times of uproar. I am made to confess that "Time is the most terrible, the most discouraging, the most unconquerable of all obstacles." For exercise, when the weather is clear, I hack at the tough, old roots of the Sarcobatus bushes, or, again, I grub among the roots of the antique sage. Already the thoughts of social intercourse grow strangely remote. For Christmas Carol, for New Year's Greeting, I hear only the shrill, sudden call of the gull, or the dry, harsh croak of the passing raven. In the stillness, the bitter cold frets the surface of winddrift and level, in the lengthened night, the storm-clouds hang low, or slowly big snowflakes fall out of the sky.

Sometimes the vault appears black. That is, I mean, as we sometimes see it on the mountain tops, as it is on certain noon-days when the sky is cloudless, and the near snow-fields rise against it. Black, as it really is, with a thin, scumbling of atmospheric cobalt. Then the island snow takes on the spectrum hues. The angles, flutings, waves, and mounds of wind-carved drifts catch the white light, and resolves it back into its component parts. Sometimes the distant mountain heights smoke in the dawn like tired horses, or the sun rises like a disk of copper, ruddy through the spindrift brine. There are times when, by the light of a half-wasted morning moon, the new island snow appears of a wondrous lilac, or, on the jutting shoulder of The Northern Cliff, it is touched with a paly gold. On cloudy days, during the midwinter thaw, they shrink in the breath of Chinook and grow leadenhued, or, as some storm rolls back to the mountain summits, they seem bathed in a mixture of fire and blood, or, later, as the light of sunset fades along the cliff-top, they become of that cold and ghastly green, the sight of which makes one shudder.

Sometimes, indeed, a feeling of awe is upon me. Often, as in the Norse Mythology, the sun comes up, all faint and wan, sick nigh unto death it seems, and languidly looks o'er the world of white. What thoughts are mine! In the dim, uncertain, and mysterious twilight, when all surrounding objects expand to the sight, I half expect to see, looking upon me from out the western desert, some angry deity of the Indian's forgotten pantheon; or, as my thoughts revert again to the olden world, to see, springing from that Nifelheim in the north, the gaunt, gray form of the Fenris Wolf, and to behold his fiery eyes as he passes onward to his terrible feast, when the Asas, Odin and Thor, and the lesser ones, too, shall become his prey in Rangnarok, the last, weird twilight of the Northern gods.

On the mountains, today, a wind-storm is raging. So fierce up there is the gale, one could scarcely keep his footing. The great snow-banners are whirled from the crests, and grand and solemn, I know, is the sound, when the strong northern winds smite upon those harps, the pines, and when, along the mountain sides, the loosened snow is caught from the forest branches and sent madly up by crag and ravine. But see! How the wind can revel on these waters, too! Behold how they sweep over the long reaches of unbroken brine; how they pick up the foam-dust from the waves of the Inland Sea, and, mixing it with snow-dust from the island cliffs, whirl it around and around! Yesterday the sun-dogs gleamed over the desert hills—but now! Did Dante, as he walked with Virgil amid the shades of the Inferno, witness more fierce commotion? As fiercely as were the spirits of the carnal malefactors "hurtled" by the infernal hurricane, the sleet and snow, the foam and spray, are whirled by these winter winds. As fiercely they are hurled back again and again from the face of the northern walls.

Tonight the wind roars. What care I? The louder the rumble in the spacious chimney, the brighter will burn my drift-wood fire. One must ,oppose his resources of mind to the blind anger of nature, and trust in the end to prevail. What to me, in this comfortable room, if the wind grows furious in its strength, and beats and clamors at window and door? No sail, I know, is out on this winter sea. What if the waves boom by the Northern Cliff, if the wind veer again and drive the foam far up the sands of the little bay? There will be no need to hang out the signal lamp. The Inland Sea and the bleak, inhospitable season, will keep both my island and myself in unbroken ostracism. The sleet and the hail may lash against the window-panes, but it is only such as might have been foreseen. There must pass many and many a day ere the yacht will put forth. So stir the embers of the smoldering fire; let the red sparks fly, remember that thy food is safe-cached, and that the hut is firm-planted and strong as the gale.

II. Books and a Raven

***

For a Homesteader, these are peculiar, almost incongruous surroundings. The hut is rough on the outside but is bright and cozy within. In self-banishment, this follower of Adam's trade has kept his household gods around him. In this room there is that to both please the eye and to feed the mind. Austere thought is forced upon one by the austerity of these rigid scenes. Sackcloth and ashes rules not in the hut, yet no place is this island for a Castle of Indolence. The great German was right. One needs a focal point of contrast. Amid the barrenness of this desert wild, the soul has need of a gentler touch. Were not the influence of nature corrected, the tendency here would be toward harshness of mind. One needs the complex—food for the desires put into the blood and brain by thousands of years of civilization.

A bed—a bunk, I should say; shelving; a table; a rack—formed from the skull of a mountain sheep, with curved and massive horns;—a bin, and the means for cooking, these are part of my goods. On the other hand is my easel. In its dark mahogany case, the piano stands. There is a statuette by Danneker—Ariadne—and a Navajo blanket of quaint design keeps from dust and grime my allotment of books. On the wall there is a plate after Titian—Sacred and Profane Love—a portrait with autograph attached, of a famous modern beauty, and over all, "a chain-dropp'd lamp" sheds a mellow ray.

Hermits the world over must live to a purpose. Thoreau, at Walden Pond, tried a social experiment. Forbes watched the flow of an alpine, glacier; from mistrust of mankind, Timon of Athens dwelt in a cave; for love, Petrarch sought the quiet of Vacluse, and to fast and pray, St. Godric lived in the Fens, and St. Berach on Orkney Isle. No gold lies buried in these sands, at some future day no bell or crozier will be found near my hut. But I have my purpose, I know my place on the soil.

To be of use, to redeem the barren waste, to make sure in the future my daily breads: these are among my desires. Possession always gives a certain amount of contented pride, and over my desert acreage, whereon the vine may yet grow, I look as fondly as does ever the family inheritor of broad estates. I come here not to practice renunciation, but to begin a life anew.

Lo, the demi-lion rampant, the ship's rudder, of which one was proud—

"That *Bar*, this *bend*, that FESS, this Cheveron."

Even among these democratic rocks, though he were Boone, one may proudly recall the land of his birth. With newness of action, one need not forget the ancestors' thought. Why regret the Hall, the Manor, the Hamlet, that Titheing, that parish, that chepping, the bridge, the stream, the vale, whose name one bears? Why regret the estate in Essex or Berkshire? Or the lands by the Cornish Sea? There are other holdings than those at Donnington, or those at the Saxon Camp, on the downs by White-Horse Hill.

"Rather use than fame," Merlin's motto will serve. If coat-of-arms the Homesteader's children should need, then let it be this: On a field azure, an island, or; in the middle chief, the gull, argent; on the base, a pruning-hook, sable, and, as tresson—flory and counter-flory—the grape, vert and gules.

But with new thought let the transplanted branch do honor to the ancestral tree. In the veins of the Homesteader's children may flow the blood of Knights and Vikings.

Alfred Lambourne's sketch of his cabin on Gunnison Island as it appeared in *Our Inland Sea.*

I turn to my books. What a comfort they are in a place like this. Here one may still have his friends around him. There they stand, the glorious company; silent, it is true, but ever ready to teach or amuse. In life, some of those who stand there so calmly, were unknown to each other, or they lived, perhaps, as enemies. But now they are friendly enough. There are "the true peace society—heretic and orthodox." Side by side, they keep truce in their work of ministry. Some of those great ones wrought in solitude; some achieved their work amid the plaudits of an admiring world. Others, though they may have known it not, nor guessed what lay in the course of time—centuries, customs, evolutions, holding them apart—seem destined now to be linked as twin stars, or to shine in clusters, as Dante has grouped them in the world of shades.

Who can tell where the written words shall be read? A singular place, this lonely and desolate rock, in which to pursue the thoughts of the men who once trod the classic vales of Hellas, or to follow the lines of those who graced the court of Queen Bess! Within reach of my hand are the best productions of the human mind—the work of the individual condensing the thought of the race. Of what august times they make one a citizen! I have to but stretch forth my arm to annihilate space and to roll back the ages. Those of the Book, Æschylus, Euripides, Musæus, Æsop, the blind old man of Scios, and the voices of the other immortals, I hear.

On the table lie a few *de lux.* There are the Decameron; the Lyrics—Beranger—the Kelevala, Herrick's Hesperides and Noble Numbers, the Siegfried's Saga of Tegner, and Walt Whitman's Leaves of Grass.

And among them at the moment, like pilgrims who have lost their way, Architecture of the Heavens, by Nichol, and Lives of the most eminent Painters and Sculptors of the Order of St. Dominic.

Yes, I turn to my books. There, for my mood, are Cæsar and Kepler, Gladstone, Webster and Paine. There are Don Quixote and the story of Faust. From Odyssey and Iliad, from the Roman Ænead, I can turn to Shakespeare and the Mediæval Song. When wearied by the great Veralum, there is the bright Montaine. There are Josephus and Augustine, Rabelais and Swift. When too much moved by the thought of Omar, the passion of Poe, there are the laughing moralities of Ingoldsby Legends. But, as with Barham, I am best pleased in the end with the solemn tones of the "As I Laye—A Thinkynge," so at last, with Hood, I leave the mirthful or caustic satire, to follow the bitter pathos of "The Bridge of Sighs," or the self-probing stanzas of "The Haunted House."

* * *

III. Wild and Windy March

Presto! The island is changed. This might be the work of an enchanter's wand. For many days mankind and I have been strangers, but, lo! society has come to my door. This rock once so desert has become a hive. The gloomy season is ended. I am lost in news of the world. Though welcome at this *ultima Thule is* the turn of the year, more welcome indeed are these human voices.

There is a plenitude of shipping. Never before has this port seen the like. In addition to, the yacht, which arrived this noon-day with a wet deck and a tired crew, a fifty-foot schooner rides out in the bay. Another craft, too, is anchored close by and to complete the surprise, besides these strange boats, a little sloop has parted her cable and lies half-wrecked on the island sands. Dragged up the beach, alongside of my *Hope,* is her broken yawl.

Suddenly this island has become important. Short the time, since for the asking alone, the place had been mine. Now, as if it had become an actual beehive, a monster and animated emblem of the state, Science, Commerce, Agriculture, Education, *"Ars Militans,"* I might add, are contending for it. Uncared for these thousands of years, no sooner would I call this Home, than there comes this change. So many the changes, that I scarcely have time to note them.

Here is the case: the corporation, with its millions of dollars, the private company, the individual, the state, each makes a claim. There have been Government surveys, railroad section surveys, local company and private surveys. There have been issued a Government Grant, the Desert Entry, the Homestead Entry, and the Mineral Claim. A coveted prize this island must certainly be.

Never before have such diverse accents of tongue fallen on these gray, old stones. America, the United Kingdom, Scandinavia, the Land of the Teuton—these send their number. Here we see that sudden progress that roots up primeval trees to make place for the school-house, or even a gallery of art. Commerce, while I terrace my slopes and watch my vines, will sweep with its besom these nested rocks. Out yonder the workman, busy with pick and shovel, with tripod and line, all proclaim a desire. The question is—for what?

From this time on, my hermitage will be of a temperate kind. The new-comers—the permanent ones—and I, will live on most friendly terms. Not a hundred rods from my own, the sifters have made for themselves a home. It is long and narrow, and is built of rounded slabs. Within this cabin, the piled-up sacks of flour, the bags of beans, the boxes of candles, the flitches of bacon that hang from the beams, the pots, pans and kettles, as well as the many aids and implements of labor, indicate that the men will make a protracted stay.

In more ways than one, I am pleased with my new companions. Mutual esteem and confidence, or a dislike amounting even to animosity, one or the other, must be our attitude. Among a number of men thus thrown together, there is hardly room for indifference. Here the Divine Right of Kings, as it were, and the Vox populi, are, in a way, united. We are here to fight this wild nature or to be assisted by it. We are here to derive the benefit given by co-operation, or assert our individuality. We may gather strength from such of the past as we can assimilate to our time and environments and can reject the other. We hope to rise superior to the mistakes of a bygone age, and to assert ourselves as men. "The arts which flourish," says Bacon, "when virtue is in the ascendant, are military; when virtue is in state, are liberal, and when virtue is in decline are voluptuous." Judged by these obvious truths—of the past at least—the island now presents a paradox. Here we have a state, a commonwealth, or whatever we may choose to call it, in which are exhibited the three stages of virtue, not separate and alone, but working in concert. Those latest comers, both the sifters and I, although we come here with widely divergent thought, are alike in this—we represent the time.

Human beings are but figures to the landscape painter. Often from that stand-point—as a sketcher—I look at these men. Man was needed to give human interest to these waves and stones, and now he is here. This island, as it existed in solitude, was complete. It was in its way a perfect thing. Now that former completeness is broken and gone, and there is that process going forward by which a new one will take its place. The figures, the sifters, accentuate these island scenes. That is, they do so through suggestion. They are as much in harmony, too, with these bird-haunted rocks, as are the samphire-gatherers to the old world cliffs. Emphasis they give to these scenes, such as the landscape painter loves.

Take the present moment: The storm of the Vernal Equinox which tore the sloop from her fastenings and still strews the beach with huge globes of foam, has partially cleared. Three of the sifters are engaged in the task of passing guano-dust through sieves, and putting it into sacks, whilst others dig among the ancient birddeposits. Leaning against the wild March wind, their rustic clothing flapping in as wild disorder, and a cloud of brown, snuff-like mineral hovering around them, or being carried by the fitful gusts, far beyond the sieves, the men make extremely picturesque figures. One of the sifters will dwell here permanently, and I expect to put him into many a sketch. He is a Hercules in strength and of brawny stature. He moves from place to place all unconscious, as of course uncaring, of his pictorial value to me. In spite of the season, and the kind of day, his head is bared to sun and wind; his feet are encased in coarse, brown sacking, and, as I write, he is, with that exception, naked. He is carrying a plank to two of his fellow laborers, and these latter men are at work on the recently stranded boat. The man's yellow hair, his ruddy flesh-tints, his athletic form, focus a natural picture in which the broken sloop, the big, black schooner, the white hull of the yacht, the blue waters of the Inland Sea, the warm, gray tones of the island cliffs, with the reeling clouds above them, are the splendid components. Only to realize the effects of this momentary scene upon the beholder, he who describes it, must not omit the sounds. Besides the wild noise of the wind and waves, there is the clattering of hammers made by the workmen over-hauling the wreck. Devil makes himself heard, the dogs yelp, and these united noises bring shrill, harsh, cries from the island birds. These are answered by a loud and indignant cackle from the sifters' score and two of newly-brought and astonished barnyard fowls.

* * *

X. Contents of a Cairn.

A HUMAN skull! Where, then, shall one tread, and not on the dust of man? These arid hills are but cemeteries. In these surrounding lands—Idaho, Wyoming, Colorado—the graveyards are found. Jurassic reptiles, mailed creatures of terrible power, lie there embedded. The feet of the shepherd, the hunter's and the cowboy's pony, have stumbled against great bones. The huge remains formed a feature in the desert landscape.* Around my horizons are lands that have been submerged in water, that have been earthquake shaken, and over which glaciers have crept in the by-gone days; lands that were once the bottom of ancient seas; that cover the remains of forests below forests, and beneath whose soils there are secrets hidden.

In Utah cairns and mounds have been lately opened. Remains of the dead have been found therein. To the south of Strong's Knob, within yonder mass of black limestone crags, bones, cave-entombed, have been brought to light. So ancient were they, those bones, that ere the smoke of the miner's blast had cleared away, they crumbled to dust on the cavern floor. Science will never know to what kind of creatures those bones belong, nor will it ever be able, perhaps, to ascribe an age to this skull.

---

* This is a literal fact. In Wyoming the "finds" of fossils were so made. This was in the dry-washes, among those frayed, crumbled, honey-combed rocks near the Green River and Church Buttes country. In Colorado, the herdsmen had built the foundation of a shelter cabin with the great round vertebra of the disjointed monsters.

Eastward I see a dim range of hills. Along the flanks of those Wasatch spurs, there was once a battle fought. In the distant past, the dead from that aboriginal strife were buried in the conglomerate caves. Here, also, are to be found similar cave-like openings; but the relic came not from either of these. It was found by my man. On the south slope of the Northern Cliff, under a ledge, and at the end of my highest vineyard trellis, with his mattock, the Drudge unearthed the skull.

Devil has strutted over that spot, I know not how many times. But his sharp, prying eyes did not see. Under that very ledge the raven had made a cache, and within a few inches of the dome of the skull. His curiosity is not small, so his instinct must have been at fault. Otherwise, surely, he would have found the prize.

How was the skull placed there? Bonneville's beating waves, rounded and polished the ledges of Strong's Knob, long after those creatures, whatever they were, had been entombed in the hollow rock. So long had those bones been in that place, that the living creatures themselves, existed and died ere Lake Bonneville fell or was. And the skull? Whatever its age, whatever was the remote period of time when its owner was a living man, I hardly expect, now, the bones to crumble. By some preservative process it has been made as hard as ivory, and as softly browned toned as a piece of old ivory, too.

From out those sockets, the eyes, that once were there, looked last—on what? Was that man's last glimpse of earth this surrounding scene? Did the Inland Sea look then, as it does this day? Did the mountains stand so? To the skull I may put the scornful command, "Say what ancestors were thine!" But no answer shall I get. No voice will come from the silent past. Little indeed could the owner of that piece of mortality have conceived of the coming race! Much less was his power to look forward to our day, than for us to look backward to his. That man was a fighter. Low, indeed, and flat is that cranium arch. It is broad at the base, and the frontal area is small and it slopes, but large and thrust forward are the supra-orbital ridges.

What has my island known? Has it, too, been a battlefield? In the days gone by, it may have been a secret stronghold—a place of retreat. I have been led to believe that the native Indians have kept away from these islands, as they did from the mountain tops; but this skull may have belonged to an older race, perhaps to a paleolithic man.

It may be that the man was contemporary with those whose mummies were found in the room beneath the Payson Mound. His relatives may have planted the grain or have gathered the kernels which were found in that old stone box. If so, then this disinterred warrior would recognize the wheat—that wheat I mean, a kind hitherto unknown and which is now grown in many of these arid valleys from that ancient seed. Perhaps he was contemporary with the making of that earth-fort among the Oquirrh foothills. He may have aided in or directed the building of that pile, that mound of oolithic sand, which stands a mystery on yonder plain. There are some strange speculations aroused by the sight of this skull.

Did that human being, its owner, poison his arrow tips? If so, perhaps he took the poison from the forerunner of my unwelcome guest. He may have sent such another creature with a message to his god, as do the desert Indians to this very day. In life, did the man look on any such creature as those whose bones still project from the soil?

It may be that this skull is as old as are the remains of that long extinct race, those people, which are found in the sepulchral chambers high among the red rocks of the San Juan—the cliffdwellers in the southern part of the State.

Here, then, was the secret—the island, although it has probably been a fort, a battleground, has also been a place of supulcher.

As we dug amid the earth and stones, how surprised were we!

A short distance from the spot where the skull was found, we exhumed more bones. There were a broken scapula, a clavicle, parts of a humurus, fragments of a spinal column, but no more. And, unlike the skull, these bones were in an advanced stage of decay.

Just below them we came upon the top of a slab, that covered the tomb.

There, as it had reposed through the ages, was a skeleton complete. For an infinite time it must have lain in that narrow home. A weapon of stone—a huge, round battleax—lay by his side. Also there were many arrow-heads—of agate and jagged obsidian—also there were many round agates, which I supposed to be beads. Once the owner was a man of note.

About the remains in the cave-dwellings of the San Juan County, archaeologists differ. What is their age? Those air-dried mummies may be of any age. Five thousand years, twenty-five thousand, the estimate ranges from one great gulf of time to that of another. And this memento mori, this island tomb? I believe it to be as ancient as any. Very much in the arrangements of the stones, the slab which formed the cover, those of the sides and floor, this tomb resembles the most ancient ones found beneath the barrows or cromlechs of the old world. These remains and this resting-place may be older than the skeletons and the tombs which contain them, which are found in the lowest excavations below Nippur. It is indeed, then, an old proprietor who makes manifest his prior claim to my home.

There was, I think, at one time, an entire skeleton, also, in the earth above the tomb. If so, it must have occupied an oblique position, feet downward toward the slab. What caused the lower parts to crumble? And why did they disintegrate so much more rapidly than did the upper? Why did we not find either ulna or radius; a rib-bone, nor anything of the skeleton as low as the pelvis? And why was this—the skull removed so far from the rest of the bones? But most of all, what relationship of events, if any, existed between the two sets of remains? Just now I am likely to receive no answer.

What have we found? Of a spear-head, similar to this one of mine, Russell has the following remarks: "The fossils from the La Hontan basin (within my sight) that will be considered by both geologists and archaeologists as of the greatest interest, is a spear-head of human workmanship. It was associated in such a manner with the bones of an elephant, or mastodon, as to leave no doubts as to their having been buried at approximately the same time."

Among my curios, there lies this trio of relics: a spear-head, within a fraction of four inches in length, and made of flint; a circular piece of stone—one and three-quarters inches in diameter, one half inch in thickness, and with a shallow central perforation on either side; and a most singular elongated piece of circular stone, two and one-quarter inches in length; both of the last-named being made of the same material—a red gray stone, and highly polished. The flint came from a Wasatch canon, where it was found in a bank of the stream. The other pieces are from the hillside in the same vicinity, and are certainly prehistoric. The remains we have just found, and the face ornaments, as I believe the pieces of stone to be, impress me as being equally old.

During the excavations in Arizona, among the burying-places of the ancient people of the petrified forests, the evidence of old time tragedies were not to be mistaken. Among the orderly burials, were found a heap of calcined and broken bones. The marks of the implements used in cracking the bones were still traceable. It was, says one who describes the "find," the first material proof of cannibalism among the North American Indians. What do we see? Perhaps we have unearthed, in that skull and those upper bones, the evidence of some dark, mysterious rite, some cruel superstition of the long ago.

The discoveries of the last few days have given me questions to ponder.

* * *

XXI. A Last Drift-Wood Fire.

My friends are here; my household goods are piled aboard the yacht. The boats of the sifters departed ere this one arrived; the Gunnison for a time, will be given over to solitude again.

These 36,806,400 seconds; 613,440 minutes; 10,224 hours; 426 days, 60 6–7 weeks, these 14 months; or, to bring the calculation to a finer division, and one of nature's own, 42,940,800, one-sixtieth part of those heart-beats that go to make up man's allotment of three score years and ten—these since my roof-tree was placed. Now my homesteading is done and I am free to depart. So many heart-beats while I lay asleep, so many passed in action, so many in reverie; so many given to this and so many to that, and the time has slipped away. Can it be that fourteen months have elapsed already. Not so long ago it seems as yesterday since the yacht, that now waits to bear me from hence, entered with its unusual cargo, this desert port. Short now seems the time since we embarked with our boat's sails set wing to wing; since we passed one by one the terminal peaks of the Desert Range, and opened out the bays and straits, as slowly we came from the south, and so, by the jutting rocks and black head of Strong's Knob, came at last to these island shores, and I began my now completed vigil.

One of the strange things in life is this—there is no experience one would care to have missed, I mean when once that experience is passed and gone. So it is with this *one—I should dislike to* part *with it now.* What I had done, had I not performed this act, who can tell? This is not an arc to determine my circle and yet—

Under certain conditions, a place becomes a part of us; we own it. We absorb it into our lives. It cannot be taken from us. It is ours, and without title or deed. We are associated with a certain spot of earth, we have our lives shaped by it, or, if that be not the case, we stamp the place with our individuality.

THIS PLACE IS MINE.

Here I make an inventory of property and benefits accrued to me, since the day of my House-warming:

A desert island, that is an island which is a desert now, but if water shall come from below these rocks, one whereon I may yet eat the grape from the vine, if not the fig from the tree.

My Hut, a place of refuge, a rock of strength.

A step toward an understanding of the noble Art of Horticulture: "Do men gather grapes of thorns, or figs of thistles?"

A proof undeniable of the fact that it is always the unexpected that happens. An opening of the eyes to the truth that surrender is sometimes a victory. A seeing, too, that while we stand fumbling at the door which is locked, another may stand wide open.

To see plainly, to know by actual climbing, that mountain which lies between the moment of resolve and the moment of achievement.

To comprehend the astonishing fact which Aurelius has pointed out: that in self-examination, one is not only himself, both plaintiff and defendant, but judge and jury as well. Also the attorney for the prosecution, and for the defense.

To see the true relationship between the stern justice of the Mosaic Law, and the greater power of the Golden Rule.

That although Charity *begins* at Home, it should not *end* there.

An understanding of the verse of Ecclesiastes:

"Wherefore I perceive that there is nothing better than that a man should rejoice in his own works, for that is his portion: For who shall see what shall come after him?"

Also the verse of Revelations:

"Because thou sayest, I am rich, and increased with goods, and have need of nothing; and knowest not that thou art wretched and miserable, and poor and blind and naked."

Therefore—

To realize that the motive should be in the deed and not the event.

To learn the wisdom that lies in Contemplation and the forsaking of Works.

And the majesty that lies in the simple words:

"Man shall not live by bread alone, but by every word that proceedeth out of the mouth of God."

And besides these benefits—

A bronzed countenance, and a gain in physical strength and well-being.

A house-cleaning of the brain; a discarding of useless furniture therein; together with a sweeping out of cob-webbed corners, and a general admittance of wholesome light and air.

Lastly—

The virtue of possessing my soul in patience, and the memory of four hundred, twenty-six days, the effect of which, mentally, I cannot just at present weigh, but which I believe will be beneficial

Not a poor investment of time, surely, nor one likely to cause me regret.

Tonight we illumined the island with a driftwood fire. An enormous pile we made; the trunks and branches of the Sacrobatus, the pine and the fir, storm-torn from their native rocks, and by the course of many waters, brought to these alien shores.

Music?—is not the charm of out-door music everywhere the same? "Music at Nightfall," touches all hearts alike. Savage and civilized nations are alike in this. Around their watch-fires chant the American Indian, the native Australian, the Botocudor of Brazil. At twilight the Laplander sings his reindeer song, the Arab touches the tambor, the Russian utters the Song of the Steppe. Then the Arcadian blows upon the pan-pipes, then is heard the Yodle of the Tyrolean mountaineer. On the waves of Mediterranean, the fjords of Norway, the fisherman beguiles his time with song. Then the ferrymen on some Highland Loch, on famed Killarney, keeps time with voice and oar-beat. Probably the ancient Briton, paddling his coracle of wicker, was as susceptible to the influence of out-door music, as were the Venetians in their gondolas, or as is the dusky steersman of today, gliding in the dahabeeh up or down old Nile.

A grotesque spectacle we must have made as we sang beneath the stars. Brothers to the savage and the minstrel, we drew the continents together and made the races one. As filled with animal life and roused emotions, we sent a melody across the waste, we heard an obligato of wind and sea. My own and the sifter's hut, the naked peak, and the curving sands; the breaking waves; the hull; the masts; the rigging of the waiting yacht; the trellised slopes; the wings of passing sea-gulls; each rock and bush, each ridge and well-known crag, were reddened in the night-fire's glow.

V

PLAYING, RACING, AND BOATING

The original Saltair pavilion. Used by permission, Utah State Historical Society, all rights reserved.

A Pleasure Palace on the Great Salt Lake

"In Xanadu did Kubla Khan a stately pleasure dome decree." The pleasure dome described in the following selection was not decreed by the Kubla Khan of Samuel Taylor Coleridge's famous poem, but rather by the First Presidency of the Mormon Church. Nor was its purpose anything like the hedonistic excesses Coleridge had in mind, but rather quite the opposite: to provide a wholesome recreational alternative to such excesses as were reputedly occurring in other Utah resorts. Though the church eventually got out of the pleasure palace business, Saltair became one of Utah's most celebrated facilities for recreation, both wholesome and otherwise, for residents and tourists alike for many decades until fire, wind, and the capricious levels of the Great Salt Lake itself conspired with other emerging forms of recreation to render the place unprofitable. Yet even today, admittedly in a vastly diminished and less lavish incarnation, a Saltair continues to exist and to draw tourists and concertgoers.

As the first chapter (not included here) in the McCormicks' book tells, Saltair was not the first recreational facility on the Great Salt Lake, for the wide beaches (at low lake levels), the warm water with the famous buoyancy created by its high salinity, and the relatively close proximity of the lake to Salt Lake City had attracted weekend fun seekers since the time of Brigham Young. At various times in the late nineteenth and early twentieth centuries, resorts of different degrees of elaborateness had existed at Lake Side, Lake Park, and Lake Shore on Farmington Bay, at Syracuse Resort east of the north end of Antelope Island, and at Black Rock, Garfield, and Lake Point on the southeastern shore. Various steamboats and sailboats provided excursions on the lake, while several short railroad lines provided convenient access from the cities along the Wasatch Front.

The selection reprinted here tells the story of Saltair's first two incarnations, from 1893 to the great fire of 1925, and the rebuilt resort from 1926 to 1970, when another fire destroyed it. The second Saltair, which was architecturally even more ornate and impressive than the first, went into decline during the Great Depression of the 1930s (part of the "ominous clouds" that "hung upon the horizon" at the conclusion of this selection) and again during the late 1950s, especially after a huge windstorm destroyed the famous roller coaster. During the 1960s, promoter Sheldon Brewster led a desperate movement to "SAVE SALTAIR," but receding lake waters and the popularity of movies and other recreation doomed the old resort. When it burned down in 1970, it was only a shell—a pathetic reminder of a bygone day. In 1981 a group of partners purchased an old airplane hangar from Hill Air Force Base and hired an architect to design a facade reminiscent of, but far less lavish than, the old Saltairs, and opened Saltair III in 1982 on a site about one mile south of the original facility. While the old Saltairs had suffered from receding lake levels that forced such expedients as a rail line to transport bathers to the water, and a dike creating an artificial pond around the buildings, the new Saltair was temporarily drowned in the unprecedented high waters of the 1980s. Eventually it reopened, however, and at this writing has just enjoyed an attractive new paint job and features tourist shops and concerts. Together with Utah State Park facilities at the Great Salt Lake marina to the south and at Willard Bay and Antelope Island to the north, its existence is a testimonial to the tenacious recreational appeal of Utah's inland sea.

Suggestions for further reading

The book from which this selection is taken can be highly recommended as both a recent and reliable history of the various Saltairs. In addition, it is a visual delight, with generous selections of photographs, postcards, tickets, and other memorabilia giving a firsthand feel for the delights of dancing, dining, and swimming at the resort. Its bibliographic essay (pp. 103–5) is also a reliable guide to further reading, of which John D. C. Gadd's "Saltair: Great Salt Lake's Most Famous Resort," *Utah Historical Quarterly* 36 (summer 1967): 198–221; and Wallace Stegner's reminiscence, "Xanadu by the Salt Flats," recently reprinted in Stegner, *Marking the Sparrow's Fall: The Making of the American West* (New York: Henry Holt and Co., 1998), 38–45, are particularly recommended.

SALTAIR
Nancy D McCormick and
John S. McCormick

A MOORISH PALACE IN ZION

On January 14, 1893, the *Deseret News* announced construction of a new resort on the shores of the Great Salt Lake to be called "Saltair." Though the pleasure of swimming in the Great Salt Lake was "world renown," the paper said, never before had there been a resort as magnificent as Saltair was destined to be, and word of it would spread "wherever newspapers are read or words transmitted by lightning."[1]

The owner of the new resort was the Saltair Beach Company, and its largest stockholder was the Mormon church, which held half of the company's 2500 shares. Mormon church leaders and prominent Mormon businessmen held the other shares and were company officers. George Q. Cannon, first counselor to Mormon president Wilford Woodruff and the most influential Mormon leader from the time of Brigham Young's death in 1877 until his own in 1901, was president. Joseph F. Smith, Woodruff's second counselor, was vice-president, while Isaac A. Clayton was secretary-treasurer, and his brother, Nephi W. Clayton, was general manager. Both Claytons were officers in the Brigham Young Trust Company and were involved with other Mormon businessmen in the Inland Salt Company, which operated on the southern shore of the Great Salt Lake near the new resort. The board of directors consisted of President Woodruff; L. John Nuttall, Woodruff's private secretary; James Jack, church treasurer; and George Henry Snell, who owned the Utah Soap Company and was a founder of the Inland Salt Company.

Mormon church officials organized the Saltair Beach Company in June 1891. Shortly afterwards they acquired from Mormon businessman Matthew White 744 acres of beach property. White lived in a small house on the property and had earlier planned an elaborate commercial development there that would have included

From Nancy D. McCormick and John S. McCormick, *Saltair* (Salt Lake City: University of Utah Press, 1993), 19–24, 29–65 a residential section of about six hundred houses; a pier with bathing and boating facilities; a clubhouse and casino to be open year-round; a hotel; and a "sanitarium." Soon after church officials bought the property from White they announced that they also meant to build a residential section near Saltair. "The construction of cottages on shore about a mile from the pavilion will soon commence," Nephi W. Clayton said. "It is our intention to build a little town there just as soon as we can. More than that some of us intend to make our home there nine months in the year, and we expect to find residence there healthful and agreeable in many ways."[2] Why those plans were never carried out is not clear.

In September 1891, two months after the establishment of the beach company, the same Mormon leaders and Matthew White and Abraham H. Cannon, a Mormon apostle and son of George Q. Cannon, formed the Saltair Railway Company to build a railroad from Salt Lake City to Saltair. The company was soon renamed the Salt Lake and Los Angeles Railway Company, reflecting an intention to eventually extend the line all the way to California.

The Mormon church established Saltair in an effort to provide a wholesome place of recreation under church control for Mormons, particularly families and young people. For the previous ten years or so church officials had been concerned about "pleasure resorts" and their harmful influence on members of the Mormon church, especially young men and women. In 1883, for example, the church-owned *Deseret News* warned parents that "to allow children of either sex of tender years to go unprotected to pleasure resorts where all classes mingle indiscriminately is criminal." Resorts, it continued, exposed Mormon children "to the villainous arts of practiced voluptuaries" and "degraded character destroyers" who sought to "overthrow" the Mormon church.[3] Church officials were particularly distressed about the resort at Garfield, which non-Mormons owned and operated. According to apostle Abraham H. Cannon, Saltair was intended for "our people" so that "they can have a place to go and bathe, if they so desire, without being mixed up with the rough element which frequents Garfield."[4]

The Mormon church intended as well that Saltair be the "Coney Island of the West," and it was advertised as that before its completion and for many years afterward. By the late nineteenth century commercial amusement parks were increasingly popular in the United States. Made possible by rapidly growing urban populations, and spurred by the development of electric trolley systems, they reached their height in the first two decades of the twentieth century when other forms of mass entertainment such as movies, dance halls, and spectator sports also expanded rapidly. By 1919 there were an estimated 1500 amusement parks across the country. The best-known and the most elaborate was New York's Coney Island. A quiet seaside resort in the years before the Civil War, it had become "the top banana of amusement parks" by the turn of the century and was attracting more than ten million visitors annually.[5] Coney Island's carnival atmosphere became the model for all other parks. Its popular entertainments included swimming, dancing, music,

variety shows, catchpenny games, shooting galleries, stunts, food vendors, mechanical rides of all kinds, and circus sideshows.[6]

The Mormon church's effort to establish a "Coney Island" on the Great Salt Lake
was part of a larger movement toward accommodation with American society that
had begun in the early 1890s. Throughout the nineteenth century most Americans
viewed the Mormon church with suspicion because of its commitment to polygamy,
theocracy, and communalism. In the late 1890s church authorities made a conscious
decision to bring the church into the mainstream of American life, a commitment
they maintained and intensified in the twentieth century. Their decision followed
the federal government's passage in the 1880s of two pieces of legislation: the
Edmunds Act of 1882, which outlawed the practice of plural marriage, denied the
right to vote or hold public office to people who either practiced polygamy or
believed in it, and placed much of the government of Utah Territory in the hands of
a five-person presidential commission; and the Edmunds-Tucker Act of 1887, under
which Mormon church property was made liable to confiscation and the church
itself was disincorporated. In the face of these pressures, Mormon President Wilford
Woodruff issued a "Manifesto" in 1890 proclaiming an end to the performance of
plural marriages. A year later the church dissolved its People's Party and divided the
Mormon population between the Democratic and Republican parties. In the next
few years it gave up its efforts to establish a self-sufficient cooperative economy. It
discontinued the promotion of cooperative enterprises, sold most church-owned
businesses to private individuals, operated those businesses it did not sell as income-
producing ventures rather than as shared community enterprises, and began a
process of participation in and accommodation to the national economy.[7]

Mormon officials saw Saltair as a way of demonstrating Utah's new sense of
national identity. When church leaders and others talked about the importance of
Saltair as an "advertising agent" spreading Utah's "name and fame," they meant
both that Utah was a place of modern recreational opportunities and that it was no
longer a strange, isolated land of curious people and practices.

Mormon leaders wanted to have the best of both worlds—Saltair was to be both
a typical American amusement park and a place that provided a safe and wholesome environment for Mormon patrons. In less than a decade, though, the first
goal had clearly triumphed over the second. Nevertheless, initially Saltair signified
the Mormon church's intention at the turn of the century to join the world and at
the same time minimize its influences and avoid its excesses.

Construction of the railroad to Saltair began in May 1892 and was completed in
September, and a few days later church officials announced that architect Richard
K. A. Kletting's drawings for the new Saltair resort had been approved.

Kletting was one of Utah's most important architects from the late nineteenth
century until his death in 1943. Born in Germany in 1858, he worked on several
major European projects including the Sacré Coeur at Montmartre before settling
in Utah in 1883. Today he is best known as the architect of the Utah State Capitol

Building, completed in 1916, but he also designed the State Mental Hospital at Provo, and the original Salt Palace, the *Deseret News* Building, the McIntyre Building, and the New York Hotel in Salt Lake City.[8]

Construction on Saltair began in January 1893. It was built on a platform over the water held up by twenty-five-hundred ten-foot pilings of native pine, each ten inches in diameter and placed twelve feet apart. Driving the pilings into the lake bottom, which was composed of an initial foot of loose sand and then extremely dense sodium sulphate, was the most difficult part of construction. After experimenting with several methods, workers hit upon the idea of forcing steam through pipes to temporarily dissolve the lake bottom at points where posts were to be sunk. After a few hours the sodium hardened again, and the posts were virtually immovable. Construction proceeded rapidly and was completed by the end of May.

When finished, Saltair was an architectural wonder. Wings on either side of the grand central pavilion extended crescentlike into the lake. The entire complex measured more than 1,100 feet from tip to tip. The pavilion itself was about 250 by 140 feet and rose more than 100 feet skyward. Three hundred tons of steel girders supported its large, shallow dome, which was similar in size and shape to the Mormon church's Tabernacle on Salt Lake City's Temple Square. At each corner were six-sided domes. Farther out bud-shaped onion domes graced two and three levels of arched and ornate trelliswork. Tall mosquelike towers in the middle of each wing and at each end added to Saltair's exotic atmosphere. A huge central archway announced the entrance to the pavilion. Thousands of lights studded the complex, and at night the building became a dazzling spectacle. Its Moorish design reflected an architectural style popular in the last half of the nineteenth century. Earlier Kletting had designed airy arches framed by patterned screens for the pavilion at Lake Park, and his sketchbook was filled with Near Eastern drawings. Saltair sprang from the same oriental inspiration.[9]

Picnic and luncheon areas, a restaurant, snack bars, and restrooms were on the first floor of the pavilion. The grand staircases rose to "a large and magnificent dancing hall, dressing rooms, clubrooms, and ladies' and gents' parlors" on the second level. The wings were two stories high and about thirty feet wide. On the first levels were walkways with rows of bathhouses—300 "double compartments" on either side. At frequent intervals stairs led down to the water so that, the *Deseret News* said, bathers could go into the lake "unseen by the mighty crowd of spectators and avoid the light remarks and ridicule of the vulgar and unrefined if clad in the too often abbreviated and unsightly bathing suit."[10] The second levels of the wings were promenades where strollers could watch bathers "sporting in the Brine" or view the magnificent sunsets for which the Great Salt Lake was famous. A plaza in front of the pavilion accommodated concessions, the midway, and crowds arriving and departing from the railroad terminal.

In designing Saltair, Kletting's intention—and the intention of architects of amusement parks across the country—was to create an "architecture of escape and pleasure." It was not enough that an amusement park have a variety of individual

Entrance to the original Saltair. Used by permission, Utah State Historical Society, all rights reserved.

attractions. It was necessary to create an environment that sustained a festive spirit. Buildings of American amusement parks were typically grand, but not solemn, and they featured a profusion of arches, towers, curves, bright colors, rich ornament, and an abundance of detail, all designed to stimulate visitors, even overwhelm them, temporarily transporting them out of their everyday world into another realm.[11] As the *Deseret News* suggested at Saltair's opening, it had just that effect: "The magnificent pavilion, rising, Venice-like, out of the waves in stupendous and graceful beauty, deepened in its semi-Moorish architectural lines, the suspicion that what one saw was not firm structural reality but rather a delightful oriental dream."

Saltair opened to the public on Memorial Day 1893 and was officially dedicated on June 8. An estimated 10,000 people were there, with many arriving on special trains from Logan, Ogden, Provo, and other outlying areas. The main speaker at the ceremonies was Territorial Governor Caleb W. West. He repeated the long-standing myth, still prevalent today, that the Salt Lake Valley was a barren desert when Mormon settlers arrived in 1847, but said that it had since been transformed into a place of "fertility and productiveness, progress and prosperity." In his view the construction of Saltair was a further step in that direction, a proof of what "manly vigor and determination" could do. More important, Saltair's construction meant that people in the rest of the country, particularly Easterners, who commonly charged Utah with being "out of civilization," would no longer be able to say that. "Magnificent Saltair," he said, proved otherwise.[12]

THE GOLDEN YEARS 1893–1924

> *"Carl McMillan and Laura Ford, charged with having committed fornica-*
> *tion at Saltair on last Monday evening, were given a preliminary examina-*
> *tion yesterday before Commissioner Sommer. . . . The officers stated that the*
> *couple, though not discovered in the act charged, were found under suspi-*
> *cious circumstances on the north pier. The defendants, when put on the*
> *stand, contended that their relations with each other on the occasion were*
> *not criminal, but merely those of proper lovers."*
>
> Salt Lake Tribune, *August 31, 1895.*

Saltair was extremely popular from the first. People flocked there, making Saltair their summer outing place. Sometimes they made a day of it. They rode the train out early in the morning, bringing picnic lunches and dinners, changes of clothing and swimming paraphernalia; then, weary but exhilarated after a day of swimming, dancing, picnicking and rides, they climbed aboard the midnight train back to Salt Lake. Often, because Saltair was so close and the journey there so convenient, Salt Lake residents went for only a couple of hours, frequently after work for a short swim and a walk around the pavilion. Total attendance the first season was a little more than 100,000 (the population of Salt Lake City at the time was less than 50,000). By 1906 attendance had more than doubled to 250,000. In 1915 it was 300,000 and in 1919 reached 450,000. The largest crowds each year came on holidays—Memorial Day, the Fourth of July, the Twenty-fourth of July (the local pioneer day, celebrating the founding of the Mormon settlement), and Labor Day. During the first season daily attendance averaged 1000 people, but on the Fourth of July, 11,000 people came. According to the *Salt Lake Tribune*, "If anybody was absent from Saltair yesterday he wasn't missed. . . . At meal hours the lunch floor got the Surge when a 'howling mass' of humanity, that sounded like a roaring cataract, gathered around the tables, bars, and counters." The dance floor, the *Tribune* continued, "was thronged, and the dancing room was markedly curtailed by the pressure from the crowds in the circumference." So many people wanted to go swimming that by noon every available suit had been rented. "As the suits became exhausted only the large and small sizes were left, and they were eagerly grabbed by the besiegers of the suit booths. Men attired in boys' pants that pressed like elastic and showed plenty of the thighs; thin women wearing no. 42 suits into which a dozen pillows might easily have been stowed to fill surplus space; one man of some 250 pounds creating unbounded laughter by parading down the ladies' pier in white underclothing, or something that looked strikingly like it."[13]

Saltair's appeal was its liberating atmosphere. It provided a temporary escape from everyday routine and convention, a distinctive environment that encouraged behavior not appropriate elsewhere.[14] And the railroad fare to Saltair was always low. Originally fifty cents for a round-trip ride, which included admission to the resort, itself, it was in reach of most people, and company officials deliberately kept fares down to increase patronage. Lagoon, in contrast, adopted a different policy. In 1903 it raised its train fare to fifty cents each way, double that of Saltair's, and the next year announced that it had no intention of lowering it. "It has given us only the best class of patronage," owner Simon Bamberger said, "and even though the crowds have not been as large as last year, they have been of the class we want and are really more profitable to us."[15]

The train ride to Saltair was not only inexpensive, it was also fun. Wallace Stegner remembered riding in the open excursion cars, watching the approaching city lights and the mountains behind them, feeling the night wind and experiencing the salt flat smells. "Necking couples sat on the steps eyed with disapproval by matrons in charge of large families. Boys worked their way fore and aft along the cars, risking their necks and interruptings the neckers. Whole cars sometimes burst spontaneously into song. If we were lucky, a moon would have floated free of the Wasatch and would be washing the broad valley with silver. Sometimes we came in like an old-fashioned hayride, the little kids asleep, the lovers quiet, the singers all sung out."[16]

The Mormon church regularly endorsed Saltair and counseled its members to patronize it. In June 1902, following Saltair's decision not to sell "intoxicating drinks" that season, the church's Young Men's Mutual Improvement Association (YMMIA) and its Young Ladies' Mutual Improvement Association (YWMIA) issued a joint statement urging "our membership, in all the stakes of Zion, to patronize Saltair with their pleasure excursions, in preference to other resorts where intoxicants are sold."[17] The *Deseret News* did the same. In an editorial the same year it said that Mormons had a "duty to themselves, to their families, and to the church" to patronize Saltair.[18]

There was another factor contributing to Saltair's popularity—the moderation of the extreme division that had existed between Mormons and non-Mormons in the nineteenth century. A basic feature of life in Utah, almost from the moment of its founding in 1847, had been the division of the population into two opposing groups, Mormons and non-Mormons, those inside the Kingdom and those outside it. By the late nineteenth century it was perhaps Utah's most striking feature. Prior to Woodruff's Manifesto, there were no national political parties in Utah—only the church People's Party and the "anti-church" Liberal Party. Two school systems existed, a predominantly Mormon public school system and a mainly non-Mormon private one. Fraternal and commerical organizations did not cross religious lines; Mormons and non-Mormons sometimes even celebrated national holidays like the Fourth of July separately. By the early twentieth century hostility, though it still existed and still affected almost every public issue, had moderated considerably. Saltair clearly benefitted from the new spirit of toleration, attracting Mormons and non-Mormons alike; it also promoted it. Groups holding outings there in 1893, for example, included the Mormon Tabernacle Choir, the Salt Lake Eleventh LDS Ward, the Salt Lake YMMIA, the International Order of Odd Fellows, the Ancient Order of United Workmen, the Railway Switchmen's Union, and the National Real Estate Exchange.

When it opened Saltair's main attractions were swimming and dancing. Swimming at Saltair was an event—people loved bobbing around like a cork and having their pictures taken with their feet out of the water. On ordinary days hundreds of people, and on weekends and special occasions thousands, swam at Saltair.

People also loved to dance. Saltair's dance floor was advertised as the largest in the world, and it may have been, though Coney Island's Dreamland also advertised its ballroom as the world's largest. On special occasions two bands played, one at each end of the floor, one picking up when the other stopped so that dancing was continuous. Couples customarily danced the first and last dances with each other and changed partners in between. Those who forgot and danced cheek-to-cheek were asked to leave the floor. Once they banned the Charleston "for fear all those people coming down hard on the downbeat would shake the whole pavilion into the lake."[19] In an effort to attract even more dancers Saltair offered free dancing lessons. In 1914 they were given every Saturday afternoon. According to instructor "Professor" William Woodward, "Before the summer is over, more people in Salt Lake will be dancing the new and modern steps than in any western city."[20] The dances he taught included the maxixe, the tango, the hesitation waltz, and the crown prince waltz. Dancing was so popular that at the turn of the century Saltair began holding regular preseason and postseason dances, usually twice weekly for the two months before the resort opened for the summer and the two months after it closed. Christian Christensen's Orchestra played regularly from the time Saltair opened until the early twentieth century. Harry A. Montgomery followed him, and from 1917 until 1924 R. Owen Sweeten's "Jazziferous Band" played.

During its first season Saltair had a variety of food and refreshment stands, rowboats, an excursion boat christened the *Talula* (which made a three-mile trip around the lake), something called a "Cosmerama," and a merry-go-round, a standard feature of American amusement parks. It also had a bar that served beer and liquor operated by Charles Auer, who owned the Occidental Saloon in Salt Lake City. Like many of the concessionaires at Saltair, Auer did not own the bar, but leased it from the Saltair Beach Company and paid back a percentage of his gross receipts.

Company officials originally intended that liquor not be sold at Saltair, but changed their minds before the resort opened. They also changed their minds about not opening on Sunday, even though only a year earlier the *Deseret News* had criticized the owners of the Garfield resort for lowering Sunday rates in an effort to attract Sunday business.[21] Thus, from the time Saltair opened, as Leonard J. Arrington points out, the Mormon church found itself "in the embarrassing position of owning a resort which served liquor and having in the interests of profit to work up patronage for it."[22]

Throughout the 1890s Saltair's bar was periodically closed when Mormon church groups held outings there. In January 1901, following a recommendation of the church's First Presidency and Council of the Twelve Apostles, Saltair's management decided not to sell liquor at the resort during the next season but to allow people to bring their own liquor with them if they chose. They subsequently decided to adopt the same policy for the 1902 and then the 1903 season. In 1904 company officials leased the entire resort to Mormon businessman Jeremiah Langford who announced that under his management a bar would once again operate at Saltair. Two years later, in May 1906, the church sold Saltair to a group of private individuals, including Langford, Charles W. Nibley, Joseph Nelson, and Nephi W. Clayton, because, according to the *Deseret News,* it had long been caught on the horns of a dilemma. Allowing liquor to be sold increasingly attracted "disreputable, rowdy" people, but closing the bar simply meant that people brought their own liquor, and more liquor was consumed than when the bar operated. The only solution, the *News* said, was for the church to get out of the resort business.

Saltair offered more than swimming and dancing, and its other attractions became increasingly popular. New attractions were added nearly every year. For the 1894 season billiard rooms and gambling devices, referred to as "nickel-in-the-slot machines," were brought in. The next year saw the addition of a number of midway games, including Bagatelle, which was played with a cue and balls on an oblong table that had cups or cups and arches at one end, and a "Nigger Babies" ball game, in which a person tried to knock down weighted dolls with a thrown baseball. "Come on, now. Knock 'em down," the barker cried. "Four balls for a dime. A great big pack of gum with every doll down." In 1899 free silent, or "flickering," movies were shown every night.

One of the biggest early attractions was the roller coaster, also known as the giant racer, and sometimes advertised at Saltair as The Ride Through the Clouds. In 1884 Coney Island installed the first roller coaster in the United States. By the early twentieth century it was a fixture in amusement parks across the country, and each new one tried to outdo the others in height, length, speed, and thrills. Saltair had one by at least 1914 and in 1919 advertised it as "the largest roller coaster ever erected in Utah and one of the largest in the West."[23]

Another popular attraction was Ye Olde Mill. More familiar by the 1930s as the Tunnel of Love, couples rode boats through dark, quiet waterways, occasionally getting a glimpse of a scene, but mostly staying in the dark. A large water wheel located at the entrance of the tunnel kept the water flowing.

Saltair's regular attractions for the 1915 season included automatic baseball, motor boats, six bowling alleys, the roller coaster, Ye Olde Mill, a fish pond, a ferris wheel, a moccasin wheel, a Gee Whiz (known today as the funhouse), laughing parlors, a merry-go-round, Ping-Pong parlors, spot-the-spots, a pennant wheel, several pool halls, a photograph gallery, a penny arcade, a silk hose wheel, and a shooting gallery.[24]

In 1916 a roller skating rink and a surfboard ride were added. Paddle boats, captive airplanes, and a bike-go-round (a device similar to a merry-go-round with bicycles on a circular platform that revolved at "motordome speed") were added in 1919, and in 1924 a Dinty Moore Walk Thru, a simulated coal mine, dodg'ems, the Swanee River, and the African Dip joined the bill.

Amusement parks had difficulty maintaining their patrons' interest and constantly had to provide new, fresh entertainments. "Novelty, that's the answer," said Sam Gumpertz, long-time manager of Coney Island's Dreamland.[25] In addition to periodically adding to its regular attractions, Saltair every year featured special ones. In 1893 it had several fireworks displays, "the greatest balloon ascension ever seen in the interior West," and a "parachute dive from the clouds by Professor Harmer and his Dog." The following year "Miss Annie May Abbott, the little electric magnet," appeared for a two-week engagement. She performed a number of tricks, the most impressive of which, according to the *Salt Lake Tribune,* involved "transmitting her powers to a child in the audience so that the strongest man can't lift her or him."[26] That year also Salt Lake's YMCA put on a Grand Gymnastic Exhibition featuring routines on the horizontal, parallel, and spring bars, Indian club swinging, dumbbell exercises, a grand bicycle drill, and pyramid building.[27] The 1895 season included a Grand Masked Ball and Carnival, Professor Wilbert's Slide for Life, and Eleason, the Wizard. During Jubilee Week in 1897 Saltair celebrated the fiftieth anniversary of the Mormon settlement of the Salt Lake valley with seven days of special attractions: an Indian brass band; high divers names Phylon and Speedy, who dived 125 feet into three feet of water; the Three Houstons, swinging trapeze performers; a musical pageant on the lake at sunset entitled the Wedding of the Waters; a Ghost Dance; a Wild West Show; a balloon ascension; fireworks displays; and Hal Clawson, a hypnotist.[28]

For a month in 1899 Professor Macarter's African Baboon, Dog, and Monkey Comedians appeared nightly. It advertised itself as "a remarkable exhibition of animal sagacity," and featured "a Baboon Clown, a Baboon groom, a Baboon Bicyclist, a skirt-dancing dog, an acrobatic dog, and a dog that dances the Hoochie Coochie." It also included what the *Salt Lake Tribune* termed "a sensational effect: dogs enacting the rescue of a child from a burning cottage." The company concluded its performance with a group of acting dogs that presented "an Emotional Dog Drama entitled 'A Widow's Devotion.'"[29]

Touring vaudeville companies often performed at Saltair. During the summer of 1903, a troupe from the Keith Vaudeville circuit appeared featuring Raymond and Webb, "American Dialect Comedians"; Miss Nettie Walsh, "Soubrette"; Kelly and Clayton, "Knockabout Wonders"; Miss Mamie Walsh, "Song and Dance Artist"; John W. Mack, "banjo player"; and the King Sisters, a "sketch team."[30]

During the summer of 1911 Saltair had a particularly large number of special attractions. The first was a Wild West Show with "Bucking Bronchos, Wild Steers, the West's cleverest riders." A Spanish Festival followed the Wild West Show highlighted by bullfights under the direction, ironically, of "noted French matador, Felix Robert, who will bring a full troupe of toreadors, bulls, matadors, picadors, and barrerillos."

In 1911 Saltair also maintained an Alligator Farm with more than "fifty alligators of various sizes, ranging from 2 feet to 10 feet in length." Other attractions during the year included an Egyptian Hall of Palace of Illusions"; a "Wild Man of Borneo in full eruption"; a gigantic Gorilla"; and Siamese twins who on one occasion "got into a big fight . . . and came near to breaking the eternal bonds that hold them together."[31]

The last week of the 1915 season was Carnival Week with women and children admitted free. "Cake walks" were held and Slivers' Clown Band played regularly. Thursday was Charlie Chaplin Day. The Excella Duo, "a couple of rare comedy ragtime singers and coon shouters . . . famous throughout the country in vaudeville circles as a high class entertainment," sang. Montgomery's Band and the Hand Opera Company performed *Faust,* the third act of *Rigoletto,* and the fourth act of *Il Trovatore.*[32]

In the spring of 1917 the United States entered World War I. Unlike much of the rest of the country, where United States' involvement initially met with widespread opposition, Utahns strongly supported the war effort. That summer one of the most popular special attractions at Saltair was a patriotic Musical Spectacular entitled the Call to Arms featuring the singing of "The Flag Without Stain" and a mock sea battle on the Great Salt Lake. According to the *Deseret News,* "To bring out the thrillingly patriotic theme more vividly and illustrate graphically just what war means, there will be a naval sham battle fought on the lake, just west of the pavilion. More than 100 soldiers from Ft. Douglas will participate in the battle, which will be made realistic in the extreme. It will consist of an attack on an enemy ship, which is being constructed just west of the pavilion. The soldiers will embark in the smaller vessels, armed with rifles and cannon, and will surround the big ship and bombard it. The culmination of the spectacle will be an explosion of the attacked vessel which sets it on fire and consumes it."[33]

During the summer of 1918 Saltair staged a new event to draw people, a widely advertised "public wedding" performed in the roller skating rink in which "one entire company of soldiers from Fort Douglas" and "thirty pretty girls" participated.[34] Three years later it staged a "Heap Big Indian Wedding," with "prominent officials participating and society women as bridesmaids."[35]

By the early 1920s Saltair had reached the peak of its popularity. The great Moorish building with its domes and latticework rose magnificently out of the lake almost a mile from the shore. The air was clean and dry, and the breezes from the lake cooled the rays of the summer sun and fanned the dancers at night. Scenery and water were everywhere—fantastic views of mountains and lake, pastel blues and pinkish tones of sun and sunset. Bands, railroad whistles, hucksters, honky-tonk, and the roar of the roller coaster all created marvellous sights and sounds far removed from the routine of everyday life. At night its mystical qualities intensified. Thousands of lights outlined the buildings, and orchestra music played for couples who strolled along the promenade and danced under the twinkling lights. "An enchanted playground," Wallace Stegner called it. "I remember it like lost Eden."[36]

SECOND CHANCE, 1925–1930

Sunset at Saltair

Far to the East, beyond the busy city,
Darkening shadows fill the canyons with
*   suggestions of despair;*
Above, the snowcapped peaks gleam white
*   and cold,*
Like a soulless woman's face.
I turn, a path of golden glory gleams across
*   the lake,*
Leading to some enchanted cloudland, where the
*   Goddess of the West,*
Enwrapt in slumber, dreams of love.
And blushes in her dream
And then the flow transforms itself to dusk. The
*   golden glory faces into the gloom.*
The last faint ray is lost in gathering clouds.
A gull on silent wings sweeps slowly by.
Chill night descends.
In silence I watch the cold and passionless stars.

J. B. Miller, in Salt Lake Tribune,
August 6, 1911.

Early in the spring of 1925, as workmen readied Saltair for another record-breaking season, a fire broke out in the Ali Baba Cave concession under the grandstand seats of the Hippodrome. At 2:25 P.M. on April 22, an employee smelled smoke and discovered a four-foot wall of flames. He beat it out with his hands and hat and reduced the fire to embers before running for help. In the two minutes he was gone, the wind fanned the smoldering coals into a blaze. Workmen hurried to put it out and quickly sounded the alarm bell. A telephone call was made to Salt Lake for help, but the raging fire spread into the Hippodrome. For two hours Saltair employees, workers, concessionaires, and volunteers from the Inland Crystal Salt Company struggled to save the pavilion. Firefighters from Salt Lake were on the scene in record time. Some arrived on specially built flatcars kept in readiness to speed fire engines to the resort, and the Sugar House fire station came with the only truck that could pump salt water.

About 4 P.M. the winds shifted away from the resort, and it looked for a time as if the famed pavilion could be saved. Maddeningly, minutes later the wind swerved and drove the fire back toward the pavilion, fanning the flames into an inferno. As the *Tribune* reported, "tongues of the flame and smoke leaped fifty to one hundred feet [and] shot out and licked up the timbers and beams of the great structure as though they were cardboard."[37] Heat and smoke drove the firefighters away, and the fire burned out of control. Within ten minutes the pavilion was a mass of twisted iron and charred beams.

Flames could be seen as far away as Salt Lake City, and films of the fire were shown that night in local movie houses even as the fire still burned. It took twenty-six hours for firemen to put out every ember. When it was all over, only the bathing pier, beach office, merry-go-round, pilings, and giant racer were still standing. Everything else was destroyed. Insurance covered only $150,000 of the estimated $500,000 in damages.

The day after the fire workmen began removing blackened timbers that littered the concrete base and waters around Saltair, and on April 25, Saltair manager, Stringham A. Stevens, announced plans to rebuilt the resort. It was not known when construction would begin, he said, but company owners had decided to build on the same site and to reuse Richard Kletting's original plans for sentimental and historical reasons. Stevens set May 30 for the opening and promised that the new bathing suits the company had ordered would still be arriving to replace "the cumbersome old style bathing suits in favor of modern ones."[38]

Saltair, however, did not open on time. Mormon church owners began to have second thoughts about their involvement in Saltair and saw this as an opportune time to divest themselves of the resort. On May 8, church President Heber J. Grant offered Saltair to Salt Lake City Mayor C. Clarence Neslen as a gift to the city. According to Mormon officials, "this resort is of such community importance it should be under control of the municipality."[39]

The city commission took three weeks to decide whether they wanted Saltair and considered various ways to finance the venture, including popular subscription and bond elections. For city officials the decision hinged on economics. Even if Saltair were given free to the city, Salt Lake would have had to assume a $267,000 debt for the electric railroad and spend an estimated $300,000 rebuilding. In 1924 Saltair had earned a profit of seven percent over maintenance, amounting to $75,000, but $25,000 of it had gone to pay off the bond, and the rest was used to pay back interest and reduce the debt principal. Since electrification of the railroad in 1917 Saltair had not paid dividends. Committees evaluating the proposal announced on May 19 that the railroad, which was worth $632,000, had only scrap value "unless it is maintained at a high degree of efficiency" for resort traffic and that "without the resort the railroad property would rapidly become valueless"; the property was reported to be worth $90,000.[40]

Utah Governor George Dern and businessman James H. Waters each offered to donate $20,000 to help the city finance Saltair in exchange for a share in the profits. Others, however, urged the City not to accept ownership of the resort. The Board of Governors of the Chamber of Commerce said that Saltair should be privately owned and sent a committee to urge church leaders not to give it to the city. "The resort should be reconstructed, possibly even along a more pretentious scale," the committee said, "but every effort should be made to conduct it as a private enterprise."[41]

To add to the difficulty Lagoon ran a half-page *Tribune* ad May 27 announcing its grand opening where people would find a "bigger, prettier, finer, more thrilling Lagoon." Lagoon owners sensed an opportunity to step in and attract summertime crowds looking for a resort and were not wasting any part of the season waiting to see what happened to Saltair.

City officials took a hard look at the economics, competition from Lagoon, community feelings, and business pressures and on May 28, 1925, declined the Mormon church's offer. "We feel that you are imbued with the highest of motives in offering this valuable property to the municipality," city commissioners wrote to church President Heber J. Grant, "and that your only motives were to insure the re-establishment of this indispensable institution and its management along high moral grounds . . . [but] given the limited funds of the city this year, we do not know how we could possibly replace the pavilion and other necessary buildings." After the city declined President Grant announced that swimming would resume immediately at Saltair. "The railroads are bringing a lot of tourists here," he said, "and most of them want a dip in the lake."[42]

Preparations furiously began to ready the resort for a shortened summer season, and on June 29, Stringham Stevens announced that Saltair would open July 1, two and a half months after the fire. "Bathing would be available with complete accommodations in the way of dressing rooms, new suits, and towels," he said, as well as a luncheon bowery overlooking the lake, refreshment concessions, a merry-go-round, a giant racer, and trains on half-hour schedules. A high fence and potted palms hid the burned sections from view. A temporary maple dance floor big enough to hold five to six hundred people (only a fraction of the number previously served), had been built, and the new "California style" of paying for one dance at a time and then clearing the floor was introduced because it was so much smaller.[43]

Saltair began the 1925 season with a lick and a promise. Owners let people know that their patronage would determine the resort's future. They urged tourists and Utahns to come and enjoy the new bathing facilities, the beauties of the lake and the sunsets and "to bear in mind the recent heavy loss" and temporary facilities. With a straightforward appeal advertisements read: "Do you want Saltair? Say it with your patronage now!"[44]

Throughout the summer Saltair launched a heavy advertising campaign to recapture the crowds that were finding their way to Lagoon and other places. An advertising war between Saltair and Lagoon ensued.[45] Lagoon's July 4 *Tribune* ad encouraged people to spend the glorious fourth at Lagoon where there were fireworks, matinee and evening dances, swimming, boating, concessions, picnicking, and 3,000 parking spaces. Lagoon, advertisements read, was "The ideal outing place, the coolest place in Utah, the fun place for all." Saltair responded with an appeal to sentimentality and loyalty and tried to convince people it was the "greatest amusement value in the world." On July 24, a large Saltair ad encouraged people to

Come where the fun is July 24!
Come out with the, family.
Spend the day where it is cool, where the crowds
    are, where the fun is.
Plenty of room for the kiddies to romp and scores
    of amusements, a picnic bowery on the waterfront,
    evening dances 2 for 50 , free matinee dances.
Dance on the new maple floor to the toe-tingling
    melodies of the Oscar C. Martin Ambassadors.

A continuous stream of gimmicks brought people to Saltair that summer. There were carnivals, costume dances, three dances for five cents, dances all night for twenty-five cents, ladies' free nights and childrens' free days, free hats, and free confetti. It advertised the swimming, the water, the fun, the temperature, the crowds, and, most of all, the place "where you'll feel like a million dollars." The advertising apparently paid off because the next winter when no one was thinking of summer sun and fun, a *Tribune* headline, on January 27, 1926, announced that a "New Saltair Will Rise on Old Site at Lake." According to the paper, owners of the Salt Lake, Garfield and Western Railroad, Ashby Snow, David P. Howells, and Willard T. Cannon, had purchased Saltair from the Mormon church and planned to build a new $350,000 pavilion. Snow said he decided to buy the resort and rebuild with the help of his partners because he felt depressed over the public loss every time he visited the site. From their "intimate knowledge" of Saltair's history, the partners knew the resort had never paid a dividend. They hoped to change that, but even if its "previous investment history is repeated," they would feel repaid "in the saving of this unique amusement place to the community."

Raymond J. Ashton and Raymond L. Evans were the architects of the new Saltair pavilion. They were prominent Utah architects from the 1920s to the 1960s and designed a number of important buildings, including fieldhouses at the University of Utah and Utah State University, the Mountain States Telephone Building in Salt Lake City, and the Utah State Penitentiary at the Point-of-the-Mountain.

Saltair's new owners wanted to rebuild it along the Moorish lines of the old Kletting pavilion. "It seems to embody the very spirit of the place. No other design would fit so well," Snow said. At the same time they wanted it to be bigger and better—one hundred feet longer and fifteen feet wider, more spacious, more elaborate and well appointed, and lacking in the incongruities that marred the old building. Manager Stringham visited amusement parks from California to Florida. The new building, he said, would be the nearest to fireproof of any similar structure, with the most modern equipment, the most sanitary methods of refuse disposal, and restrooms of the most modern type.

The owners broadcast revival of the resort throughout the nation when the new pavilion was finished. Dignitaries and newspaper people from across the state

Entrance to the restored Saltair, late 1920's. Used by permission, Utah State Historical Society, all rights reserved.

toured it on May 28, 1926, and responded with enthusiasm and praise. Saltair was "a playground which crowns the glory of the lake and magnificence of the mountains," the *Tribune* reported after the tour. "Out of every bad comes good, and Saltair is larger, stronger, and more beautiful then ever."

The pavilion, finished in stucco and painted in a variety of vivid Mediterranean colors and intricate patterns, was predominantly and orange-pink, a unique color, the *Tribune* wrote, that "glints back brightest rays of the sun." One thousand white dressing rooms, covered with green lattice work for shade, flanked the pavilion. Thousands of lights outlined the new building as they had the old, making a wonderful picture, a fantasy playground. A huge dance floor was the center; to the north was a cafe, and to the south were restrooms and lounges. Fare and admission prices were twenty-five cents. Concessions and rides included the fun house, heydey, Missouri mule, giant racer, children's playground, and shooting gallery.

Opening day, May 29, 1926, brought huge crowds and headlines reading "New Saltair Is Appreciated." Many visitors had to park at the salt works and walk two miles to the resort; the trains were so jampacked that they were off schedule. Stringham Stevens responded to the enthusiastic crowds. "If the success of the opening continues with the season," he said, "there will be no doubt of the wisdom of restoring Saltair."[46] Newspaper editorials and advertisements by Salt Lake businessmen heralded the owners as "men of vision, ability, and public spirit," who were determined that "the resort would be conducted on a high plane of morality and wholesomeness."[47]

The restored Saltair, late 1920s, showing bathers (top) and the roller coaster (bottom foreground).

Saltair had emerged from a devastating fire with a second chance to be Utah's top resort. Throughout the Twenties Utahns and tourists responded with approval through their patronage. Advertising for Saltair during the decade noted events like Jack Davis and his eight-piece orchestra playing "matchless music," free patriotic concerts, fire-works, and the Greatest Independence Day Celebration in the resort's history in 1926 where "half the population of the state would be."

There were beauty contests advertised as "the most gorgeous revues of beauty ever staged in Utah," where "one hundred of Utah's choicest" could be seen. There was Black Jack gum day (free gum with admission), Hoo Hoo Day (where everyone wore their scariest costumes), All-German Day, Pacific Island Day (with an erupting volcano), a Night in China, frequent carnivals, and Charleston contests. In 1927 a parkway green Buick sedan, valued at $1,530, was given away, and when Charles Lindbergh flew the "Spirit of St. Louis" to Salt Lake that year, Saltair stayed open six extra days. Spectators could watch the landing and then catch the train to Saltair.

Group outings continued in popularity. In August 1926, for instance, the Grant, Liberty and Pioneer stakes of the Mormon church, the Cohn Dry Goods Employees, the University of Utah students, the American Society of Mechanical Engineers, and the Young Men's Democratic Club all held outings at the resort.

In 1927 Sunset Pier was added. Patrons could stroll along the 400-foot walkway out over the lake and view unsurpassed sunsets. And each year brought new rides and new concessions—such as the balloon racer, candy wheels, or tango games.

In 1928 there was a startling adaptation to changing public tastes when people were permitted to walk around all sections of the resort, except the dance floor, in their swim suits. In that year 7000 people attended Saltair on opening day. Other enticements to keep people coming included costume parties, free candy, peanuts and wafers for boys' and girls' days, and the chance to see A. L. Roberts do his "daring thirty-five-foot dive."

As the nineteen twenties wound to a close, Claude Kiff and the Saltair Orchestra played syncopated rhythm to continuous crowds. Saltair was repainted and redecorated and a 200-foot sandy beach area was added near the pavilion. Officials at season's end estimated patronage to be equal to the previous year's.

Like Phoenix rising from the ashes, Saltair had discovered new life. In the Twenties the grand lady of the lake glittered once more under the bright summer sunlight of popularity and fame. Ominous clouds, however, hung on the horizon.

Notes

1. *Deseret News*, Jan. 14, 1893.
2. Ibid.
3. Ibid., Aug. 18, 1893.
4. Abraham H. Cannon Journal, May 2, 1892, Utah State Historical Society.
5. Richard Cox, "Coney Island, Urban Symbol in American Art," *New York Historical Society Quarterly* 60 (Jan./April 1976): 35–53.

6. The best treatment of Coney Island is John E Kasson, *Amusing the Millions: Coney Island at the Turn of the Century* (New York: Hill and Wang, 1978). See also Ido McCullough, *Good Old Coney Island* (New York: Charles Scribner's Sons, 1957); Rem Koolhaus, *Delirious New York: A Retrospective Manifesto for Manhattan* (New York: Oxford University Press, 1978); Robert E. Snow and David W Wright, "Coney Island. A Case Study in Popular Culture and Technological Change," *Journal of Popular Culture* 9 (Spring 1976): 960–75; and Joseph Gastaitis, "The Character of Coney Island: Stalking the Strange with Sam Gumpertz," *American History Illustrated* 15 (February 1981): 37–41.

7. On the accommodation of the Mormon church to the larger society, see Leonard J. Arrington, *Great Basin Kingdom: An Economic History of the Latter-day Saints, 1830–1900* (Cambridge, Mass.: Harvard University Press, 1958), 380–412.

8. On Kletting, see *Encyclopedia of American Biography* (New York: The American Historical Co., Inc., 1947), 68–71, and Craig L. Bybee, "Richard Karl August Kletting: Dean of Utah Architects, 1858–1943," M.A. thesis, University of Utah, 1980.

9. Robert S. Olpin, "Art Life of Utah, 1776–1976," unpublished manuscript, University of Utah Special Collections, Marriott Library, 1976.

10. *Deseret News*, Jan. 14, 1893.

11. For a useful discussion on the architecture of the American amusement park, see Kasson, *Amusing the Millions*, 63–70.

12. *Deseret News*, June 9, 1893.

13. *Salt Lake Tribune*, July 5, 1893.

14. On this aspect of amusement parks, see John E. Kasson, *Amusing the Millions: Coney Island at the Turn of the Century* (New York: Hill and Wang, 1978), 240–54.

15. *Salt Lake Herald*, Aug. 17, 1903.

16. Wallace Stegner, "Xanadu By the Salt Flats," *American Heritage* 32 (June/July 1981): 84.

17. "Saltair and Temperance," *Improvement Era* 5 (July 1902): 731.

18. *Deseret News*, June 12, 1902.

19. Stegner, "Xanadu By the Salt Flats," 84.

20. *Salt Lake Tribune*, June 24, 1914.

21. *Deseret News*, June 2, 1892.

22. Arrington, *Great Basin Kingdom*, 393.

23. *Deseret News*, May 29, 1919.

24. H. A. Strauss, "Saltair Beach Company," unpublished manuscript, Utah State Historical Society, 1915.

25. Quoted in Joseph Gastaitis, "The Character of Coney island: Stalking the Strange with Sam Gumpertz," *American History illustrated* 15 (February 1981): 40.

26. *Salt Lake Tribune*, July 24, 1894.

27. *Deseret News*, Aug. 10, 1894.

28. See daily issues of both the *Deseret News* and the *Salt Lake Tribune*, July 18 through July 30, 1897.

29. *Salt Lake Tribune*, July 15, 1899.

30. *Salt Lake Herald*, July 19, 1903.

31. *Salt Lake Tribune*, June 1, June 2, June 15, July 13, July 16, Aug. 3, Aug. 10, Aug. 11, Aug. 17, 1911 .

32. Ibid., Aug. 30, 1915.

33. *Deseret News*, Aug. 27, 1917.

34. Ibid., Aug. 24,1918.

35. *Salt Lake Tribune*, Aug. 28, 1921.
36. Stegner, "Xanadu By the Salt Flats," 86.
37. *Salt Lake Tribune*, Apr. 23, 192 5. 38. Ibid., Apr. 26, 1925.
39. Ibid., May 9, 1925.
40. Ibid., May 20, 1925.
41. Ibid., and May 22, 1925.
42. Ibid., May 29, 1925
43. Ibid., June 29, 1925.
44. Ibid., July 3, 1925.
45. For a more complete look at advertising distinctions between the resorts check daily *Salt Lake Tribune* ads for July and August 1925.
46. Ibid., May 28, 1926.
47. Ibid.

Speed on Salt

S peed was a concern for operators of wheeled vehicles on the salt flats west of
the Great Salt Lake from the very beginning, for the Donner party found the
surface, which appeared so flat and firm, to be in fact so soggy that it was all their
animals could do to get the wagons across it at all. Automobile operators, like historian Charles Kelly who took his new Model A Ford over much of the Donner
trail in the late 1920s, found that pneumatic tires were only sometimes helpful, and
that bogging down was something to be expected. How ironic, then, that speed aficionados in search of world records would find the salt flats an ideal surface for
their behemoth machines, and that their feats during a brief thirty-five year period
(1935–1970) would make the salt flats synonymous with the word "speed" in the
popular mind.

The following selection is a story of legendary names in automotive speed records,
from the days of John Cobb, George Eyston, Sir Malcolm Campbell, and Salt Lake
City's own Ab Jenkins, to the amazing achievements of Craig Breedlove and Gary
Gabelich, whose 630.388 mph will almost certainly stand as the greatest speed ever
achieved on salt. The hard, flat surface with no obstructions visible in virtually any
direction seemed to be Lake Bonneville's great legacy to the automobile age.

But alas, unpredictable Nature—with perhaps a little assistance from the salt
industry—could not be counted upon to support man's love of power and speed
forever. By 1970 it had become apparent that the old lake bed was deteriorating to
a point where extreme speeds could no longer be safely achieved. The culprit may
have been simply a dry weather cycle that robbed the surface of the brine necessary
to replenish and smooth the salt. Others blamed the salt industry for pumping that
very brine into its evaporation ponds. Whatever the cause, the salt flats became
unusable for the kinds of speed that world record holders need to achieve. Happily,
though, for those speed aficionados content to test the limits of other types of vehicles that reach their maximum at a lower point, the flats continue, at least for now,
to serve their purpose.

John Cobb, world land speed record contender. Used by permission,
Utah State Historical Society, all rights reserved.

Suggestions for further reading

For a subject as dramatic as world speed records, it has attracted amazingly little in
serious scholarship. As the citations in this selection indicate, most of the literature
is found in newspaper and magazine stories, with little in the way of general syn-
thesis. Two books, however, can be recommended. The first is Ab Jenkins and
Wendell J. Ashton, *The Salt of the Earth* (Los Angeles: Clymer Motors, 1939),
Jenkins's reminiscences of the early days on the salt flats and a general history of the
speed trials through the days of Cobb and Campbell. The other is Paul Clifton, *The
Fastest Men on Earth* (New York: John Day Co., 1966), a longer and better history
which brings the story up to the time of Craig Breedlove, though not all the way
to the end of the salt flats era.

"These Bloomin' Salt Beds":
Racing on the Bonneville Salt Flats
Jessie Embry and Ron Shook

The 1996 hit movie *Independence Day* featured a train of recreational vehicles crossing the west Utah desert to a secret air force base. The spot was chosen for its eerie loneliness and emptiness, for its utter flatness, and for the strange sheen of its salt beds under the moonlight. One actor even remarked on the lack of perspective one has on the salt flats.

Utahns know the salt flats as more than a movie set. Those who have traveled Interstate 80 from Salt Lake City to Wendover see it as one of the most featureless stretches of the interstate highway system in the United States. That very characteristic appeals to automobile racers who wish to compete on what has been one of the fastest places on earth. From 1935 to 1970 automobile racers broke the land speed record (the fastest speed traveled in an automobile) fifteen times on the Bonneville Salt Flats. In fact, more speed records have been broken at Bonneville than anywhere else in the world. It is unlikely that any other racing venue in the world will ever accrue a speed record to rival that of Bonneville.

Yet the Bonneville Salt Flats have not been used to establish an absolute land speed record since 1970. Speed records are broken there every year for many classes of racing cars but not *the* land speed record. While it is true that since 1970 there have been fewer than a half dozen assaults on the land speed record, they could not take place at Bonneville. Once so attractive for high speed driving, Bonneville has not been used for that purpose for over twenty-five years.

Located 130 miles from Salt Lake City, the salt flats are the remnants of Lake Bonneville that once covered nearly a third of Utah. They consist of hundreds of square miles of the flattest, most desolate land on the planet. Standing on the salt flats, one can see the curvature of the earth. Nothing grows there. The result is a shimmering white surface that stretches endlessly in all directions, dazzling to the eye and confusing to the senses.

Jessie Embry and Ron Shook, "'These Bloomin' Salt Beds': Racing on the Bonneville Salt Flats," *Utah Historical Quarterly* 65 (fall 1997): 355–71.

Shortly after the development of automobiles, men began racing them. Count Gaston de Chasseloupe-Laubat set the first land speed record in 1898 near Paris, France, by traveling 39.24 mph. His record was broken the next year, and speeds continued to increase as automobiles improved. Eventually the Federation Internationale de l'Automobile (FIA) was established in France to set the rules, monitor the speeds, and validate records. At first cars simply had to travel one mile. In 1911 the FIA ruled a car had to run a course twice—once each direction—with the speeds to be averaged. Shortly thereafter the FIA also decreed a car must go at least 1 percent faster than the previous record in order to be accorded an official speed record.

Since speeds were still relatively moderate, for years these races took place in populated areas. But as the speeds increased, the drivers needed longer and longer tracks. As a result, entrepreneurs started looking at new venues.

In the United States, the Bonneville Salt Flats had an inauspicious start as a race course. In 1896 travel promoter Bill Rishel crossed the flats while helping locate a coast-to-coast route for a bicycle race. He discovered the salt flats were not bicycle friendly as his two-wheeler bogged down in the mud. But he wondered how automobiles would perform. In 1907 he and two Salt Lake City businessmen tested the area with a Pierce-Arrow. Encouraged, Rishel urged other drivers to come to the flats. In 1914 he convinced a barnstorming driver, Teddy Tezlaff, to test his Blitzen Benz there. The railroad agreed to haul the car out if the Salt Lake Chamber of Commerce could sell 100 tickets. The event was successful; 150 people turned out. Though Tezlaff went 141.73 miles per hour, faster than the record at Daytona Beach, automobile clubs refused to recognize the record. According to Rishel, "Consequently the salt beds were forgotten and the flats faded into [temporary] racing oblivion."[1]

Rishel claimed that Ab Jenkins, a local Utah racer, finally brought fame to the salt flats. Jenkins crossed the desert for the first time on his way to the James J. Jeffries—Jack Johnson boxing match in Reno by riding the rails on a motorcycle "like a bronco-busting cowboy." He returned to the flats when Rishel asked him to race the train to the 1925 dedication of the new Lincoln Highway. Jenkins explained, "That was my first time on the salt with an automobile, and right then and there I realized the tremendous possibilities of those beds for speeding." He believed the salt which "appeared to be a large lake of frozen ice" was a good racing surface because there was open space and "the concrete-like salt" cooled the tires.[2]

Jenkins referred to the salt flats as the "ugly ducking" because of its unattractive and remote location. Even after he set an unofficial 24-hour endurance record (112.935 mph) on the salt in 1932, Salt Lake newspapers refused to carry the story for a week. "Bigwigs of the automobile concern" told him that it was foolish to take "a wild ride on a sea of salt somewhere in the middle of Utah's desert." But Jenkins continued to push the salt flats as the place for setting speed records.[3]

At the same time, a change was taking place in the racing world that made the salt flats a logical place to compete in spite of its distance from population centers and its inhospitable nature. Drivers had used stock machines for early automobile races and

Ab Jenkins's "Mormon Meteor." Used by permission, Utah State Historical Society, all rights reserved.

John Cobb's Railton Red Lion with cowling removed. Used by permission, Utah State Historical Society, all rights reserved.

speed trials. A person could buy a car in the morning and race it that afternoon with a good chance of winning. However, as racing grew in popularity, drivers began to modify their cars and finally to build special cars for individual types of races. By the 1930s the fastest land speed racers were already too fast for most venues. They were thirty to forty feet long with huge wheels and 1,000-horsepower aircraft engines. Lacking maneuverability and good brakes, they needed wide open space. Even Daytona Beach, where some impressive records had been set, was too small. Racers started looking for new places to drive. The salt flats became a likely candidate.

The year 1935 was pivotal for racing in Utah. After hearing Ab Jenkins's glowing reports, English racers started testing the area. John Cobb, a fur broker, arrived first, hoping to break Jenkins's records. In his test run, Cobb broke twenty-four records, including distance traveled in an hour, on July 12. Two days later he started his twenty-four-hour endurance run. Despite bad weather, he set new records. The *Salt Lake Tribune* was impressed, reporting that Cobb "put away some 64 records in brine" such as 12-hour average speed, fastest average speed for 200 miles, and averaging 127.229 mph during a twenty-four hour period. The *Tribune* continued to cover activities on the flats, including Jenkins regaining his records which included the twenty-four hour average at 154.76 mph.[4]

In August Sir Malcolm Campbell, the world's foremost auto racer of the time, arrived. Americans knew Campbell; he had already established the land speed record at Daytona Beach. Unable to top 300 mph there, he was ready to try a new place. His tests on the salt flats were successful, and on September 3 he made an official try. Initially, the timekeeper showed that he had just barely missed the magic 300 number. But when his required two runs were averaged, a recalculation showed that Campbell had attained 301.1202 mph.[5]

Increasingly, race enthusiasts praised the Bonneville surface. Campbell himself, though never to return, was especially impressed. "The course appeared to be perfect . . ." he said. "It was the most wonderful sensation that I have ever felt. Here we were, skimming over the surface of the earth, the black line ever disappearing over the edge of the horizon; the wind whistling past like a hurricane; and nothing in sight but the endless sea of salt with the mountains fifty miles away in the distance. . . . I felt . . . that we were skimming along the top of the world and the earth appeared to be acutely round." The British magazine *The Autocar* described the track as "a vast white expanse of salt, dead smooth, varying but little from day to day." The London *Times* explained, "The use of a smooth surface instead of the rippled, sandy beach of Daytona clearly meant much in the conversion of power into speed."[6]

U.S. publications also complimented the flats. *Time* magazine, for example, wrote: "No novelty, the Bonneville Salt Flats have been in their present position and equally well suited to high-speed automobile driving for centuries. . . . For 200 square miles the residual salt is as flat as a concrete highway, so hard that iron tent-stakes often bend when driven in. . . . Moisture in the salt cools friction-heated tires. The salt's resistance minimizes skidding." According to the *New York Times,* "The record made in Utah speaks for itself " If a car was going to go fast, the track had to be "straighter and smoother" than Daytona Beach. After quoting this article, the *Salt Lake Tribune* editorialized, "In this recognition, Utah is made conscious of a natural asset, which merits progressive development."[7]

Racers continued to come to the salt flats during the rest of the 1930s. John Cobb and George Eyston came from England each year to compete for the land speed record. Cobb, Eyston, and Jenkins also went after endurance records. They bounced the records back and forth. It was a glorious decade for racing in Utah.

Each year brought electrifying runs and new records. A good example was 1938, the most spectacular year on the salt flats to date. Both Eyston and Cobb set the land speed record within a month of each other. Eyston was not accorded the record at first because his car did not trigger the timing devices on the return trip. Officials claimed the "bright glare of the morning sun and the light reflection from the white salt beds . . . prevented the . . . shadow of the speeding white car from registering its image." Eyston painted his car black and set a record (345.49 mph) on the "snow-like plains." He commented the run was "one of the most casual trips I've made on the salt flats . . . The course was in splendid condition and there was never a tendency to slip or skid." Cobb broke the record at 350.2 mph two weeks later, but within two days Eyston regained it at 357.5 mph.[8]

While Cobb and Eyston set the records, the salt flats shared in the glory. The *Tribune* declared August and September "the biggest in all history with the eyes of the entire racing world centered on the greatest, safest and fastest course known." The paper was especially pleased that H. J. Butcher of Auckland, New Zealand, said the beaches of his home country "hardly compare to your salt flats. This is without question the greatest and safest racing course in the world." Eyston echoed those feelings: "There is no place in the world like these bloomin' salt beds."[9]

The outbreak of war in Europe interrupted racing for the Englishmen. Jenkins raced by himself in 1940, but the next year the United States entered the war and no one used the salt flats for the next several years. After World War II, John Cobb returned. However, either the salt was beginning to change ever so slightly or the higher speeds of the cars made it seem that way. A track that was perfect at 150 miles an hour seemed full of bumps and potholes at 350. The huge cars with their rock-hard tires and minimal suspension systems reacted harshly to imperfections.

Despite these concerns, both Cobb and Jenkins raced in 1947 for the Mormon Pioneer Centennial. Because of bad weather, Cobb stayed in Utah for over a month. After setting a new land speed record of 394.2 mph in September, he decided not to continue to race because the course had taken "a severe pounding." Clem Schramm from Salt Lake City declared, "The course had been scraped so frequently that the 'top level'—the hard surface that makes the flats the greatest racing course in the world—was all but scraped off."[10] Cobb's record stood for fifteen years.

Although there were no new land speed records in the 1950s, amateurs developed new types of racing. Along with driving on open roads, hills, and oval tracks, some speed enthusiasts modified cars to see just how fast they would go. In 1947 some of these hot rodders examined the salt flats, then wrote to the American Automobile Association (AAA), the organization which sanctioned their speed records at the time, and asked if they could use the flats to establish hot-rod records. The AAA somewhat loftily refused the request, arguing that it was "highly unlikely a 'hot rod' could ever achieve the speed of 203 miles an hour," the existing record for C-class cars.

But the amateurs did not give up. In 1948 they appealed to the Salt Lake City Bonneville Speedway Association. After studying the situation, the association agreed to let them experiment on the salt. A year later the Southern California Timing Association organized the first Bonneville National Speed Trials sponsored by Hot Rod magazine and Union Oil of California. The *Salt Lake Tribune* reported in 1949 that "these boys" had the same difficulties that Jenkins, Campbell, Cobb, and Eyston had experienced, but they all agreed "there's no place like it for real speed."[11] After the first year, Speed Week became an annual event, weather permitting.

The hot rodders were completely different from the land speed racers. In contrast to the likes of Cobb and Campbell, they came in home-designed, jerry-built contraptions that had only one thing in common with their forerunners: they went fast. In 1953 *Life* commented, "The glistening Salt Flats of Bonneville, Utah, were overrun this month by some of the oddest shapes the motor age has produced."[12] Some drivers modified stock car chassis and used hopped-up V-8 engines. Others created new car types, using materials they found in junk yards and surplus shops. One type of car designed for the flats was the "lakester," built from airplane wings and belly fuel tanks. Lakesters looked like teardrops with motors and wheels.

Speed Week faced the usual problems: heat, winds, and the slippery track. As one article explained, "It's an inhospitable place, Bonneville. The racing surface—it is salt, taste it—combines for cars, tools, and human beings the worst properties of beach sand, snow, and hydrochloric acid. It gets into everything, including the beer." But there were also the victories. The article continued, "The salt provides a superior straight-line racing [surface] when it is healthy . . . Traction is marvelous. (It's like ice with bumps.)"[13]

The 1960s were erratic years for the Bonneville Salt Flats, mostly because of the weather but also because the financial stakes had risen. Drivers searching for the land speed record started using huge machines weighing several tons, some propelled by jet engines. While racers of the 1930s used aircraft engines, these had been conventional piston engines, usually having twelve to sixteen cylinders, and generating about 1,000 horsepower. The jet engines, on the other hand, were larger, longer, bulkier, heavier, and produced several times the horsepower.

These new cars had several effects on racing and on the salt. Jet cars were harder to control. In a conventional car, the engine is connected to the wheels, and the driver can control the car to some degree with the throttle. In a jet car the wheels roll freely, and the engine cannot be used for braking. Heavier, they tore up the salt as they sped over it. Faster, they required better tires and improved brakes. (The 1960s saw the first widespread use of parachutes for brakes.)

The years 1964 and 1965 were the fastest yet on the salt. Drivers broke the land speed record nine times. Donald Campbell started 1964 by breaking the record (403.1 mph) on Lake Eyre in Australia, the last time that the record was to be held by a conventional, wheel-driven car. When the record returned to the salt flats on October 2, it was set by Tom Green at 413.2 mph in a jet car. He exclaimed, "The wind pressure and the rattling gave an impression of speed. I didn't have a sensation of things flying by, but of pressure and noises."[14]

Three days later Art Arfons set a new record at 434.02 mph; on one run he went 479 mph. "Things go so durn fast that you just don't know you're going," he declared. Convinced that his car was designed to go 500 mph, Arfons tried for that record two days later but blew a tire. Because a spare was not immediately available, he had to yield his place on the track.[15]

Then Craig Breedlove tried for the record. His first attempts were not successful. On October 12 he made one run at 452.9 mph, but the salt "tossed" the car on the return run. Breedlove explained, "It was kind of a bumps-a-daisy feeling when I hit that stretch on my second run and I almost lost control of the car." The next day he set a new record of 468.72 mph, though still experiencing trouble with the rough salt. When he hit that same spot his head whipped around and smacked his helmet against the plastic canopy.[16]

One day later Breedlove broke his own record, averaging 526.33 mph. On the return run his steering failed, and when he tried to stop the chutes did not release. As a result, Breedlove explained, "I marked every place I could get into trouble." He eventually hit a row of telephone poles that "sheared off like so many toothpicks" and then landed in a lake. After climbing out of the cockpit, Breedlove said, "I looked back at the car and it was like something unreal, like a cartoon. The tail was sticking out of the water and there was smoke coming out of the tailpipe."[17]

But the racing was not finished for the year. On October 27, 1964, Art Arfons returned and averaged 536.71 mph, 2 percent better than Breedlove's record. On the second run, Arfons went 559.18 mph, and the extra power from the afterburner blew out the right rear tire. Arfons explained, "The salt was terribly rough. I almost didn't try for the record, but then my crew found out if I stayed on the outside it wasn't as bad. So I made the run right near the edge of the track, right by the timing lights." Art's brother, Walt Arfons wanted to try for the record in November, but rain prevented an attempt. Instead Paula Murphy used Walt's car to set a new speed for a woman at 226 mph "on a short, slippery track."[18]

Drivers also broke records the next year. On November 12, 1965, Bob Summers, from Ontario, California, drove Goldenrod, a Chrysler Hemi V-8, at 409.277 mph, the fastest a conventional car had ever been driven. The jet car record fell several times, too.

Breedlove, Art Arfons, and Breedlove again broke the land speed record during November 2–15, 1965. Arfons talked about his plans to maintain the record, then added a word of caution:

Gary Gabelich's "The Blue Flame." Used by permission, Utah State Historical Society, all rights reserved.

The land speed record climbed 120 miles per hour last year. For nearly 25 years the record wasn't broken. Now, with the jet engines, it's climbing too fast. Things that jump that fast aren't good. We should be taking more time because we're now approaching the sound barrier, about which we know very little. But no one seems to want to slow down. So, we'll just have to be ready.[19]

First, Breedlove went for the mark on November 4. He clocked 544.283 and 566.394 mph on his two runs for an average of 555.339. Breedlove insisted that he went faster, noting that his gauges registered 575 mph. Then Art Arfons reclaimed the record at 576.55 mph. But on the second run he blew the right rear tire, lost a parachute, and ripped the right front tire. His cockpit filled with smoke, and he drifted two and a half miles farther than he expected. After it was all over, he commented, "Look at my car . . . It looks like it was driven by a drunken driver." Breedlove wanted the record back, so he returned just a week later and again set a new land speed record at 600.60 mph. After the race, he said, "There is a lot of difference between 599 and 600 and breaking this barrier is a big thrill."[20] But after these records, the pace slowed. Gary Gabelich broke the land speed record (630.388 mph) for the last time on the Salt Flats in 1970.

Besides the broken records, there were also accidents and deaths during the 1960s. In 1960 the course took on moisture. Athol Graham died in his attempt to set a land speed record. Mickey Thompson refused to try. Donald Campbell, Malcolm's son, rolled his car but escaped with a minor skull fracture. Andy Brown, who was part of Campbell's team and had also been with his father's team in 1935, told reporters that the salt was in "much worse condition" than it had been when Malcolm Campbell raced there. In September 1962 Glenn Leasher died in an attempted run in a jet car. A 1965 *Sports Illustrated* article referred to the 1960 and 1962 accidents and contended, "Bonneville has become worse than Darlington or Daytona or any of the major places where the death factor is present." Commenting that on other tracks such as the Indianapolis 500 and Daytona, a driver could walk away from a crash, the article explained, "At anything over 350 the sheer speed figures to kill him no matter how he's protected."[21]

The article correctly pointed out some of the problems at the salt flats. By this time the speeds were getting very high, and speed records frequently jumped by fifteen or twenty miles an hour. Racers began experimenting with new equipment that was lighter, sleeker, and sometimes more dangerous. In order to be even reasonably safe at these speeds, the salt had to be perfect.

Fortunately, the salt provided some protection at high speeds. According to *Time* magazine, "The Bonneville Salt Flats of Utah rank high on any list of the world's most desolate place, but they have a special fascination for a special kind of a fanatic: the speed demon." As unbelievable as it may sound, the article told of a motorcyclist who flipped at 150 mph in 1965 and walked away "muttering, 'I thought I had stopped.'" In 1969 when racing returned after several wet years, *Hot Rod* reported, "Mother Nature relented this year and the SCTA's 21st (and coming of age) Bonneville meet was one of the most successful in years. The salt was perfect—[in] fact a little too perfect as a few contestants will testify. Several areas in midcourse were so smooth and hard they were actually slick, resulting in some rather spectacular spinouts."[22]

There was one death on the flats in 1969 that *Hot Rod* blamed on the car. Bob Herda burned to death. Observers explained he wanted "a perfectly smooth and aerodynamically clean bellypan" so he did not "cut a drain opening under the engine." He also used pure oxygen in the breathing system. The combination of leaking fluids and oxygen was lethal when his car caught on fire. But the article continued, "There have been only two fatalities in SCTA's 21 years on the salt. No other major sport can equal that record."[23]

For years, only land speed racers and the amateur group from California used the salt flats. In 1987, however, a new group, the Utah Salt Flats Racing Association, started the "World of Speed" meet. According to the *Salt Lake Tribune*, "The salt will come alive for the second time in 45 days following annual 'Speed Week,' in August. "Having another event would "focus more attention on the world-famous salt flats, which have been used only sporadically for high-speed runs since the early

'70s."[24] Since 1987 USFRA and SCTA have continued to sponsor meets on the salt flats including "World of Speed" and "Speed Week." Later USFRA added the "Land Speed Opener" in July.

Spectators noticed the smoothness and safety of the salt. Art Arfons brought a friend, Jim Cook, to the flats in 1965. For him it was unbelievable. "I can't begin to compare it with the pictures. It looks exactly like something you'd expect to find on the moon. It's really eerie." Wester Potter, a Salt Lake City businessman who has been visiting the flats since the 1950s, recently said, "It's like no other experience on earth. The salt is so white and so flat and the cars are so fast that you have trouble believing it's all real."[25]

Drivers at the Land Speed Opener in July 1994 also talked about the wonder and safety of driving on the salt. Phil Freduiger first came to the salt flats in 1958. He recalled, "It was like a super highway." The experience hooked him and he returned every year. While he had never spun out, he explained, "If you spin here, you have got plenty of places to go. It is very seldom that people dig in and get sideways. There have been a few deaths here over the years but very few."[26]

But drivers also talked about the dangers. After a frightening accident where the driver broke his leg, the Land Speed Opener was canceled. Chuck Small explained what was happening to the track just before the crash:

> As we started getting up over 200 miles an hour, the car has tendency to kind of wander a little bit . . . As I was getting into it pretty good in high gear, I let it drift. The rear tire hit the black line. It just spun, and like that I started going sideways at about 205. I just lifted my foot off the gas and turned into the way it was sliding. It straightened itself right out again. But it kind of made me take a deep breath. I found out later that the surface was going away and I had hit some soft spots.

But, Small added:

> From the standpoint of racing this is the safest place that we have that we can go. If we have a problem, we have so much run off area. This car here has spun out thirteen times anywhere from 174 to 247 miles per hour. One time it made thirteen revolutions. It has not offered to tip over on this surface . . . This surface is really forgiving. It is a neat place to be.[27]

For the racers traveling in the rarified atmosphere of the ultimate land speed, the view was different. Craig Breedlove explained, "Most people have a faulty impression of what it's like on the Salt Flats. The salt isn't smooth—it's full of ridges and grooves, and in places the mud shows right through the crust. The course is 80 feet wide and believe me, it's a tough fight to keep on it through the full 11-mile course."[28] Of course, Breedlove was going over 400 mph during these runs.

Racing on the salt flats has continued to be problematic. There are frequently weather delays, and the track is not as long nor as smooth as when Campbell raced in 1935. Racers debate why, but their common scapegoat is a potash plant which made potassium chloride into a fertilizer. After his unsuccessful runs in 1963, Craig

Breedlove told the press, "It's the only place of its kind in the world that you can make record speed runs and it's not going to last much longer unless it's preserved." He blamed the potash company's canal for "drain[ing] water off to process salt."[29]

A year later the Utah Department of Highways started work on the section of Interstate 80 that would run from Salt Lake City to Wendover, encroaching on the salt flats raceway. The Bonneville Speedway Association realized that the track would be smaller because of the highway, but they also received some improvements, including a highway exit and a paved road at the salt flats.[30]

After the new highway was completed, conditions continued to worsen. In 1965 racing officials complained of "a lack of brine." A state engineer drilled samples to "determine how much of the water is being drained from the surface and exactly where it is going." William Backman, who had worked with the Bonneville Speedway Association and the Salt Lake Chamber of Commerce in promoting the flats since the 1930s, explained, "The salt flats have played an important part in bringing mention to Utah and there is no reason why we should sit back and watch it disappear."[31]

Except for the potash plant officials, nearly everyone claimed that the salt was deteriorating. But they could not agree on why. In 1966 Harry E. Wilbert, the highway department regional engineer, felt that as the potash plant drained water it also extracted salts. But William P. Hewitt, the Utah Geological Survey director, concluded the salt content had not changed since 1914. He agreed that when the water level was low the salt flats were dry and cracked. To provide for "high subsurface water" that would help percolate salt upward," the Bonneville Speedway Association and the Utah Division of State Parks and Recreation asked for the state to build $500,000 dikes on the east and west sides so the water would not run off. Governor Calvin Rampton questioned why and asked for more studies.[32]

And more studies there were, in abundance. The U.S. Geological Survey, the state, and Kaiser, who owned the potash plant, sponsored other studies in 1973, 1974, 1975, 1977, and 1978. They did not agree on whether the salt was disappearing or, if it were, who was to blame. One study, for example, suggested that the potash plant's canals were draining the salt and damaging the track. Others contended that the salt flats were stable, since they created a "bowl of relatively pure salt through which water passes with difficulty, if at all."[33]

But even if Kaiser were causing the problem, state officials pointed out in 1975 that the company had millions of dollars invested in its operations and provided jobs and tax income to the state. The salt flats, on the other hand, were only used one week a year for race car amateurs, and at that time the state paid $30,000 a year for upkeep on the track. Others insisted that economics should not be the only consideration, arguing that "The famed speedway is unsurpassed as a widely-known definitive feature of Utah."[34]

The Bureau of Land Management designated the area a Special Recreational Management Area in 1985, then called for a study to solve the conflicts over use. A *Salt Lake Tribune* reporter, Tom Wharton, explained, "The lore surrounding Salt Flats speed trials is long and colorful. But even if the racing events are discounted or ignored, the Bonneville Salt Flats are every bit as unique a part of Utah's land-scape. . . . They should be preserved for both those who like to race and others who enjoy them for their aesthetic values."[35] Deane H. Zeller, the manager of the Pony Express BLM Division, agreed, "My personal feeling is that the . . . best use of the salt flats is not racing and it's certainly not minerals production. I think it is a nat-ural geologic phenomenon that is awesome . . . People should be able to experience the Bonneville Salt Flats" by "standing out in the middle of this huge white noth-ingness surrounded by outlines of mountains" for a "truly wilderness experience."[36]

So the debate continues. In the 1990s all groups believe that the salt flats have value, but they differ on what that is and how it may best be promoted. Many Americans drive quickly across the area en route to somewhere, at most pausing at the rest stop near Wendover to gaze out over the salt. The Southern California Timing Association and the Utah Salt Flats Association continue to sponsor meets, weather permitting. The potash plant continues to remove salts that are shipped throughout the world to be used as fertilizer. In 1995 the potash plant and the racers finally agreed on a BLM-approved plan to transport salt back to the track.

In the meantime, though, other things have changed. In 1983 Richard Noble from England broke the land speed record on a "dry, dusty lake bed in the Black Rock desert" in Nevada. The *Salt Lake Tribune* editorialized, "It was the first time since World War II that a Land Speed Record was set outside the Bonneville Salt Flats but will probably not be the last."[37] In 1996 Breedlove had hoped to test his new car on the salt flats, but a late summer rain canceled his first attempts as well as the Land Speed Opener. Speed Week was held, but World of Speed was rained out. All in all, it is questionable whether the salt flats will ever be used again for the land speed record. Its use as a hot-rod track is also in doubt because of the contin-ued deterioration of the salt. It is probable that some racers will continue to use Bonneville in their quest for records near 400 miles an hour in different classes. The kings of the hill, the monster jets, the 600 mph missiles, are almost certainly gone forever. Bonneville's great era of land speed record attempts, with its incredible excitement and spectacular daring, has slipped quietly into history.

Notes

Jessie Embry is assistant director of the Charles Redd Center for Western Studies at BrighamYoung University. Ron Shook is director of the technical writing program in the English department at Utah State University.

1. Ab Jenkins and Wendell J. Ashton, *The Salt of the Earth* (Los Angeles: Clymer Motors, 1939), pp. 9, 24, 28.
2. Ibid., 29, 34–35.
3. Ibid., 17, 34–36.
4. Ibid., 57; *Salt Lake Tribune*, July 18, 1935, August 7, 1935, September 2, 1935.
5. *Salt Lake Tribune*, August 18, 1935, August 30, 1935, September 2, 1935, September 3, 1935, September 4, 1935.

6. "301.129 M.P.H.: Sir Malcolm Campbell's Own Story," *The Motor: The National Motor Journal* 68 (October 29, 1935): 23–24; "Bravo!," *The Autocar,* September 6, 1935, p. 416a; *The Times,* September 4, 1935.

7. "Bluebird at Bonneville," *Time,* September 16, 1935, p. 45; *New York Times,* September 5, 193 5; *Salt Lake Tribune,* September 20, 193 5.

8. "Eyston at 347 m.p.h.," *Newsweek,* September 5, 1938, p.26; *Salt Lake Tribune,* August 28, 1938, September 15, 1938, September 17, 1938.

9. *Salt Lake Tribune,* August 27, 1938, September 13, 1938, September 17, 1938.

10. Ibid., September 17, 1947.

11. Wally Parks, "After Thirty Years It's Still the Greatest," 1978, Pamphlet 18415, Utah State Historical Society, Salt Lake City; *Salt Lake Tribune,* August 9, 1949, August 29, 1949.

12. "Speaking of Pictures," Life, September 28, 1953, p. 17.

13. Cory Farley, "If This Is a Race Weekend, Why Doesn't My Ulcer Hurt?," *Car and Driver,* February 1979, pp. 97–98.

14. *Salt Lake Tribune,* July 18, 1964, October 3, 1964.

15. Ibid., October 6, 1964.

16. Ibid., October 13, 1964, October 14, 1964.

17. Ibid., October 16, 1964.

18. Ibid., October 28, 1964, November 12, 1964, November 13, 1964; Paul Clifton, *The Fastest Men on Earth* (New York: John Day Company, 1966), p. 238.

19. *Salt Lake Tribune,* September 9, 1965.

20. Ibid., November 5, 1965, November 8, 1965, November 16, 1965.

21. Ibid., August 2, 1960, August 15, 1960, August 10, 1962, September 17, 1960, September 11, 1962; Jack Olsen, "My Brother, My Enemy, in Speedland," *Sports Illustrated,* November 29, 1965, p. 84.

22. "Mr. and Mrs. Speedlove," *Time,* November 12, 1965, pp. 75–76; 78; Eric Rackman, "The Salt Was Fine in '69," *Hot Rod,* November 22, 1969, pp. 30–33.

23. Ibid.

24. *Salt Lake Tribune,* September 28, 1987.

25. Ibid., August 7, 1965; Wester Potter personal conversation with Ron Shook, July 24, 1994.

26. Phil Freduiger interviewed by Jessie Embry, 1994, Bonneville Salt Flats Oral History Project, Charles Redd Center for Western Studies, Manuscript Division, Harold B. Lee Library, Brigham Young University, Provo, Utah (hereinafter referred to as Bonneville Salt Flats Oral History).

27. Chuck Small interviewed by Jessie Embry, 1994, Bonneville Salt Flats Oral History.

28. *Salt Lake Tribune,* December 1, 1965.

29. Ibid., August 24, 1963.

30. Ibid., February 20, 1964.

31. Ibid., May 14, 1965.

32. Ibid., December 22, 1966.

33. Ibid., August 13, 1973.

34. Ibid., March 17, 1975.

35. Ibid.

36. Deane H. Zeller interviewed by Jessie Embry, 1994, Bonneville Salt Flats Oral History.

37. *Salt Lake Tribune,* October 23, 1983. In fact, on October 15, 1997, Andy Green, driving Noble's jet-powered Thrust SSC, set a new record of 763.035 mph at Black Rock. Ibid., October 16, 1997.

Boats on the Great Salt Lake

A visitor to the south shore of the Great Salt Lake on any balmy weekend day will immediately notice one of the lake's most popular functions. As far as the eye can see toward Stansbury Island in the west, the surface will be dotted with white sails, and perhaps if he turns his gaze to the northwest along the western shore of Antelope Island, he may be treated to the sight of a racing fleet on its downwind run, their multicolored spinnakers billowing out in front of the boats in every hue imaginable. In the following selection, Peter G. Van Alfen mentions in passing the existence of a yacht club on the Great Salt Lake as early as the 1870s, and pleasure boating on this immense and scenic desert lake has been popular ever since.

As Van Alfen notes, sailing on the Great Salt Lake has its difficulties and perils. For one thing, the mineral-laden water rapidly corrodes metal fittings and clogs cooling systems on motors (one reason why one sees few powerboats on the lake today). The dominance of fiberglass hull construction, which rapidly occurred during the 1960s, greatly diminishes boat maintenance chores, though wise boaters take frequent advantage of freshwater outlets at the marina to hose down their boats and flush their engines. The shallow water, which extends for an amazing distance from most points on the shore, strongly commends the use of manual or electronic depth sounding devices, accurate charts, and swing keels which can be winched up inside the hull to avoid running aground when approaching an island. Most serious, though, is the capricious weather in the form of rapidly approaching storms that can turn the surface into a maelstrom with amazing speed, and the unpredictable "Tooele twisters," the sudden sharp gusts of wind that can catch a helmsman unaware and put his boat on its side before he can react.

Thus the pioneers of lake navigation were those motivated by commerce or scientific exploration rather than mere pleasure. And their experiences with the lake led them to some interesting and even strange modifications of naval architecture principles in practice elsewhere, so that the Great Salt Lake even has a place—minor, to be sure—in naval history. Van Alfen, though a student of naval architecture, tells the

story of those local modifications in nontechnical language and conveys an appreci-
ation for the considerable diversity of boat types that have plied the waters of our
inland sea.

During the century that has elapsed between 1901, when he closes his narrative,
and our own day, the lake has continued to see a wide variety of boat types and
both commercial and recreational use. The state of Utah maintains marinas at the
northern end of Antelope Island and on the south shore of the lake near Saltair,
with slips for some three hundred boats, mostly sailboats in the twenty to thirty
foot range. The brine shrimp industry maintains a fleet of boats to harvest the lake's
tiny indigenous mollusks and their eggs, which are sold for food for tropical fish
and commercially grown prawns. And a modern commercial cruise boat, the *Island
Serenade*, offers sunset dinner cruises or longer explorations of the lake.

Suggestions for further reading

Several books excerpted or cited in previous selections offer at least passing consideration to boating on the lake, for example, Morgan, *The Great Salt Lake*; Gwynn,
Great Salt Lake; and McCormick, *Saltair*. Marilyn Kraczek, *Small Boat Cruising on
Great Salt Lake, Past and Present* (Salt Lake City: Hawkes Publishing Inc., 1995), is
a recent popularly written look at the modern sailing scene, with chapters on history and the writer's personal experiences on the lake. Some of the best reading
about Great Salt Lake sailing, however, is available on the Internet rather than in
print. Two websites, in particular, are highly recommended: Pat Swigart, an avid
sailor and researcher, runs a comprehensive and frequently updated site: www.geoc-
ities.com/SouthBeach/Shores/9144/, with information on boats, history, philoso-
phy, ecology, and news updates. The Great Salt Lake Yacht Club also runs a useful
site: www.gslyc.org, with several kinds of information, including a bulletin board
posting boats for sale and information. Members of the yacht club also receive a
periodical, *The Brine Flyer*, which contains entertaining and informative discussions of the lake and sailing.

Sail and Steam: Great Salt Lake's Boats and Boatbuilders, 1847–1901
Peter G. Van Alfen

Since the 1930s, when Utah historians and others began to write about Great Salt Lake's past, several writers have addressed the lake's nineteenth-century steamships and sailing craft. Despite the local historical interest in these vessels, no attempt has been made to fit them into the greater sphere of maritime history. Some of Great Salt Lake's early vessels represent an overlooked boatbuilding tradition due to the unusual way they were constructed. The relative isolation of the region, especially in the period before the railroad, the European background of local shipwrights, and the lake itself were all factors that shaped the region's boatbuilding tradition. Admittedly, it was neither a grand nor long-lived tradition, but it deserves recognition for its role in North American maritime history.

Documentary accounts show that many of Great Salt Lake's early boats possessed nuances in design and construction that made them notably different from other North American watercraft. Such distinguishing characteristics were a necessary response to the difficulties of boatbuilding in the Salt Lake Valley and of navigation on the lake. Many of these locally built vessels were neither graceful nor admirable craft; ugly and practical would better describe them. However, they were well suited for the lake.

Because it is one of the larger bodies of water in North America, Great Salt Lake would seem to offer itself readily to navigation. This is simply not the case. Writer and naturalist Terry Tempest Williams recently called the lake "the liquid lie of the West"—water in a desert that no one can drink; water that nothing but brine flies and brine shrimp call home.[1] For sailors the lake was, if not a lie, then a seriously underestimated hoax. Great Salt Lake is notoriously shallow, especially within a mile of its shorelines, and ringed by shifting sandbars and foul, bluish mud. Early nauti-

Peter G. Van Alfen, "Sail and Steam: Great Salt Lake's Boats and Boatbuilders, 1847–1901," *Utah Historical Quarterly* 63 (summer 1995): 194–221.

cal explorers found these aspects of the lake perpetually frustrating. Their vessels frequently grounded far from shore, and any anchorage inevitably required a long trek to dry ground through knee-deep, reeking mud. The lake's water level is also in constant fluctuation. Portions of the lake that may have been recorded as navigable one year could be dry land in the following year; or, just as likely, the annual rains and run-off could send the lake topping over surrounding lands. The captain of the steamboat *Kate Connor,* for example, reported a voyage in which he unexpectedly cruised over what had been farmland the previous year. Fence posts and ditches were visible in the water below the boat.[2] Violent storms on the lake also make navigation treacherous. As sudden as they are ferocious, the storms catch even experienced sailors off-guard. In the nineteenth century at least ten boats were wrecked or seriously damaged in storms. In this century the number has been far greater. The intense salinity of the waters, Great Salt Lake's most famous characteristic, poses still more troubles to navigation. Iron fastenings on a vessel corrode more quickly in this water than in sea water, and hulls and machinery become thickly encrusted with salt. Boats used on the lake require endless maintenance, even more so than comparable coastal vessels.

The challenges of the lake had to be considered by the early local boatbuilders, for a boat's design is very much influenced by the body of water on which it will be used. To overcome the lake's shallow waters and submerged obstacles, the valley's shipwrights launched predominately flat-bottomed boats. The sea-like waves encountered on the lake and frequent hard groundings also meant that vessels had to be sturdily built. Although the lake's later boats appear to have been strongly, even overly built, there are accounts of the earliest boats nearly falling to pieces a short time after they were launched.[3] To resist salt-induced corrosion local shipwrights opted for galvanized fastenings and brass fixtures when these were available. Additionally, modest sail plans seem to have been the rule, possibly to make the boats safer in heavy winds and sudden storms but perhaps also due to the paucity of sail material in the valley.

Aside from the limitations of design imposed by the lake itself, more fundamental problems existed for the region's shipwrights. The greatest of these was the availability of boatbuilding materials. Before the completion of the transcontinental railroad in the spring of 1869 local shipwrights were entirely dependent upon nearby canyons for timber and planking and on local blacksmiths for fittings and fastenings. The species of trees available in the canyons, though serviceable, were not the best for boatbuilding; transportation of this timber also required tremendous expenditure.[4] Obtaining iron and other metals for boatbuilding was equally difficult. Despite Brigham Young's attempts to establish an ironworks in Utah Territory, iron and other metals still had to be imported from the States at prohibitive expense. Therefore, much of the iron found in the earliest vessels came from recycled sources. The anchor for *The Timely Gull,* for example, was fashioned entirely of scrap iron.[5]

Without question, the arrival of the railroad had a significant impact on the valley's boatbuilding practices. Once the railroad arrived, wood types more appropriate for boatbuilding could be obtained, as could various corrosion-resistant metals and prefabricated fittings. The railroads were also capable of transporting enormous steamboat boilers and engines with relative ease and economy. Moreover, entire boats, either complete or disassembled, could ride the rails to the valley. After the spring of 1869 boatbuilding in the valley was less difficult but lost much of its native ingenuity.

The coming of the railroad ushered in a new period of boatbuilding in the Salt Lake Valley region. In the earlier period, from 1847 to 1869, Mormon shipwrights using locally available materials built vessels primarily for working purposes. It is this short period that provides the purest examples of Great Salt Lake's boatbuilding tradition. The later period, from 1870 to 1901, is characterized by an influx of materials, boats, and non-Mormon shipwrights. Further, the later era shows the decline of working vessels and the rise of boats built solely for pleasure. Three major boat-types carry through both periods: working sailboats, steamboats, and pleasure sailboats.

Working Sailboats

Working sailboats are vessels expressly designed and built for carrying cargo or for exploration. Between 1847 and 1879, when the last working sailboat was constructed for Great Salt Lake, local shipwrights launched at least a dozen vessels of this type. Of these, Dan Jones built two (possibly more), Gammon Hayward likely built three, and four (possibly five) others were constructed by the Miller family.

Only Gammon Hayward, whose father had been a shipwright in Kent, England, appears to have had any formal training in boatbuilding. Dan Jones served as a river boat captain on the Mississippi River for a few years after his immigration from Wales but does not seem to have had extensive boatbuilding training; he may have been self-taught. Likewise there is no mention of formal training for the Miller brothers, Henry W. and Daniel A. The latter's son, Jacob, who built two of the last working sailboats on the lake, made intensive studies of the world's watercraft while on his proselytizing mission in Australia for the Mormon church. On his return he employed line drawings and half-models when building his boats, design tools of the sophisticated boatbuilder. He also employed the services of Henry Barrot, a retired British Royal Navy ship's carpenter, to direct the actual construction of one boat.[6]

Where these men learned to build boats, whether abroad or in the United States, would be reflected in the style of the boats they built and the manner in which they were constructed. Boatbuilders are usually trained within a regionally specific tradition. Asked to construct a 25-foot fishing boat, for example, a boatbuilder from one region or country might produce a boat differently from another builder. The differences may be as subtle as the size and location of the frames or as obvious as the shape of the bow and stem. Most, if not all of the valley's Mormon shipwrights received their training abroad, primarily in England or Wales. The nearly direct importation of English and Welsh boatbuilding practices by Gammon Hayward, Henry Barrot, and possibly Dan Jones and the Miller family to the Salt Lake Valley means that the basis of the local boatbuilding tradition was more British than American, as were the boatbuilders themselves.[7] It is unlikely, however, that the vessels these men launched on Great Salt Lake were close copies of boats found abroad. The problems of navigating the lake and of boatbuilding in the valley were regionally specific. These problems would require the builders to modify their designs or construction techniques to fit the region's peculiarities. The adaptation of British boatbuilding practices to meet Great Salt Lake's requirements resulted in a distinctively American boatbuilding tradition.

Mud Hen, one of several so-called skiffs (a small open boat) built in the first few years of Mormon settlement, was the first locally built boat to sail on Great Salt Lake. At least two, and possibly as many as four, of these small boats were constructed between 1847 and 1850. Only the name *Mud Hen* has survived.

Because a boat was needed immediately to explore the Jordan River and Utah Lake, construction of *Mud Hen* began within days of the Mormon arrival in the valley. The boat was not large, measuring only 15 feet long and 4 feet wide, and, according to tradition, was built of only "five fir planks" acquired from a single tree felled in City Creek Canyon. Although the boat was launched barely three weeks after its construction began, the exploratory mission, due to trouble navigating the river, was abandoned and the boat was brought back to the camp. Early the following spring (April 1848), Albert Carrington and five others used the boat for a five-day voyage on Great Salt Lake. For this excursion the boat was fitted with a sail to complement its oars. Shortly after the trip, *Mud Hen* was taken to the Bear River ford, near modern Corinne, were it served for several years as a ferry boat.[8]

The journals and the final report of U.S. Army Capt. Howard Stansbury's exploration of Great Salt Lake (1849–50), mention the use of two, possibly three, other skiffs. For his work on the Jordan River and Utah Lake in the autumn of 1849, Lt. John W. Gunnison employed an old skiff, not *Mud Hen,* and later welcomed a new boat to his flotilla.[9] The following year Stansbury also had a skiff, possibly one of Gunnison's boats, to accompany his yawl on Great Salt Lake. Stansbury found his skiff to be quite useful and reliable after it was fitted-up and caulked. Gunnison's journal entry of April 16, 1850, mentions that the skiff contained ceiling planks, knees, cross-timbers, and thwarts, a substantial improvement over the five fir planks of which *Mud Hen* was constructed.

For his survey of the lake Stansbury arranged for a "yawl," a larger boat than the skiffs, to be built by Dan Jones. Construction of this boat began in September 1849, within a month, after Stansbury's arrival in the valley, and apparently was paid for in installments.[10] By the following spring Jones had the boat ready for use.

Stansbury, an accomplished sailor, found the *Salicornia* acceptable, but nothing to boast about. Flat-bottomed, excessively heavy, and slow despite its two masts, this humble craft was, as Stansbury remarked, "a miserable, lumbering affair."[11] Nor was he impressed with Jones's workmanship. The rudder was attached in "a most lubberly manner"; there were constant problems with the forward mast-step, and the boat needed recaulking only a month after it was launched.[12] When the survey ended Stansbury left both the yawl and the skiff to their fates, anchored in shoal water near Antelope Island, a muddy mile-long walk from shore.

Three years after Stansbury left the valley Dan Jones was again requested to build a boat, this time for Brigham Young who needed a boat large enough to ferry cattle and horses the short distance between the mainland and Antelope Island. Because the lake's waters had risen, the sandbar that earlier had been used to drive stock across to the island was, by 1854, completely submerged. Jones launched *The Timely Gull* in the Jordan River on June 30, 1854. Days after the boat was launched the *Deseret News* reported that it would soon be fitted with a stern wheel turned by two horses on a treadmill.[13]

In the nineteenth century horse-powered ferry boats were commonly used for short-distance crossings on lakes and rivers throughout the United States. Compact treadmills, as well as the other necessary machinery and fittings for horse-powered boats, were commercially available. However, it does not appear that *The Timely Gull* ever did use horse power. The craft was later known as a sailboat.[14]

Besides a mention of the boat's length of 45 feet, a few clues suggest the nature of *The Timely Gull's* hull. Because Young intended the boat to ferry stock, the hull was likely built low and wide. A "Bill of Items for Boat" mentions a "hog chaine" used in the boat's construction.[15] A hog chain, or hogging-chain, is a chain or cable attached at both inside ends of a vessel, which is tightened to keep the ends from sagging or hogging. This device is a necessity in lightly built, shallow hulls like those of most ferry boats. The "Bill of Items" otherwise notes that construction of *The Timely Gull* required at least 69 pounds of nails, 18 pounds of spikes, 126 bolts, and 14 gallons of tar—a reasonable amount of material for a 45-foot-long vessel— all procured from communal stores.

Four years after it was launched *The Timely Gull* was wrecked in a storm on the southern end of Antelope Island. Reportedly, the wreckage was visible for many years.[16]

Little information is available about the two boats launched by Miller brothers, one in 1859 or 1860 and the other in 1862.[17] The brothers used the first boat, called either a "skow" or a "flatboat," to stock their sheep-raising operations on Fremont Island. The second boat, also a "skow," gave the Millers considerable trouble soon after it was launched. The centerboard of the vessel leaked badly, necessitating, on one voyage, that 48 head of sheep be thrown overboard to lighten the sinking boat. This vessel was wrecked in 1876.

In September 1876 Jacob Miller began construction of a replacement for the wrecked sheep boat. He employed Henry Barrot to help design and construct the new boat, and despite disagreements concerning the shape the boat was to take the two worked through the autumn of 1876 to complete the vessel.[18] Seymour Miller, Jacob's son, described *Lady of the Lake* as:

> about 50 ft. long and 12 ft. wide. She carried two main masts, the largest one being about 50 ft. high. She flew four sails, two main sails, and two jibs. She was a double-decked craft with three and a half or four feet clearance

Fig. 1. Vessel abandoned on Great Salt Lake shore. Although it is not "scow-shaped," as George Frary described it, its size and configuration are similar to the cattle boat built by Jacob Miller in 1879. Used by permission, Utah State Historical Society, all rights reserved.

between the decks. This was plenty of clearance for the sheep and 300 head could be carried at a time. The cabin was at the rear of the boat. . . . She was a shallow water boat and when empty, would float in eight or ten inches of water.[19]

In the mid-1880s, after several years of neglect, *Lady of the Lake* was sold to Judge U. J. Wenner, who had obtained possession of Fremont Island. Moving to the island with his wife Kate and their son and daughter, Wenner repaired the boat, carved a ram's head on its stem, and rechristened it *Argo*.[20] During the time they lived on the island the boat served the family as their link to the mainland. Changing hands again, *Argo* remained in service as late as 1909. Shortly thereafter Seymour Miller claimed that the boat was wrecked at Promontory Point.

In the summer of 1879 Jacob Miller built another stock boat (Fig. 1), this one for the Davis County Co-op. He designed this odd craft to be sloop-rigged, 40 feet long and 16 feet wide, and "with a cabin forward of the mast and, back of the mast, a pen in which to put stock (wild stock if necessary), with ropes to prevent the main sail from dropping below the boom where it might be injured by the stock . . . it was arranged to load and unload from the stern."[21] This last boat of Miller's is undoubtedly the "clumsy, scow-shaped cattleboat, sloop-rigged . . . and steered with an oddly placed wheel on the forecastle deck" used by long-time island dweller and boat captain George Frary.[22] With this boat Frary transported a dozen buffalo to Antelope Island in 1892, the sires of the famous Antelope Island herd.

In 1868 and in the spring of 1869 former U.S. Army general Patrick E. Connor financed the launching of two 100-ton, flat-bottomed schooners, *Pioneer* and *Pluribustah*. Both vessels were designed to transport railroad ties, ore, and other materials from Connor's private mining operations near Stockton, at the southern end of the lake, to railroad points at the northern end."[23] There is no record of the shipwright who built these vessels, though Gammon Hayward is the likeliest candidate. He was actively building boats in the Salt Lake Valley as early as 1865; by 1868 he had already built at least one vessel for Connor, the steamboat *Kate Connor*.[24]

Flat-bottomed schooners, usually scow-schooners, were not an uncommon sight on North American waterways in the last century. However, the two known photographs of schooners on Great Salt Lake do not illustrate scow-schooners . . . ; the hulls of these vessels are more traditionally boat-shaped not scow-shaped.[25] There were traditions of keelless, flat-bottomed vessels in North America and Europe that had approximately the same hull form as the two schooners, but there are no certain parallels of which I am aware.[26]

Neither *Pioneer* nor *Pluribustah* remained in Connor's service after 1872 when commercial navigation on the lake had dwindled. During his tenure on Gunnison Island in 1896 artist and poet Alfred Lambourne noted a "schooner" in the island's bay used by the guano-diggers to transport their materials.[27] This vessel could have been one of Connor's boats under a new owner. In a 1909 interview David L. Davis claimed that *Pioneer* lay rotting in a boat graveyard at the mouth of the Jordan River. Of *Pluribustah* he said that "the wreck of the old schooner now lies within sight of the tracks at Saltair."[28]

Great Salt Lake's dozen or so working sailboats are the most homogenous of the three types of vessels used on the lake. All of the boats were flat-bottomed, constructed of locally available materials, and built by a handful of men, all Mormon converts, most, if not all, of whom had come from England or Wales. Nearly all of the boats were built before the arrival of the railroad, and even the two (or three) working sailboats built after 1869 do not seem to have been greatly affected by it. Jacob Miller, the only shipwright to build this type of boat after 1869, continued to use locally available materials. The working sailboats were the purest examples of Great Salt Lake's boatbuilding tradition. More than the steamboats and pleasure craft, these vessels were designed and built specifically within the limitations of the lake and the region's resources. Therefore, the relationship between the lake and the working sailboats was much more integrated, much more natural than that between the lake and other vessel types.

Steamboats

At the end of the 1860s, as the locomotives of the Union Pacific and Central Pacific transcontinental railroads were drawing closer to their meeting point near Great Salt Lake, steam power was introduced to the lake itself. Steamboats were certainly not new to North America; decades of refinement on North American waterways, most notably the Mississippi River, had nearly perfected the high pressure marine steam engine and steamboat hull design. By the 1860s the combined efforts of iron work-shops and shipwrights throughout the country, including those in California, were producing scores of steamboats a year. Steamboats and their land-based counterpart, the locomotive, were a source of American technological pride and world-renowned symbols of the nation's rapid progress as a civilized, industrialized country.

It is not surprising that the man who introduced the steamboat to Great Salt Lake, Patrick Connor, was a man who most wanted to see "progress" brought to the territory of Utah. Sent to Utah during the Civil War, he detested Brigham Young, not only because of the religion the prophet espoused, but also because he saw Young's stranglehold on the territory's political and economic realms as an impedi-ment to the development of the West. In everything he did in Utah, Connor sought to break Young's tight grip and to bring Utah into the nineteenth century, so to speak. In essence, his steamboat, *Kate Connor*, was a symbol of his struggle for west-ern development and progress. This steamboat, in addition to his fleet of sailboats would help to expand non-Mormon commercial enterprises and mining in the ter-ritory.[29] But the boat was neither an economic nor technical success, and ironically, Gammon Hayward, the man who built the steamboat's hull, was a Mormon.

The same themes of progress and Mormon-bashing are found in the origins of Great Salt Lake's most ambitious steamboat, *City of Corinne*, financed by the non-Mormon, if not anti-Mormon, Corinne Steam Navigation Company. The "Un-godly City," as Corinne was called by the Saints, was a railroad boom town located at the northern end of the lake on the Bear River.[30] Founded in 1869, Corinne quickly became the capital city for the territory's "gentiles" (non-Mormons) and the focal point for the lake's commercial navigation, primarily in the shipment of ores from the southern mines to the railroad. The townspeople lauded their *City of Corinne* as the most modern vessel to sail "the briny deep" and presented her tri-umphantly as the vanquisher of "Heathendom," Mormon Salt Lake City. Due to competition from the local railroads and the lack of materials needing shipment across the lake, this vessel too was an economic failure.

At a cost to Connor of $18,000, *Kate Connor* was launched in the Jordan River on December 11, 1868. The *Salt Lake Daily Reporter* described the boat as,

> fifty-five feet long, with eighteen feet main breadth and guards of four feet. The build consists of one "flush deck" in the center of which is left a space 10 x 6 feet, neatly covered and rising four feet, above deck, for the engine room, through which passes the main shaft to the side wheels, leaving considerable space in front and rear for freight. She is of sixty ton measurement . . . the boiler is from the Union Foundry, San Francisco, the machinery from Chicago.[31]

The only existing photographs of the boat (Figs. 3 and 4), taken in May 1869, show that *Kate Connor* was not a flashy steamboat and in fact appears to have been a little unusual. Gammon Hayward had never before built a steamboat hull, so it is likely that for his first (and only) steamboat, he simply modified the hull design he used for the schooners. *Kate Connor's* sheer (the longitudinal sweep of the vessel's sides), as seen in the photographs, is certainly closer to that found on a sailboat than that found on most steamboats of the period.[32] Also, the photographs show the boat's lack of an exhaust funnel, a necessary piece of steamboat equipment to ensure sufficient draft in the boiler to heat the required steam.

From a technological point of view *Kate Connor* was somewhat obsolete. Stemwheelers, which by the 1860s had become the steamboat of choice on the western rivers, offered several advantages over sidewheelers. Sidewheel boats, especially those with a single engine like *Kate Connor,* presented difficulties in maneuverability. Also, the boiler, engine, and drive shaft occupied the entire center section of the vessel, eliminating valuable cargo space.[33] Sternwheel vessels, with their engines and boilers spaced more efficiently, did not have this fault. Sidewheel steamboats did have one major advantage: their hulls were far less complex and easier to build. They did not require the bracing and support to compensate for the enormous weight of a wheel hung off of the stern. For Gammon Hayward, the comparative simplicity of a sidewheel hull was likely the determining factor for his first attempt at a steamboat.

Within a year after launching the lake's first steamboat Connor discovered several problems with the vessel itself and with operating a steam engine on the lake. Although the boat performed well on its trial run, it soon became apparent that *Kate Connor* was quite underpowered. During the spring of 1870 the vessel was entirely refitted with a new engine, a new boiler, and, to accommodate the increased power, its sidewheels were almost doubled in size.[34] At this time Connor may also have fitted the boat with a steam condenser of his own design.

Steamboats operating on fresh water simply pumped whatever water was necessary for steam directly from the lake or river to the boiler and then exhausted the steam from the engine into the atmosphere. This was not the case on Great Salt Lake. Because of the water's high salinity, which could do considerable damage to the boiler and engine, steamboats on the lake had to carry the fresh water they required on board. To eliminate the portage of an excessively large tank of water, Connor hoped to save space and weight on *Kate Connor* with his condenser.[35] With the condenser, the steam exhausted from the engine into copper coils strategically placed to be splashed upon with water from the sidewheels. Once the steam had cooled and condensed, the water was returned to the boiler. Despite this device, *Kate Connor* still had to stop at Antelope Island for fresh water on the long north-south voyages across the lake.

In March 1872 *Kate Connor* was sold to Mormon bishop Christopher Layton of Kaysville to be used by the Co-op for ferrying stock to Antelope Island.[36] How long Layton owned the boat is uncertain. Tradition claims that the boat was used again to haul ore after the Garfield smelter opened in the 1880s and that it sank loaded with ore near the smelter. More plausibly, David L. Davis stated that "the machinery of the

Figs. 3 and 4. Two views of *Kate Connor* in the Bear River near Corinne, May 1869. Used by permission, Utah State Historical Society, all rights reserved.

Fig. 5. *City of Corinne* at Lake Point, ca. 1871. Used by permission, Utah State Historical Society, all rights reserved.

Kate Connor was taken out after a few years [of service] and the boat went to pieces, with some others, in the 'graveyard' at the mouth of the Jordan River."[37]

Of all the vessels used on Great Salt Lake, none compares to *City of Corinne* (Fig. 5) for the amount of attention it has received. *City of Corinne* was, by the lake's standards, a glamorous vessel, huge, expensive, and thoroughly modern. No other vessel's launching drew such crowds and fanfare; no other vessel has seemed so out of place on Great Salt Lake.

The Corinne Steam Navigation Company, an investment consortium comprised of Corinne's leading businessmen, proudly launched their behemoth in the Bear River, May 24, 1871, with the intent of using the boat to transport goods and people between Lake Point and Corinne. The *Corinne Daily Reporter* described the vessel:

> Her length overall is 130 feet, beam 28 feet, depth of hold 7 feet, tonnage 300 tons, and has passenger accommodations for 150 persons. She is provided with fifteen-inch cylinder engines of four and a half feet stroke, manufactured by Girard B. Allen & Co., St. Louis. She also contains a water tank capacity of 14,000 gallons, to supply water for her boilers, which consist of two flue boilers, forty inches in diameter and twenty four feet long.[38]

Mechanically, *City of Corinne* displayed the latest in steamboat technology. The size and number of its boilers and engines were equal to those in comparable steamboats launched that same year on the Mississippi River.[39] Even the choice of a well-known engine builder, Girard B. Allen & Co., reveals Corinne's concern for obtaining the best and latest technology. Nor did they cut corners in the construction of the hull. Descriptions of the vessel under construction, as well as photographs of the hull's remains found in the 1930s (Fig. 6), show that *City of Corinne* was very heavily built, much more so than most Mississippi steamboats.[40]

It comes as no shock then to learn that the final cost, nearly $40,000, overran the original estimate by close to 40 percent.[41]

City of Corinne stands as the turning point in Great Salt Lake boatbuilding practices, not so much because of the vessel's technical marvels, but because it was entirely imported. Designed and prefabricated near Sacramento, California, *City of Corinne* came to Utah in pieces. Every bolt and every pre-sawn timber used in the hull was shipped by rail to Corinne, along with the shipwrights to put the parts back together.[42] In all, three dozen shipwrights, cabinet makers, and machinists came from California to reassemble the vessel, a task that took seven weeks to complete. Nothing about this vessel, not even the money that financed it, was indigenous to Utah Territory.

After one season of service *City of Corinne* was quietly declared a financial failure by its owners, who sold it to H. S. Jacobs & Co., a mining firm. Brigham Young's son, John, owned the steamboat for a short time around 1875 before it finally came into Thomas Douris's possession. The founder of the Garfield Beach resort, Douris used *City of Corinne* as an excursion boat and renamed it *General Garfield* after one of his more notable passengers. In the late 1870s or early 1880s Douris at last moored the boat to one of Garfield Beach's piers, stripped its machinery, and left it to be used, successively, as a floating hotel, a changing room for bathers, and a boathouse for the Salt Lake Rowing Club (Fig. 7). In 1904 *City of Corinne,* by then a dilapidated curiosity, burned to the waterline with the rest of the Garfield Beach resort. Before the end of the decade the Western Pacific Railroad ignominiously buried the charred bow of the steamboat beneath their roadbed.

City of Corinne has the distinction of being the only one of the "early boats" rediscovered in this century. In the late 1930s Salt Lake Yacht Club Commodore Thomas C. Adams and Daughter of Utah Pioneers historian Bernice Anderson took an interest in the reexposed remains of the vessel. Both took many photographs of the half-buried, half-burned hull. Anderson's article on the history of the vessel and of Garfield Beach soon thereafter appeared in the *Salt Lake Tribune* (September 9, 1938). What remained of *City of Corinne* now lies beneath two roadbeds, those of the railroad and Interstate 80.

Less than three months after the grand *City of Corinne* made its debut in the Bear River, John Young's tiny steamer, *Lady of the Lake,* was launched eighty miles south in the Jordan River. *Lady of the Lake* was the first of many small steamers used on Great Salt Lake solely for pleasure outings. The earliest of these boats were little more than playthings for the valley's wealthier sailors. After the turn of the century resorts on the south side of the lake employed small, bus-like steamers for their daily or hourly excursions

Fig. 6. Remains of *City of Corinne*, ca. 1938. Used by permission, Utah State Historical Society, all rights reserved.

Fig. 7. *General Garfield* (*City of Corinne*) at the Garfield Beach pier, ca. 1890. Used by permission, Utah State Historical Society, all rights reserved.

Lady of the Lake, only 30 feet long with a 10 foot beam, was first launched and tested by its Williamsburg builders on the Hudson River in June 1871.[43] Having successfully passed its trials, the boat was shipped to Utah on a railcar; three months later John Young relaunched it near the Jordan bridge. For over a decade *Lady of the Lake* guarded her enviable position as the lake's only diminutive steamer until two other steamers, *Whirlwind* and *Susie Riter,* joined her in the 1880s. The sidewheel *Susie Riter* was employed at Garfield Beach for almost two years before it sank at anchor in a storm. The fates of *Lady of the Lake* and *Whirlwind* are not known.

Lady of the Lake and *Whirlwind* were probably Great Salt Lake's first propeller-driven vessels. Two photographs (Fig. 8 [Fig. 9 not shown here]) taken in the 1880s show small, propeller-driven steamers that may be illustrations of the two boats.[44] The use of a fixed propeller is significant because it demonstrates the changing nature of vessels used on the lake. Because of the lake's shallowness, a vessel with a fixed propeller is more likely to run onto submerged obstacles than either a paddlewheeler or sailboat. Clearly these propeller-driven steamers were neither designed nor built with Great Salt Lake in mind. Like the *City of Corinne, Lady of the Lake* and *Whirlwind* may have been imported boats of a generic design, basically ill-suited for use on the lake.[45]

Although not really within the focus of this article, the Southern Pacific Railroad's fleet, used during the construction of the Lucin Cutoff (1902–3), deserves mention. Photographs taken during the construction of the cutoff show that the railroad's fleet consisted of one large sternwheeler, *Promontory* (Fig. 10), and at least four smaller launches. All of the vessels appear to have been steam powered. In his recent research on the launches, California boatbuilder David Peterson determined that they were built in San Francisco then shipped by rail to the lake.[46] This may also have been the case with *Promontory.*[47] According to Peterson, at least one of the launches, *Lucin,* was shipped back to California after work on the cutoff was completed. There it saw use as a fishing boat for nearly a century until it sank in 1992. Two of the other launches remained on the lake, serving a variety of purposes until at least the late 1930s. There is no record of *Promontory's* disposition.

The development of Great Salt Lake's steamboats was closely linked to the railroad. All mechanical components for the steamboats had to be imported by rail, and, with the exception of *Kate Connor,* it may be argued that the hulls were imported as well. The steamboats, again with the exception of *Kate Connor,* therefore cannot be counted as part of the Great Salt Lake boatbuilding tradition. They were a short-lived phase, replaced after the turn of the century by more economical gasoline-powered boats.

Pleasure Sailboats

Sailboats built for the sole purpose of racing or pleasure sailing outnumbered every other type of boat on the lake in the nineteenth century. At least fifteen of these "yachts" or "sloops" were built between 1865 and 1901. Nearly twenty years had passed

Fig 8. Small, propeller-driven steamer, possibly *Whirlwind*, near the Garfield Beach resort, ca. 1885. Used by permission, Utah State Historical Society, all rights reserved.

Fig. 10. The sternwheeler *Promontory* was involved in the construction of the Lucin Cutoff. Used by permission, Utah State Historical Society, all rights reserved.

since the launching of Great Salt Lake's first boat, *Mud Hen,* before the appearance of the first "yacht."[48] Primarily the lapse of time is a reflection of regional economics. In the first decade of Mormon settlement there was little spare cash or spare time to be spent on luxuries such as pleasure boats. By the 1860s, as the region's wealth increased and the Old Fort near City Creek became a thriving Salt Lake City, there was more money and time to spend on non-necessities. The many sailboats built for sport or pleasure on the lake were indicative of the region's economic success. More wealth generally means more leisure time, or at least more expensive entertainment.

Interest in the sporting aspects of sailing inspired the formation of the Salt Lake Yacht Club in 1867 and may have motivated the construction of boats designed to compete in the club's regattas. Although there were many of these yachts, their details remain far more obscure than those of other of Great Salt Lake's vessels. Gammon Hayward is known to have built the first yacht, possibly *Petrel,* in 1865 for Salt Lake City's well-known merchants, the Walker brothers.[49] Hayward also had a hand in the construction of several other yachts, the names of which are uncertain. At least three other sailboats, *Eureka, Star of the West,* and *Pride,* were launched before the completion of the railroad in 1869. Of these, *Pride* and *Star of the West* may have been Hayward's projects. *Eureka* was built by a Brother Tuckfield with David L. Davis lending his assistance.[50]

As for the design of these boats, the nature of the lake excluded many European or American yacht types with which local shipwrights may have been familiar. The lake necessitated shallow-draft designs, preventing the use of deep- or ballast-keeled yachts.[51] For larger boats, such as the 28-foot-long *Waterwitch* (Fig. 11), the necessity of a light draft must have had a serious effect on its sailing performance. Without a deep- or ballasted-keel to offset the weight of the rigging and the force of the wind on its large sails, *Waterwitch* could not have been too stable in heavy winds or too successful in the Yacht Club's regattas.[52] The need to find a shallow drafted, yet stable, design explains why David L. Davis chose a catamaran hull type for his two best known yachts, *Cambria I* and *Cambria II.*

Born in Wales, where he converted to Mormonism, Davis did not enter the valley until 1864. He was a successful grocer and spent what free time he had either sailing or building boats. His interest in Great Salt Lake and in sailboats instigated the formation of the Yacht Club; he served as its Commodore for several decades. An intense observer of the lake and of the way various types of vessels performed on it, he came to realize that this odd body of water demanded innovative watercraft: boats designed both to perform superbly on the lake and to survive its perils. In September 1877 he launched *Cambria I,* the embodiment of his observations of the lake and its vessels.

The first *Cambria* (Fig. 12) was not a large boat, measuring 19 feet long with a 10-foot beam, but it was the first catamaran (a craft having two hulls side by side) in the West, and one of the first catamaran yachts in the United States.[53] Strung between its two lapstrake-constructed hulls, *Cambria I* had a large open deck and

Fig. 11. Yacht anchored near Black Rock, late 1870s. The size of this boat corresponds to that given for *Waterwitch*.

a single mast carrying a sloop rig. As the results of the Yacht Club's regattas show, *Cambria I* was a very successful design. Davis used the boat for over twenty years until he lost interest in favor of his greater project, *Cambria II*. Left on the beach near a pavilion at Black Rock, the first *Cambria* burned to ashes at the hands of errant Utah and Nevada railroad employees in 1904.[54]

Launched by Davis on July 31, 1901, *Cambria II* (Fig. 13) was the most elegant yacht ever to sail Great Salt Lake. Over 40 feet long and possessing a 14-foot beam, she had six berths, a galley, and a lavatory in its cabin.[55] In the construction of the boat's two hulls, Davis took every precaution to ensure strength and resistance to corrosion; the boat's framing was of oak and the fasteners all galvanized. To propel the boat Davis yawl-rigged over 1,500 square feet of canvas and, more notably, *Cambria II* carried on deck, just forward of the wheel, Great Salt Lake's first naphtha engine. This four-cylinder, six-horsepower motor, now on display in the Daughters of Utah Pioneers Museum in Salt Lake City, was connected by a retractable brass shaft to the boat's brass propeller.[56]

Cambria II did not have the illustrious racing career of its predecessor. Davis and his son, Dewey, used the yacht primarily as an excursion boat, sometimes for fare-paying tourists. After Davis died in 1926 *Cambria II* fell into disrepair.

Great Salt Lake's short-lived boatbuilding tradition quietly ended the day David L. Davis launched *Cambria II*. Any locally built boats to follow Davis's last yacht

Fig. 12. The catamaran *Cambria I* (behind boat in foreground) at Garfield Beach, ca. 1885. Used by permission, Utah State Historical Society, all rights reserved.

were far too contaminated by commercial boatbuilding techniques to be counted as indigenous. Without question, the purest period of Great Salt Lake's wooden boatbuilding tradition occurred in the two decades before the completion of the transcontinental railroad. Quickly thereafter, the introduction of outside materials and of boats not expressly designed for Great Salt Lake eroded the region's distinctive boatbuilding practices. Although a later craft that benefitted from the commercial boatbuilding industry, *Cambria II* was thoroughly attuned to the nature of Great Salt Lake. This boat was a final tribute to the lake Davis loved.

By the turn of the century most of Great Salt Lake's early boats were rotting hulks. The dream of a Great Salt Lake commercial shipping fleet had been overcome by the reality of the lake itself and the competition from the railroads; the abandoned schooners and steamboats stood as monuments of thwarted ambition. Through the 1890s a few boats still shuffled cattle and sheep between the islands, but little use remained for them when the herds on the islands dwindled. These boats too were abandoned and left to the elements. Only yachts and excursion boats continued to find use on the lake in the twentieth century. As these older yachts grew irreparable and were themselves abandoned, they were replaced, not by locally built boats but by brand-name boats. In the early 1930s, three decades after Davis launched the lake's finest sailboat, Thomas C. Adams, the new Commodore

Fig. 13. David L. Davis at the helm of *Cambria II*. Used by permission, Utah State Historical Society, all rights reserved.

of the Yacht Club, photographed the stripped *Cambria II* (Fig. 14) as it lay on shore
near the newly created Great Salt Lake Boat Harbor. On that day nearly one hundred newer sailboats and motorboats were moored in the harbor, all of them safely
insulated, physically and spiritually, from the lake.

Notes

Peter G. Van Alfen is a graduate student in the Nautical Archaeology Program at Texas
A & M University.

1. Terry Tempest Williams, *Refuge: An Unnatural History of Family and Place* (New York,
   1991), p. 5.
2. *Daily Utah Reporter,* August 8, 1870. Since the 1850s, when records of the lake's level
   begin, the water level in the lake has fluctuated by as much as 20 feet. In some places

Fig. 14. *Cambria II*, ca. 1930. Used by permission, Utah State Historical Society, all rights reserved.

this has altered the shoreline by as many as 15 miles. Needless to say, changes in the lake's level have often been catastrophic both to wildlife and to human enterprise. See, for example, Richard H. Jackson, "Great Salt Lake and Great Salt Lake City: American Curiosities," *Utah Historical Quarterly* 56 (1988): 128–48; and Williams, *Refuge*.

3. The boat used by Stansbury's expedition, *Salicornia,* and the Miller brothers' scow launched in 1862, experienced serious leaks and structural problems less than a month after they were launched. Local shipwright David L. Davis maintained that "there was no cause for concern or alarm in navigating the lake if the boats were strong, even if they were not of special construction." See "The Great Salt Lake and Its Islands" in Kate B. Carter, comp., *Our Pioneer Heritage* 20 vols. (Salt Lake City: Daughters of Utah Pioneers, 1958–77), 11:442.

4. There are no hardwoods in the local canyons that grow to sufficient size or have wood of the structural strength required in boatbuilding. Of the many softwood species available, Douglas fir *(Pseudotsuga menziesii)* offers the most suitable wood for boatbuilding, although it can be brittle. Unfortunately, there are no specific mentions of the woods used by the prerailroad shipwrights. Stansbury laments that the wood used to build *Salicornia,* "although the best material the country afforded, was so 'shaky' and liable to split and crack, that it was totally unfit for the purpose" (Howard Stansbury, *An Expedition to the Valley of the Great Salt Lake* [Philadelphia, 1852], p. 150). Securing usable trees also required journeys of at least 3 0 miles roundtrip up the canyons. Jacob Miller went as far as Blacksmith Fork near Logan, almost 100 miles away, for the wood he used to build *Lady of the Lake* (David H. Miller and Anne M. Eckman, eds.,

"Seymour Miller's Account of an Early Sheep Operation on Fremont Island," *Utah Historical Quarterly* 56 (1988): 168.

5. A piece of paper dated August 31, 1854, in LDS Church Archives, Salt Lake City, describes the 164-pound anchor and its construction by Jonathan Pugmire. Similarly, the 500-pound anchor for the *City of Corinne* was fashioned from iron taken from dismantled wagons. See *History of Tooele County* (Tooele: Daughters of Utah Pioneers, 1961), p. 149.

6. Kate B. Carter, comp., *Heart Throbs of the West*, 12 vols. (Salt Lake City: Daughters of Utah Pioneers, 1939–50), 4:164; *Headstone Dedicatory Service for Captain Dan Jones, 4 Aug. 1810–13 Jan. 1862* (Provo, 1974), pamphlet in Utah State Historical Society collection; J. R. and Elna Miller, eds., *Journal of Jacob Miller* (Salt Lake City, 1967), p. 176.

7. David L. Davis, who will be discussed below, is another Welsh boatbuilder to be added to this list.

8. Dale L. Morgan, *The Great Salt Lake* (Albuquerque: University of New Mexico Press, 1973), pp. 204, 211–12: and Carter, *Heart Throbs,* 4:162.

9. J. W. Gunnison Journal, November 12, 1849, in Brigham D. Madsen, ed., *Exploring the Great Salt Lake: The Stansbury Expedition of 1849–50* (Salt Lake City: University of Utah Press, 1989), October-November 1849, passim.; Stansbury, *An Expedition,* p. 161.

10. Gunnison's journal entry for September 22, 1849, in Madsen, *Exploring,* mentions $50.00 sent to Dan Jones "as an installment on building a yawl boat." The total cost for the boat is not recorded.

11. Stansbury, *An Expedition,* p. 173. Stansbury's descriptions of *Salicornia* suggest that it was very similar in appearance to the flat-bottomed, double-ended sailing dories used by New England fisherman in the nineteenth century. See Howard I. Chapelle, *American Small Sailing Craft: Their Design, Development, and Construction* (New York, 1951), pp. 85–94. Stansbury uses "yawl" as a general description. Originally, a "yawl" was a ship's boat, but by the mid-nineteenth century the term meant any open boat, rowed or sailed, larger than a "skiff."

12. Stansbury, Journal, May 2, 1850, in Madsen, *Exploring;* see also Stansbury, *An Expedition,* p. 191. After his experiences with *Salicornia* Stansbury regretted that he had not procured two Francis metallic lifeboats for the survey, "which would have," he laments, "saved much time and effort."

13. *Deseret News,* July 6, 1854.

14. The Journal History of the Church, June 25, 1856, LDS Church Archives, notes that *The Timely Gull* "had been fitted-up as a sailing boat." Morgan, *The Great Salt Lake,* p. 254, also reports that Young had plans to install a steam engine in *The Timely Gull*

15. This undated piece of paper in LDS Church Archives lists various items supplied by the Tithing House and the Public Works Smith Shop used in the construction of the boat.

16. Morgan, *The Great Salt Lake,* p. 257.

17. Brief mentions of the two boats appear in the Henry William Miller Diary, typescript, p. 49, Utah State Historical Society collections; and Miller and Miller, *Journal of Jacob Miller,* pp. 56, 61, 63, 176.

In addition to the four known boats constructed by the Miller family, Seymour Miller claims that the family also constructed a "75 foot boat with three holds to use in [the] salt business" (Miller and Eckman, "Seymour Miller's Account," p. 173). This may be *Old Bob,* a boat traditionally owned by the Millers (Margaret S. Hess, *My Farmington, 1847–1976* [Farmington: Daughters of Utah Pioneers, 1976], p.54). There are no other records of either *Old Bob* or the 75-foot salt boat.

18. Miller and Miller, *Journal of Jacob Miller*, p. 176. Barrot had crafted a half-model of the boat and intended to work by eye from the model. Miller, on the other hand, had drawn lines for the boat and wanted Barrot to follow his calculations.

19. Miller and Eckman, "Seymour Miller's Account," p. 169.

20. Ibid., p. 173, and n. 40.

21. Miller and Miller, *Journal of Jacob Miller*, p. 176. Construction of this boat cost $615.72. Also, Seymour Miller claimed this boat could carry "about 25 head of cattle and 200 head of sheep" (Miller and Eckman, "Seymour Miller's Account," p. 173).

22. Morgan, *The Great Salt Lake*, p. 326.

23. Ibid., p. *294*. *Pluribustah* was also known as *Bustah* and *Filerbuster*. The *Utah Tri-Weekly Reporter*, May 17, 1870, mentions another schooner, *Viola*, carrying ore to Corinne from Stockton. There is no other record of this vessel.

24. Carter, *Heart Throbs*, 4:164. Since Dan Jones died in 1862, the Miller brothers are the only other likely candidates, but they built vessels solely for their own operations. Other boatbuilders active in the valley in the late 1860s, such as Davis, seem to have limited themselves to building yachts.

25. [A photo of a schooner] which appeared in Miller and Eckman, "Seymour Miller's Account," may not be *Lady of the Lake*. This unlabeled photograph was found in Seymour Miller's papers on Great Salt Lake (personal communication, David H. Miller, February 1994). The other photograph appeared in Hess, *My Farmington*, with the caption, "Miller boat used to haul livestock to Antelope Island." Close examination reveals that these are photographs of two different vessels, one of which may in fact be *Lady of the Lake*. The other is probably one of Connor's schooners.

26. Some English and Welsh sailing barges were similarly shaped (F. G. G. Carr, *Sailing Barges* [London, 1951], *passim*). In North America the closest parallel may be the Brown's Ferry Vessel, a flat-bottomed, eighteenth-century boat excavated at Brown's Ferry near Georgetown, South Carolina, in 1976 by the South Carolina Institute for Archaeology and Anthropology (Frederick M. Hocker, "The Development of a Bottom-based Shipbuilding Tradition in Northwestern Europe and the New World" [Ph.D. diss., Texas A & M University, 1991], pp. 227–48; and A. B. Albright and J.R. Steffy, "The Brown's Ferry Vessel, South Carolina," *International Journal of Nautical Archaeology* 8 [1979]: 121–42)

27. Morgan, *The Great Salt Lake*, p. 342.

28. "Experiences of Capt. David L. Davis on the Great Salt Lake, compiled by Mr. and Mrs. Stephen L. Richards," bound, undated, and unpaginated manuscript in the Daughters of Utah Pioneers Museum, Salt Lake City.

29. Brigham D. Madsen, *Glory Hunter: A Biography of Patrick E. Connor* (Salt Lake City: University of Utah Press, 1990), describes Connor's activities in Utah, including the political and economic situations surrounding the launching of *Kate Connor*.

30. Brigham D. Madsen, *Corinne: The Gentile Capital of Utah* (Salt Lake City: Utah Historical Society, 1980), is the most complete history of Corinne's development and its relations with the Mormon capital, Salt Lake City. The chapter entitled "By Land and by Sea" is the best account available of Great Salt Lake's short-lived, non-Mormon commercial navigation enterprises.

31. *Salt Lake Daily Reporter*, December 11, 1868. The note in the article that the machinery (i.e., engine) for this boat came from Chicago has caused some confusion. Bernice Anderson (in Carter, *Heart Throbs*, 4:165) claimed that the engines for *City of Corinne* were built in Chicago, shipped around the Horn to California, and then to Utah.

Although her story is often cited, Anderson confuses *Kate Connor* with *City of Corinne*. In fact, the engines for *City of Corinne* were built in St. Louis and shipped by rail to Utah. Furthermore, it is not likely that Connor would have paid to ship *Kate Connor's* engine around the Horn if it could be forwarded west from Chicago by rail. Also, it should be noted that all of the wood used in the construction of *Kate Connor* came from local sources *(Mining and Scientific Press,* November 28, 1868).

32. Although some post-1850 American steamboats, especially a few eastern examples, had hull forms similar to *Kate Connor,* most tended to have much flatter sheers than that of sailing craft. This was due to the fact that the average steamboat hull was built more boxlike than boatlike. In at least two other ways *Kate Connor* departs from what was common practice on late nineteenth century western steamboats. The paddlewheels appear to be placed either directly amidships or farther forward—an unusual trait in later sidewheelers. Also, *Kate Connor's* length-to-beam ratio (without the guards) was 3:1; the average for steamboats of its class in 1870 was nearly 5:1 (Louis C. Hunter, *Steamboats on the Western Rivers: An Economic and Technical History* [New York, 1949], pp. 80–86).

33. Single-engine, sidewheel boats were difficult to maneuver because both wheels were connected to the same drive shaft. A pilot could not tighten his turning radius by stopping or slowing one wheel and leaving the other rotating, as an automotive differential works when the vehicle is turned. Some later sidewheelers did employ clutches at the wheels to overcome this problem. Sidewheel boats were more vulnerable to collision damage than sternwheelers, and they could not provide as much paddle area as stemwheelers potentially could and hence might be slower (Hunter, *Steamboats,* pp. 145–46; and personal communication, Kevin Crisman, May 1994).

34. *Utah Tri-Weekly Reporter,* May 21, 1870; *Daily Utah Reporter,* June 17, 1870. During this refitting Connor also remodeled the boat's passenger accommodations. In doing so he hoped to make more money on excursions than he had made using the boat to haul freight. This refitting, as some have claimed, was not a conversion of *Kate Connor* from a sailing schooner to a steamboat; she was never rigged with sails.

35. *Mining and Scientific Press,* February 20, 1869. This condenser did not eliminate completely the portage of fresh water, nor did it allow the lake's water to be used as Madsen *Corinne,* p. 180, implies.

36. *Corinne Daily Reporter,* March 30, 1872.

37. Richards, "Experiences of Capt. David L. Davis," from a ca. 1909 interview with Davis.

38. June 15, 1871. The *City of Corinne's* length has been variously reported as being 128, 130, and 150 feet. The discrepancies may be explained as follows: 128 feet, as the length from the inside of the stem to the inside of the sternpost (the official manner in which steamboat hull lengths were recorded); 130 feet, as the overall length of the hull itself, and 150 feet, as the overall length of the vessel including the sternwheel.

39. Hunter, *Steamboats,* p. 156.

40. The *Daily Utah Reporter,* March 13, 1871, described the floor timbers (of Oregon fir, not redwood as some have claimed) as being eight inches moulded and only ten inches apart. These floors in turn were secured to the keel by innumerable galvanized bolts. This is well shown in the photographs from the 1930s. The vessel's planking was three inches thick. As a comparison, Mississippi riverboats were, on average, built with floor timbers measuring only three to six inches moulded and with planking of one to two inches thickness (Hunter, *Steamboats,* p. 80). Although the comparison has often been made, *City of Corinne* was in no way a Mississippi-style steamboat. Unlike Mississippi

steamboats, *City of Corinne's* hull was far more boatlike than bargelike, though it did not have quite the same qualities as *Kate Connor's* hull. Heavier and more boatlike steamboat hulls similar to *City of Corinne's* were found on the Columbia and other far-western rivers.

41. *Corinne Daily Journal*, May 23, 1871.

42. Prefabricated steamboats were not unusual in the late nineteenth century. In the 1870s one Pennsylvania steamboat builder, James Rees & Sons Co., shipped prefabricated vessels to such places as India and the Belgian Congo. Nor was *City of Corinne* Great Salt Lake's only large, imported steamboat. See n. 47.

43. Morgan, *The Great Salt Lake*, p. 361.

44. There is no specific mention, as there is in the case of *Susie Riter*, of these boats having paddlewheels. Furthermore, these photographs are of two different steamboats, and no other small steamers are known to have been used on the lake until after the turn of the century.

45. No clear records exist for the origins of *Whirlwind* and *Susie Riter*. One cryptic reference *(History of Tooele County*, p. 143) claims that either William G. Davis or Alonzo Hyde built a steamer for use at the Black Rock resort in the early 1880s. This boat could be either *Susie Riter* or *Whirlwind*, although Morgan *(The Great Salt Lake*, p. 356) makes it clear that both boats were owned by Thomas Douris of Garfield Beach. Douris may very well have brought both boats to Utah. David L. Davis, after an excursion with Douris on *Susie Riter*, was not too impressed with the little sidewheeler's performance, suggesting that even this boat was ill-suited for use on the lake ("Journal of David L. Davis," November 7, 1886, in *Chronicles of Courage* (Salt Lake City: Daughters of Utah Pioneers, 1990–), vol. 4.

46. Personal communication, January 1994.

47. *Promontory* has often been mislabeled as one of the lake's excursion steamers. Clearly this rough boat was built for work not pleasure. Photographs show that it was much less heavily constructed than either *City of Corinne* or *Kate Connor*. In the fashion of turn-of-the-century and earlier Mississippi-style steamboats, *Promontory* used a great deal of external support for the hull; for example, note the large sampson post in the center of the vessel and the trusses along its sides. Lightly built steamboats of this type were far easier to transport over land—because they were built with less wood—and far easier to reassemble. See, for example, *Charles H. Spencer*, a paddlewheeler similar to *Promontory* launched on the Colorado River in 1912. Toni Carrel, ed., *Submerged Cultural Resources Site Report: Charles H. Spencer Mining Operations and Paddlewheel Steamboat*, Southwest Cultural Resources Center Professional Papers, No. 13, (New Mexico, 1987).

48. Although technically many of these sailboats can not be considered true "yachts," I will use the term here to distinguish these boats from the working sailboats. This is the term used by David L. Davis when he referred to all the lake's pleasure or sport sailboats.

49. Carter, *Heart Throbs*, 4:164. *Petrel* is said to be the first yacht on the lake *(Utah Daily Reporter*, September 7, 1869). The Walker brothers' yacht may therefore be *Petrel* which was owned in the 1870s by Milton Barret, vice commodore of the Yacht Club. *Petrel* was seriously damaged in a storm, November 1882, that wrecked and damaged several other Yacht Club members' boats (Richards, "Experiences of Capt. David L. Davis").

50. Ibid. Nothing else is known about the boatbuilder "Brother Tuckfield."

51. Since the completion of the dredged Salt Lake County Boat Harbor, deep- and ballast-keeled sailboats have been able to use the lake, so long as they keep to deeper water.

52. Davis reported that *Waterwitch*, 28 feet long with an 8-foot beam, carried 50 square yards of canvas, an appreciable amount. That it had a shallow draft is shown by the fact that Davis and his crew were able to row the boat over the bars at the mouth of the Jordan River in August 1875. His accounts of sailing this boat frequently note dropping or reefing the mainsail at the slightest wind change, an indication that the boat could not handle heavier winds. Amazingly, there is no mention of the boat being fitted with a centerboard that would have alleviated much of the instability. *Waterwitch* was wrecked at Lake Shore in the storm of November 1882.

53. As early as the 1810s catamaran steamboats had been used as ferries on several eastern rivers. On the Mississippi and related rivers catamaran steamboats were used as "snag boats" (vessels designed to clear the rivers of submerged obstacles) and as ironclads (Hunter, *Steamboats,* p. 82). But the catamaran yacht did not see widespread use in the United States until the 1950s. In the late 1880s New England boatbuilder Nathaniel Herreshoff presented a catamaran yacht to the New York Yacht Club. It declared a "freak" because of its superior performance and was subsequently barred from participation in the club's regattas. Robert Harris, *The Modern Sailing Catamaran* (New York, 1960), p. 14).

54. Davis records that *Cambria I* won most if not all of the Yacht Club's regattas throughout the 1880s. Those who torched her may have been the same people who burned the dilapidated *City of Corinne* less than a mile away. Richards, "Experiences of Capt. David L. Davis."

55. Ibid.

56. In 1886 Davis came to the conclusion, after his excursion with Douris on *Susie Riter,* that the best way to propel boats on the lake was with the combination of sail and steam. In the internal combustion engine, Davis found a power plant more compact and more economical than any steam engine available.

VI
FANTASIES, TALES, AND PHENOMENA

Weird Weather, Odd Creatures, and a Vanishing Act

Perhaps because the Great Salt Lake is such a conspicuous geological anomaly—a huge body of salt water in the midst of an even more immense desert—its lore has become encrusted through the years with some amazing stories. Tales of a prehistoric race of people called the "Munchies" who lived on the lake's islands; of a large river, the Rio Buenaventura, which drained the lake to the west and flowed all the way to the ocean; of Indians riding elephants along its shores; of immense whirlpools large enough to suck even a large schooner into their bowels; and, perhaps inevitably, of a sea monster, have created a fantastic lore as exotic as the lake itself. Such tales have been encouraged, no doubt, by the fact that there are indeed enough exotic phenomena around the lake, both natural and manmade, so that people have found it possible to cross the ephemeral boundary in their imaginations between reality and fantasy, and to believe almost anything. This section—which is by no means exhaustive!—explores that borderland.

Fireballs

Almost any annual cycle of seasons in one of the Wasatch Front cities from Ogden to Provo will demonstrate the dramatic effect the Great Salt Lake has on the weather. The so-called "lake effect," for example, can greatly exacerbate storms over the mountain-hugging cities. Most storm systems approach the urban areas from the northwest, crossing the Great Salt Lake on the way (Utah Valley cities experience something similar when storms cross the much smaller freshwater Utah Lake). If the sun has warmed the water, the storm will pick up large quantities of evaporated moisture in the atmosphere and carry it eastward. As the storm is forced upwards by the mountains into thinner and cooler air, that moisture precipitates over the cities, with the possibility of turning what might have been a minor shower into a real deluge.

The geography of the lake environs, too, produces violent weather patterns on the lake itself. The often significantly different temperatures over the lake and the land, the vast unobstructed expanses of desert and lake, and the successions of mountain ranges and valleys to the east and south of the lake offer many possibilities for violent winds to develop and to become channeled in unexpected ways. Winds of one hundred miles per hour have been recorded at the Great Salt Lake marina, for example, and sailors often experience the sudden terror of "Tooele twisters"—unheralded gusts of wind roaring out of Tooele Valley and whirling around the north end of the Oquirrh Mountains that can put a sailboat "rail down" (on its side) before the helmsman can react.

No doubt the eeriest of weather phenomena on the lake, though, are the fireballs that have been observed on multiple occasions and are reported here by two of Salt Lake City's most respected television weathermen, Mark Eubank and Clayton Brough:

> John Silver, who used to operate a beach and marina on the south shore of the Great Salt Lake, for many years had the opportunity to observe the lake and all of its varied weather conditions. One of the oddest events he ever observed was the appearance one summer of several "balls of fire" on the surface of the lake. A night watchman became so spooked over this that he quit on the spot. The color of the "fire" was red, the shape was spherical; the fireballs appeared to be quite large and would dance all around on the surface of the water. Several sightings were reported. On one or two occasions, dinner patrons of the Islander Cruise Boat were witnesses to the phenomena. It is possible that some electrical-optical event was taking place similar to ball lightning or possibly some chemical reaction between the air and the lake-brine solutions.*

Pink Floyd

The islands of the Great Salt Lake and the wetlands along much of its shore are habitat for an amazing variety of shore birds, as we have seen. They are objects of much scientific study and delight for bird watchers. Visitors to Saltair and sailors on their way to the marina, however, often find themselves rubbing their eyes and reaching for their binoculars and cameras when they observe, ankle deep in seagulls, stilts, and avocets, what appears to be a pink flamingo. Their eyes are, in fact, telling them the truth. One of the delights of visiting the south shore of the lake during the winter months is a viewing of an escaped Chilean flamingo that has come to be known as Pink Floyd.

---

* From Mark E. Eubank and R. Clayton Brough, "The Great Salt Lake and Its Influence on the Weather," in J. Wallace Gwynn, *Great Salt Lake: A Scientific, Historical and Economic Overview* (Salt Lake City: Utah Geological and Mineralogical Survey Bulletin 116, 1980), 282.

Floyd's residency in Utah began at the Tracy Aviary in Liberty Park in downtown Salt Lake City in 1985. The wily flamingo somehow escaped notice when the wings of other new acquisitions were clipped to keep them from flying away. For three years he seems to have been happy enough with the aviary's regular meals and the company of the other birds, but in 1988 he spread his wings and flew away. One would think that a bird that big and bright in color would be easy to spot anywhere, but in fact his whereabouts since that time are only sporadically known. In the winter of 1988 he first appeared on the south shore of Great Salt Lake, and that has been his regular winter hangout ever since. In the spring, though, he flies away to an unknown destination for the summer. He has been spotted on the lake's north shore and once in an irrigation canal some thirty miles farther north, but the location of a regular summer residence has not been discovered.

One might think that the frigid winter weather of Great Salt Lake would be an uncomfortable habitat for a tropical bird, but in fact the climatic extremes are very close to those of the species' native Chile, Bolivia, and Peru. The lake's abundant supply of brine shrimp, too, has proven to be a healthy diet (like whales, flamingoes scoop up feed-bearing water and strain it through a screen-like structure at the sides of their mouths). And flamingoes are very social birds. Although Floyd is the only flamingo at the lake, the abundant population of other species apparently satisfies his need for a social life, and the other birds give every evidence of having welcomed him into their company as well. Floyd has been observed flying with a flock of tundra swans, but most of the time his companions are the much smaller gulls, stilts, and avocets who feed in the shallow water between Saltair and the marina.

Wildlife management people have attempted to capture Floyd, but the freedom of his life on the lake obviously appeals to him more than the sedentary style of the aviary. He will allow his stalkers to approach him very closely, but when they make a move to capture him, he frustrates them with an amazing burst of takeoff speed. So one has to expect that Pink Floyd will be a Great Salt Lake resident as long as he wishes.*

The Sea Monster

A flamingo in the Great Salt Lake seems improbable enough, though his origin and presence are both well accounted for, leaving his whereabouts in the summers the only remaining mystery. Other lake creatures of reputed existence stretch the imagination much further than Pink Floyd. As early as 1877, for example, there have been periodic reports of a sea monster, perhaps a migrating one that divides its time among the Great Salt Lake, Utah Lake, and Bear Lake, where it has been variously

---

* Sharon J. Huntington, "A Flamingo Flies the Coop to Fame," *Christian Science Monitor*, 6 January 1998.

sighted and described. It was one J. H. McNeill, an employee of a salt company at its plant in Kelton, on the north end of the lake, who reported the first sighting, a huge creature that leaped out of the water in an attempt to devour him and some other workmen. The Bear Lake monster was already a matter of record, having been observed as early as 1868 by a figure of no less veracity than Joseph C. Rich, son of a well-known Mormon apostle. Its existence was eventually corroborated by Indians who told legends of tribesmen who had been devoured when they ventured too close to it. The Utah Lake monster was not reported until 1882 by traveler Phil Robinson, who did not observe the creature himself but passed on descriptions by those who had. The historian Dale Morgan ties all these stories together in his classic *The Great Salt Lake* with his tongue firmly in cheek and his winsome sense of humor at full tide:

On the basis of the evidence which I have painstakingly assembled, it is clear that the monster was a most interesting beast, and it is much to be regretted that no specimen has yet been taken for purposes of classification. Since it is my earnest desire that this book be a contribution to the natural sciences, as well as a work of history, I will undertake to summarize what is known of the monster. Its head resembles that of a horse or an alligator or a great serpent or a sea lion; at all events, it has ears or bunches on the side of its head as large as a pint cup. Its body resembles that of a seal or a serpent or a dolphin or a crocodile; at all events, it is covered with brownish fur, has legs 18 inches long and ranges up to 80 feet in length. The beast can roar very loudly; it makes much noise when it thrashes about near shore; it has the ability to spout water from its mouth; it can travel through the water at the rate of a mile a minute; and, the inference seems justified, it has a distinct migratory tendency.

Assuming that the Salt Lake Monster, the Utah Lake Monster and the Bear Lake Monster were of the same species, if not even the same animal, one may make certain postulates. The beast was possessed of considerable agility, for it was able to make its way up and down the canyons by which the Bear River flows to Great Salt Lake, and up and down, similarly, the Jordan Narrows—no mean feat for so large a creature. That it was able to pass through, if not flourish in, the waters of Great Salt Lake seems a fact of high importance, for it has already been pointed out that Great Salt Lake presents a hostile environment to most living organisms. It should be remembered, as Dr. A. M. Woodbury puts it, that "those who would survive the rigors of this aquatic desert must either be equipped to meet the exactions imposed or to avoid them," and the monster evidently did not have to avoid them.

In general, the monster does not seem to have exhibited a carnivorous appetite. Apart from the problematical Indian traditions, J. H. McNeill's affidavit is the only evidence tending to a contrary conclusion, and special circumstances were operative in that instance. The lake is devoid of fish, and a monster would have to eat extraordinary quantities of brine shrimp and brine flies to fare very well. Doubtless the men working on shore attracted the attention of the monster in an especially ravenous moment, so that it blindly charged on the saltworks in an effort to satisfy its terrific hunger.

Of later years, the monster has not been seen, but it is premature to suppose that it has become extinct. The attention of aspiring zoologists is called to a real opportunity. Someone might very profitably devote a summer in Utah to an investigation. The new radar devices need not be restricted to the pursuit of mackerel and sardines in the ocean seas; there is no such difficulty about locating a specimen as existed 75 years ago; and the rewards, in the event of success, should be substantial. The scientist who captured a specimen could feel assured of a full-page picture in *Life*; he would be implored to accept a chair at Harvard; and assuredly he could look for an invitation to lecture in Australia.*

Whales in the Great Salt Lake

Only slightly less improbable than the sea monster is the following story of whales transplanted into the Great Salt Lake as a commercial venture. Discovered by historian David E. Miller in an 1890 Provo newspaper article, this is an intriguing story of a hoax:

Intelligent newspaper readers have not forgotten the inauguration fifteen years ago by Mr. James Wickham . . . of the whale industry in the Great Salt Lake. As considerable time was required for the development of the experiment the subject has passed out of the public mind but it has by no means been forgotten by naturalists or capitalists interested in the whale fishery. The whale is the largest and probably the longest lived animal. They have been known to grow to 100 feet in length and live to the age of 400 years. It is a mammal, or in other words suckles its young. The project of Mr. Wickham was greatly assisted by this fact, for the difficulty that would attend the obtaining of whale eggs in the deep seas is at once apparent. It was only necessary to obtain a pair of whales in order to begin the propagation of the animals under domestication. The southern or Australian whale was selected as the best suited to the Great Salt Lake. The greater part of two years were occupied off the coasts of Australia by a vessel sent especially for the purpose in continued efforts to capture the

* From Dale L. Morgan, *The Great Salt Lake* (Indianapolis: Bobbs-Merrill Co., 1947), 379–86.

young whales without injury. The feat, however, was at last accomplished, and the beasts, each about thirty-five feet long[,] were shipped to San Francisco in 1875 in tanks built expressly for them. Fifty tanks of sea water accompanied their overland shipment to insure plentiful supples of the natural element.

Mr. Wickham came from London in person to superintend the "planting" of his leviathan pets. He selected a small bay near the mouth of Bear River connected with the main water by a shallow strait half a mile wide. Across this strait he built a wire fence, and inside the pen so formed he turned the whales loose. After a few minutes['] inactivity they disported themselves in a lively manner, spouting water as in mid ocean, but as if taking in by instinct of intention the cramped character of their new home, they suddenly made a bee line for deep water and shot through the wire fence as if it had been made of threads. In twenty minutes they were out of sight. . . .

Though the enterprising owner was[,] of course, disappointed and doubtful of the results, he left an agent behind him to look after his floating property.

Six months later Mr. Wickham's representative came upon the whales fifty miles from the bay where they had broken away, and from that time to the present they have been observed at intervals, by him and the watermen who ply the lake, spouting and playing.

Within the last few days, however, Mr. Wickham cabled directions to make careful inspection and report the developments, and the agent followed the whales for five successive days and nights. Discovering that the original pair are now sixty feet in length, and followed about by a school of several hundred young, varying [in] length from three to fifteen feet. The scheme is a surprising and complete success, and Mr. Wickham has earned the thanks of mankind.

Catching whales in Great Salt Lake and following that business on the dangerous Greenland coast are two quite different things. The enormous value of the new industry can be better appreciated by remembering that a single whale produces twenty tons of pure oil.*

A Vanishing Act on Fremont Island

Hardly less strange than the natural history of the lake, both real and fantastical, is the human history, which includes a mystery unsolved to this day. In 1862 a body which had to be exhumed by the police from the Salt Lake City cemetery was

* From David E. Miller, *Great Salt Lake Past and Present* (Salt Lake City: Publishers Press, 1997), 5–6.

found to be completely naked. An investigation led to the Third Avenue residence of the gravedigger, one Jean Baptiste, whose wife let the police in. A search of the premises turned up several boxes, all filled with burial clothing. Rushing to the cemetery, they caught Baptiste red-handed in the middle of the night, and he confessed to the deed. For some time he had been exhuming bodies, taking whatever he could find, but primarily saving the clothing for resale and using the coffins themselves for firewood. Judge Elias Smith received his guilty plea and had him placed in the city jail, partly for his own protection against the public outrage that ensued when the story was released. Although Baptiste identified as many of the graves as he could that he had robbed, and some of the stolen clothing was identified by survivors and returned to them, the rest of the clothing had to be buried in a separate grave of its own.

What to do with the perpetrator of such an outrage? The court records are completely silent on the entire affair, which we know about only from the diary of Judge Smith. At the suggestion of Brigham Young, whose word in 1862 still carried much weight in Utah affairs, the judge decided to make Baptiste "a fugitive and a vagabond upon the earth." Accordingly, he was taken to Fremont Island, where the Miller brothers of Davis County were keeping livestock and had erected a cabin. Baptiste was to make that cabin his home and to be supplied with provisions for the rest of his life. It was said that he was branded with the words "grave robber" on his forehead, shackled with ball and chain, and his ears cut off, though the policemen who transported him to the island denied the shackling and said the branding was only a tattoo. They said nothing of mutilation.

Jean Baptiste's island exile was brief. When the Millers took provisions to the island three weeks later, he was gone. The cabin had been torn down, a heifer killed, and the prisoner, presumably with some fresh beef and carried on a homemade raft, had left the island. Human remains found in 1890 and again in 1893 near the mouth of the Jordan River suggest that Baptiste had not gotten far before meeting his demise, but the police vehemently denied that one skeleton, which was still carrying a ball and chain, could have been the grave robber. Dale Morgan summarizes the mystery, which is just as deep today as it was at the end of the nineteenth century:

> Perhaps the policemen told the whole truth as to what was done with Jean Baptiste. And yet the whole thing had been a good deal more than irregular. Baptiste was dealt with by what must be described as lynch law and the fact that it was done by officers of the law only underlines this awkward fact. The policemen who were interviewed in 1893 had every incentive to put as kind an interpretation as possible on the part they had taken in the marooning of Jean Baptiste. There is something too forbearing about the attitudes they profess to have held toward their prisoner. To brand his forehead with his infamy and cut off his ears, as the

matter-of-fact contemporary record indicates was done, accords much better with the sense of bitter outrage that prevailed in 1862 than to think he was simply turned loose on a desert island to shift for himself.

And yet, if there were tools on the island, if Jean Baptiste was able to demolish a hut and escape on a raft constructed of its parts, how was it that he was unable to free himself of his irons?

Still again, if the shackled bones found near the mouth of the Jordan were *not* the last earthly remains of Jean Baptiste, what became of him? There is no possibility that he died on the island; it is too small and over the years has been tramped by too many feet. His body would have been found. If he drowned in attempting to escape, it seems once more inevitable that his body must have sank with the weight of his irons. But that raises anew the difficult question of the irons.

If, despite everything, Jean Baptiste ultimately escaped, where did he vanish to? Even if his ears were not cut off, even if his forehead was branded with ink only, how could he have found anonymity anywhere? . . .

And how is it that Jean Baptiste could be jailed—for weeks, admittedly; for months, almost for a certainty—and leave no trace in the criminal records? How could he be given a judicial hearing and leave not so much as a shadow upon the records of the court? . . . And who, finally, could take upon himself the responsibility for sentencing a man, without trial, to be marooned upon a desert island?

Even when these puzzles are laid aside, the mystery attendant upon the entire affair of Jean Baptiste is wholly remarkable. For the Mormons have had enemies, both bitter and unscrupulous, during the whole course of their history, enemies who have delighted to seize upon real or imagined irregularities of which the Saints have been guilty, to make all the lurid capital possible to be made from them. Yet the strange case of Jean Baptiste is one they have left almost wholly aside.

Folklore and history alike have turned their face from Jean Baptiste. His story itself has almost sunk from sight. He is a presence on a lost page of history, the only specter of the Great Salt Lake.*

---

* From Dale L. Morgan, *The Great Salt Lake*, 274–82.

Artists and the Great Salt Lake

There have been two instances in which human artistic endeavors have made
their mark almost indelibly upon the lake. Perhaps it is because the lake is such
an anomaly, and the salt flats that surround much of it such an outrageous emptiness on the face of the earth, that artists have not been able to resist the temptation
to sculpt something on that blank expanse, to utilize that vast backdrop that nature
has provided.

One instance is *Spiral Jetty*, which is on a remote part of the northern shore of
the lake and presently visible mostly from the air. Karl Momen's sculpture, *The Tree
of Utah*, on the other hand, is just about as conspicuous as a work of art can be.
Located on the north side of Interstate 80 about twenty-six miles east of Wendover,
it utilizes the flattest and whitest part of the salt flats as its backdrop. Whether as
an object of delight or of ridicule, it is sure to evoke discussion within any carload
of travelers that passes by, for not only is it the only object of discussion outside the
car windows at that point, but its blaze of multicolored balls held eighty-seven feet
aloft on a concrete tree trunk irresistibly forces itself upon the travelers' attention.

The sculpture's creator, Karl Momen, was born and reared in Meshed, in northern Iran, near the Russian border. His cultural roots are a diverse mix of pre-Islamic
Persian mythology and Russian folklore. An avid reader, Momen devoured
European and American novels from the eighteenth and nineteenth centuries.
Later, he studied in Germany, where he developed a love for Nordic mythology and
their operatic realization under the pen of Richard Wagner. Today, this citizen of
the world divides his residence between Sausalito, California, and Sweden.

The idea for the sculpture occurred to Momen during a drive across the salt
flats. He was impressed both by the monotony of the relentlessly white scenery and
by its potential as a backdrop for a colossal and colorful work of art. The idea possessed him, consuming most of three years of his life and much of his money. "I
had heard that people of Utah are conservative," he remarked, "but everyone who
worked with me here was very excited about the idea." Momen's enthusiasm

The Tree of Utah, by Karl Momen. Photo by Marianna A. Hopkins.

infected others, particularly Mr. Semnani, head of S. K. Hart Engineering, who acquired the land from the state at no charge to Momen and put him in touch with concrete master Don Reimann of Style-Crete in Salt Lake City. Reimann's firm had extensive experience in stone work and concrete casting and was not reticent about undertaking the immense shells and fruit of Momen's vision.

Eighty-three feet high, the sculpture contains two hundred tons of crushed concrete and stone. Katherine Nelson, writing in *Utah Holiday* magazine, speculated that "in the future, *The Tree of Utah* could become as pertinent an insignia of the state as the beehive." Nelson admonishes us to "Take a look as you drive by—a split trunk, dense spheres where foliage should be, deathly still silhouette even when the wind blows fiercely. At its base are fragments of castoff shells in varying stages of reburial in the salt ground. It is a strange tree in a strange land where nothing grows except a highway."*

Since its erection, at the cost of some one million dollars, the condition and ultimate fate of the sculpture have come into question. Predictably, gun-wielding van-

---

* Katherine Nelson, "Desert Solitaire," *Utah Holiday*, September 1984, 50–51. See also Nelson's "Metaphor: A Gravestone for the Century," *Utah Holiday*, February 1986, 26–27; and Jim Woolf, "'Tree of Utah' in Salt Flats Needs Face Lift, Artist Says," *Salt Lake Tribune*, 31 July 2000.

dals have not been able to resist such a conspicuous target, and it is showing the effects of their depredations. A plaque at the base has also disappeared. In 1996 Momen donated the site to the state of Utah in hopes of securing perpetual support for renovation and maintenance, but to date a fund created for those purposes contains only five thousand dollars donated by Momen himself, toward an estimated need of forty-two thousand.

As related below by *Salt Lake Tribune* reporter Dan Egan, the *Spiral Jetty* was erected in 1970 by contractor Grant Busenbark for a wealthy New York City hippie named Robert Smithson, who would soon achieve international renown as an artist. Although, as Egan points out, the jetty is underwater except at low lake levels, it is still visible from low-flying airplanes.

Coming Around: First a Joke, Then a Jewel for the Guys Who Built "Spiral Jetty"
Dan Egan

Some people are destined to be disappointed in their earnest hunts for meaning behind modern art. They want to view beauty, but they can't see beyond the soup cans or paint splotches.

Ogden construction worker Grant Busenbark got lucky. Modem art pursued him. It caught him off guard, on the job. He "got it," and he has looked at the world differently ever since.

It began in 1970, when a 32-year-old, long-haired New York City hipster named Robert Smithson showed up in Brigham City with a bulging wallet and wacky plan to hire a construction crew, dump trucks and dozers to move some rocks around and make some "art" on the mucky north shore of the Great Salt Lake.

The work would become the now-famous "Spiral Jetty," a 1,500-foot-long swirling rock wharf. The massive sculpture, which the lake's rising water line quickly swallowed, subsequently achieved masterpiece status among many in the art community. It appears in most introductory art history books.

"It's hard to find anything more important. It is probably the best-known earth work in the country," said University of Utah art professor Robert Olpin.

But 30 years ago, Busenbark, a crew-cut, Korean War vet, was hard- pressed to find anything more foolish after he was picked to be foreman for the job.

Up to that point, Busenbark's life was built around constructing practical things—roads, parking lots. He never anticipated someone would hire him to build a monumental dead end. He laughed at Smithson and his project. He thought both were a joke.

Then came a $6,000 check, and it wasn't funny anymore.

"I thought there was something wrong with him," recalled Busenbark. "He was a hippie, and I'd never been around one."

Dan Egan, "Coming Around: First a Joke, Then a Jewel for the Guys Who Built 'Spiral Jetty,'" *Salt Lake Tribune*, 28 November 1999.

Odd Couple: Smithson was more than a hippie. He was an up-and-coming artist who had won financial backing from the prestigious Dwan Gallery to construct a piece of "land art." The concept is to use expanses of open areas as a canvas to take art out of the confining galleries and onto the open land.

It was—and remains—a very 1960s notion.

Busenbark, a decidedly 1950s kind of guy, was dubious. But a job is a job, and in the spring of 1970 his crew began taking their orders.

Smithson picked the north end of the Great Salt Lake because its algae and bacteria induce a "tomato-soup" redness. Red turned him on, and the only other place where he knew of such a colorful lake was Bolivia, too far for even this far-out guy.

So Utah, and Busenbark, would have to do.

The odd couple progressed quickly, but Busenbark couldn't resist occasionally razzing his bohemian boss. Project manager Bob Phillips remembered one particular confrontation during the two weeks it took for the coil to emerge from the lake bed.

"Grant was standing there, and he said [to Smithson] something to the effect of: 'It turns me on! It turns me off!' It turns me on, now turn me off so I can go home!'" recalled Phillips in a 1996 interview with Utah's Hikmet Sidney Loe, who did her master's thesis on Spiral Jetty.

Smithson didn't take the lampooning lightly.

"He called me," Phillips told Loe. "And he said, 'Can we get somebody else out there to do this work? I don't think Grant understands what we're trying to accomplish here. We need somebody who has a feel for this project.'"

Phillips didn't have anybody who had such a "feel." More importantly, he didn't have anybody who could match Busenbark's skills at dancing the earth moving machinery over axle-cracking rocks and across the treacherous muck.

"This Busenbark was a real wizard, a master at running the equipment," Phillips said recently while on a tour of the site of "Spiral Jetty." "He was the only guy who could do that job."

So Phillips entreated Busenbark, a high school dropout, to take seriously the apparently ludicrous work, and the problems stopped.

In fact, Smithson later made a point of commending the crew on their skill and ability to show him how to get the effect he wanted.

Busenbark said he doesn't remember much about Smithson, other than "he smelled like he hadn't hit the shower for days." It didn't help that he wore black leather pants even on hot, sunny days at the construction site.

Busenbark stopped the teasing, but he didn't drop his disdain for the project. Even today, he said there was not much to it; Smithson planted stakes along the shallow shore of the lake indicating where the swirl should emerge, and Busenbark made it happen.

"All you had to do was put the rocks between the friggin' laths, and then knock it all down so you could get a truck over it," he recalled. He left the site when work was completed in April 1970 and he didn't look back.

But he didn't stop thinking about the quirky work, and about three years later he saw a picture of the jetty in a magazine and something clicked.

"All I can say is, it's — art," said Busenbark, flicking a Merit cigarette between fingers thicker than many men's thumbs. He has a flag-sized picture of "Spiral Jetty" on a living room wall at his cabin in Alpine, Wyo. It is one of his proudest possessions, though he still has a hard time putting one of those big fingers on exactly why the artwork is important. But it is.

The experience, he said, taught him to slow down, to take a harder look at the beauty around him, to appreciate different forms of art. "I look at pictures differently today," he said.

But if Smithson had a master plan for his masterpiece, he certainly hid it well. He initially presented Phillips with a drawing that resembled a J. Then he had the crew build a swirl with an island in the middle.

"He was very upset after he got done," said Phillips. "It didn't look right."

Somewhere in his mind, Smithson found the problem. He ordered the island removed. Cost: another $3,000.

"He just knew what he wanted, and he got what he wanted," said Busenbark, defending the artist's apparent whimsy.

At the time of construction, Busenbark was flabbergasted to be ordered back out to the site to re-work the jetty. It was, he figured, more evidence that Smithson was out of his mind. But if he were to run into Smithson today, Busenbark would thank the artist for opening his eyes.

That won't happen.

Smithson died at 35 in a 1973 plane crash in Texas while surveying the site of his next work. The two never saw each other after the day Busenbark drove his dump truck from the lake.

"It was an experience for me," Busenbark said, dead serious about the subject. "I wasn't that quick in the head, I guess. He [Smithson] could see further ahead. . . . He was an artist, no question about it."

The project had a similar effect on Phillips, who recalled two key moments when he began to consider the possibility Smithson was onto something more important than pushing rocks around the lake shore.

"I did think it was kind of weird," Phillips confessed to thinking at the project's beginning. Then a French film crew arrived in a helicopter. "That's when I thought that this guy must know something that we don't."

Smithson gave Phillips a picture of "Spiral Jetty," but after a few years on the wall at home Phillips' wife insisted he take it down.

Then in 1985, Phillips' son came home from Weber State University with his art history textbook. "Spiral Jetty" was one of its featured works. "I was just stunned. I'm still amazed," said Phillips.

The picture went back on the wall, where it remains today.

"It's a hell of a conversation piece," he said.

Sunken Treasure: Smithson knew "Spiral Jetty's" remote location at the end of a kidney-bruising road meant most art appreciators would never get to enjoy his work first hand. So he made a movie about the project and also wrote an essay in a presumed effort to explain its significance.

The movie shows some construction of the jetty, but Smithson's primary goal for the film was to help people experience the art. At one point, a helicopter swirls above so the sculpture appears to spin. As the screen whirls, a monotone, almost bored-sounding Smithson begins a chant, repeating the words "mud, salt crystals, rocks, water" 18 times.

Phillips got a copy of the film and showed it to his construction buddies. Most left the room cussing and confused before it ended 35 minutes later.

Smithson's essay on the jetty is more of the same.

"In the Spiral Jetty the surd [irrational] takes over and leads one into a world that cannot be expressed by number or rationality," Smithson wrote. "Ambiguities are admitted rather than rejected, contradictions are increased rather than decreased."

Maybe, like Busenbark, you had to be there to get it. Maybe it's like a New Yorker cartoon: if it has to be explained to you, you're not going to get it.

Busenbark and Phillips needed no explanation. Both have individually taken trips to the lake in hopes of getting a rare glimpse of their work.

This month they went together to enjoy "Spiral Jetty" for the first time since the construction days of 1970. It was nowhere to be seen. A stranger had to show them where the jetty would be if the lake were lower. They squinted south into the low autumn sun. Nothing, just a hazy, flat lake.

"This is the pits," grumbled Busenbark, and then he smiled and shook his head, as if he just remembered the punch line to a joke.

For most of its life the 1,500-foot-long, 15-feet-wide swirl has been under several feet of water. Nobody knows when the water will recede and the swirl will re-emerge, but that didn't stop about 500 artsy types from raising their wine glasses to Smithson on a Manhattan roof-top this fall. The party was hosted by the Dia Center for the Arts, which had just acquired the invisible piece through a donation from Smithson's estate.

Smithson's widow, New Mexico artist Nancy Holt, said she picked Dia because it is "a very prestigious" organization. "And they've already had experience in this area of taking care of earth works."

Dia manages several of the country's best-known pieces of land art, including Walter De Maria's Lightning Field in New Mexico.

But ownership of the sunken treasure is fuzzy business. It can't be moved, and the land upon which it is built is owned by the state of Utah. Dia's "ownership" includes title to a piece of art that cannot presently be viewed, as well as a 20-year lease on the land, for which it pays $250 annually. Dia can apply to renew the lease and state land managers see no reason why it would not be approved.

Spiral Jetty by Robert Smithson, as it looked in September 1996 when it was just a few inches below the surface of the Great Salt Lake. Photo by Al Hartman, *Salt Lake Tribune*, 28 November 1999. Used by permission.

Smithson reportedly said before his death that he wanted to raise the spiral above the lake waters, and Dia is considering firing up the bulldozers to do that and improve the bumpy road to the site. When "Spiral Jetty" last poked above water several years ago, it appeared totally intact, though it took on a crusty white trim from salt crystallized out of the lake.

"The hope is very much to make the piece accessible to the public, but how and when we do that has yet to be determined." said Stephen Dewhurst, Dia's assistant director.

"That'd be kind of a shame," said Phillips. "I'd vote for waiting for the lake to go back down."

Some in the art community feel the same.

"Part of the mystery is going out there and not finding it," said Steven Rosen, chief curator at Utah State University's art museum.

And, perhaps, not getting it.

VII

THE GREAT SALT LAKE TODAY

A Threatened Refuge

The title perfectly expresses the theme of the book: what happens when Nature does something "unnatural"? The following selection deals with a part of only one theme of a complex book, arguably nature writer Williams's best. During the mid-1980s, a succession of abnormally wet years in Utah caused some very unnatural phenomena, like the flooding of City Creek which flows through northern Salt Lake City, turning streets into rivers, and an unprecedented rise in the ultimate destination of City Creek and other streams draining the Wasatch Mountains: the Great Salt Lake. Seriously affected by that rise was the Bear River Wildlife Refuge, a vitally important nesting and stopover point for the shore birds and migratory species that make the environs of the Great Salt Lake so biologically interesting and important. Williams, who was employed in the education department of the Utah Museum of Natural History at the time, had an almost lifelong involvement with the refuge and indeed with the birds of the entire Great Salt Lake, and her book, with its lake elevation figures at the head of every chapter, is partly the story of her tracking, through frequent visits, the effects of the rising lake level on the bird population.

Arresting though that theme is, the book encompasses much more, for it also narrates the slow death of her mother of ovarian cancer. Williams and her family are what have been called "downwinders"—residents of southern Utah who were exposed to drifting nuclear radiation from the bomb testing in southern Nevada during the 1950s. That radiation, research has laboriously demonstrated and politicians have reluctantly come to acknowledge, produced a dramatically higher incidence of cancer among those Utahns "downwind" of the tests than others out of the way. In Williams's experience, it created what she calls the "Clan of the One-Breasted Women" through the repeated cases of breast cancer and mastectomies. At any rate, the book tells two stories: the gradual death of the bird refuge through flooding, and the slow death of her mother from cancer, both themes expertly interwoven through each chapter.

There are other threads as well, which Williams brings to bear on her two major themes. One is her attempt to reconcile what she observes and experiences in her external world with the ideals and doctrines of the Mormon faith in which she grew up. Another is her playful relationship, not only with her parents, but with her grandmother and her husband, the creative tensions that produce growth and deepen love. In all of them, there is something that resonates deeply in readers of all faiths and domestic situations.

Tempting though it might be to range out into metaphysical and theological directions, this anthology is concerned only with the Great Salt Lake, and so the following selection includes only a sampling of Williams's empathetic and expert writing about the birds of the lake and her passionate desire to study, understand, and protect them. It would be impossible in a brief space like this to indicate much of the complexity, interest, and beauty of her book as a whole. Fortunately, it is readily and inexpensively available in a paperback reprint, and the editor of this anthology hopes these selections will entice the reader to purchase and enjoy the book from which they are drawn. The selections have been slightly rearranged from the order in which they appear in the book.

Suggestions for further reading

Williams's other popular books, which include *Pieces of White Shell: A Journey to Navajoland, Coyote's Canyon,* and *Desert Quartet,* focus on the canyon country of the Southwest. Those who enjoy this kind of nature writing about the Great Salt Lake should be aware of two recent loving tributes to the lake in prose and photography: Ella Sorensen (with photographs by John P. George), *Seductive Beauty of Great Salt Lake: Images of a Lake Unknown* (Salt Lake City: Gibbs Smith, 1997); and Marlin Stum (with photographs by Dan Miller), *Visions of Antelope Island and Great Salt Lake* (Logan: Utah State University Press, 1999). The great expert on Utah birds was Dr. William Behle, whose *The Bird Life of the Great Salt Lake* (Salt Lake City: University of Utah Press, 1958) is still authoritative.

REFUGE:
AN UNNATURAL HISTORY OF FAMILY
AND PLACE
Terry Tempest Williams

BURROWING OWLS

lake level: 4204.70'

***

There are those birds you gauge your life by. The burrowing owls five miles from the entrance to the Bear river Migratory Bird Refuge are mine. Sentries. Each year, they alert me to the regularities of the land. In spring, I find them nesting, in summer they forage with their young, and by winter they abandon the Refuge for a place more comfortable.

What is distinctive about these owls is their home. It rises from the alkaline flats like a clay-covered fist. If you were to peek inside the tightly clenched fingers, you would find a dark-holed entrance.

"Tttss! Tttss! Tttss!"

That is no rattlesnake. Those are the distress cries of the burrowing owl's young.

Adult burrowing owls will stand on top of the mound with their prey before them, usually small rodents, birds, or insects. The entrance is littered with bones and feathers. I recall finding a swatch of yellow feathers like a doormat across the threshold—meadowlark, maybe. These small owls pursue their prey religiously at dusk.

Burrowing owls are part of the desert community, taking advantage of the abandoned burrows of prairie dogs. Historically, bison would move across the American Plains, followed by prairie dog towns which would aerate the soil after the weight of stampeding hooves. Black-footed ferrets, rattlesnakes, and burrowing owls inhabited the edges, finding an abundant food source in the communal rodents.

Reprinted with special permission from Terry Tempest Williams from *Refuge: An Unnatural History of Family and Place* (New York: Vintage, 1992), 8–13, 21–22, 69–75, 87–90, 110–14, 144–47.

With the loss of desert lands, a decline in prairie dog populations is inevitable. And so go the ferret and burrowing owl. Rattlesnakes are more adaptable.

In Utah, prairie dogs and black-footed ferrets are endangered species, with ferrets almost extinct. The burrowing owl is defined as "threatened" a political step away from endangered status. Each year, the burrowing owls near the Refuge become more blessed.

The owls had staked their territory just beyond one of the bends in the Bear River. Whenever I drove to the Bird Refuge, I stopped at their place first and sat on the edge of the road and watched. They would fly around me, their wings sometimes spanning two feet. Undulating from post to post, they would distract me from their nest. Just under a foot long, they have a body of feathers the color of wheat, balanced on two long, spindly legs. They can burn grasses with their stare. Yellow eyes magnifying light.

The protective hissing of baby burrowing owls is an adaptive memory of their close association with prairie rattlers. Snake or owl? Who wants to risk finding out.

In the summer of 1983, I worried about the burrowing owls, wondering if the rising waters of Great Salt Lake had flooded their home, too. I was relieved to find not only their mound intact, but four owlets standing on its threshold. One of the Refuge managers stopped on the road and commented on what a good year it had been for them.

"Good news," I replied. "The lake didn't take everything."

That was late August when huge concentrations of shorebirds were still feeding between submerged shadescale.

A few months later, a friend of mine, Sandy Lopez, was visiting from Oregon. We had spoken of the Bird Refuge many times. The whistling swans had arrived, and it seemed like a perfect day for the marsh.

To drive to the Bear River Migratory Bird Refuge from Salt Lake City takes a little over one hour. I have discovered the conversation that finds its way into the car often manifests itself later on the land.

We spoke of rage. Of women and landscape. How our bodies and the body of the earth have been mined.

"It has everything to do with intimacy," I said. "Men define intimacy through their bodies. It is physical. They define intimacy with the land in the same way."

"Many men have forgotten what they are connected to," my friend added. "Subjugation of women and nature may be a loss of intimacy within themselves."

She paused, then looked at me.

"Do you feel rage?"

I didn't answer for some time.

"I feel sadness. I feel powerless at times. But I'm not certain what rage really means."

Several miles passed.

"Do you?" I asked.

She looked out the window. "Yes. Perhaps your generation, one behind mine, is a step removed from the pain."

We reached the access road to the Refuge and both took out our binoculars, ready for the birds. Most of the waterfowl had migrated, but a few ruddy ducks, redheads, and shovelers remained. The marsh glistened like cut topaz.

As we turned west about five miles from the Refuge, a mile or so from the burrowing owl's mound, I began to speak of them, *Athene cunicularia*. I told Sandy about the time when my grandmother and I first discovered them. It was in 1960, the same year she gave me my Peterson's *Field Guide to Western Birds*. I know because I dated their picture. We have come back every year since to pay our respects. Generations of burrowing owls have been raised here. I turned to my friend and explained how four owlets had survived the flood.

We anticipated them.

About a half mile away, I could not see the mound. I took my foot off the gas pedal and coasted. It was as though I was in unfamiliar country.

The mound was gone. Erased. In its place, fifty feet back, stood a cinderblock building with a sign, CANADIAN GOOSE GUN CLUB. A new fence crushed the grasses with a handwritten note posted: KEEP OUT.

We got out of the car and walked to where the mound had been for as long as I had a memory. Gone. Not a pellet to be found.

A blue pickup pulled alongside us.

"Howdy." They tipped their ball caps. "What y'all lookin' for?"

I said nothing. Sandy said nothing. My eyes narrowed.

"We didn't kill 'em. Those boys from the highway department came and graveled the place. Two bits, they did it. I mean, you gotta admit those ground owls are messy little bastards. They'll shit all over hell if ya let 'em. And try and sleep with 'em hollering at ya all night long. They had to go. Anyway, we got bets with the county they'll pop up someplace around here next year."

The three men in the front seat looked up at us, tipped their caps again. And drove off.

Restraint is the steel partition between a rational mind and a violent one. I knew rage. It was fire in my stomach with no place to go.

I drove out to the Refuge on another day. I suppose I wanted to see the mound back in place with the family of owls bobbing on top. Of course, they were not.

I sat on the gravel and threw stones.

By chance, the same blue pickup with the same three men pulled alongside: the self-appointed proprietors of the newly erected Canadian Goose Gun Club.

"Howdy, ma'am. Still lookin' for them Owls, or was it sparrows?"

One winked.

Suddenly in perfect detail, I pictured the burrowing owls' mound—that clay-covered fist rising from the alkaline flats. The exact one these beergut-over-belt-buckled men had leveled.

I walked calmly over to their truck and leaned my stomach against their door. I held up my fist a few inches from the driver's face and slowly lifted my middle finger to the sky.

"This is for you—from the owls and me."

* * *

WHIMBRELS

lake level: 4203.25'

The Bird Refuge has remained a constant. It is a landscape so familiar to me, there have been times I have felt a species long before I saw it. The long-billed curlews that foraged the grasslands seven miles outside the Refuge were trustworthy. I can count on them year after year. And when six whimbrels joined them—whimbrel entered my mind as an idea. Before I ever saw them mingling with curlews, I recognized them as a new thought in familiar country.

The birds and I share a natural history. It is a matter of rootedness, of living inside a place for so long that the mind and imagination fuse.

Maybe it's the expanse of sky above and water below that soothes my soul. Or maybe it's the anticipation of seeing something new. Whatever the magic of Bear River is—I appreciate this corner of northern Utah, where the numbers of ducks and geese I find resemble those found by early explorers.

Of the 208 species of birds who use the Refuge, sixty-two are known to nest here. Such nesting species include eared, western, and pied-billed grebes, great blue herons, snowy egrets, white-faced ibises, American avocets, black-necked stilts, and Wilson's phalaropes. Also nesting at Bear River are Canada geese, mallards, gadwalls, pintails, green-winged, blue-winged, and cinnamon teals, redheads, and ruddy ducks. It is a fertile community where the hope of each day rides on the backs of migrating birds.

These wetlands, emeralds around Great Salt Lake, provide critical habitat for North American waterfowl and shorebirds, supporting hundreds of thousands, even millions of individuals during spring and autumn migrations. The long, legged birds with their eyes focused down transform a seemingly sterile world into a fecund one. It is here in the marshes with the birds that I seal my relationship to Great Salt Lake.

I could never have anticipated its rise.

* * *

CALIFORNIA GULL

lake level: 4207.75'

* * *

The California gulls rescued the Mormons in 1848 from losing their crops to crickets. The gull has become folklore. It is a story we know well.

As word of Great Salt Lake's nasty disposition filtered through the westering grapevine in the 1840's, the appeal of the Great Basin was tainted. The Mormons were an exception. They saw it as Holy Land.

Brigham Young raised his hands above the Salt Lake Valley and said, "This is a good place to make Saints, and it is a good place for Saints to live; it is the place that the Lord has appointed, and we shall stay here until He tells us to go somewhere else."

God's country. Isolation and a landscape of grit were just what the Mormons were looking for. A land that no one else wanted meant religious freedom and community-building without persecution. It was an environment perfectly suited for a people unafraid of what only their hands could yield. They were a people motivated by the dream of Zion. They had found their Dead Sea and the River Jordan. The Great Basin desert was familiar to them if not by sight, at least by story.

But it wasn't easy. Winter quarters for the poorly provisioned families who had just arrived proved difficult. Their livestock had been decimated by wolves and Indian raids. Untended animals grazed down their crops and the harvest of 1847 consisted of only a few "marble-size potatoes." The starving pioneers were reduced to eating "crows, wolf meat, tree bark, thistle tops, sego lily bulbs, and hawks."

One member describes in his journal, "I would dig until I grew weak and faint and sit down and eat a root, and then I would begin again."

The harvest of 1848 looked more promising and the Saints' spirits were buoyed. But just when a full pantry for each family seemed assured, hordes of crickets invaded their wheat fields. The crickets were described as "wingless, dumpy, black, and swollen-headed creatures, with bulging eyes in cases like goggles, mounted upon legs of steel wire . . . a cross between a spider and a buffalo."

The pioneers fought them with brooms, shovels, pitchforks, and fire. Nothing seemed to halt their invasion. In desperation, the farmers and their families fell to their knees with exhaustion and prayed to the Lord for help.

> Upon looking up, I beheld what appeared like a vast flock of pigeons coming from the northwest. It was about three o'clock in the afternoon . . . there must have been thousands of them; their coming was like a great cloud; and when they passed between us and the sun, a shadow covered the field. I could see the gulls settling for more than a mile around us. They were very tame, coming within four or five rods of us.
>
> At first, we thought that they also were after the wheat and this fact added to our terror; but we soon discovered that they devoured only the crickets. Needless to say, we quit fighting and gave our gentle visitors the possession of the fields.

Their prayers had been answered. Their crops had been saved.

Over one hundred years later, Mormons still gather to tell the story of how the gulls freed them from the crickets. How the white angels ate as many crickets as their bellies would hold, flew to the shores of Great Salt Lake and regurgitated them, then returned to the field for more. We honor them as Utah's state bird.

While sitting on the edge of Great Salt Lake, I noticed the gulls flying in one direction. From four o'clock until dusk, with their slow, steady wing beats, they flew southwest. I pocketed this information like a small stone.

The next day, I returned and witnessed the same pilgrimage. After all these years of cohabitation, the gulls had finally, seized my imagination.

I had to follow.

The gulls were flying to their nesting colonies on the islands of Great Salt Lake. What they gain in remoteness (abeyance from predators and human interference) they sacrifice in food supply. Because of its high salinity, Great Salt Lake yields no fish. With the exception of brine shrimp, which make up a meager percentage of the gull's total diet, the water is sterile. Consequently, gulls must fly great distances between island nesting sites and foraging grounds. Round trips between fifty to one hundred miles are made from Hat and Gunnison Islands to the Bear River Migratory Bird Refuge. Daily. White pelicans, double-crested cormorants, and great blue herons, also colony nesters, must make these same migrations to the surrounding marshes of Great Salt Lake.

The population of colony-nesting birds on the islands fluctuates with the lake level and human disturbances. Herons, cormorants, and pelicans are much more sensitive to these pressures than gulls. One striking difference between the species is their territoriality. Herons are wary, skittish. Pelicans and cormorants are shy. If disturbed, great blue herons leave the island first, followed by the pelicans and cormorants. The gulls never leave. They just fly around in circles screaming at the intruders.

The populations of herons, cormorants, and pelicans are decreasing on the islands of Great Salt Lake, whereas evidence shows gull communities on the rise. Gulls are more resilient to change and less vulnerable than other birds to environmental stresses.

William H. Behle, curator of ornithology at the Utah Museum of Natural History, in his classic study on the birds of Great Salt Lake, reported sixty thousand adult California gulls nesting on Gunnison Island on June 29, 1932. This was the highest gull concentration ever known on Great Salt Lake.

Since the flooding, most of the islands have either been abandoned by colony nesters or their populations have been greatly reduced. This seems to have happened for three reasons: lack of nesting space due to rising waters, increased human visitation to the islands, and, most important, lack of food due to the submerged marshes.

In drought conditions, bird populations also decline but for different reasons. In low water, most of the islands are attached to the mainland, making the birds more vulnerable to predators and human interference. Food supply is also threatened as the marshes shrink.

The balance between colony-nesting birds, the fluctuating Great Salt Lake, and its wetlands is a delicate one.

In 1958, Dr. Behle wrote prophetically,

> If present trends continue, there is danger that the islands of Great Salt
> Lake will be entirely abandoned by colonial birds. Herons already have
> abandoned all their historic nesting sites on the lake. Cormorants persist
> at Egg Island but are barely holding their own from year to year. Pelicans
> faced a critical condition in 1935 and seem to be slowly recovering but
> their existence is precarious. The gulls are moving to man-made dikes and
> the islands of the refuges on the east side of the lake.

For now, any remembrance of Great Salt Lake hosting an island archipelago of
birds is limited to the journals of early explorers. Captain Howard Stansbury wrote
on April 9, 1850,

> Rounding the northern point of Antelope Island, we came to a small
> rocky islet, about a mile west of it, which was destitute of vegetation of
> any kind, not even a blade of grass being found upon it. It was literally
> covered with wild waterfowl: ducks, white brandt, blue herons, cor-
> morants, and innumerable flocks of gulls, which had congregated here to
> build their nests. We found great numbers of these, built of sticks and
> rushes, in the crevices of the rock, and supplied ourselves without scruple,
> with as many eggs as we needed, primarily those of the heron, it being too
> early in the season for most of the other waterfowl.

And on May 8 of the same year:

> The neck and shores on both of the little bays were occupied by immense
> flocks of pelicans and gulls, disturbed now for the first time, probably by
> the intrusion of man. They literally darkened the air as they rose upon the
> wing, and hovering over our heads, caused the surrounding rocks to re-
> echo with their discordant screams. The ground was thickly strewn with
> their nests, of which there must have been thousands.

I have seen hundreds of gulls nesting not on the islands of Great Salt Lake, but on
the old P-dike at the Bear River Migratory Bird Refuge. To wander through a gull
colony is disorienting. In the midst of shrieking gulls, you begin to speak, but your
voice is silenced. They pull the clouds around you as you walk on eggshells. You
quickly realize that you do not belong.

Hundreds of gulls hovered inches above my head, making their shrill repetitive
cries, *"Halp! Halp! Halp!"* Several wing tips struck my forehead, a warning that I
was too close to their nests. There were so many nests, I didn't know where to step,
much less how to behave. Finally, I just stood in one place and watched.

A California gull's nest is a shallow depression on the ground. They gather nesting material and line the hollow. The gull settles down, usually female, and with
her body and sometimes the aid of her feet and bill, neatly arranges the feathers,

grasses, and twigs into a cup-shaped nest. Depending on the resources available, they can range from simple to elaborate.

The nests at Bear River were simple. Bones from gulls and other animals were woven into their fabric, making them look like death wreathes. Clutches of umber eggs splotched with brown lay in their centers.

Most of the gulls I watched at the Bird Refuge were incubating eggs, an activity which takes from twenty-three to twenty-eight days. Both sexes share in the responsibility.

I wondered in the midst of so many gulls and so many eggs, how the birds could differentiate between them. They do. Parental recognition. The subtle distinctions in patterning and coloration among individual egg clutches test my eye for discrimination. Each brood bears its own coat of arms.

Young gulls are precocial, which means they are relatively well developed at hatching. They are covered with a thick coat of natal down, can leave the nest soon after they hatch, and can feed themselves within a short time. Precocial young are typical to most waterfowl, an adaptation against predators of ground-dwelling birds.

In contrast, altricial young are those birds born helpless, usually naked and with closed eyes, completely dependent on their parents for a sustained period after hatching. Altricial young are more common to passerine birds, which have the advantage of tree nesting. They can afford to be helpless.

It is tempting to pick up a baby gull. I must confess I have tried, but only got as far as its fierce little beak would let me. They come into life as speckled warriors, waving egg teeth on the tips of their upper mandibles. Their battle with the eggshell is tireless as they struggle anywhere from twenty minutes to ten hours. They stand in wet armor ready to face the world.

All around me, eggs were moving, cracking, and breaking open. I would stoop a few feet from a nest and find myself staring eye-to-eye with a chick.

A month from now, in June, the young will be in juvenile plumage, looking like gulls who ventured too close to a campfire. Smoked feathers. They will stretch and beat their wings wildly until one day their own force will surprise them, lifting them a foot or two off the ground. Gradually, with a few running steps, their wings will carry them. In a matter of weeks, adolescent gulls will be agile fliers.

By July, the California gulls will prepare to leave their breeding grounds, taking their young with them. Banding records from Bear River indicate that most of the Great Salt Lake population winters along the Pacific coast from northern Washington to southern California.

I love to watch gulls soar over the Great Basin. It is another trick of the lake to lure gulls inland. On days such as this, when my soul has been wrenched, the simplicity of flight and form above the lake untangles my grief.

"Glide" the gulls write in the sky—and, for a few brief moments, I do.

* * *

PINK FLAMINGOS

lake level: 4208.00'

* * *

I love to make lists. Maybe it's my background in beehives and breadmaking, the whole business of being industrious and frugal (of which I am neither) that a list promotes. Or maybe it's the power that comes when you can cross something off a list. Done. Finished. Move on to the next chore. I can see in a very tangible form what I have accomplished in a day. Or perhaps it's the democratic nature of lists that I find so attractive. Each task is of equal importance on paper. So "pick up fresh flowers" carries the same weight as "do the laundry." It's the line slashed through the words that counts. Never mind that the pleasurable items are crossed off by noon and the difficult ones, meant for procrastination anyway, get moved to the next day's agenda. The point is that my intentions are honorable. My lists will defend me.

The life list of a birdwatcher is of a different order. It's not what you cross off that counts, but what you add. It is a tally of all the species of birds seen within a lifetime. A bird seen for the first time is called "a lifer."

The life list can be a private accounting of birds seen, a scrapbook of sorts, of places visited and birds watched. It provides the pleasure of traditional list-making (in this case, adding something new to the list instead of crossing something off). Those who use their bird list in this manner usually have no idea of their total sum of species. And it is done at random—when a person thinks about it.

At the end of each day, I write down the names of all birds seen and read them out loud, regardless of who is there. It's like throwing a party and afterwards talking about who came. There are always those you can count on and those who will surprise you. And, once in a blue moon, an accidental guest will arrive.

Within every checklist there are those birds listed as "accidentals," one species, or at best a few, that have wandered far from their normal range. They are flukes in a flock of predictable migrants. They are loners in an unfamiliar territory.

William H. Behle, author of *Utah Birds,* defines an accidental as "a species seen only one or two times since 1920 or one or two times in the last fifty years or another fifty year interval provided that species is just as likely to occur now as then." Accidental birds in Utah are substantiated by at least one recorded specimen.

On July 25, 1962, Don Neilson, manager of the Clear Lake Refuge, observed an American flamingo in Millard County, Utah. It stayed in the area through Columbus Day. He, has color photographs to prove it.

Another sighting occurred on August 3, 1966, by W. E. Ritter and Reuben Dietz who saw a flamingo at Buffalo Bay, on the northeast shore of Antelope Island. The bird was washed out and pale, thousands of miles from its homeland, so they inferred it must be an escapee from Tracy Aviary or Hogle Zoo in Salt Lake City. Calls were made, but all captive flamingos were accounted for.

Then, in the summer of 1971, a third flamingo was seen at the Bear River Migratory Bird Refuge from early June through September 29. Once again, photographs verified the sighting.

I personally have seen flamingos throughout the state of Utah perched proudly on lawns and in the gravel gardens of trailer courts. These flamingos, of course, are not *Phoenicopterus ruber*, but pink, plastic flamingos that can easily be purchased at any hardware store.

It is curious that we need to create an environment foreign from our own. In 1985, over 450,000 plastic flamingos were purchased in the United States. And the number is rising.

Pink flamingos teetering on suburban lawns—our unnatural link to the natural world.

The flocks of flamingos that Louis Agassiz Fuertes lovingly painted in the American tropics are no longer accessible to us. We have lost the imagination to place them in a dignified world. And when they do grace the landscapes around us, they are considered "accidental." We no longer believe in the possibility of such things.

There have been other accidentals in Utah.

On July 2, 1919, a flock of five roseate spoonbills flew over the Barnes Ranch near Wendover, Nevada. Mr. Barnes, having never seen such a bird, shot one. and kept it inside his house for years as a conversation piece. It strangely disappeared and was subsequently found; it now rests at the Utah Museum of Natural History.

The flamingo and roseate spoonbill are not the only rarities to visit the wetlands surrounding Great Salt Lake. Other accidentals include the European wigeon seen at the Bear River Bird Refuge on October 19, 1955, and another one sighted by Bill Pingree at the Lakefront Gun Club on December 15, 1963.

And when there is a species whose occurrence is open to question largely by virtue of the absence of a record specimen (a bird in the hand), but where the competence of the observer or observers constitutes "sufficient evidence to justify the inclusion of the species in the checklists," these birds are listed as "hypothetical." Hypothetical species sighted around Great Salt Lake include the red-necked grebe, reddish egret, Louisiana heron, harlequin duck, black scoter, black oystercatcher, wandering tattler, stilt sandpiper, bartailed godwit, parakeet auklet, northern parula warbler, and a palm warbler.

How can hope be denied when there is always the possibility of an American flamingo or a roseate spoonbill floating down from the sky like pink rose petals?

How can we rely solely on the statistical evidence and percentages that would shackle our lives when red-necked grebes, bar-tailed godwits, and wandering tattlers come into our country?

When Emily Dickinson writes, "Hope is a thing with feathers that lights upon our soul," she reminds us, as the birds do, of the liberation and pragmatism of belief.

REDHEADS

lake level: 4208.50'

September, 1985. Don Paul's study is out. The recent population and habitat studies performed by the Utah Division of Wildlife Resources shows that colony nesting species around Great Salt Lake have been affected by the rise in lake level. Some are adapting and some are not. The data collection was funded by Los Angeles City Power and Light, which was recently sued by the National Wildlife Federation for drawing down the water levels of Mono Lake.

Great blue herons, egrets, and cormorants, all tree nesters, have been aided by the flooding of the wetlands, as waterfowl management areas have become inaccessible to man and arboreal predators. Their preferred habitat for nesting: dead trees. Suddenly, there's lots of them, killed by the rising salt water. The cottonwoods and box elders that once provided shade and cover for songbirds have become bare-branched rookeries for herons and cormorants.

They have not been without their problems, however. In some instances, where they had used the low tamarisk shrubs to nest in, eggs and young were drowned as the waters rose over a few weeks.

As was expected, white-faced ibises and Franklin gulls, both dependent on hard-stem bulrushes for nesting, have suffered the most. With 80 percent of the world's population of white-faced ibises nesting in Utah, these losses become significant.

In 1979, the Utah ibis population was estimated at 8690 pairs. The 1985 colony-nesting survey recorded 3438 pairs. The decline in Franklin gulls is even more radical: a late 1970s survey showed a thousand breeding pairs, compared to the fifty-one nests counted this year.

It is hoped that many breeding adult ibises and Franklin gulls have survived and moved on to more stable marshes in the Great Basin. Breeding numbers are reported higher at Fish Springs and at the Ruby Marshes in Nevada. The Cutler and Bear Lake marshes northeast of Bear River also show an increase in ibis and gull populations.

The avocets and stilts, along with other ground nesters around Great Salt Lake, have been completely displaced. Their nesting sites have been usurped by water, with mudflats almost nonexistent. Some pairs of avocets have been seen nesting just off the interstate on gravel shoulders.

California has lost 95 percent of its wetlands over the past one hundred years. Eighty-five percent of Utah's wetlands have been lost in the last two. When wetlands are destroyed, many species go with them, and not just the birds that nest there. In Utah's case, tiger salamanders, leopard frogs, orchids, buttercups, myriads of insects and rodents, plus the birds and mammals that prey on them, are vanishing.

Marshes are among the most productive ecosystems on the planet. They are also among the most threatened.

Nationwide, seventy-six endangered species are dependent upon wetlands. Marshes all across the country are disappearing without fanfare, leaving the earth devoid of birdsong. The long-billed curlews who lose their broods to floods become a generation that much more precious to their species' survival. Whether it's because of drought, as is the case in the prairie pothole region to the north, or levels of high toxicity in California's central valley, or just plain development—our wetlands are disappearing.

Wetlands are one more paradox of Great Salt Lake. The marshes here are disappearing naturally. It's not the harsh winter or yearly spillover that threatens Utah's wetland birds and animals. It is lack of land. In the normal cycle of a rising Great Salt Lake, the birds would simply move up. New habitat would be found. New habitat would be created. They don't have those options today, as they find themselves flush against freeways and a rapidly expanding airport.

Refugees.

Before the rise of Great Salt Lake, thousands of whistling swans (now called "tundra swans" by the American Ornithologists' Union) descended on Bear River Bay each autumn. As many as sixty thousand swans have been counted at the Bear River Migratory Bird Refuge during mid-October and mid-November, making it the single largest concentration of migrating swans in North America.

In November, 1984, only two hundred fifty-nine whistling swans were counted at the Refuge. One year later: three.

Birds are opportunistic by nature, but resourcefulness fails in the presence of high-speed traffic and asphalt.

This year, the Utah State Legislature appropriated $98 million for flood control. The alternatives state waterfowl managers are reviewing are: wait for the lake to recede, as it inevitably will; try to acquire more habitat, especially newly created wetlands; or reduce the level of the lake.

Tim Provan, the waterfowl biologist for the Division of Wildlife Resources in Salt Lake City, points out that "The marshes don't produce young. They never have. They hold the birds during migration. The marshes let them rest and feed for extended periods—two, three, four months at a time. The seven to eight hundred thousand ducks we did produce have dropped 85 percent since the flood."

He goes on to say, "The Great Salt Lake marshes had one of the strongest populations of redheads, but they are extremely susceptible to high water. They have been hit the hardest. They are not producing young. Their population is down 60 to 80 percent. We have found a direct statistical relationship between loss of habitat and rate of production: 70 percent loss of habitat, 70 percent loss of young. Our redheads are going other places where they are less successful breeders and more subject to predation." He stares out his office window. "I've seen redheads, canvasbacks, shovelers, and teals just laying dormant in the water as though they were in shock."

"How long before the marshes of Bear River will return?" I ask him.

"It will be three to seven years after the lake recedes before it even begins to take a significant turn, because the soil is so saturated with salts. The recycling of nutrients, the reseeding of plants—that will be a fifteen- to twenty-year turnaround."

"The truth is, the system isn't out there to replace. No other system on the continent can replace or absorb this wetland complex. There is a certain threshold that once crossed, we can never recover. When the death rates exceed the birth rates, we are in trouble. Nobody knows the answers. We are working with the questions."

* * *

LONG-BILLED CURLEWS
lake level: 4211.65'

* * *

On my way home, I stop at a favorite pond to watch a pair of cinnamon teals. Barn swallows fly in and out from under the bridge. Dozens of nests are plastered with mud against the concrete beam. A barn swallow is busy lining its cuplike nest with white down feathers. It flies, returning seconds later, with another piece of down in its beak. I wonder where the cache is—most likely a goose nest.

The cliff swallows' nests are different from the barn swallows', although both are built beneath the bridge. Their nests are enclosed, with a small hole left open as an entrance. One pair, their nest barely a shelf, takes turns bringing back dabs of mud. Ten dabs of mud in five minutes. Within an hour, I watch them pack 120 beak-loads of mud onto their new residence. The swallows tirelessly fly to the mudflats on the edge of the pond, load up their bills, return to the construction site, vibrate their heads as they pour the mud onto the nest. Then they vigorously pat it and shape it around their nest. They alternate turns as the male flies from the nest to the mudflat, loads, while the female pats. He returns, she flies out. Over and over again, the same painstaking work, as their tiny feathered bodies quiver with purpose. The shelf slowly, steadily, becomes a closed dwelling.

The spinning of phalaropes. The courtship of grebes. The growth of a swallow's nest. Each—a natural history unfolding.

North of Promontory Point, where the golden spike commemorated the completion of the transcontinental railroad on May 10, 1869, there is a remote vale called Curlew Valley. It is the breeding ground of the long-billed curlew.

In recent years, the long-billed curlew, the largest North American shorebird, has been declining in number in the Great Basin, as it loses much of its breeding habitat to the plow and other land developments. In the midwest, it has been extirpated as a breeding species altogether.

The eskimo curlew is close to extinction. At the turn of the century, in its northward migrations a single flock covered forty to fifty acres in the grasslands of Nebraska. They were known as "prairie pigeons" or "dough birds." As wagonloads were shot and sold, they took the place of the passenger pigeon on the marketplace. Hunters followed the curlews' migration from state to state, literally making a killing. Those who remember the eskimo curlew's call, say it sounded like "the wind whistling through a ship's rigging."

If grasslands continue to shrink, the long-billed curlew could follow the same path as its relative. Its plaintive cry resounds like a warning.

Long-billed curlew, *Numenius americanus,* takes its genus from the Greek *neos,* meaning "new" and *mene,* "moon." The shape of its long bill was thought to resemble the curvature of the sliver moon.

If new moon is defined as no moon or dark moon, the curlew could be associated with destructive powers, for it was long believed that ghosts, goblins, and witches were at the peak of their power in the dark of the moon.

In folklore, this relationship between curlews and black magic stands. A prayer of the Scottish Highlands asks "to be saved from witches, warlocks, and aw lang-nebbed things." In Scotland, the word *whaup* is the name of both the curlew and a goblin with a long beak who moves about under the eaves of attics at night.

In *The Folklore of Birds,* Edward Armstrong writes, "Flocks of curlews, passing over at night and uttering their plaintive, musical calls have also been regarded as the Seven Whistlers, and in the north of England their voices were said to presage someone's death."

He goes on to say, "The curlew's low-pitched fluting is sufficiently near the range of human voice to arouse in the heart the sense of weirdness which we are apt to feel on hearing sounds which have some simulation to but do not really belong to the world of men."

Curlews have been seen as winged souls with foreboding messages. Curiosities of natural history have been defined by curlews. An old-timer of the moors once told a friend of mine there was always an accident after hearing "them long-billed curlews." He spoke of a flock passing overhead and, a few minutes later, their boat overturned. Seven men drowned.

But the flipside of darkness is light. The new moon is also the resurrected moon, soon to be crescent, quarter, then whole. It is the time in many cultures to sow seeds. During the waxing moon all those things that needed to grow are attended to.

In the dark of the moon there is growth. Plants do not flourish in the noonday sun, but rather in the privacy of the new moon.

Maybe it is not the darkness we fear most, but the silences contained within the darkness. Maybe it is not the absence of the moon that frightens us, but the absence of what we expect to be there. A wedge of long-billed curlews flying in the night punctuates the silences and their unexpected calls remind us the only thing we can expect is change.

I found the long-billed curlews at Curlew Valley. A dozen hovered over me like banshees,

"Cur-lee! Cur-lee! Cur-lee!"

I was in their territory and they did not like it. Because of their camouflage, those in the grasses were difficult to see. Movement was my only clue. I counted seven adults. Most were pecking and probing the overgrazed landscape, plucking out multitudes of grasshoppers in between the stubble. Others were contesting the boundaries of competing curlews as they chased each other with heads low in a running crouch. Two curlews faced each other, with necks extended, their long bills pointing toward the sky. They looked ready to fence. Tense gestures, until one bird backed down and flew. The triumphant curlew stepped forward and fluttered its strong, pointed wings above its head. Cinnamon underfeathers flashed like the bright slip of a Spanish dancer.

Female curlews, slightly larger than the males, were prostrate, their necks stretched outward from their bodies. I suspected they were on nests and did not disturb them.

Burr buttercups grew between the grasses like snares, and in prairie dogs' abandoned holes black widows, the size of succulent grapes, reigned.

The hostility of this landscape teaches me how to be quiet and unobtrusive, how to find grace among spiders with a poisonous bite. I sat on a lone boulder in the midst of the curlews. By now, they had grown accustomed to me. This too, I found encouraging—that in the face of stressful intrusions, we can eventually settle in. One begins to almost trust the intruder as a presence that demands greater intent toward life.

On a day like today when the air is dry and smells of salt, I have found my open space, my solitude, and sky. And I have found the birds who require it.

Deciding the Future of the Lake

The final selection in this anthology is chosen from a series of feature articles in the *Salt Lake Tribune* in 1999 examining various dimensions of the lake's importance to Utah and Utahns at the end of the twentieth century. These articles focus on one of the central dilemmas of modern America: the often contradictory goals of exploiting natural economic resources and yet protecting the integrity of the environment and ecological relationships and processes. Resolving that contradiction is proving no easier on the Great Salt Lake than in similar wild areas across the country.

At the heart of this debate is the Union Pacific railroad causeway. The original route of the transcontinental railroad system, comprised of the Union Pacific and Central Pacific railroads, skirted the lake to the north, and in fact it was at the summit of the Promontory Mountain range north of the lake that the two companies joined their rails on the historic date of May 10, 1869, an event commemorated annually on that site at Golden Spike National Monument. Almost immediately after the beginning of commercial traffic over the new line, railroaders began investigating construction of a shortcut directly across the lake, which would save almost fifty miles in distance and seven hours in time over the original route. Building such a shortcut, however, turned out to be an engineering nightmare. While the shallower reaches at each end of the cutoff could simply be filled in, the deeper parts had to be crossed by means of a trestle, but the porous lake bottom swallowed up pilings as deep as they could be driven. The solution eventually was to spread the load out by lashing two timbers side by side to form individual pilings and to group the double pilings five abreast throughout the twenty-three miles of trestle. The new route, known as the Lucin Cutoff, opened in 1903.

Larger trains during the twentieth century gradually rendered the Lucin Cutoff impractical and unsafe, and in the 1950s the Union Pacific, at the expense of $50 million, replaced the trestle section with a gravel causeway, giving the road a solid foundation all the way across the lake. The new causeway opened in 1959. Several large culverts were installed in the causeway to equalize the lake level on each side. An unanticipated consequence of the causeway, though, as the following articles indicate, was an increasing inequality in salinity between the north and south portions of the lake. This inequality results from the fact that the largest freshwater tributaries—the Weber and Jordan Rivers—flow into the south arm, while the north is fed significantly only by the sluggish Bear River, and there are insufficient currents in the lake to effect much transfer of water through the causeway. Thus one economic interest—the railroad—has threatened to destroy another—the brine shrimp industry—by rendering the water to the north of the causeway too saline for the shrimp and the water to the south too fresh. The decline in the brine shrimp population ripples out into other environmental consequences as well, as the article on an environmental bellwether, the eared grebe, indicates.

With such significant economic and environmental consequences at stake, it is no wonder that state agencies and private groups like the Audubon Society are working and debating energetically to find remedies that will satisfy, if possible, all interested parties. Some of the proposed solutions suggested by a massive draft management plan prepared by the Utah Department of Natural Resources are presented and discussed in the final selection.

Suggestions for further reading

The selections presented here represent only about half of the articles included in the original "Lake at the Crossroads" series, which it will repay readers to consult in libraries or through the online archives of the *Salt Lake Tribune*: www.sltrib.com (there is a subscription fee for the archives service). David E. Miller, *Great Salt Lake Past and Present* (Salt Lake City: Publishers Press, 1997), is a recent update of a handy booklet distilling the lifelong love and study of the lake by one of Utah's great historians (and a descendant of the Miller brothers of Davis County who pioneered the livestock business on the islands of the lake).

The Lake at a Crossroads
Jim Woolf, Heather May, and Glen Warchol

Is Causeway Killing the Lake?
Jim Woolf

A dramatic decline in the number of tiny brine shrimp in the Great Salt Lake is generating concern that Utah's inland sea is in trouble—perhaps approaching the brink of ecological collapse.

The doomsday scenario offered by some scientists centers on Union Pacific's 21 -mile-long railroad causeway that runs east-west across the middle of the lake. The rocky berm provides a shortcut for trains traversing the nation, but also acts as a dam that divides the lake into two distinct sections.

Water to the north of the causeway has become so salty that brine shrimp no longer can survive there, while salinity levels on the south side have dipped below the level favored by these tiny crustaceans.

The stakes are high. Brine shrimp are an important food for millions of birds that stop at the Great Salt Lake during their annual migration. Biologists know the loss of this critical rest stop could create problems for dozens of species of bird species, but they don't know how severe.

Declining brine shrimp numbers also have crippled a commercial fishing industry that skims the microscopic eggs off the lake's surface. They are sold as food for prawns and farm-raised fish. In a good year, this industry has generated $58 million from the sale of eggs.

Fears of damaging this world-famous ecosystem prompted the Utah Division of Natural Resources this month to recommend deepening an existing 300-foot-wide opening in the causeway to allow better mixing between the lake's north and south arms. The recommendation is included in the state's draft management plan for the lake. But a group of prominent Utah scientists who reviewed the state's studies question whether brine shrimp are a good barometer of the lake's health. They note

From Jim Woolf, Heather May, and Glen Warchol, "The Lake at a Crossroads," *Salt Lake Tribune*, 25–28 November 1999.

that so little is known about the natural cycles of this remnant of ancient Lake Bonneville, it is hard to know whether an environmental disaster is unfolding.

"I don't think we can tell right now," says Katrina Moser, assistant professor of geography at the University of Utah and a member of the scientific review committee.

The problem, she says, is determining what is "healthy" and "sick" in a lake that fluctuates wildly in response to subtle shifts in climate.

The lake shrank so much during a drought in the early 1960s that many experts worried it would dry up. Salinity levels in the remaining puddle were high enough that pure salt crystals would form on anything left in the water. It was the opposite problem in the mid- 1980s when a rising lake threatened the Salt Lake City International Airport and Interstate 80. The water then was so fresh that a species of salt-tolerant fish moved into the lake for several years.

Many scientists define a "healthy" ecosystem as one that "operates within its nat-ural variability," says Moser. Since the lake previously was as salty as the north arm is today, and as fresh as today's south arm, it might still be considered healthy—at least for salt.

Another question asked by the scientists is how much the West Desert Pumping Project of the 1980s affected today's salinity levels. To control flooding, the state built huge pumps to move lake water onto the Bonneville Salt Flats, where it evap-orated away. Recent studies suggest 12 percent of the lake's total salt may have been left in the desert.

More subtle human-caused changes also could be taking place in the lake, Moser says. For example, the science advisory team urged further study to deter-mine how fertilizers and other organic wastes washing into the lake from Wasatch Front cities affect the ecosystem. It seems likely the lake's plant and animal com-munities evolved in an environment with far lower levels of nutrients, and no one knows how these additional chemicals are affecting the system.

The state's draft management plan acknowledges a "lack of full scientific cer-tainty" about the lake's ecosystem. But it says these questions "should not be used as a reason not to initiate measures to prevent environmental degradation."

It describes deepening the causeway opening as a cautious first step toward restor-ing a more natural salt balance between the north and south arms. Several years of monitoring will be done to determine whether additional measures are necessary.

Differences between the north and south arms of the lake are starkly visible from an airplane. Salt-loving bacteria on the north side give the water an other-worldly shade of red or pink. Green algae predominate in the fresher water to the south, giving the lake the appearance of pea soup.

The reason for this salinity difference is that 95 percent of the water from rivers and streams flowing into the Great Salt Lake enters the south arm, says Lloyd Austin of the Utah Division of Water Resources.

The Union Pacific causeway has only three openings that allow water to move from the south to the north. They are the 300-foot-wide cut the state wants to deepen and two smaller culverts. Because there is usually more water entering the south arm than moving into the north arm, the water level in the south arm is a little higher.

Water that moves north quickly evaporates, leaving its salt behind. Little of this salty water has flowed back to the south in recent years.

A computer model developed by the U.S. Geological Survey suggests the salt imbalance between the north and south arms will persist and possibly worsen unless circulation through the causeway is improved. That would mean continued problems with brine shrimp.

If the USGS calculations are correct—and other researchers have questioned the reliability of the computer model—the outlook for migrating birds and the brine shrimp industry is bleak.

Don Leonard, director of the Utah Artemia Association that represents the brine shrimpers, says questions raised by the scientists should be studied but it is clear that immediate action is required.

"It only takes third-grade math to figure out you need greater mixing" between the north and south arms, he says. "This is, after all, one lake that because of man-made impacts has been converted into two. It is well past time to take the measures needed to heal the lake."

Great Salt Lake Ecosystem Still Full of Secrets
Heather May

With the city smog and stink of rotting algae at their backs, three scientists recently left Antelope Island marina to search for what they call the "web of life."

Their boat scares away a flock of pelicans, which rises from the water in a spiral as the men get closer. No matter. It is the microscopic life within the water that fascinates Paul Birdsey, Mark Davidson and Jim Van Leewen, biologists with the Utah Division of Wildlife Resources (DWR).

They are on one of their twice-weekly visits to collect water samples from 21 sites on the Great Salt Lake.

Their research vessel is built to handle the vagaries of the Great Salt Lake, whose waves slap hard because the water is heavy. Radar warns of dangerous rocks and shallow spots and a global-positioning system guides them to the same spot each time. Today it is No. 2767, located a couple miles northwest of Antelope Island.

Davidson and Van Leewen use a 6-foot-long net with mesh so fine it releases the water but captures life as small as a dust-size brine shrimp egg.

Weighed down by a 5-pound black dumbbell, the white net disappears in the milky, golden-green water.

The Great Salt Lake once was considered a dead sea—a place too salty to support life. But biologists now know it is teeming with life, much of it so small it takes a microscope to see. Included are brine shrimp, brine flies, aquatic insects, algae and bacteria.

Interest in the Great Salt Lake's aquatic life has grown with concerns the brine shrimp population is crashing. Many blame the Union Pacific causeway, which has divided the lake in two since 1959 and prevents the water from mixing. Another source of the problem may be flood-control efforts in the 1980s when lake water was pumped onto the Bonneville Salt Flats and allowed to evaporate. Left behind was about 12 percent of the lake's total salt load.

Today, the north arm is too salty and the south arm too fresh for the brine shrimp to thrive.

To better understand the ecosystem, researchers from DWR, Utah State University and the U.S. Geological Survey are studying the lake in detail to learn more about the brine shrimp and 30 other species of aquatic life that make up the Great Salt Lake's ecosystem.

Part of that information is gathered as the DWR researchers pull their net from the water and collect the tiny organisms. They will be counted later in the lab with the same machine that counts blood cells. On this day few critters fill the plastic jug, a scarcity that is normal as the temperature drops in the fall.

Female brine shrimp give birth to live offspring in the summer when the lake is warm and they have plenty of food. The reproductive cycle changes as the weather cools in the fall. Rather than producing live young, the females release some 70 cysts, or eggs, a week. The adults will die when the mercury drops below 30 degrees Fahrenheit, but their eggs are hardy. Millions of the tiny, reddish-brown cysts—a quarter of a million fill a teaspoon—pucker up and gather like a snowdrift floating on the lake, coloring the water pinkish-red.

When the water warms again in February and March, the shells swell and crack, the nauplii—the first stage of the shrimp's life pop out and eat yolk from their former home. Shrimp become adults three-eighths of an inch long in 30 to 45 days. The females have a tell-tale brown egg pouch and the males grow graspers on their heads to latch on to females during mating.

"They're really bizarre-looking creatures," says Doyle Stephens, a research hydrologist for the USGS.

He says that with affection. Stephens has been studying lake life off and on since he wrote his dissertation on its algal production in 1974. Detailed drawings of the shrimp's 12 life stages hang on his wall, along with pictures of his dogs.

Stephens says brine shrimp have a long association with the Great Salt Lake—their eggs have been found in 15,000-year-old sediment core. He suspects they were brought to the lake on the feet of migratory birds.

The critters used to live throughout the lake but now are largely limited to the south arm. Salinity levels in the north arm have climbed to 26 percent since the causeway was built, making it too salty for all but certain types of algae and bacteria that give the water a rosy color visible from space.

"You put a boat on that thing and it's like running through strawberry milk," says Stephens.

Although brine shrimp won't survive in the north arm's salty water, enough eggs were flushed through the causeway breaches to allow a limited harvest there this year.

For now, researchers are focused on the south arm. DWR hired Stephens to collect water samples at 17 sites there and measure the water temperature and salinity levels. USU professor Gary Belovsky studies shrimp in the lab, noting how they survive under various environmental conditions.

The findings alarm them. Reproduction is dropping. In good harvest periods the percentage of females with cysts would peak three times during the year, with the most, 80 percent, during the fall. This year, the researchers found only one peak in June.

DWR requires there be 21 cysts per liter of water in the south arm of the lake at the end of the harvest so the shrimp can repopulate by spring. But this year, even before the harvest, the water held just 11 cysts per liter, forcing DWR to confine the harvest to the lake's north arm.

DWR, Stephens and Belovsky have some theories about the change.

Salinity in the south arm has dropped from 13 to 7 percent in three years, probably because the bay continues to receive fresh water from its tributaries and doesn't mix with the salty water in the north arm. This is critical because the amount of salt affects the shrimps' food supply, the algae.

Brine shrimp like a species of algae known as Dunaliella viridis. The shrimp swim through the green-tinted water on their backs with their 20-plus feather-like appendages delivering algae to their mouth.

When brine shrimp populations are high, Stephens says "they eat everything in sight, they just clean up the place. [The water gets so clear] you can see 25 feet to the bottom."

Not anymore. The water is cloudy and looks more golden as diatom species have taken over. Dunaliella species make up just 10 percent of the algae in the south arm when they used to be 90 percent, Belovsky says.

Under a microscope the diatoms look like crystal pill boxes. Beautiful, but inedible to shrimp, Because of the limited food supply, adult shrimp can't reproduce well. There has been a five-fold reduction in survival from the hatchling to the juvenile stage compared to when Dunaliella was the dominant algae type in the early 1990s, Belovsky says.

Lower salinities invite more predators, too. Belovsky found that insects like corixids, or waterboatmen, live where salinity is 4.5 percent, usually along the shore. They suck out the shrimps' insides and likely eat 2 percent of the population a month.

"Shrimp don't do well with competition," Stephens says. "They're just a soft fluffy bag of food. They don't have a shell to speak of, and they don't swim very fast. They've got a lot of protein, and they're high in fat."

The cysts are also heavier than the water now. Most used to float on the surface, but for the first time Stephens finds there are more on the bottom. One site sampled in May found 300,000 cysts at 10 meters deep and just 1,200 on the surface.

At such depths, the water looks like black coffee and carries ammonia and hydrogen sulfide, both possibly toxic to the developing shrimp, Stephens says.

"What does that mean next year after [they have] wintered in dark, stringy stuff?" he asks. "Are they still going to hatch?"

The researchers don't know if what they find is normal, and they have plenty more questions to answer. Like how many cysts and shrimp do the migratory birds eat? What nutrients are flushed in the lake and what is their role? How much pollution enters the lake and what is the impact?

"We've learned important things," says W. Clay Perschon, leader of the Great Salt Lake project for DWR. "But boy, there are some big gaps we need to address."

ECCENTRIC EARED GREBE MAY HELP UNLOCK MYSTERIES OF THE ECOSYSTEM
Glen Warchol

Probably no bird is tied so intimately to the Great Salt Lake as the eared grebe.

Upwards of 150 bird species depend on the lake's ecosystem for food and shelter. The lake's shore is North America's primary nesting site for the California gull and the diminutive snowy plover.

But the eared grebe is linked so closely to the lake that scientists believe this quail-size waterbird might serve as a living index to the lake's tenuous health.

In a two-pronged southern migration, North America's 3 million eared grebes stop at the Great Salt Lake or California's Mono Lake to molt feathers and prepare for the rest of their grueling southern journey to Mexico's Sea of Cortez. Biologists believe the North American eared grebe is unique in timing its migration to environmental conditions at these twin salt water lakes.

In trying to understand the Great Salt Lake, scientists have been studying the eared grebe. One unanswered question is whether a collapse of the shrimp population would prove catastrophic to the species.

"I can't give you an alarmist scenario," says California-based ornithologist Joe Jehl, considered one of the foremost authorities on the eared grebe. "I can just say it's one of the things we are trying to find out."

The somber-colored eared grebe gets its name from the burnished-gold feathers that gleam on the sides of its head during mating season. Mating and nesting take place at the northern end of its range in the lakes and ponds of the northwestern United States and Canada.

Wendy Hill, an animal behaviorist at Lafayette College in Pennsylvania, studies what she calls the grebe's "condo-living" behavior at Oregon's Malheur National Wildlife Sanctuary. Hill's work mostly amounts to counting eggs, measuring distances between nests and swatting mosquitos. But she has come to love the eared grebes and delight in their mating "penguin dance," a sort of waterborne do-si-do.

"Their courtship behavior is remarkable," Hill says. "They dance, then mate on the water."

When the grebe's young hatch and leave their floating nests, they ride on their parents' backs.

For the casual naturalist, the eared grebe's slender-necked beauty is an acquired taste. In fall and winter, when the "ear" is merely a patch of white, binoculars will reveal a blazing coal of an eye glaring back—usually a half-second before the grebe arches forward and smoothly submerges.

"These are strange birds, not related in evolution to any other water birds," says Jehl. "It's an evolutionary puzzle as to exactly what they are related to."

With their stubby wings and lobed feet trailing behind them, grebes can hardly claim gulls or raptors as close cousins.

They are designed to swim and dive more than to fly," says Don Paul, the Great Salt Lake biologist for the Utah Department of Wildlife Resources. "They are basically a little softball with wings."

After breeding season, the birds head south and begin to appear along the Antelope Island causeway in late August. The Great Salt Lake is a 1,500-square-mile pit stop on their migration. About 1.5 million eared grs will molt their feathers on the lake and bulk up for the trip to Southern Califomia's Salton Sea and the Gulf of California.

The grebes, which arrive at a trim 250 grams, begin eating. "Their diet is more than 98 percent brine shrimp," says DWR's Paul. "No other bird is so dependent on the shrimp."

The eared grebes are soon flabby and flightless. Their chest muscles, necessary for flight, atrophy, possibly to allow them to dive more efficiently for brine shrimp.

"It's such a tiny package of food," says Mike Conover, a wildlife ecologist at Utah State University who is studying the relationship between the grebe and brine shrimp. "Grebes have to eat 15,000 brine shrimp a day—every day."

After about four months, the brine shrimp are eaten or naturally die off. Without a food source, the grebes have about two weeks to get back into flying condition.

"The eared grebe is the only bird that loses weight to migrate," Jehl says. "It's like a heavyweight fighter losing excess weight to get ready for the ring."

As they approach fighting weight, the grebes gather in remote parts of the lake, many around Fremont Island. Because they withdraw from shore, it was decades before naturalists knew they were on the lake, let alone their millions. "Early bird studies barely list eared grebes, which is ridiculous," Jehl says.

Then, in groups numbering in the hundreds of thousands, they resume their journey south.

The grebes only fly at night, and biologists never have directly observed their migration.

"We've watched them on radar," Jehl says. "From what we've seen, there are huge pulses of birds [rising into the air]. The next time you see them is at the Salton Sea."

To understand the eared grebe, scientists must understand the brine shrimp. Both life forms remain a puzzle.

"If the brine shrimp density goes down early, will the grebes have had enough time to build up enough fat to finish their migration? I don't know." Jehl says. "If they leave before they have enough fat . . . think about what the terrain looks like between the Great Salt Lake and the Salton Sea."

This year's migration—with brine shrimp densities way down—may provide the keys to these mysteries. Jehl thinks the eared grebes will have to migrate early.

"They seem to put off the trip as long as possible into periods of prolonged darkness," Jehl says. "But if the food runs out early they will be forced to leave before the nights get long." The aerodynamically incorrect grebes fly at night to avoid predation. To leave before the long nights of winter would put them at higher risk.

In studying the eared grebe and the brine shrimp, Jehl, Paul and Conover are trying to fit pieces into the larger puzzle: How much can humans exploit the Great Salt Lake before rending its web of life? So far, Jehl, says they can definitively agree on one thing. "We just don't know."

WHAT DO WE WANT TO DO WITH THE LAKE?
Jim Woolf

The biggest obstacle to managing the Great Salt Lake may be confronting our own ambivalence toward this world-famous inland sea.

Most of the 1.6 million people who live along the Wasatch Front rarely think about their vast neighbor, although Utah's capital city and even this newspaper carry its name.

When the topic of the lake comes up, the first image that flashes through many minds is of a stinking, brine-fly-infested cesspool that occasionally floods highways and low-lying subdivisions.

This negative image is tempered for some Utahns by romantic stories from older relatives who recall riding the train to Saltair in the 1930s and 1940s to dance to Glenn Miller's swing band, and modern experiences of hiking to Antelope Island's Buffalo Point, sailing off the tip of Stansbury Island, or watching flocks of Canada geese feeding in a field at the Bear River Migratory Bird Refuge.

A new planning effort by the Utah Department of Natural Resources offers a chance to rethink our relationship with the lake and decide what we want from this huge, briny puddle in the desert.

The 386-page draft management plan compiled by a team of state employees is intended to establish policy for a decade.

Preparation of the document was triggered three years ago by a sudden drop in the number of brine shrimp in the lake.

Most experts blame the problem on a salt imbalance caused by Union Pacific's railroad causeway that runs across the middle of the lake. Water to the north of the causeway is too salty for brine shrimp, while water to the south is becoming too fresh.

The plan identifies possible solutions to the causeway problem and numerous other issues related to the lake. Approaches to dealing with lake issues are grouped into the following four categories:

—Utahns could decide to do nothing. The causeway would remain as it is. Existing state, federal and local laws would continue to provide a modest level of protection for the lake. Roads and subdivisions would further encroach on the shoreline, industrial and recreational development would be allowed to expand and water quality likely would worsen as the Wasatch Front population grows.

—The lake could be managed to produce the greatest economic benefit for the state. The causeway would be left alone, converting the lake's north arm into a giant evaporation pond for industry. Businesses want stable lake conditions, so this option would make extensive use of the West Desert Project built in the 1980s to keep lake levels within a predictable range. Tourism could be boosted by construction of marinas, new scenic drives and large resorts in popular areas such as Antelope Island.

—The lake could be managed to protect and restore the natural environment. A large new opening would be cut in the causeway to allow a more normal circulation of water. Strict limits would be placed on the amount of pollution entering the lake, and development along the shoreline would be closely regulated. Limited recreational development would be permitted. The lake would be allowed to rise and fall in its natural cycle with minimal interference from humans.

—The state's preferred alternative is a carefully crafted political compromise that attempts to solve the lake's perceived ecological problems without creating serious problems for any existing users. It is a middle-of-the-road approach aimed at Republicans in the Legislature who will need to approve funding for whichever management plan is adopted.

On the causeway issue, the state's proposal recommends deepening an existing 300-foot-wide opening in the Union Pacific railroad causeway by at least 4 feet.

This is designed to allow just enough salt to migrate into the south arm to improve conditions for the declining brine shrimp population, but would leave the north arm salty enough to sustain the large mineral company there. The West Desert Pumping Project would be used when the lake threatens to flood again, but the state's preferred plan calls for the pumps to be turned on later than industry prefers to allow greater natural fluctuation in the lake level. And the state's proposal accepts that salt companies have transformed large sections of the lake into barren evaporation ponds.

It raises no objections to existing dikes along the eastern shore that create artificial wetlands, and recommends no changes in the Antelope Island causeway that has transformed Farmington Bay into a freshwater lake.

Such human-caused modifications of the lake are "acceptable" because they were done for a reason and do not jeopardize the overall "sustainability" of the ecosystem, according to the plan.

That is not the case with the unanticipated changes caused by Union Pacific's railroad causeway.

The plan says changes in salinity attributed to the causeway are too large and affect too much of the lake to be allowed to continue.

Kathleen Clarke, director of the Utah Department of Natural Resources, told state lawmakers recently the planning team worked hard to devise a compromise that would be acceptable to most people.

"I believe we have found a balance point," she said.

The plan makes no reference to the proposed Legacy Highway that would cut through wetlands in Davis County. Although this would be a state highway and impacts on the lake have been the source of the greatest controversy, planners said the Department of Natural Resources has no control over highways so they decided not to include the issue in this document.

Lynn de Freitas, president of Friends of the Great Salt Lake, agrees everyone was given a chance to participate in the planning process but said the lake-side industries appear to have had a louder voice.

"It's not that they [the planners] care less about what our concerns are," says de Freitas, "but we have less leverage because we aren't part of the economic livelihood of the state."

The state's proposal is headed in the right direction but doesn't go far enough, she says. Her group is about to launch a campaign aimed at protecting the lake by improving and restoring waterways through the entire 22,000-square-mile watershed.

A team of prominent Utah scientists that conducted an independent review of the state's plan also wondered whether too much attention is being paid to the lake's industries while ignoring hard-to-measure values that today's indifferent public does not yet recognize.

"We suggest that the Great Salt Lake is a phenomenal asset to the state of Utah," the scientists say in their report to the planning team.

"Its mineral resources have been appreciated for almost 150 years. The brine shrimp now are appreciated because they are economically valuable. To only a very limited extent is the lake appreciated for tourism, for culture, for earth systems history and for education. We fear that the present constituencies drive the DNR [Department of Natural Resources] approach to management and that these policies may eventually diminish the net social value of the lake to the citizens of the state of Utah," conclude the scientists.